Merchants of Menace

Merchants of Menace

The Business of Horror Cinema

EDITED BY RICHARD NOWELL

BLOOMSBURY
NEW YORK • LONDON • NEW DELHI • SYDNEY

Bloomsbury Academic
An imprint of Bloomsbury Publishing Inc

1385 Broadway	50 Bedford Square
New York	London
NY 10018	WC1B 3DP
USA	UK

www.bloomsbury.com

Bloomsbury is a registered trade mark of Bloomsbury Publishing Plc

First published 2014

© Richard Nowell and Contributors 2014

All rights reserved. No part of this publication may be reproduced or transmitted in any form or by any means, electronic or mechanical, including photocopying, recording, or any information storage or retrieval system, without prior permission in writing from the publishers.

No responsibility for loss caused to any individual or organization acting on or refraining from action as a result of the material in this publication can be accepted by Bloomsbury or the author.

Library of Congress Cataloging-in-Publication Data
Merchants of menace : the business of horror cinema / edited by Richard Nowell.
pages cm
Includes bibliographical references and index.
ISBN 978-1-62356-879-5 (hardback : alk. paper)-- ISBN 978-1-62356-420-9 (pbk. : alk. paper)
1. Horror films--History and criticism. 2. Horror films--Production and direction. 3. Horror films--Marketing. I. Nowell, Richard, editor of compilation.
PN1995.9.H6M48 2014
791.43'6164--dc23
2013048638

ISBN: HB: 978-1-6235-6879-5
PB: 978-1-6235-6420-9
ePub: 978-1-6235-6985-3
ePDF: 978-1-6235-6394-3

Typeset by Fakenham Prepress Solutions, Fakenham, Norfolk NR21 8NN

Contents

Illustrations ix
Acknowledgments x
Contributors xi

Introduction: There's Gold in Them There Chills 1
Richard Nowell

PART ONE Production Lines, Trends, and Cycles 11

1. "House of Horrors": Corporate Strategy at Universal Pictures in the 1930s 13
   Kyle Edwards

2. The Undead of Hollywood and Poverty Row: The Influence of Studio-era Industrial Patterns on Zombie Film Production, 1932 to 1946 31
   Todd K. Platts

3. By the Book: American Horror Cinema and Horror Literature of the Late 1960s and 1970s 45
   Peter Hutchings

4. Risen from the Vaults: Recent Horror Film Remakes and the American Film Industry 61
   Kevin Heffernan

5 Monster Factory: International Dynamics of the Australian Horror Movie Industry 75

Mark David Ryan

PART TWO Film Content, Style, and Themes 91

6 "Bad Medicine": The Psychiatric Profession's Interventions into the Business of Postwar Horror 93

Tim Snelson

7 Horror Film Atmosphere as Anti-narrative (and Vice Versa) 109

Robert Spadoni

8 "A Kind of Bacall Quality": Jamie Lee Curtis, Stardom, and Gentrifying Non-Hollywood Horror 129

Richard Nowell

9 "New Decade, New Rules": Rebooting the *Scream* Franchise in the Digital Age 147

Valerie Wee

PART THREE Movie Marketing, Branding, and Distribution 161

10 "Hot Profits Out of Cold Shivers!": Horror, the First-run Market, and the Hollywood Studios, 1938 to 1942 163

Mark Jancovich

11 Strange Enjoyments: The Marketing and Reception of Horror in the Civil Rights Era Black Press 187

Mikal J. Gaines

12 Bids for Distinction: The Critical-Industrial Function of the Horror Auteur 203
Joe Tompkins

13 Low Budgets, No Budgets, and Digital-video Nasties: Recent British Horror and Informal Distribution 215
Johnny Walker

14 Hammer 2.0: Legacy, Modernization, and Hammer Horror as a Heritage Brand 229
Matt Hills

Index 251

Illustrations

Figures

7.1 *The City of the Dead.* Nan stops at a gas station to ask for directions 119

7.2 Nan steps into the lobby of the Raven's Inn 120

7.3 Nan in her room at the inn 120

7.4 The church in Whitewood 123

7.5 Dick, gun in hand, opens the trapdoor 125

Tables

5.1 Australian horror film production by decade 79

5.2 Horror films at the Australian box office, 2012 83

5.3 Recent Australian horror films at the box office 84

Acknowledgments

This collection would not exist were it not for a fantastic group of people. First and foremost, I would like to thank the wonderful authors who contributed to the collection. It has been an honor, a privilege, and a pleasure to collaborate with such a dedicated group of scholars. I would also like to express my heartfelt gratitude to the publishing staff at Bloomsbury. Special thanks go to Katie Gallof, whose confidence in the collection has been as unwavering as her confidence in its editor disarming. *Merchants of Menace* has been a part of my life for close to three years, which has meant it has also been a part of the lives of those around me for just as long. Thanks, as ever, then, to Jindriska Blahova, for her insights, support, and patience.

Contributors

Kyle Edwards is Associate Professor of English and Director of Cinema Studies at Oakland University, USA, where his teaching and research focus on the industrial history of Hollywood, film authorship, and film adaptation. He is currently writing a monograph on the Hollywood B film.

Mikal J. Gaines is a Ph.D. candidate in the American Studies Program at The College of William and Mary, in Williamsburg, VA, USA. His areas of specialization include African American Literature, Film and Media Studies, Critical Theory, Gothic Studies, and violence and gender issues. He has published articles on Spike Lee, Roger Corman, and other auteurs. His dissertation, 'The Black Gothic Imaginary: Horror and Black Subjectivity in American Cinema from 1960 to the New Millennium', investigates African American responses to the horror film and the intersections between gothic rhetoric and American civil rights discourse. He is currently an Adjunct Instructor at Massachusetts College of Pharmacy and Health Sciences, University in Boston, MA.

Kevin Heffernan teaches media culture and history in the Division of Film and Media Arts at Southern Methodist University, USA. *Divine Trash*, a documentary on the early career of John Waters on which Heffernan served as associate producer and co-screenwriter, won the Filmmakers' Trophy in Documentary at the 1998 Sundance Film Festival. He is the author of *Ghouls, Gimmicks and Gold: Horror Films and the American Movie Business, 1952–1968* from Duke University Press, and co-author, with Frances Milstead and Steve Yeager, of *My Son Divine* from Alyson Publications. He is writing a book-length history of American moving-image pornography from 1994 to the present tentatively titled *Channels of Pleasure*, and another book tentatively titled *From Beavis and Butt-head to Tea Party Nation: Dumb White Guy Politics and Culture in America*.

Matt Hills is Professor of Film and TV studies at Aberystwyth University, UK. He is the author of five books, including *Fan Cultures* (Routledge, 2002), *The Pleasures of Horror* (Continuum, 2005), and *Triumph of a Time Lord* (I. B. Tauris, 2010). He is also the editor of *New Dimensions of Doctor Who*

(I.B. Tauris, 2013). Matt has published widely on cult media and fandom, and his recent horror-related work includes contributions to the edited volumes *Horror Zone* (2010) and *Horror After 9/11* (2012).

Peter Hutchings is Professor of Film Studies at Northumbria University, UK. He is the author of *Hammer and Beyond: The British Horror Film*, *Terence Fisher*, *The British Film Guide to Dracula*, *The Horror Film*, and *The Historical Dictionary of Horror Cinema*. He has also published numerous journal articles and book chapters on horror cinema, British film and television, science fiction cinema and television, and the thriller.

Mark Jancovich is Professor of Film and Television Studies at the University of East Anglia, UK. He is the author of several books: *Horror* (Batsford, 1992); *The Cultural Politics of the New Criticism* (Cambridge University Press, 1993); *Rational Fears: American Horror in the 1950s* (Manchester University Press, 1996); and *The Place of the Audience: Cultural Geographies of Film Consumption*, (with Lucy Faire and Sarah Stubbings, BFI, 2003). He is also the editor of several collections: *Approaches to Popular Film* (with Joanne Hollows, Manchester University Press, 1995); *The Film Studies Reader* (with Joanne Hollows and Peter Hutchings, Arnold/Open University Press, 2000); *Horror, The Film Reader* (Routledge, 2001); *Quality Popular Television: Cult TV, the Industry and Fans* (with James Lyons, BFI, 2003); *Defining Cult Movies: The Cultural Politics of Oppositional Taste* (with Antonio Lazaro-Reboll, Julian Stringer, and Andrew Willis, Manchester University Press, 2003); *Film Histories: An Introduction and Reader* (with Paul Grainge and Sharon Monteith, Edinburgh University Press, 2006); and *Film and Comic Books* (with Ian Gordon and Matt McAllister, University Press of Mississippi, 2007). He was also the founder of *Scope: An Online Journal of Film Studies*; and is series editor (with Eric Schaefer) of the Manchester University Press book series, *Inside Popular Film*; and series editor (with Charles Acland) of the Continuum book series, *Film Genres*. He is currently writing a history of horror in the 1940s.

Richard Nowell teaches American Cinema at the American Studies Department of Charles University in Prague, Czech Republic. He is the author of *Blood Money: A History of the First Teen Slasher Film Cycle* (Continuum, 2011), the guest editor of a special issue of *Ilumiance: Journal of Film History, Theory, and Aesthetics* on the topic of genre and the movie business, and has published articles in journals such as *Cinema Journal*, *Inmedia*, *Journal of Film and Video*, the *New Review of Film & Television Studies*, and *Post Script*.

Todd K. Platts (Ph.D., University of Missouri) is Adjunct Professor of Sociology at Harrisburg Area Community College, USA. His article "Locating Zombies in the Sociology of Popular Culture" was recently published in *Sociology Compass*. He also has two forthcoming essays on *The Walking Dead*—"AMC's: *The Walking Dead*" for Alain Silver and James Ursini's *The Zombie Film*, and "'[Zombies] Couldn't Be Done on Network': Producing AMC's *The Walking Dead*" for an untitled anthology to be edited by Margo Collins and Deborah Christie.

Mark David Ryan is a lecturer in film, screen, and animation, and a research fellow for the Creative Industries Faculty, Queensland University of Technology, Australia. He is a leading expert on Australian horror films and Australian genre cinema. He is a co-editor (with Goldsmith and Lealand) of the *Directory of World Cinema: Australia and New Zealand 2*, published by Intellect and the University of Chicago Press. Mark has written extensively on Australian horror films, genre cinema, industry dynamics of cultural production, and cultural policy.

Tim Snelson is Lecturer in Media History at the University of East Anglia, UK. His research addresses the relationship between media and social history, and has been published in a number of edited collections, and in journals including *Media History*, *Cultural Studies*, and the *New Review of Film and Television Studies*.

Robert Spadoni is the author of *Uncanny Bodies: The Coming of Sound Film and the Origins of the Horror Genre* (University of California Press, 2007), *A Pocket Guide to Analyzing Films* (California, forthcoming), and essays on horror films and other topics. He is an Associate Professor in the English Department at Case Western Reserve University in Ohio, USA.

Joe Tompkins is an Assistant Professor of Communication Arts at Allegheny College, USA, where he teaches Critical Media Studies. His work has appeared or is forthcoming in journals such as *Television and New Media*, *Cinema Journal*, *Post Script*, and *Popular Communication*.

Johnny Walker is a lecturer in media at Northumbria University, UK. He has been published in journals such as *Horror Studies* and the *Journal of British Cinema and Television*. He is currently writing *Contemporary British Horror Cinema: Industry, Genre and Society* for Edinburgh University Press.

Valerie Wee is an Associate Professor in the Department of English Language and Literature at the National University of Singapore, and lectures on Film and Media Studies. Her research areas include teen culture and the American culture industries, horror films, and gender representations in the media. Her work has appeared in *Cinema Journal*, *Journal of Film and Video*, *Journal of Popular Film and Television*, and *Feminist Media Studies*. She is the author of *Teen Media: Hollywood and the Youth Market in the Digital Age* and *Japanese Horror Film and their American Remakes: Translating Fear, Adapting Culture*.

Introduction
There's Gold in Them There Chills

Richard Nowell

In spring 1981, the UPI news agency issued a press release on behalf of a leading figure in American horror cinema. Intended to form the basis of newspaper publicity articles, this document provided the producer-distributor Irwin Yablans with a stage upon which to showcase his insights into turning a profit from the production, assembly, and distribution of scary movies (see e.g. Scott, 1981). The man behind the sleeper hit *Halloween* (1978), as well as less lucrative ventures such as *Tourist Trap*, *Nocturna* (both 1979), and *Hell Night* (1981), wore with pride his self-proclaimed title, the "Merchant of Menace" (quoted in ibid.).

While the economic dimensions of Anglophone horror cinema command significant attention in the trade and popular press, and in fan circles, this topic has continually occupied a marginal position in academic writing.[1] To date, scholars have tended to either sidestep the industrial logic, strategies, and practices that shape horror, or reduce these phenomena to the profit-seeking motive underwriting all capitalist endeavors. As a consequence, the single greatest influence on the production, content, and delivery of one of the world's most enduring audio-visual forms remains quite poorly understood. Instead of focusing on industry structure, supply chains, corporate

---

[1] In Anglophone academia, understandings of horror cinema have largely derived from studies of English-language examples: those of Hollywood, the American independent sector, and, to a lesser extent, Britain, Canada, and other English-speaking countries. Accordingly, as a revisionist study, this collection also focuses on films originating from these nations. While a recent upsurge in English-language scholarship focusing on non-Anglophone cinema is timely and salient, it is equally important to recognize that a great deal of work on Anglophone cinema remains to be done. Further investigation of the economic dimensions of non-Anglophone horror is welcomed but is beyond the scope of this collection.

strategy, target markets, and box office patterns, academic treatments of Anglophone horror have largely reflected the dominant approaches in Film Studies and in Genre Studies. This tendency has resulted in three general approaches dominating the field: definitions, symptomatic analyses, and critical reception studies.

In line with an early preoccupation of Genre Studies, several scholars attempted to pin down the horror film's unique formal, structural, or thematic characteristics (for a detailed discussion see Jancovich, 2002). For example, Robin Wood suggested that this genre was distinguished by the eruption of repressed ideas, like the proletarian resentment and oppressive families in 1974's *The Texas Chainsaw Massacre* and 1977's *The Hills Have Eyes* (1984 [1979]). Noel Carroll, on the other hand, argued that horror's uniqueness derived from the presence of an incongruously fearsome and loathsome threat: a werewolf, an extra-terrestrial, nature run amok, and so on (Carroll, 1990). The pursuit of such a definition was criticized for seeking to impose a trans-cultural, trans-historical ideal on to a discursive phenomenon that was subject to levels of contestation and flux that made this endeavor unviable or impossible: horror, like other genres, had simply meant too many things to be distilled into a universal essence (see e.g. Tudor, 1989). The definitions themselves either exceeded everyday use of the term "horror" or excluded films that were widely recognized as such (see e.g. Jancovich, 2002). Thus, where Wood admitted that his model applied just as much to other action-driven films like Westerns (1984 [1979]), Carroll's rejection of serial murderers omitted arguably the most prominent cinematic monster of the day (1990).[2] Accordingly, this collection focuses on "horror" as a series of loosely defined, historically situated discourses upon which industry professionals have drawn: not necessarily what "we collectively believe it to be" (Tudor, 1973, p. 139), but rather what they collectively believed it to be.

---

[2]These interventions emphasized the differences between conceptions of a film category rather than common ground. By overstating diversity—polysemy over structure—we risk replacing illusionary order with illusionary chaos (on genre, order, and chaos theory see Deleyto, 2009, Introduction). Thus, while it is important to recognize that some of the examples discussed in this collection may not be remembered as horror films today, in spite of their being seen in this way contemporaneously, most will provoke little surprise. Similarly, it needs stressing that most if not all of the films discussed in this collection will have been understood as more than just horror, on account of their borrowing from, and being framed as examples of, a number of different categories of film (on the industrial dimensions of genre-mixing or hybridity see Altman, 1999, pp. 128–32; Nowell, 2011, pp. 24–9). For example, *Prom Night* (1980) borrowed content from, was marketed as, and—based on journalistic responses—was understood at the time of its original release as, among other things, a horror film, a murder-mystery, a thriller, a teen film, a disco film, and a female coming-of-age story (see Nowell, 2011, ch. 4).

Symptomatic analysis remains the pre-eminent approach to the study of Anglophone horror. This approach tackles scary movies as by-products of psychological and social demons purportedly haunting filmmakers and their homelands—in short, as our collective nightmares (see e.g. Wood, 1984 [1979]; Lowenstein, 2005, ch. 4). Such work analyzes depictions of groups such as women and the family or concepts like globalization in order to expose their political or ideological underpinnings. Thus, a propensity for female victims and monsters prompted some scholars to argue that horror was misogynistic (Williams, 1984; Creed, 1993). Others saw in marginalized monsters surrogates for stigmatized social groups such as homosexuals and blacks (Benshoff, 1997; Coleman, 2011). Others still read horror films as mediations or allegories of topical concerns, arguing, for example, that twenty-first-century "torture-porn" like *Hostel* (2005) wrestled with concerns over "post-9/11" America's vulnerability and bellicosity (see e.g. Middleton, 2010; Briefel and Miller, 2012). The symptomatic approach was criticized in some quarters for failing to capture the visceral, emotional, social, and pleasurable dimensions of horror film consumption; the unconscious and cerebral activity of the putative spectator was far removed from the experiences of actual viewers (see e.g. Cherry, 1999; Hills, 2005). Whereas such studies also tend to elide the industrial decision-making that gives rise to the articulation of themes and the taking of positions, the relevant chapters in this collection take this practice very much into account.

The perceived shortcomings of these two approaches, coupled with other factors such as the genre's capacity to incite extremes of support or condemnation, contributed to the rise to prominence of reception studies as a key approach in the study of Anglophone horror cinema. This discursive turn produced a shift away from analyzing the content of scary movies to analyzing viewer responses to, views on, and memories of such films, thereby positioning such work at a cutting-edge of both Film Studies and Genre Studies (see Staiger, 1992; Naremore, 1998; Altman, 1999). These studies shed light on the cultural politics that underpin claims about horror, whether in journalism, public policy, or the battleground that is fandom (see e.g. Jancovich, 2000; Hills, 2005, Egan, 2007). An understanding of the ways in which industry decision-makers have viewed, responded to, and attempted to influence public perceptions of horror is central to the development of industrially-oriented and industrially-sensitive studies of this and other genres; such a consideration undergirds or is made explicit in several contributions to this collection.

While these general tendencies for the most part elided industry conduct, they nevertheless reinforced a number of misconceptions about the industrial dimensions of horror cinema. Studies of horror films and of claims-makers' discourse have served—sometimes by design, sometimes by default—as proxies for industrial logic and agency, in much the same way as Richard Maltby has pointed out that interpretive readings of motion pictures often stand in for the experiences of actual viewers (2011). Thus, elaborations of the supposed sexism of Hollywood women-in-danger films like *Eyes of Laura Mars* (1978) and *Dressed to Kill* (1979) are suggestive of universal consensus and industrial intention (see e.g. Fischer and Landy, 1982; Lyons, 1997, ch. 2), when these films were in fact the subject of heated critical debate about their sexual politics, and were typically pitched to moviegoers as female-oriented indictments of misogyny (see Nowell, 2013). The cultural politics that have driven the valorization of certain horror films like the aforementioned critiques of family, the denigration of others like the women-in-danger movies, and the dismissal of others like a spate of self-reflexive teen horror films that pre-dated *Scream* (1996), have also contributed to the proliferation of three figures that have served to overwrite the complexity of industrial activity with reductive caricature. Thus, horror films have oftentimes been framed as mouthpieces for misogynistic sadists lurking in the shadows of the exploitation sector, or as expressions of defiant resistance enacted by noble progressives, or as platforms for the reactionary evils of the biggest, scariest monster of all: Hollywood.

Whereas calls to pay greater attention to reception have for the most part been heeded, those for emphasis to be placed on industry conduct have largely fallen on deaf ears (see e.g. Neale, 1990; Jancovich, 2007; McDonald, 2013). Nevertheless, it needs to be stressed that this collection follows a series of paths broken by earlier work in the field. For example, Robert E. Kapsis considered the extent to which the market shaped horror film production in the late 1970s and early 1980s (1991), and the industrial appropriation of Alfred Hitchcock's public personae (1992); Kevin Heffernan offered new insights into the production, distribution, and exhibition of scary movies in the 1950s and 1960s (2004; see also Heffernan, 2002); and I (Nowell, 2011) recently attempted to explain the industry logic behind the early proliferation of teen slasher films (see also Berenstein, 1996; Gomery, 1996; Hutchings, 2004; Wee, 2006; Spadoni, 2007; Snelson, 2009; Lobato and Ryan, 2011; Edwards, 2012). Notwithstanding studies such as these, the business of Anglophone horror remains sketchily theorized and supported by relatively few case studies.

Accordingly, this collection hopes to shed new light on the industrial dimensions of Anglophone horror in order to facilitate the illumination of this under-researched aspect of cinema history. The collection contains 14 hitherto unpublished chapters that as a group employ a range of approaches, and focus on a range of historical periods and industrial sectors. These are organized into three parts, each containing four or five chronologically ordered chapters, which, broadly speaking, foreground production, content, and dissemination, respectively. However, it is to the credit of many of the chapters that they could justifiably be included in more than one part, since not only do they tend to heed calls to approach horror cinema as an intrinsically trans-media and intra-generic phenomenon (see Waller, 1987, Introduction), they also approach the genre as a product of the vertical and horizontal relationships—both national and international—that connect various sectors of the creative industries.

The opening part concentrates on the industrial logic and strategies that have supervised certain horror film production trends. These chapters offer industrially sensitive alternatives to the symptomatic accounts discussed above. The part opens with a study of the early to mid-1930s output of Universal Pictures, in which Kyle Edwards argues that this company developed literary adaptations such as *Dracula* (1931) and *Murders in the Rue Morgue* (1932) to carve itself a profitable niche as the era's premier "house of horrors." In Chapter 2, Todd K. Platts considers the forces that shaped the production of zombie films across the 1930s and into the early 1940s, proposing that the onset, progress, and decline of the trend resulted from various institutional and market conditions; conditions that also explain Hollywood's and Poverty Row's distinct employment of this material. Chapter 3 examines the literary adaptations that were a staple of American cinema in the wake of *Rosemary's Baby* (1968); Peter Hutchings charts a diverse field of production before suggesting that an exemplary adaptation such as *Audrey Rose* (1977) indicates a broader effort to attract older, female audiences. In Chapter 4, Kevin Heffernan analyzes two horror film remake cycles that unfolded around the millennium. He proposes that remakes of older American horror films like *The Haunting* (1963) provided a commercially viable entry for A-listers transitioning into medium-budget production, and that remakes of contemporaneous South-East Asian chillers such as *Ringu* (1998) enabled Hollywood companies to woo audiences in this region as well as young female Americans. In Chapter 5 of Part One Mark David Ryan proposes that the "international dynamics" of the Australian production sector help to explain a recent boom in horror films in this country. Crafting products that are both marketable and appealing overseas, contends Ryan, has given rise to scary movies that showcase their Australian production origins, or that affect "American-ness," or that project a placeless quality.

Part Two focuses on horror film content—a term I use loosely here to denote not only formal and structural elements, but also style, themes, and modes of address. Taken as a group, the four chapters in this part indicate that individual expression and engagement with resonant extra-filmic discourse not only need to be considered alongside economic motivations, but that economics often help to explain why certain forms of creativity and topicality reach the screen and others do not. In the first of these chapters, Tim Snelson considers the conditions that precipitated a postwar shift in Hollywood's portrayals of psychiatry in horror films. The mobilization of increasingly sensitive depictions, argues Snelson, was a result of industry decision-makers responding to an outcry over the demonization of this profession by journalists, academics, and psychiatrists themselves. The following chapter, Chapter 7, may seem an unlikely presence in a collection such as this, but I contend that Robert Spadoni's formalist analysis of the generation of "atmosphere" in the British film *The City of the Dead* (1960) is an important and relevant contribution; not least because it develops our understanding of a crucial but poorly understood aspect of horror cinema, and, in so doing, reminds us of the need to consider the economic imperatives that underwrite such practice. The commercial logic driving the recruitment of certain on-screen talent is the subject of Chapter 8, my own contribution to the collection. I try to make the case that, even though Jamie Lee Curtis is remembered as a damsel in distress, her appeal to the producers and distributors of films such as *The Fog*, *Terror Train* (both 1980), and *Road Games* (1981) rested on her capacity to pre-empt claims that these were unpolished, misogynistic exploitation films, on account of her star persona embodying the concepts of innocuous horror, Hollywood, and neo-feminism. The final chapter of Part Two considers how corporate struggle and a general neglect of young audiences in the late 2000s led the Weinstein Company to bankroll the teen slasher sequel *Scre4m* (2011), a decade after the series had seemingly concluded. Valerie Wee proposes that the filmmakers' inability successfully to address both the viewers of the earlier films and a new generation of American youths helps explain the box office failure of this film.

The third and final part contains five chapters that concentrate on delivery. In contrast to the majority of earlier studies, these chapters consider the manner in which dissemination influences production and assembly, and the roles played by the other multi-million-dollar texts that film industries generate: marketing campaigns. In the first of the chapters, Chapter 10, Mark Jancovich examines how theatrical distribution and exhibition influenced Hollywood's horror films from 1938 to 1942. Central to understanding this aspect of output, and especially the establishment of RKO's Lewton Unit, argues Jancovich, was the studios' targeting of both upmarket first-run theaters and America's female heads of household. Chapter 11 sees Mikal J. Gains consider the potential influence of horror film marketing on black audiences' conceptions of the genre during the late 1950s and the 1960s; Gains analyzes how advertisements and publicity articles framed scary movies for the predominantly black readership of the *Chicago Defender* newspaper. In Chapter 12, Joe Tompkins explores what he describes as the "industrial-critical function of the horror Auteur." Tompkins suggests that the notion that 1970s filmmakers like George A. Romero fashioned radical or transgressive horror has been appropriated to imbue events such as awards ceremonies, films such as "torture-porn" movies, and directors such as the so-called "splat pack," with something of their predecessors' subcultural cache. From there, Chapter 13 focuses on developments in contemporary British horror cinema, as Johnny Walker contends that this sector has been sustained in recent years by direct-to-video releases. Various forms of non-theatrical delivery, claims Walker, have provided medium-budget horror with a commercially viable route into distribution and have enabled DIY films to reach a wider audience, while helping to imbue the latter with a cult status that they may not otherwise have achieved. This part, and therefore the collection as a whole, concludes with Matt Hills' analysis of the branding strategies that Britain's Hammer Horror employed following its relaunch in the early 2000s. To understand the twenty-first-century rebranding of this company, proposes Hills, is to understand an effort to balance heritage and modernization, one that derives from Hammer's attempts to capitalize on its back catalog and to compete in today's global marketplace; a strategy that has required careful negotiation of the investment that fans place in this talismanic firm.

Taken together, the 14 chapters that comprise this collection remind us that a closer consideration of industry logic, strategies, and practices promises to enrich our understandings of horror cinema in a variety of ways. Given that horror cuts across budgetary categories, across industry and national sectors, and across media, the collection also promises to broaden our understandings of the economic dimensions of cultural production generally. Of course, the scope of this collection is limited, which highlights the fact that a significant amount of work still needs to be done to illuminate the industrial dimensions of horror cinema. Focusing greater attention on the logic of green-lighting decisions will enable us to paint a clearer picture of the composition of output, and to gain a deeper understanding of the specific forces shaping the advent, duration, and end of specific horror trends, as well as the relationships between them, and their relationships to non-horror trends. What is more, by considering the manner in which commercial considerations influence horror film content we will gain a deeper insight into the development of patterns of stasis and change, and of evocation, differentiation, and innovation. A closer consideration of the dynamics of delivery will also help us to enrich our understandings of these topics, and of how and why interested parties endeavor to imbue their products with specific forms of symbolic value derived from the manner of their circulation and the relay of information that orbits them. On the whole, we will benefit from paying greater attention to the profound influence that target markets, targeted audiences, and supply chains exert upon the production, content, and circulation of horror films. In so doing, we are likely to get a much better sense not only of why horror films amount to our collective nightmares, but of why merchants of menace like Irwin Yablans have assessed tales of terror and concluded that "there's gold in them there chills."

References

Altman, R. (1999), *Film/Genre*, London: BFI.
Benshoff, H. M. (1997), *Monsters in the Closet: Homosexuality and the Horror Film*, Manchester: University of Manchester Press.
Berenstein, R. J. (1996), *Attack of the Leading Ladies: Gender, Sexuality, and Spectatorship in Classic Horror Cinema*, New York: Columbia University Press.
Briefel, A. and Miller, S. J. (2012), *Horror after 9/11: World of Fear, Cinema of Terrors*, Austin: University of Texas Press.
Carroll, N. (1990), *The Philosophy of Horror or Paradoxes of the Heart*, New York: Routledge.
Cherry, B. (1999), "Refusing to Refuse to Look: Female Viewers of the Horror Film," in M. Stokes and R. Maltby (eds), *Identifying Hollywood's Audiences: Cultural Identity and the Movies*, London: BFI.
Coleman, R. M. (2011), *Horror Noire: Blacks in American Horror Films from the 1890s to the Present*, New York: Routledge.
Creed, B. (1993), *The Monstrous-Feminine: Film, Feminism, Psychoanalysis*, New York: Routledge.
Deleyto, C. (2009), *The Secret Life of Romantic Comedy*, Manchester: Manchester University Press.
Edwards, K. (2012), "Morals, Markets, and 'Horror Pictures': The Rise of Universal Pictures and the Hollywood Production Code," *Film & History*, 42.2: 23–37.
Egan, K. (2007), *Trash or Treasure: Censorship and the Changing Meanings of the Video Nasties*, Manchester: Manchester University Press.
Fischer, L. and Landy, M. (1982), "'The Eyes of Laura Mars': A Binocular Critique," *Screen*, 23.4: 4–19.
Gomery, D. (1996), "The Economics of the Horror Film," in J. B. Weaver III and R. Tamborini (eds), *Horror Films: Current Research on Audience Preferences and Reactions*, New York: Routledge.
Grant B. K. (ed.) (1984), *Planks of Reason: Essays on the Horror Film*, London: Scarecrow Press.
Heffernan, K. (2002), "The Hypnosis Horror Films of the 1950s: Genre Texts and Industry Contexts," *Journal of Film and Video*, 54.2–3: 56–70.
—(2004), *Ghouls, Gimmicks and Gold: Horror Films and the American Movie Business, 1953–1968*, Durham, NC: Duke University Press.

Hills, M. (2005), *The Pleasures of Horror*, New York: Continuum.
Hutchings, P. (2004), *The Horror Film*, London: Routledge.
Jancovich, M. (2000), "A Real Shocker: Authenticity, Genre and the Struggle for Cultural Distinctions," *Cultural Studies*, 14.1: 22–35.
—(2002), *Horror, the Film Reader*, London: Routledge.
—(2007), "Reviews," *Screen*, 48.2: 261–6.
Kapsis, R. E. (1991), "Hollywood Genres and the Production of Culture Perspective," in B. A. Austin (ed.), *Current Research in Film: Audiences, Economics and Law Vol. 5*, Norwood: Ablex.
—(1992), *Hitchcock: The Making of a Reputation*, Chicago, IL: University of Chicago Press.
Lobato, R. and Ryan, M. D. (2011), "Rethinking Genre Studies through Distribution Analysis: Issues in International Horror Movie Circuits," *New Review of Film and Television Studies*, 9.2: 188–203.
Lowenstein, A. (2005), *Historical Trauma, National Identity, and the Modern Horror Film*, New York: Columbia University Press.
Lyons, C. (1997), *The New Censors: Movies and the Culture Wars*, Philadelphia, PA: Temple University Press.
McDonald, P. (2013), "In Focus: Media Industry Studies—Introduction," *Cinema Journal*, 52.3: 145–9.
Maltby, R. (2011), "New Cinema Histories," in R. Maltby, D. Biltereyst, and P. Meers (eds), *Explorations in New Cinema History: Approaches and Case Studies*, Oxford: Wiley-Blackwell.
Middleton, J. (2010), "The Subject of Torture: Regarding the Pain of Americans in *Hostel*," *Cinema Journal*, 49.4: 1–24.
Naremore, J. (1998), *More than Night: Film Noir in its Contexts*, Berkeley: University of California Press.
Neale, S. (1990), "Questions of Genre," *Screen*, 31.1: 45–66.
Nowell, R. (2011), *Blood Money: A History of the First Teen Slasher Film Cycle*, New York: Continuum.
—(2013), "Targeting American Women: Movie Marketing, Genre History, and the Hollywood Women-in-danger Film," *In Media: The French Journal of Media and Media Representations in the English Speaking World*, 3. Available online at http://inmedia.revues.org/600 (accessed August 31, 2013).
Scott, V. (1981), "Film Mogul Turns Menace into Millions," *Chicago Tribune*, May 31, p. D32.
Snelson, T. (2009), "'From Grade B Thrillers to Deluxe Chillers': Prestige Horror, Female Audiences, and Allegories of Spectatorship in *The Spiral Staircase* (1946)," *New Review of Film and Television Studies*, 7.2: 173–88.
Spadoni, R. (2007), *Uncanny Bodies: The Coming of Sound Film and the Origins of the Horror Genre*, Berkeley: University of California Press.
Staiger, J. (1992), *Interpreting Films: Studies in the Historical Reception of American Cinema*, Princeton, NJ: Princeton University Press.
Tudor, A. (1973), *Theories of Film*, New York: Viking Press.
—(1989), *Monsters and Mad Scientists: A Cultural History of the Horror Movie*, Oxford: Blackwell.
Waller, G. A. (1987), "Introduction," in *American Horrors: Essays on the Modern Horror Film*, Urbana: University of Illinois Press.

Weaver, J. B. III and Tamborini, R. (eds) (1996), *Horror Films: Current Research on Audience Preferences and Reactions*, New York: Routledge.

Wee, V. (2006), "Resurrecting and Updating the Teen Slasher: The Case of *Scream*," *Journal of Popular Film and Television*, 35.2: 50–61.

Williams, L. (1984), "When the Woman Looks," in M. A. Doane, P. Mellencamp, and L. Williams (eds), *Re-Vision: Essays in Feminist Film Criticism*, Los Angeles, CA: AFI.

Wood, R. (1984 [1979]), "An Introduction to the American Horror Film," in B. K. Grant (ed.), *Planks of Reason: Essays on the Horror Film*, London: Scarecrow Press.

PART ONE

Production Lines, Trends, and Cycles

1

"House of Horrors"
Corporate Strategy at Universal Pictures in the 1930s

Kyle Edwards

In addition to the pursuit of profit—and control over their products and personnel, and the industrial conditions in which they operated—film companies operating during Hollywood's classical era sought to develop a long-term presence in the industry, a recognizable public identity, and productive industrial relations, and to maximize efficiency. Their ability to achieve these goals depended on the formulation and execution of corporate strategy; that distinct pattern which provides "unity and coherence to the decision-making process" and "gives the firm its identity, its power to mobilize its strength, and its likelihood of success in the marketplace" (Andrews, 1980, p. 13). Strategy formalizes policy and operations, establishes consistency throughout an organization, and clarifies the relationship between day-to-day practices and the long-term goals of management (Besanko et al., 2004, p. 16). In so doing, it enables a company to adapt to "constantly changing business conditions" and, in select cases, to posit an identity that distinguishes the firm and its products from competitors and their output (ibid.).

During the classical period, film companies developed sophisticated corporate strategies that were built around their strengths and weaknesses, and their short- and long-term objectives (see e.g. Edwards, 2006, 2011;

see also Christensen 2006, 2012). This chapter considers this phenomenon through an analysis of Universal Pictures' early 1930s efforts to develop a corporate strategy around a series of modestly budgeted, sensationalistic horror films. For Universal, this production category represented a "core competence"—or, a "skill the corporation possesses that results in a sustainable competitive advantage" (Nordhielm, 2004, p. 15; see also Prahalad and Hamel, 1990)—that it would refine over the next few years, and through which it would build an identity as the paragon of horror, one that persists to the present day.

Accordingly, the first part of this chapter argues that Universal's strategy provided a way to counteract the company's deficiencies, to surmount financial obstacles, and to secure the attention of exhibitors and moviegoers. The second part focuses on the first of Universal's horror films, *Dracula* (1931), showing that the company was drawn to the prestige and broad international appeal of this literary property, and that it pitched it to audiences on the allure of the evil Count. The third part argues that, with *Frankenstein* (1931), the first follow-up to *Dracula*, Universal developed discourses of quality around the property, thereby establishing transferable production and marketing models that it could apply to subsequent films. The final part examines *Murders in the Rue Morgue* (1932), *The Black Cat* (1934), and *The Raven* (1935), suggesting that these three films bear witness to the increased proficiency of Universal's horror unit (i.e. evidence of its core competence), and the company's desire to brand itself as the period's premier "house of horrors" (see also Hirschhorn, 1983; Dick, 1997; Humphries, 2006; Spadoni, 2007).

This chapter therefore connects the production, content, and marketing of early sound-era horror to Universal Pictures' commitment to its core competency and to branding exercises. In so doing, I hope to shed new light on the industrial forces that underpinned Universal's contribution to the early development of this genre. In a more general sense, the chapter spotlights the extent to which a focus on the formulation and implementation of corporate strategy can help us to better understand the motives and actions of individual film companies, and therefore the underlying forces that help to shape film and media history.

Universal Pictures, Inc.

In 1912, the German émigré Carl Laemmle pioneered an early form of vertical integration when his firm, Universal Film Manufacturing Company, started to distribute and exhibit the short films it produced at its East Coast facilities.

This company released its first feature-length film, *Traffic in Souls*, in 1913, the same year that it was renamed Universal Pictures, Inc., and two years before it relocated to a larger facility in North Hollywood (see e.g. Hirschhorn, 1983; Schatz, 2010). Despite the commercial success of *Traffic in Souls*, Laemmle opted to specialize in low-budget feature films and in one- and two-reel shorts, which, in addition to being shown at Universal's own theaters, could be sold easily to independent exhibitors.

In 1920, Laemmle appointed the 21-year-old Irving Thalberg as general manager in charge of production. Thalberg hoped to raise the visibility of Universal by producing a greater number of big-budget pictures. Upscale fare like *The Hunchback of Notre Dame* (1923) soon began to appear on the company's production schedule. Most of these lavish productions turned a profit, but Thalberg became frustrated with the restraints imposed by Laemmle's low-budget programming. Needing a steady flow of capital to repay debts and to finance new films, Universal began offloading its theaters in the 1920s. Thus, where other film companies viewed the purchase of theaters as a means of corporate development—based on the regular cash flow, guaranteed sites of exhibition, and public advertising spaces that they provided—Universal focused on rural and foreign markets. As Thomas Schatz has pointed out, "Universal had all but written off the [US] first-run market by 1920" (2010, p. 21; see also Huettig, 1944).

Within a decade, Universal had shrunk in stature from a major to a major-minor. Under these conditions it perhaps comes as little surprise to discover that in 1923 Thalberg was headhunted by Louis B. Mayer Productions, which became MGM, following a merger. By the mid-1920s, Universal was left with few assets, a disparate production slate, and, after its top star Lon Chaney also joined MGM, no marquee names with which to excite exhibitors or moviegoers. Constant management shuffles ensured that Universal did not develop a long-term production policy. The company hemorrhaged money across the late 1920s as mismanagement threatened to undermine relationships with exhibitors, and resulted in a failure to establish production units that could be relied upon to deliver a steady supply of feature films.

Across the mid-to-late 1920s, Universal continued to be an important supplier of cinematic entertainment to rural markets, one of the last vestiges of silent film exhibition. Consequently, it was among the final major or major-minor film companies to move exclusively into the production of talkies (see Crafton, 1999). Although Laemmle preferred the low-risk policy of producing inexpensive features and shorts, and was in little doubt that talkies represented the future of the industry, in 1928, he ceded control of production to his 21-year-old son Carl 'Junior' Laemmle (hereafter Junior Laemmle). Like Thalberg before him, Junior Laemmle placed his confidence in big-budget films aimed at lavish movie palaces. A few of these early "Jewel" productions, as Junior Laemmle called prestige pictures, were financially successful, including the upscale musical *Broadway* (1929) and the epic war film *All Quiet on the Western Front* (1930); the former was Universal's first foray into Technicolor, the latter a $1.4 million production that turned a significant profit and won an Academy Award for Best Picture.

In spite of the success it enjoyed with high-end product, Universal was neither sufficiently capitalized nor in possession of the upmarket first-run theaters needed to support such fare. "Pictures like *Broadway* and *All Quiet on the Western Front*," Schatz has argued, "were acts of cinematic and institutional bad faith, hardly the basis for a consistent studio operation or a reliable market strategy" (2010, p. 87). Rather than risk his company's solvency on new big-budget projects, Junior Laemmle took Universal in a different direction. He halved production, imposed a budget cap of $1 million per film, and developed a core competence in the production and promotion of modestly priced, technically proficient, sensational feature films that promised to distinguish the company from its competitors across all sectors of exhibition.[1]

The Great Depression hit the American film industry in 1931, when declining domestic ticket sales, coupled with a need to repay high-interest loans taken to finance the conversion to sound, resulted in the combined earnings of the top eight American film companies dropping by 90 percent from 1930 to 1931. Universal, however, eked out a $400,000 profit in 1931 (Schatz, 2010, p. 12; see also Wasko, 1982, ch. 3), thanks to a corporate strategy that was built, in part, on horror film production and distribution.

Dracula

Dracula introduced conventions and practices that would guide the development, production, and marketing of Universal's subsequent horror films. The company had flirted with the idea of adapting this property in 1915, and gave it serious consideration in 1927, when Carl Laemmle instructed his staff to assess the possibilities of filming Bram Stoker's bestselling 1897 novel (see Brunas et al., 1990, p. 9; see also Riley and Turner, 1990, pp. 26–7). Whereas some of Universal's in-house assessments emphasized the viability of adapting the property based on its gruesome imagery,

---

[1] According to Nordhielm, the successful identification and cultivation of core competence can produce a viable corporate strategy and, eventually, a lasting and meaningful brand identity (2004, p. 15).

mysterious characters, and sensationalistic content, others dismissed *Dracula* as "revolting," "horrible," "unpleasant," and "an insult to [...] its audience." Based on these mixed responses, Laemmle decided against developing a film that threatened to be too gruesome for the rural market (see Riley and Turner, 1990, pp. 19–72).

Two years later however, Junior Laemmle came to a rather different conclusion. Having reviewed an in-house report on the commercial potential of a cinematic version of *Dracula*, the executive authorized Universal to pay $40,000 for the rights to both the novel and a stage play credited to Deane and Balderston (Brunas et al., 1990, p. 9). Early in the adaptation process, Junior Laemmle requested that elements of the play be added to the script, that settings and situations be tailored to keep costs down, and that the final film be sufficiently short to feature on a double bill (see Taves, 1995; Riley and Turner, 1990, pp. 55–6).

This desire for efficient production practices influenced the selection of creative personnel. Bela Lugosi, who had played the Count on the stage, was hired to reprise this role in Universal's film; he knew the part well and could be acquired at little expense (see Soister, 1999, pp. 81–9). Director Tod Browning was known for his collaborations with Chaney on a series of macabre MGM films, and set designer Charles D. Hall's previous work for Universal demonstrated an ability to construct suitably sinister sets. Hall was also well acquainted with the company's stock of props and sets, some of which could be repurposed for new films; recycling sets constituted a key cost-cutting measure. The initial treatment of the script reveals that scenes in a Hungarian village could be shot on Universal's existing "Swiss Village Set"; in notes, Junior Laemmle sought clarification about the construction of new sets and the modification of existing ones. Ultimately, the film cost $355,050, still a generous budget given the average $237,000 cost of the company's films at the time (Universal Pictures, n.d.a).[2]

Because it could not exert direct control over exhibitor ballyhoo on account of having sold off its theaters, Universal circulated a press book to theater owners in an effort to secure engagements and to advise them on how best to promote and publicize *Dracula*. The document encouraged exhibitors to play up the plausibility of the *Dracula* story, and of vampirism in general. For example, one newspaper advertisement read: "BEWARE! Be on guard for one who roams the night! Lock and Bolt the doors and windows! Investigate

---

[2]These figures show that Universal considered *Dracula* to be an important part of its release slate (see Riley and Turner, 1999, p. 42). Pre-production costs for *Dracula* totaled $71,000, which represented about 20 percent of the film's overall budget (Universal Pictures, n.d.a; for 1930 to 1932 production schedules and average budgets see Schatz, 2010, p. 86).

all strange noises! [...] Get set for Dracula, the vampire mystery thriller!" (Universal Pictures, 1990 [1931], p. 3; capitalization in original). The press book also suggested publicity stunts that involved inviting audiences to think about whether the vampire myth might actually be rooted in fact (ibid., p. 5). These included an essay-writing contest in which newspaper readers would consider whether the creatures really existed, and a campaign encouraging them to send letters on this topic to local physicians (ibid.). Exhibitors largely followed Universal's advice when promoting the picture. As the trade paper *Film Daily* reported, an employee of one first-run house had been sent around the town of Shreveport, Louisiana sporting a Count Dracula costume and make-up, and opening his cape to expose an announcement that read "[Dracula at] Majestic Theater, One Week Starting Sunday" (ibid.).

Universal opened *Dracula* on February 14, 1931 to immediate commercial and critical success. Reviewers lauded it for featuring an "ultra-sensational [...] cunningly developed story" and for being "the best of the many mystery films" ("Sid", 1931, p. 14; Hall, 1931, p. 21). *Dracula* was Universal's top grossing film of the year (Hirschhorn, 1983, p. 72).

Frankenstein

Universal had benefitted hugely from *Dracula*, which had generated a significant amount of income for the company, increased its visibility in the first-run market, and, most importantly, established a reusable production-textual model. As Jack Alicoate of *Film Daily* observed in a profile of the Laemmles, "One cannot visit the Universal lot without immediately being impressed with its complete rejuvenation" (1931, pp. 1–2). The trade paper *Variety* shared this optimism in a headline reading "U[niversal] Has Horror Cycle All to Self [sic]" (1931, p. 2). While the company touted the commercial success and increasing quality of its feature films, Universal quietly went about cutting budgets and making the most of its resources. In June 1931, Junior Laemmle instructed his sales team to aggressively promote "revival bookings" of Universal hits such as *Dracula* (*Film Daily*, 1931b, pp. 1, 3; 1931c, p. 2; 1931e, pp. 1, 3), thereby keeping this film in the public eye and on the radar of exhibitors just as the company was looking to develop a follow-up.

In late 1931, Universal identified another literary classic as the second entry in its nascent production category: Mary Shelley's 1818 novel *Frankenstein*, the theatrical rights to which it already owned. As with *Dracula*, Universal sought to capitalize not only on the *Frankenstein* novel, but also on numerous theatrical adaptations, the recognizability of its central characters, and the universality of its themes. James Whale, fresh from the success of the war film *Journey's End* (1930) and the romantic drama *Waterloo Bridge* (1931), was offered his pick of any Universal film in development, and chose *Frankenstein*. Whale exerted a great influence over pre-production decisions, most notably the casting as ambitious scientist Henry Frankenstein of Colin Clive, with whom the director had collaborated on a stage production of *Journey's End* (see Curtis, 1998). At Whale's behest, Universal cast the little-known, and thus inexpensive, character actor Boris Karloff as the monster—the character that had become *Frankenstein*'s principal attraction. The supporting cast was drawn largely from *Dracula*, with Dwight Frye playing Frankenstein's grossly disfigured lab assistant Fritz, and Edward Van Sloan his trusted mentor Dr. Waldman. Evidence of Universal's growing efficiency in producing horror films can be gauged by the $262,007 production budget of *Frankenstein*, which was approximately 25 percent less than that of *Dracula*.

Universal's marketing campaign posited that *Frankenstein*'s themes, images, and effects would stay with viewers long after they had left the theater. "Warning! The monster is loose!", cautioned one of the film's taglines. An announcement in the *Atlanta Constitution* carried a "friendly warning" that *Frankenstein* would agitate those with "a weak heart [who] cannot stand excitement or gruesomeness" (1931, p. 16). According to the ad, those moviegoers who "like an unusual thrill [...] will find it in *Frankenstein*" (ibid.). A more explicit instance of this approach occurred in a December 2 ad in the *Chicago Daily Tribune*, which proclaimed "To See It Is To Wear a Badge of Courage!", before asking, "Do You Dare To See It?" (1931, p. 12). Theater owners supported the company's marketing angles through their own publicity stunts. For example, the Paramount-owned Palace Theater in McAllen, Texas offered a $5 prize to the first person who viewed *Frankenstein* alone with the theater lights down and its doors locked (*Film Daily*, 1932a, p. 9).

The emphasis on the ambivalent allure of *Frankenstein* in advertisements and other exploitation practices is reinforced in the film itself, most notably in the opening shot, which features tuxedoed gentlemen who address the audience directly:

> How do you do? Mr. Carl Laemmle feels that it would be a little unkind to present this picture without just a word of friendly warning. We are about to unfold the story of Frankenstein, a man of science, who sought to create a man after his own image without reckoning upon God. It is one of the strangest tales ever told. [...] I think it will thrill you. It may shock you. It might even horrify you. So if any of you feel that you do not care to subject your nerves to such a strain, now is your chance to, uh—well, we've warned you.

Here, the narrator provides a crucial link between the company—and more specifically its long-time figurehead Carl Laemmle—and the audience at the site of exhibition, an especially important strategy given the fact that Universal could exert only limited control over the first-run theaters where it hoped *Frankenstein* would find success.

The company's motives are also evident in the concluding scenes of the film, wherein a fire appears to engulf Henry Frankenstein and his monster, before an epilogue shows the doctor convalescing at home. This sequence differed from the original ending, in which the two characters perished in the blaze. It was modified at the behest of Junior Laemmle, who instructed James Whale to leave the characters' futures in doubt (see Schatz, 2010, pp. 94–5). This adjustment ensured that the company could deploy the key characters in *Frankenstein*, and the studio-contracted actors associated with them, in subsequent Universal horror films.

Frankenstein opened in November 1931, and enjoyed huge commercial success. It generated an estimated $12,000,000 at the domestic box office,[3] a return on investment which far exceeded that of *Dracula*. Even more satisfying for Universal, however, was the fact that *Frankenstein* was cheaper to produce and more technically polished than its predecessor, evidence of the further refinement of Universal's competence in horror. Along with *Dracula*, *Frankenstein* helped to associate Universal with a financially viable production model, and cemented demand for a product that the company was well equipped—more so in fact than its competitors—to deliver quickly, efficiently, and profitably.

Becoming the house of horrors

By the early 1930s, the work of the poet and author Edgar Allan Poe signified themes such as depravity, melancholy, psychological trauma, and sadism; themes that corresponded closely to those prevalent in cinematic horror. Universal sought to commodify these discourses by producing three Poe adaptations: *Murders in the Rue Morgue* (1932), *The Black Cat* (1934), and *The Raven* (1935). An examination of these three films demonstrates the degree to which Universal continued to refine its core competence and to reinforce the company brand that it had started to develop with the production and promotion of *Dracula* and *Frankenstein*.

The production of *Murders in the Rue Morgue* in the spring of 1931, seven months before the release of *Frankenstein*, was a sign that Universal was

---

[3]This estimate is cited by numerous sources (see e.g. Internet Movie Database, 2013a).

primed to produce a succession of horror films in the wake of the success of *Dracula*. Robert Florey was assigned as director, and Karl Freund, Jack Pierce, and Charles Hall were chosen for cinematography, make-up, and art direction respectively. The presence of these horror stalwarts ensured that *Murders in the Rue Morgue* maintained visual continuity to Universal's earlier horror films, even though its $130,000 budget constituted only half of that used for *Frankenstein*, and just one-third of that of *Dracula*. While the cost of *Murders in the Rue Morgue* eventually climbed to nearly $190,000, it still represented a significantly smaller financial risk than its predecessors.[4] Universal also exploited one of its most valuable assets by casting Lugosi as the sinister Dr. Mirakle, the amateur scientist and carnival barker who abducts women in order to test the kinship of humans and apes, and who, in so doing, recalls the grotesquely alluring Count Dracula and the brilliant but reckless Henry Frankenstein. Such parallels may also be seen in Mirakle's loyal yet deranged accomplice Janos, the Black One (Noble Johnson), who, not unlike those played by the aforementioned Dwight Frye in *Dracula* and *Frankenstein*, serves as both a henchman and a lab assistant.

In its marketing of *Murders in the Rue Morgue*, Universal promised moviegoers a similar experience to that offered by both *Dracula* and *Frankenstein*. A February 1932 full-page advertisement in *Photoplay* advised readers to "Watch Your Theatre for 'MURDERS IN THE RUE MORGUE' which follows close on the heels of 'DRACULA' and 'FRANKENSTEIN' and is fully as gruesome and intense. [...] And what greater cast could you ask for than BELA LUGOSI (Dracula himself) as 'Dr Mirakle'" (1932a, p. 15; capitalization in original). Another full-page ad, this time in a March 1932 issue of the magazine, claimed that *Murders in the Rue Morgue* would exceed its predecessors: "Grimmer than that grim picture, 'DRACULA,' more gruesome and awe-inspiring than 'FRANKENSTEIN'" (1932b, p. 13; capitalization in original). Universal also drew parallels between *Murders in the Rue Morgue* and its previous horror films in a promotional campaign targeting exhibitors. For example, one *Film Daily* ad described the *Murders in the Rue Morgue* as the "logical successor to 'DRACULA' and 'FRANKENSTEIN'" (1932b, p. 7; capitalization in original), while another thanked "the publicity and advertising men of the theatres" for their "bold" promotion of *Frankenstein*, promising that, with *Murders in the Rue Morgue*, "another super-shocker is on the way" (1931f, p. 9).

---

[4] This original budget was slashed to a miniscule $90,000, before Junior Laemmle ordered extensive re-shoots and a revised ending after witnessing the phenomenal success of *Frankenstein*. This increased the cost of the film to $186,090 (Brunas et al., 1990, pp. 31–2). The shooting of new material over ten days in December 1931, as well as soundtrack recording and mixing that January, pushed the budget up to $188,090 (Universal Pictures, n.d.b).

Its modest budget, the broad appeal of its source material and star, and its connections to previous Universal horror films helped *Murders in the Rue Morgue* to turn a solid profit of $63,000 (see Mank, 2009, p. 105). Thanks to this strong performance, the film had also reinforced the narrative and technical hallmarks of Universal's horror output at a fraction of the cost of *Dracula* or *Frankenstein*. *Variety* recognized Universal's desire to showcase connections between its horror films as a means of positioning itself as the progenitor of American horror cinema: "'Dracula' and 'Frankenstein' having softened 'em up, this third of U's baby-searing cycle won't have the benefit of shocking them stiff, and then making them talk about it. Had it come first there's no doubt it would have created a stronger impression" (1932, p. 24). This writer also cited the conduct of a New York audience as evidence that the American public too was becoming familiar with the conventions of Universal's horror films (ibid.).

Following the release of *Murders in the Rue Morgue*, Junior Laemmle announced that Universal had "started a cycle of [...] horror stories and we're going to continue along that line" (*New York Times*, 1932, p. X6). This proclamation would come to fruition with the release of films such as *The Old Dark House* and *The Mummy* (both 1932), both of which starred Karloff, and of *The Invisible Man* (1933). In the same period, at least five other companies had released horror films.[5] Amid this increasingly crowded marketplace, Universal sought to position itself as the indisputable "house of horrors" by pairing Karloff and Lugosi, the two stars that were most closely associated with the genre, in a second adaptation of Poe's *The Black Cat*. Having now amassed considerable expertise in horror film production—not to mention countless costumes, props, and sets—Universal was in a position to produce such fare quickly and cheaply. *The Black Cat*'s meager $91,125 production budget was indicative of a development that had been signaled two years earlier by *Murders in the Rue Morgue*: Universal's division of its horror output into prestige and programmer units. By means of comparison, *The Bride of Frankenstein* (1935) cost $397,000 to produce, a fairly standard figure for most studios' A-films, but a substantial investment for Universal.[6] While Universal

---

[5] Among the horror films released during this period were: MGM's *Freaks*, *Kongo*, and *The Mask of Fu Manchu* (all 1932); Edward Halperin's *White Zombie* (1932); Warner Bros.' *Doctor X* (1932) and *Mystery of the Wax Museum* (1933); Paramount's *Dr. Jekyll and Mr. Hyde* (1931), *Island of Lost Souls* (1932), and *The Ghoul*, and Majestic's *The Vampire Bat* (both 1933).

[6] Delving further into the production of each film underscores this disparity: Junior Laemmle personally oversaw the two-month shoot of *The Bride of Frankenstein*, Balderston worked on the screenplay, Franz Waxman provided an original score (a rare luxury for Universal, especially for its horror films), and a team of technicians devised the most elaborate effects the company had used on a horror film. By contrast, *The Black Cat* was supervised over 15 days by the producer E. M. Asher, was written by the second-tier Universal screenwriter Peter Ruric, was directed by the

did not publicly call attention to the division of its horror production units, this development clearly reflected the company's desire to use its horror series to build a presence in the first-run market, while also serving the needs of those exhibitors to whom it had for two decades supplied low-budget programmers.

The promotional campaign for *The Black Cat* bore similarities to previous Universal horror films. Some ads cautioned viewers to "[b]eware" the anxiety they were sure to experience when watching the film. What is more, *The Black Cat* press book encouraged theater owners to post a placard beside posters for the film that read "Beware of goose pimples, shivers, chills, scares—'BLACK CAT' will give you all of these, and if you can't take it, don't see this picture" (Universal Pictures, 1934, p. 8; capitalization in original). Other ads highlighted Lugosi's and Karloff's association with horror by declaring that "[t]hose ghastly madmen are back again!", or by identifying the film's stars as "'Frankenstein' Karloff" and "'Dracula' Lugosi" (Advertisement: "The Black Cat," 1935; Universal Pictures, 1934, p. 8).

The Black Cat built upon many of the conventions Universal had established in its earlier horror films by integrating into the narrative intertextual commentary on the respective star images of Karloff and Lugosi. For instance, Lugosi's Poelzig character's train journey through a remote range of Hungarian mountains was modeled on the carriage ride that this actor's character had taken to Dracula's Transylvanian estate. Similarly, Poelzig is introduced in silhouette rising slowly from a bed, an image that calls to mind the familiar profile of Frankenstein's monster. Later, in a veiled reference to their respective roles as supernatural monsters in *Dracula* and *Frankenstein*, Poelzig asks Werdegast, "Are we not the living dead?"

The commercial success of *The Black Cat*, which was Universal's most profitable feature of 1934, reinforced the bankability of Lugosi and Karloff, indicated ongoing audience interest in horror across all markets, and validated Universal's dual production strategy *vis-à-vis* horror (ibid., p. 79).[7] The implementation of that strategy would continue into 1935, when the company once again paired Lugosi and Karloff, this time in *The Raven*, a loose adaptation of Poe's famed 1845 poem. First-time director Lew Landers (AKA Louis Friedlander) was supported by a crew with ample experience in such films, including producer E. M. Asher, cinematographer Charles Stumar, make-up designer Jack Pierce, and art director Albert D'Agostino. Where elaborate sets and script redrafts had pushed *The Raven's* budget 20 percent beyond that of

---

unproven Edgar Ulmer, was scored primarily with stock and public domain music, and was staffed by a one-man special effects crew (Brunas et al., 1990, p. 83).
[7] Soister reports that *The Black Cat* returned a profit of $140,000 (1999, p. 175); the Internet Movie Database reports domestic gross rentals as $236,000 (Internet Movie Database, 2013b).

The Black Cat, this film cost a paltry $115,000, well below the average cost of Hollywood films at the time. With its cast and crew of horror mainstays and its basis in familiar source material, *The Raven* illustrates Universal's ongoing efforts to utilize its core competence within the domain of film production.[8]

Universal also sought to highlight this attribute at the level of distribution, especially in the emphasis that it placed on Karloff's and Lugosi's relationships to the company's previous horror films. Sample posters featured in *The Raven* press book—not unlike those of *The Black Cat*—referred to Lugosi as "Bela (Dracula) Lugosi," and included an image of the costumed actor that bore an uncanny resemblance to the Count (Universal Pictures, 1935, p. 8). Similarly, in clear allusions to his roles in *Frankenstein* and *The Mummy*, Karloff is described as "the uncanny master of makeup in a new amazing thriller!" (ibid.). The press book was also used to encourage theater owners to create a "Chamber of Chills" in their lobbies, and to assign a member of staff to walk around in a raven costume, thereby imbuing their venues with a "chilling atmosphere" befitting of such a film (ibid., pp. 4–5).

Like *The Black Cat*, *The Raven* boasted many of the conventions that Universal had established in its previous horror films. The stars of *The Raven* indicated the film's generic credentials, as did its sets, cinematography, and soundtrack, all of which had become key components of Universal's model. The operating room, labyrinthine home, and expansive cellar all have close or exact corollaries in previous Universal horror films. So too does the regular use of frightening off-screen noises and the piercing screams of women in peril: as a storm descends on the Vollin home late at night, the ambient sounds of rain, thunder, and lightning—as well as the crash of a tree limb through a bedroom window—set a familiar mood, recalling the baying wolves of *Dracula*, and violent storms in both *Frankenstein* and *The Black Cat*. The film concludes, fittingly, with Karloff's character locking Lugosi's in a device of his own construction, a scene with clear parallels to *The Black Cat*, and one that captures the film's promotion as a stand-off between Universal's two most iconic horror actors.

Conclusion

Despite the commercial success of its horror films, Universal was still

---

[8]The fact that Universal placed an announcement in *Variety* stating that *The Raven* would be a "super-production" indicates that the company wanted this film to be perceived as a lavish, high-quality release on a par with *The Bride of Frankenstein*, its lower production budget notwithstanding (1935, p. 4).

burdened with heavy debt throughout the 1930s. Programmers and formula pictures provided a steady cash flow, but the rate at which Universal generated income from these hits was surpassed by the speed at which those monies were rechanneled into the prestige productions with which Junior Laemmle hoped to reap huge financial rewards and to challenge the majors. In effect, Universal was banking its future on a production category that was far removed from the core competence it had refined over the previous half-decade. In late 1935, Carl Laemmle offered the company as collateral against a $750,000 loan borrowed from the Standard Capital bank. Standard Capital would ultimately exercise its right to assume control of Universal's production facilities, theaters, and foreign interests for an additional $4,100,000 in the spring of 1936, when the company's latest high-end production, *Show Boat* (1936), went over budget. As a result of this buy-out, Carl Laemmle retired and his son was unceremoniously relieved of his duties. Robert H. Cochrane became president of Universal, and Charles Rogers, a former RKO producer, was installed as head of production. Rogers would push down Universal's annual production budgets and increase output (Hirschhorn, 1983, pp. 54–5; Schatz, 2010, pp. 233–8). A fan of musicals, he used the 15-year-old Deanna Durbin—a star thanks to a 1936 turn in *Three Smart Girls*—to project a new image for Universal, one in which horror seemed anathematic. The company ceased its production of horror films (*Film Daily*, 1936, pp. 1–2).

Universal's hiatus from horror film production proved short-lived however. The characters that it had popularized in the 1930s were valuable assets, and, perhaps more importantly for the debt-ridden company, they were presold properties that required little marketing. Several of its early horror films, including *Dracula* and *Frankenstein*, were rereleased in the late 1930s, and spin-offs such as *Son of Frankenstein* (1939) were greenlighted. When horror flourished in the early 1940s, Universal intensified its focus on such fare, releasing films like *The Ghost of Frankenstein* (1942), *Son of Dracula* (1943), *House of Frankenstein* (1944), *House of Dracula* (1945), and *House of Horrors* (AKA *Joan Medford is Missing*) (1946).[9]

While Universal's horror production units of the 1930s had long since disbanded, the brand identity that had been attached to the company through the production and promotion of *Dracula*, *Frankenstein*, and subsequent horror films persisted. Universal exploited that image in its 1940s horror films by invoking the most identifiable aspects of its brand identity: the supernatural villains it had showcased in the 1930s. Teaming Frankenstein's

---

[9] *Variety* reported that Universal's horror films had generated $10 million as of 1944, and that the company was planning to produce six new horror features during the 1944 to 1945 season (1944, p. 3).

monster, Count Dracula, the Wolf Man, the Mad Doctor, and the Hunchback in both *House of Frankenstein* and *House of Dracula* reminded audiences of Universal's association with the genre's most iconic characters—or "The Mightiest Monsters of Terror!", as one ad called them—while also underscoring its continued status as the only Hollywood studio with the right to unite them in a single feature film.

In more recent times, Universal has continued to invoke the reputation that may be traced back to the strategy formulated and implemented by Junior Laemmle in the early to mid-1930s. In 2004, the company—now owned by General Electric, and renamed NBCUniversal Entertainment—launched the Universal Monsters Legacy DVD series. Timed to coincide with the opening of its calculated blockbuster *Van Helsing* (2004), each DVD package featured digitally remastered versions of films featuring Dracula, Frankenstein's monster, the Mummy, the Invisible Man, the Wolf Man, and the Creature from the Black Lagoon (characters that also appear in *Van Helsing*). The company also released a six-disc box set that included 13 films and hand-cast miniature busts of many of these creatures. Touted as a "celebration [of] Universal Pictures history of classic horror films," the series demonstrated Universal's ongoing interest in mining the economic and symbolic value of the characters that it had brought to the screen over 70 years earlier, and its continued confidence in the practices developed at this time, most famously with respect to *The Bride of Frankenstein*. In 2007, NBCUniversal announced the opening of "House of Horrors," a "multi-sensory experience" located at the Universal Studios Hollywood theme park. According to a press release, this attraction promised to "breathe life into Universal's most notorious celluloid creatures," and to usher visitors through a variety of famous sets, including Dracula's Lair and Dr Frankenstein's laboratory (Universal Studios, 2007). In this venue, the public could finally immerse itself in the peculiar combination of pleasure and terror that Universal had offered to moviegoers who dared view its horror films on their original release in the 1930s.

References

Advertisement: "The Black Cat" (1935), Barry Theater, Pittsburgh. Available online at http://cryptofwrestling.tumblr.com/post/37217040596/great-ad-for-the-black-cat-1934-and-werewolf-of (accessed August 10, 2013).
Alicoate, J. (1931), "Universal City – A Day with the Laemmles," *Film Daily*, October 14, pp. 1– 2.
Andrews, K. A. (1980), *The Concept of Corporate Strategy*, Revised Edition, Homewood: Richard D. Irwin.

Atlanta Constitution (1931), "Advertisement B: *Frankenstein*," November 29, p. 16.
Balio, T. (ed.) (1995), *Grand Design: Hollywood as a Modern Business Enterprise, 1930–1939*, Berkeley: University of California Press.
Besanko, D., Dranove, D., Shanley, M., and Schaefer, S. (2004), *Economics of Strategy, Third Edition*, Hoboken: John Wiley & Sons.
Brunas, M., Brunas, J., and Weaver, T. (1990), *Universal Horrors: The Studio's Classic Films, 1931–1946*, Jefferson, NC and London: McFarland.
Chicago Daily Tribune (1931), "Advertisement C: 'Frankenstein,'" December 2, p. 12.
Christensen, J. (2006), "Studio Authorship, Warner Bros., and *The Fountainhead*," *The Velvet Light Trap*, 57: 17–31.
—(2012), *America's Corporate Art*, Stanford, CA: Stanford University Press.
Crafton, D. (1999), *The Talkies: American Cinema's Transition to Sound, 1926–1931*, Berkeley: University of California Press.
Curtis, J. (1998), *James Whale: A New World of Gods and Monsters*, Boston, MA: Faber and Faber.
Dick, B. (1997), *City of Dreams: The Making and Remaking of Universal Pictures*, Lexington: University of Kentucky Press.
Edwards, K. (2006), "Brand-Name Literature: Film Adaptation and Selznick International Pictures' *Rebecca* (1940)," *Cinema Journal*, 45.3: 32–58.
—(2011), "'Monogram Means Business': B-Film Marketing and Series Filmmaking at Monogram Pictures Corporation," *Film History*, 23.4: 386–400.
Film Daily (1931a), "Exploitettes: Street Ballyhoo for *Dracula*," April 3, p. 5.
—(1931b), "Universal's 1931–1932 Program Aimed at First-Run Houses," May 11, pp. 1, 3.
—(1931c), "Universal Starts Drive for Revival Bookings," June 15, p. 2.
—(1931d), "Last of U Horror Cycle," November 19, p, 2.
—(1931e), "Universal has 100 New Stories from which to Improve Lineup," December 4, pp. 1, 3.
—(1931f), Advertisement: "Murders in the Rue Morgue," December 14, p. 9.
—(1932a), "Exploitettes: What Price for Courage?," February 16, p. 9.
—(1932b), Advertisement: "Murders in the Rue Morgue," February 23, p. 7.
—(1936), "Chas Rogers … the New Universal Head Man," April 14, pp. 1–2.
Gomery, D. (1996), "The Economics of the Horror Film," in J. B. Weaver III and R. Tamborini (eds), *Horror Films: Current Research on Audience Preferences*, Mahwah, NJ: Lawrence Erlbaum Associates.
Hall, M. (1931), "The Screen: Bram Stoker's Human Vampire," *New York Times*, February 13, p. 21.
Hirschhorn, C. (1983), *The Universal Story*, New York: Crown.
Huettig, M. D. (1985 [1944]), "Economic Control of the Motion Picture Industry," in T. Balio (ed.), *The American Film Industry*, Madison: University of Wisconsin Press.
Humphries, R. (2006), *The Hollywood Horror Film, 1931–1941: Madness in a Social Landscape*, Lexington, MA: Scarecrow Press.
Internet Movie Database (2013a), "Box Office/Business for *Frankenstein* (1931)." Available online at http://www.imdb.com/title/tt0021884/business (accessed August 14, 2013).

—(2013b), "Box Office/Business for *The Black Cat* (1934)." Available online at http://www.imdb.com/title/tt0024894/business (accessed August 14, 2013).

Kinnard, R. (1995), *Horror in Silent Films: A Filmography, 1896–1929*, Jefferson, MO, and London: McFarland.

'Land.' (1934), "Review: 'The Black Cat'," *Variety*, May 22, p. 15.

Mank, G. (2009), *Bela Lugosi and Boris Karloff: The Expanded Story of a Haunting Collaboration*, Jefferson, NC: McFarland.

New York Times (1932), "A Chat With Laemmle, Jr.," April 3, p. X6.

Nordhielm, C. (2004), *Marketing Management: The Big Picture*. Stamford, CT: Thomsen.

Photoplay Magazine (1932a), "Advertisement: 'Murders in the Rue Morgue'," February, p. 15.

—(1932b), "Advertisement: 'Murders in the Rue Morgue'," March, p.13.

Prahalad, C. K. and Hamel, G. (1990), "The Core Competence of the Corporation," *Harvard Business Review*, 68, pp. 79–91.

Riley, P. J. and Turner, G. (1990), "Production Background," in P. J. Riley (ed.), *Dracula: The Original 1931 Shooting Script*, Absecon: MagicImage.

—(ed.) (1990), *Dracula: The Original 1931 Shooting Script*, Absecon: MagicImage

Schatz, T. (2010), *Genius of the System: Hollywood Filmmaking in the Studio Era*, New York: Holt.

'Sid.' (1931), "Review: 'Dracula'," *Variety*, February 18, p. 14.

Soister, J. T. (1999), *Of Gods and Monsters: A Critical Guide to Universal Studios' Science Fiction, Horror, and Mystery Films, 1929–1939*, Jefferson, NC: McFarland.

Spadoni, R. (2007), *Uncanny Bodies: The Coming of Sound Film and the Origins of the Horror Genre*, Berkeley: University of California Press.

Taves, B. (1995), "The B Film: Hollywood's Other Half," in T. Balio (ed.), *Grand Design: Hollywood as a Modern Business Enterprise, 1930–1939*, Berkeley: University of California Press.

Universal Pictures (n.d.a), "Budget: 109-1 Tod Browning: 'Dracula'," Universal Pictures Collection, University of Southern California, Special Collections Library.

—(n.d.b), "Budget: 315-1 Florey, 'Murders in the Rue Morgue'," Universal Pictures Collection, University of Southern California, Special Collections Library.

—(1934), "*The Black Cat* Pressbook." Available online at http://movieposters.ha.com/c/item.zx?saleNo=7003&lotIdNo=37001 (accessed August 8, 2013).

—(1935), "*The Raven* Pressbook." Available online at http://www.emovieposter.com/agallery/archiveitem/8632272.html (accessed August 8, 2013).

—(1990 [1931]), "*Dracula* Pressbook," in P. J. Riley (ed.), *Dracula: The Original 1931 Shooting Script*, Absecon: MagicImage: PB1–14.

Universal Studios Hollywood (2007), "Universal's House of Horrors," March 31. Available online at http://www.thestudiotour.com/ush/attractions/walkthrough_horror.shtml (accessed August 5, 2013).

Variety (1931), "U has Horror Cycle all to Self," April 8, p. 2.

—(1932), "Review: 'Murders in the Rue Morgue'," February 16, p. 24.

—(1935), "U Spread Eagling with Budget of 'The Raven'," September 6, p. 4.
—(1944), "Chillers Warm U till with $10,000,000 Net," July 24, p.3.
Wasko, J. (1982), *Movies and Money: Financing the American Film Industry*, Norwood: Ablex.

2

The Undead of Hollywood and Poverty Row

The Influence of Studio-era Industrial Patterns on Zombie Film Production, 1932 to 1946

Todd K. Platts

This chapter focuses on 13 zombie films that were produced for the American market between 1932 and 1946.[1] I argue that the industrial structure and practices of the period played a greater role in the advent of zombie cinema, in the early contributions of both the major studios and the Poverty Row firms, and in the temporary demise of the film type, than academic accounts have otherwise suggested.[2] Before doing so, however, it is useful to address broader debates about production trends.

---

[1] Those films are *White Zombie* (1932), *Love Wanga* (1934), *Revolt of the Zombies*, *The Walking Dead* (both 1936), *The Return of Doctor X* (1939), *The Ghost Breakers* (1940), *King of the Zombies* (1941), *I Walked with a Zombie*, *Revenge of the Zombies* (both 1943), *Voodoo Man* (1944), *Zombies on Broadway* (1945), *The Face of Marble*, and *Valley of the Zombies* (both 1946).

[2] This chapter contributes an enhanced understanding of early zombie films by employing qualitative content analysis and the "production-of-culture perspective" to examine the undergirding rationales behind their production. For clarity, I refer to qualitative content analysis as the subjective interpretation of a text's content through systematic classification schemes of coding and the identification of themes or patterns (see Hsieh and Shannon, 2005). The production-of-culture culture perspective focuses on how the content of cultural products such as films are heavily influenced by law, technology, careers, markets, organizational structure, and industry

In a recent essay, Richard Nowell distills efforts to account for production trends to what he calls the "socio-symptomatic principle" and the "one-hit principle" (2013, pp. 74–8). The former comprises two methods that are used to explain the emergence, development, and conclusion of surges in the production of certain types of film: the ritual approach and the zeitgeist approach. The ritual approach posits that audiences seek resolution to unresolved social concerns by attending films that address such issues but leave them unresolved, thereby providing a motive for filmmakers to fashion similar fare (see e.g. Wright, 1975; Schatz, 1981). Thus, it has been said that zombie films of the 1930s and 1940s offered by way of thinly veiled allegory an opportunity for audiences to consider the despair and alienation that they were suffering during the Great Depression. "The spectacle of the walking dead in films like *White Zombie*," argues David J. Skal (2001, pp. 168–9), "was in many ways a nightmare vision of a breadline" (see Russell, 2006, pp. 20–7; Dendle, 2007, pp. 46–8). The zeitgeist approach suggests that industry personnel latch on to important social developments when assembling the content of films, thereby fashioning exploratory vehicles for their own concerns (see Ryan and Kellner, 1988; Guynn, 2006). Thus, it has been suggested that the dichotomized characterizations of whites and blacks in *White Zombie* (1932) allowed the makers of this film to explore the American "imperialist hegemony" that had partly motivated an ongoing US occupation of Haiti, the island that was most associated with zombies and voodoo at this time (see Bishop, 2008). Whereas the two variants of the socio-symptomatic principle treat films as offshoots of events that are exogenous to industry conditions, the one-hit principle considers trends to be the results of short-to-medium-term intra-industrial responses to a recent box office hit (see Grindon, 2012, p. 53; Krämer, 2005, p. 11). Accordingly, it has been argued that the commercial success of *White Zombie* incentivized the production of similar films such as *Revolt of the Zombies* (1936), *King of the Zombies* (1941), and *Revenge of the Zombies* (AKA *The Corpse Vanished*) (1943), and *I Walked with a Zombie* (1943) (see Russell, 2006, pp. 20–7; Bishop, 2010, pp. 61–2). Nowell also suggests that scholarly explanations of production trends tend to exhibit "temporal discrepancies"; that the timing of films and those

---

structure (see Peterson and Anand, 2004). In addition, I use the term "cycle" to refer to patterns of output and "film type" to refer to textual models upon which industry professionals drew when organizing the production and content of zombie films (see Nowell, 2011, pp. 41–56). I use the term "major studios" to refer to two groups of production companies: the Big Five and the Little Three. The Big Five, including Paramount, Loew's/MGM, Twentieth Century-Fox, Warner Bros., and RKO, controlled their own theaters, production lots, and distribution lines. The Little Three—Columbia, Universal, and United Artists—did not own theaters but maintained strong ties with the Big Five. By "Poverty Row" I mean thinly capitalized independent companies that specialized in the supply of low-budget films primarily for rural markets (see Jacobs, 1934).

developments that are said to have triggered their production do not quite pass scrutiny (Nowell, 2013, pp. 75–7). Consequently, if American interest in Haiti reached its peak in 1929, as the historian Hans Schmidt has suggested (1995, pp. 196–206), one may ask why *White Zombie* was made some three years later, when American interest in Haiti was in fact already on the wane. Second, studies usually fail to explain why some hits are followed by similar films while others are not (see Nowell, 2011, pp. 108–9). This situation may lead one to consider why the relative box office success of *White Zombie* did not initiate an immediate surge in the production of partial imitations (for a discussion of film cycle development see ibid., pp. 41–54).

Existing accounts of early zombie films either elide those examples that do not lend themselves to socio-symptomatic interpretations, or do not fully address the industrial conditions that were fundamental to their creation. In contrast, this chapter aims to shed new light on those industrial conditions. It also seeks to illuminate the extent to which acts of opportunism determined the emergence of zombie films, and how the development of this type of film was shaped by regimes of content tailoring, routinized production, and product differentiation.

The emergence of the zombie film: *White Zombie*

To date, scholars and commentators have inaccurately claimed that zombie films emerged as a direct reaction to a series of travelogs that documented the experiences of journalists and military personnel in Haiti (see Dash, 1997, p. 51). The most important of these accounts is usually suggested to have been William Seabrook's 1929 *The Magic Island*, which sold 500,000 copies after being promoted by the prestigious book club The Literary Guild (see Renda, 2001, p. 19). These developments may have made *The Magic Island* a conspicuous work that would have been known to American film studios, which monitored literary and cultural trends in search of bankable properties (see Balio, 1993, pp. 100–1), but industry professionals showed no real interest in optioning the book.

The Magic Island offered little in the way of exploitable qualities upon which to base a coherent feature film. Structured as a loosely connected series of events, this literary bestseller could not easily be adapted to the cause-and-effect storytelling that characterized American film production of the period (see Bordwell et al., 1985). It also contained scenes that were simply too violent or too sexually charged to stand a chance of passing the censors. Furthermore, Kenneth Webb's attempt in 1932 to adapt *The Magic Island* into the stage play *Zombie* had been commercially unsuccessful (Rhodes, 2001, pp. 70–1). This development was of primary importance. As Peter Hutchings has argued (2004, pp. 11–14), 1930s horror films such as *Dracula* and *Frankenstein* (both 1931) appealed to industry decision-makers precisely because their success on the stage had indicated the existence of a sizable audience for such material, and had spotlighted readily deployable textual models. *The Magic Island*'s status as a problematic source material, combined with the commercial failure of the stage adaptation, served to temper the appeal of bankrolling films about Caribbean bogeymen.

White Zombie—the first zombie film—was a product both of general industrial forces and the commercial strategies that were employed by a team of entrepreneurs. Put simply, this film was developed by shrewd businessmen who were especially well positioned to grasp the new opportunities that were opening up for independent producers. The producer Victor Halperin and the director Edward Halperin were not looking to tap into American interest in Haiti; they were in fact seeking to capitalize on reports that the major studios were in the market for what the trade paper *Film Daily* dubbed "quality product from small producers" (1931, p. 1; see also Gillette, 1931, p. 13). The Halperins were also reacting to the growing confidence that gatekeepers at these companies were said to be placing in horror films following the commercial success of *Dracula*, of *Frankenstein*, and of *Dr. Jekyll and Mr. Hyde* (1931), all of which had cemented their interest in contributing to this nascent cycle of films (see Shaffer, 1932; Rhodes, 2001, pp. 123, 232).

Unlike most of their peers, the Halperins were capable of bringing the production values of an independently made horror film in line with those of major studio pictures, thereby increasing their chances of negotiating a distribution deal with this caliber of company. The brothers were bankrolled by New York investors who had provided them with a sizable loan of $50,000 to $62,500 (Rhodes, 2001, p. 91). The Halperins also knew how to craft a film that was likely to appeal to distributors. Promoting themselves as "movie engineers," the Halperins drew up charts of hits to assist in the assembly of what they hoped were "fail-proof" pictures (see *Syracuse Herald*, 1927, p. 18; McManus, 1936, p. X3). They also bolstered *White Zombie*'s prospects of attracting a major distributor by replicating elements of recent hits. As Rhodes has pointed out (2001, pp. 13–38), the film bore striking similarities to familiar stories such as *Faust* (1926) and *Svengali* (1931). In addition, and as was a common practice at the time, *White Zombie* was laced with a romantic sub-plot in order to make it more marketable and appealing to female moviegoers (see Berenstein, 1996, pp. 60–87). The casting of Bela

Lugosi in the role of the lead villain also gave this film a degree of star pulling power that low-budget independent productions usually lacked (see Balio, 1993, pp. 143–77). Finally, the Halperins tailored *White Zombie* in such a way as to ensure that it acquired a Production Code Seal, thereby demonstrating to potential distributors that the film would be accepted at lucrative first-run theaters (see Heffernan, 2004, p. 4).

Despite generating relatively impressive box office returns after it was released by United Artists (see Lusk, 1932; Rhodes, 2001, pp. 259–62), *White Zombie* exerted a minimal impact on the American film industry.[3] It would take a full year for production to begin on another zombie film, when in 1933 George Terwilliger shot *Love Wanga* (AKA *Ouanga*), which was eventually released stateside in 1942 (see Senn, 1998, pp. 41–2). Jamie Russell has suggested that industry decision-makers viewed *White Zombie* as something of a box office fluke (2006, p. 27), because they attributed the film's commercial achievements to the American public's fleeting preoccupation with its subject matter. In addition, *Variety* mistook *White Zombie*'s weak performances in Chicago as a sign that audience interest in horror films was dipping (*Variety*, 1932d, p. 9). The appeal of producing and distributing such fare was further undermined by a legal battle that erupted over the Halperins 1936 picture *Revolt of the Zombies*, which was accused of infringing United Artists' rights to *White Zombie* (Rhodes, 2001, pp. 171–7). This development suggested that any profits such films earned could be the victims of costly legal action.

Major studio "zombie films"

Between 1936 and 1945, the major studios produced five "zombie films": *The Walking Dead* (1936), *The Return of Doctor X* (1939), *The Ghost Breakers* (1940), *I Walked with a Zombie* (1943), and *Zombies on Broadway* (1945). I place the term zombie films in quotation marks here to denote the fact that the majors relegated zombies to the margins of the narrative, or placed them

---

[3] Upon completing *White Zombie*, the Halperins pursued a distribution deal with two of the majors: Universal and Columbia (*Variety*, 1932a, 1932b). However, both of these companies deemed the film to be too risky an investment. Eventually a distribution deal was signed with United Artists, which was in the process of purchasing independently produced films (*Variety*, 1932c). The contract resulted in the Halperins surrendering to Amusement Securities Corporation the distribution rights for *White Zombie*, and waiving their right to use the term "zombie" in the title of a film for ten years. The deal also guaranteed that *White Zombie* was an original property that did not infringe the rights of other filmmakers.

in pre-existing textual models, or that reviewers claimed that these pictures contained zombies when they did not in fact do so.[4]

The marginalization of zombie characters in most of the major studios' "zombie films" was a by-product of the increasing significance of double bills and B-unit production. Throughout the period, the majors had maintained control of the industry through block-booking (compelling exhibitors to accept groups of films on an all-or-nothing basis), through clearance and zoning (determining which theaters played what movies and when), and through setting ticket prices (Balio, 1993, pp. 18–21). These practices had led independent exhibitors to turn to double bills, whereby audiences were offered the chance to watch two films for the price of one. Despite being contested by the majors, double billing—particularly of low-budget fare—became standard practice among independent exhibitors who were looking to feed the American public's growing appetite for new pictures (see *Variety*, 1934, p. 5; Nugent, 1943, pp. SM11, SM21). Turnover was particularly rapid in the smaller subsequent-run theaters that received films only after their ability to attract audiences was diminishing. With exhibitors needing up to 300 inexpensive films each year to fill out their rosters, the majors established B-units to specialize in the production of cut-price fare that was destined for the bottom half of the double bills (Balio, 1993, p. 8). The majors largely restricted horror movie production to their B-units due to the moderate returns of this type of film. Because they operated under extreme time-pressure and tight financial constraints, the B-units relied on cost-cutting practices such as series pictures or films that featured recurring characters, settings and plots—all of which were pre-sold properties that boasted an established presence in the market. They also turned to hybrid genre films and adaptations of other media texts, and they recalibrated textual models that had been used for commercially underperforming films (Crowther, 1938, p. 126; Balio, 1993, p. 2; Schatz, 1997. p. 172). Unit production helped to

---

[4] Except for *I Walked with a Zombie*, these films' promotional campaigns did not exploit zombies as a primary selling point. For example, the marketers of *Zombies on Broadway* downplayed the presence of zombies, choosing instead to foreground screwball comedy aspects of the film. This point was highlighted in *Variety*'s review of the film (1945a, p. 27), which suggested that "*Zombies on Broadway* turns out to be a ghost comedy, with half of it punched hard for laughs, some of which fail to materialize." Similarly, the promotion of *The Ghost Breakers* highlighted romantic comedy and haunted house elements over Noble Johnson's zombie character. Reviewers spotlighted the presence of zombies in *The Walking Dead* and *The Return of Doctor X*, even though the films' makers did not label them zombie films. For example, Frank Nugent of the *New York Times* remarked of Boris Karloff in *The Walking Dead*: "There is no denying that he makes an impressive zombie" (Nugent, 1936, p. 13). Meanwhile, *Variety*'s review of *The Return of Doctor X* explained that "[The] [p]lot swings on the bringing to life of Dr. X, after electrocution, by a blood specialist, and the subsequent ceaseless search for blood by the zombie to sustain his second life" (*Variety*, 1939, p. 3).

control budgets and to maintain production values, and, because individual units specialized in certain types of film, it also ensured a measure of product differentiation across a given studio's output (*Motion Picture Herald*, 1931).

With the exception of *I Walked with a Zombie*, the major studio "zombie films" were slight variations of recent hit films. For instance, *The Walking Dead* served primarily as a contribution to a cycle of Boris Karloff mad scientist films that also included *The Man They Could Not Hang* (1939), *Before I Hang*, and *The Man with Nine Lives* (AKA *Behind the Door*) (both 1940). These films had been initiated by the commercial success of *Frankenstein*. Similarly, *The Return of Doctor X* bore strong resemblances to a spate of crime dramas that had been produced by Bryan Foy, including *Devil's Island*, *King of the Underworld*, and *The Man who Dared* (all 1939). *The Ghost Breakers* and *Zombies on Broadway* belonged to a spate of horror comedies that included *The Devil Bat* (1940) and *Spooks Run Wild* (1941). Moreover, both *The Return of Doctor X* and *The Ghost Breakers* were sequels: the former to *Doctor X* (1932), the latter to *The Cat and the Canary* (1939). The appearance of each of these "zombie films" is also partially attributable to the financial achievements of a *Dracula–Frankenstein* double, which had rekindled industry confidence in horror film production (*Variety*, 1938).

Rather than resulting from adventurous creative practice, the majors' "zombie films" are better seen as products of what Todd Gitlin has described as "copying" (2000). This strategy, argues Gitlin, is used to capitalize on recent successes by "reproducing a formula [through] a normal variation on run-of-the-mill themes" (2000, p. 69). In the hope of striking box office gold once more, the major studios added zombies to the textual frameworks they had used for earlier hits, such as those that had centered on the comedic and romantic travails of characters played by Bob Hope and Paulette Goddard. In this sense, the commercial potential of the majors' "zombie films" was not seen to reside in the presence of zombies per se but in those models into which the undead characters were placed. Zombies were recognized by the trade press for what they were: mere textual flourishes. For example, the *Motion Picture Herald* noted that *The Return of Doctor X* was "a cutback to such eerie productions as *Frankenstein*, *Doctor X*, and *Svengali*" (1939, p. 41), and the *Hollywood Reporter* drew parallels between *The Ghost Breakers* and *The Cat and the Canary* (1940, p. 6). These films therefore represented an attempt on the part of the units to differentiate their output from that of their competitors.[5]

---

[5] To understand the production of *I Walked with a Zombie*—the only zombie-centered film to emerge from a major studio—is to understand the atypical working practices of the unit that made the picture: RKO's Lewton-unit. In 1942, Val Lewton was hired by RKO to produce horror films in

The major studios' interest in zombie pictures was further undermined by events that impacted upon the American film industry as a whole. The escalation of production costs across the late 1930s and 1940s led to the downsizing or closure of many B-units (Moak, 1940; *New York Times*, 1946). Then, in 1940, the Big Five signed a consent decree in which they agreed to abandon blind-selling (the selling of films without offering the buyer a chance to view them) and to limit block-booking to a maximum of five pictures at a time. These companies soon began to emphasize production values and star talent in order to ensure that their new releases were appealing to exhibitors, who could now afford to be more selective about the films they screened. As Yannis Tzioumakis has pointed out, "[t]he repercussion of this move by the studios was that the decidedly B films of the Poverty Row firms were the only contenders for the bottom half of double bills" (2006, p. 83).

Poverty Row zombie films

Between 1940 and 1946, the Poverty Row outfits produced a total of five zombie films: *Revenge of the Zombies* (1943), *Voodoo Man* (1944), *The Face of Marble*, *Valley of the Zombies*, and *King of the Zombies* (all 1946). In contrast to major studio efforts, Poverty Row's zombie films actually paid significant attention to zombies and to the characters that animated them. For instance, *King of the Zombies*, *Revenge of the Zombies*, *Voodoo Man*, and *The Face of Marble* all concentrated on the nefarious schemes of zombie-raising mad scientists, while *Valley of the Zombies* centralized a zombie-turned-killer. Moreover, and in contrast to the majors' "zombie films," Poverty Row's marketing campaigns typically spotlighted zombies over other qualities such as comedy, crime, or mad science. Reviewers also noted the prominence of the character type in these pictures. The *Hollywood Reporter* explained that *Revenge of the Zombies* was "another yarn concerning those overworked newcomers to the screen, the Zombies" (1943, p. 3), and *Film Daily* described *King of the Zombies* as "fostering voodooism and zombieism [sic]" (1941, p. 7). The foregrounding of zombies is perhaps best understood as Poverty Row's response to the industry's renewed faith in horror films and to the majors' reduction in B-level production, as well as standing as

---

the vein of those being made at Universal (Bansak, 2003). Lewton was afforded a large amount of creative freedom in exchange for delivering $150,000, seventy-five-minute films that boasted 'pre-tested' titles (ibid., p. 89); the title of *I Walked with a Zombie*, for example, was derived from a recent news magazine article.

an instance of the mimicking strategies that were standard practice in the independent production sector.

With zombies, Poverty Row could make use of a movie monster that had demonstrated a measure of success in the past (courtesy of solid ticket sales for *White Zombie*), but which was not being exploited fully by the majors. After the signing of the aforementioned 1940 consent decree, the number of films produced by Poverty Row companies exploded (*Los Angeles Times*, 1940; *Variety*, 1941a, 1943a). For example, Monogram announced a studio record of 50 films for the 1941/1942 season (*New York Times*, 1941), and by the mid-1940s the studio was responsible for 10 percent of American film production (Onosko, 1972, p. 6). However, Poverty Row films averaged less than $2,000 in net profits due to the majors' continued stranglehold on the most lucrative exhibition sites, and on account of B-films typically being sold for a one-time set fee, which meant that producers could not share in the spoils of a hit film (see Flynn and McCarthy, 1975, p. 24). While strong demand in rural markets for low-budget product enabled Poverty Row firms to survive on these meager profits (see Gomery, 1996, p. 51; Edwards, 2011), such narrow margins were simply too low to permit these companies to act adventurously when it came to developing their properties (see Balio, 1993, p. 101). As they could not afford to buy the rights to original stories, the Poverty Row firms hastily produced their own versions. Poverty Row's handling of zombie films supports Nowell's assessment of the roller disco movie production trend of the late 1970s insofar as it exhibited a greater degree of expedience than is suggested by the socio-symptomatic principle and more guardedness than the one-hit principle imparts (Nowell, 2013, p. 75).

The zombie films made by the Poverty Row outfits represented attempts to develop the zombie film type beyond its initial Caribbean and voodoo trappings, as well as a rejoinder to the horror films released by the major studios. Thus, the makers of *King of the Zombies* relied heavily on the look of *White Zombie* but transformed its voodoo master into a Nazi scientist, while also piggybacking Paramount's recent hit *The Ghost Breakers*.[6] Monogram then released *Revenge of the Zombies* soon after *I Walked with a Zombie* had demonstrated continued audience interest in zombie films. Voodoo served as a peripheral plot device in *Revenge of the Zombies*, which instead developed the Nazi backdrop of *King of the Zombies*. The importation and centralization of such material into the zombie film type was discussed by the trade press. For example, *Film Daily* noted that "[t]he [zombie] tale is brought up to date by making the medical meddler a German who intends

---

[6] *King of the Zombies*' press book advised exhibitors to advertise the film along the lines of *The Ghost Breakers* (Weaver, 1993, p. 37).

to take his master zombie back to the old country with him and use it as a pattern for an army of automatons that will spell victory for Nazi arms" (1943, p. 5; see also *Variety*, 1943c, p. 20). By contrast, *Voodoo Man* was primarily sold on its stars—George Zucco, John Carradine, and Bela Lugosi—whom *Film Daily* dubbed "past masters in the art of producing chills" (1944, p. 6). In a loose sense, *Voodoo Man* may be viewed as a reaction to the surprisingly impressive box office returns of 1943's *Frankenstein Meets the Wolf Man*, which had inspired its producer-distributor Universal swiftly to complete two follow-ups (*Variety*, 1943b, p. 46). Because they did not own the rights to bankable monsters who could be paired in new films, Poverty Row companies were required to cast a number of stars who were associated with horror films, thereby approximating the lucrative practices of the majors. In narrative terms, the filmmakers behind *Voodoo Man* took the zombie film type in another direction, as a widower combines voodoo and science to reanimate his late wife. *The Face of Marble* offered another combination of voodoo and science, which *Variety* described as "a strange mixture of electronics, voodoo, kilocycles, yarbs and spooky dogs that walk right through locked doors without so much as knocking" (1946, p. 3). On the other hand, the producers of *Valley of the Zombies* synthesized aspects of vampires with zombies in the character of Ormund Murks, whose killing of people for their blood lent the film an air of the whodunit horrors that had been commercially successful some years earlier (*Variety*, 1943b). Even though Poverty Row's zombie films performed well in the markets they played (see e.g. *Variety*, 1941b, 1941c, 1943d, 1945b), these companies abandoned production of the film type in the mid-1940s due to the changing industry circumstances of the post-war years (see Heffernan, 2004; Davis, 2012).

The decline of early zombie film production

The decline of zombie film production had little to do with the monster losing popularity with audiences. In 1946, the American film industry reached unprecedented heights of profitability which augured Republic and Monogram's entrée into the production of A-level films (see Flynn and McCarthy, 1975, p. 34; Tzioumakis, 2006, pp. 89–90). It was shortly after Republic and Monogram shifted some of their attention to operations of this sort that production costs began to rise and film attendance started to dip. These conditions threatened to bite into the already wafer-thin profit margins of zombie films to the extent that their profit potential plummeted effectively to zero, thereby making production of such fare seem less appealing than more viable types of film such as low-budget Westerns like *Dakota Kid* (1951) and high-priced dramas à la *Macbeth* (1948) and *Moonrise* (1948) (Flynn and McCarthy, 1975, pp. 24–32; Schatz, 1997, p. 371). Accordingly, only two pictures made between 1947 and 1954 could legitimately be described as zombie films. Yet, even then, zombies appeared on screen for less than a minute in *Scared Stiff* (1953), and the "zombies" in *Zombies of the Stratosphere* (1952) were in fact Martians. In the summer of 1948, the United States Supreme Court ruled against the major studios in the United States vs. Paramount Pictures, Inc., determining that the vertically integrated structure of the major studios, their use of block-booking, and their excessive clearances constituted illegal restraints of trade. The majors were forced to divest themselves of their theaters, sparking a period of monumental change for the American film industry that saw the majors sink funds into bigger productions (see Hall and Neale, 2010, pp. 135–58). These events unfolded at a time when independent filmmakers working on low-budget films were themselves going through a period of restructuring, which saw them pursue "a new role within the film industry, one that was no longer purely secondary but instead often innovative" (Davis, 2012, p. 1). Subsequently, producers would refashion zombies in ways that enabled them to ride the coat-tails of nascent production trends like teen horror films, leading to the production of *Teenage Zombies* (1959), *The Incredibly Strange Creatures who Stopped Living and Became Mixed-Up Zombies*, and *The Horror of Party Beach* (both 1964), and weirdies or films that "broadly fall into the monster-horror-science fiction category" (*Variety*, 1957, p. 3) as in *The Creature with the Atom Brain* (1955), *Invisible Invaders* (1959), and *The Last Man on Earth* (1964). New production strategies combined with evolving ideas about zombies to ensure that the cinematic undead would rise once more (see Platts, 2013, pp. 549–50).

References

Balio, T. (1993), *Grand Design: Hollywood as a Modern Business Enterprise, 1930–1939*, Berkeley: University of California Press.

Bansak, E. G. (2003), *Fearing the Dark: The Val Lewton Career*, Jefferson, MO: McFarland.

Berenstein, R. J. (1996), *Attack of the Leading Ladies: Gender, Sexuality, and Spectatorship in Classic Horror Cinema*, New York: Columbia University Press.

Bishop, K. (2008), "The Sub-Subaltern Monster: Imperialist Hegemony and the Cinematic Voodoo Zombie," *Journal of American Culture*, 31.2: 141–52.

Bishop, K. W. (2010), *American Zombie Gothic: The Rise and Fall (and Rise) of the Walking Dead in Popular Culture*, Jefferson, MO: McFarland.

Bordwell, D., Staiger, J., and Thompson, K. (1985), *The Classical Hollywood*

Cinema: Film Style and Mode of Production to 1960, New York: Columbia University Press.
Crowther, B. (1938), "How Doth the Busy Little 'B'," *New York Times*, January 2, p. 126.
Dash, J. M. (1997), *Haiti and the United States: National Stereotypes and the Literary Imagination, Second Edition*, New York: St. Martin's Press.
Davis, B. (2012), *The Battle for the Bs: 1950s Hollywood and the Rebirth of Low-Budget Cinema*, New Brunswick, NJ: Rutgers University Press.
Dendle, P. (2007), "The Zombie as Barometer of Cultural Anxiety," in N. Scott (ed.), *Monsters and the Monstrous: Myths and Metaphors of Enduring Evil*, New York: Rodopi.
Edwards, K. D. (2011), "'Monogram Means Business': B-Film Marketing and Series Filmmaking at Monogram Pictures," *Film History*, 23.4: 386–400.
Film Daily (1931), "Major Firms Looking for Quality Product from Small Producers," August 10, pp. 1, 8.
—(1941), "*King of the Zombies*," May 9, p. 7.
—(1943), "*Revenge of the Zombies*," August 25, p. 5.
—(1944), "*Voodoo Man*," February 15, p. 6.
Flynn, C. and McCarthy, T. (1975), "The Economic Imperative: Why was the B Movie Necessary?," in T. McCarthy and C. Flynn (eds), *Kings of the Bs Working within the Hollywood System: An Anthology of Film History and Criticism*, New York: E. P. Dutton.
Gillette, D. (1931), "Pay-Day for Independents," *Film Daily*, August 23, pp. 1, 13.
Gitlin, T. (2000), *Inside Prime Time*, Berkeley: University of California Press.
Gomery, D. (1996), "The Economics of the Horror Film," in J. B. Weaver III and R. Tamborini (eds), *Horror Films: Current Research on Audience Preferences and Reactions*, Mahwah, NJ: Lawrence Erlbaum Associates.
Grindon, L. (2012), "Cycles and Clusters: The Shape of Film Genre History," in B. K. Grant (ed.), *Film Genre Reader IV*, Austin: University of Texas Press.
Guynn, W. (2006), *Writing History in Film*, New York: Routledge.
Hall, S. and Neale, S. (2010), *Epics, Spectacles, and Blockbusters: A Hollywood History*, Detroit: Wayne State University Press.
Heffernan, K. (2004), *Ghouls, Gimmicks, and Gold: Horror Films and the American Movie Business, 1953–1968*, Durham, NC: Duke University Press.
Hollywood Reporter (1940), "*The Ghost Breakers*," June 6, p. 3.
—(1943), "*Revenge of the Zombies*," October 7, p. 3.
Hsieh, H. and Shannon, S. E. (2005), "Three Approaches to Qualitative Content Analysis," *Qualitative Health Research*, 15.9: 1277–88.
Hutchings, P. (2004), *The Horror Film*, New York: Pearson Longman.
Jacobs, L. (1934), "A History of the Obscure Quickie: An Analysis of the Shoestring Products which Emerge from Hollywood's Poverty Row," *New York Times*, December 30, p. X4.
Krämer, P. (2005), *The New Hollywood: From* Bonnie and Clyde *to* Star Wars, New York: Wallflower.
Los Angeles Times (1940), "Monogram's Schedule Set," June 4, p. A8.
Lusk, N. (1932), "Stage and Screen," *Los Angeles Times*, August 7, p. B15.
McCarthy, T. and Flynn C. (eds) (1975), *Kings of the Bs Working within the*

Hollywood System: An Anthology of Film History and Criticism, New York: E. P. Dutton.
McManus, J .T. (1936), "Walking Dead in Angkor," New York Times, May 24, p. X3.
Moak, B. (1940), "Exit—2nd Letter in the Film Alphabet; B's Become Near-A's," Variety, January 3, p. 19.
Motion Picture Herald (1931), "Industry to Test Unit Producing to Shave Cost, Improve Quality," June 27, p. 29.
—(1939), "Review of The Return of Dr. X," July 8, p. 41.
New York Times (1941), "News of the Screen," March 5, p. 17.
—(1946), "Universal to Drop Four 'B' Film Units," July 26, p. 16.
Nowell, R. (2011), Blood Money: A History of the First Teen Slasher Film Cycle, New York: Continuum.
—(2013), "Hollywood Don't Skate: US Production Trends, Industry Analysis, and the Roller Disco Movie," New Review of Film and Television Studies, 11.1: 73–91.
Nugent, F. (1936), "Karloff is Brought Alive in The Walking Dead at the Strand – 'The Garden Murder Case'," New York Times, March 2, p. 13.
Nugent, F. S. (1943), "Double, Double, Toil and Trouble," New York Times, January 17, pp. SM11, SM21.
Onosko, T. (1972), "Monogram: Its Rise and Fall in the Forties," The Velvet Light Trap, 5: 5–9.
Peterson, R. A. and Anand, N. (2004), "The Production of Culture Perspective," Annual Review of Sociology, 30: 311–34.
Platts, T. K. (2013), "Locating Zombies in the Sociology of Popular Culture," Sociology Compass, 7.7: 547–60.
Renda, M. A. (2001), Taking Haiti: Military Occupation and the Culture of U.S. Imperialism 1915–1940, Chapel Hill: University of North Carolina Press.
Rhodes, G. D. (2001), White Zombie: Anatomy of a Horror Film, Jefferson, MO: McFarland.
Russell, J. (2006), The Book of the Dead: The Complete History of Zombie Cinema, London: FAB Press.
Ryan, M. and Kellner, D. (1988), Camera Politica: The Politics and Ideology of Contemporary Hollywood Film, Bloomington: Indiana University Press.
Schatz, T. (1981), Hollywood Genres: Formulas, Filmmaking, and the Studio System, New York: Random House.
—(1997), Boom and Bust: American Cinema in the 1940s, Berkeley: University of California Press.
Schmidt, H. (1995), The United States Occupation of Haiti, 1915–1934, New Brunswick, NJ: Rutgers University Press.
Seabrook, W. B. (1989 [1929]), The Magic Island, New York: Paragon.
Senn, B. (1998), Drums O' Terror: Voodoo in the Cinema, Baltimore, MD: Luminary Press.
Shaffer, G. (1932), "Movie Studios Busy with New Horror Films," Chicago Daily Tribune, February 22, p. 16.
Skal, D. J. (2001), The Monster Show: A Cultural History of Horror, New York: Faber and Faber.

Syracuse Herald (1927), "Halperin Brothers Plan for Future of Pictures," December 20, p. 18.

Tzioumakis, Y. (2006), *American Independent Cinema: An Introduction*, Edinburgh: Edinburgh University Press.

Variety (1932a), "Col. Taking Outsider," May 3, p. 21.

—(1932b), "UA Buying Up Outside Films," July 19, p. 6.

—(1932c), "Universal Grabs Zombie Neg.," August 10, p. 31.

—(1932d), "Picture Grosses," September 6, pp. 8–11.

—(1934), "Need Twice as Many Pix," August 17, pp. 17, 5.

—(1938), "Huge Horror Pic Take Shoves U's Graveyard Production Upward," November 17, pp. 1, 8.

—(1939), "Review of *The Return of Dr. X*," November 24, p. 3.

—(1941a), "Rep Plows Back Profits for Record Production Sked ...," October 29, p. 249.

—(1941b), "Picture Grosses," November 12, p. 11.

—(1941c), "Picture Grosses," November 19, p. 12.

—(1943a), "H'wood to Continue Low-Budgeters despite Shortage of Raw Material," January 6, p. 37.

—(1943b), "Creepy Pix Cleaning Up," March 31, pp. 7, 46.

—(1943c), "Review of *Revenge of the Zombies*," September 1, p. 20.

—(1943d), "Picture Grosses," September 22, p. 16.

—(1945a), "Picture Grosses," March 21, p. 14.

—(1945b), "*Zombies on Broadway*," May 2, p. 27.

—(1946), "*The Face of Marble*," January 17, p. 3.

—(1957), "Sputnik Latest 'of Monster'," November 6, p. 3.

Weaver, T. (1993), *Poverty Row Horrors!: Monogram, PRC, and Republic Horror Films of the Forties*, Jefferson, MO: McFarland.

Wright, W. (1975), *Six Guns and Society: A Structural Study of the Western*, Berkeley: University of California Press.

3

By the Book

American Horror Cinema and Horror Literature of the Late 1960s and 1970s

Peter Hutchings

In his book *Lost Illusions: American Cinema in the Shadow of Watergate and Vietnam 1970–1979*, David A. Cook begins a discussion of the horror genre by suggesting that during the 1970s "horror moved from the margins of the exploitation field into the mainstream to become a vital and disturbingly influential genre" (2000, p. 20). The part in which this claim appears is headed "Horror and the Mainstreaming of Exploitation" (ibid.). One might question such a broad reading of American horror cinema, which is after all littered with a series of ambitious or prestigious horrors that sit alongside the undoubtedly more numerous exploitation-based horror productions. Nevertheless, something does change in the American version of the genre from the late 1960s onwards, not just in those thematic and ideological qualities that have been analyzed so assiduously by horror's critics and historians but also in its commercial qualities, and its position within the cultural industries of the period. This chapter contends that one way of grasping the nature of this change, and evaluating its implications for our understanding of 1970s American horror cinema in particular, is to focus on tie-ins between horror novels and horror films. There were far more of these in American horror during the 1970s than ever before, and considering why this should be the case opens up aspects of the horror genre that perhaps have not been explored as much as they should have been.

While this chapter is therefore about the relationship between American horror literature and American horror cinema, it will not be dealing with adaptation as a creative process. It will not comment in any detail on the significance of differences between literary and film versions of any particular horror tale. Instead, it focuses on something that in various ways precedes, surrounds, and contextualizes acts of creative adaptation, and that is the business of adaptation. Here, the important issues relate less to how a literary fiction is transformed into a film and more to why in certain periods in its history, most notably in the 1970s, the American film industry turned to horror literature for source material, and why horror novels emerged as valuable properties to be sold and bought.

Indeed, an exploration of the business of adaptation necessarily foregrounds notions of markets and commercial exchange in ways that fly in the face of, and have the potential to challenge, some of the common critical understandings and evaluations of American horror cinema, especially in its 1970s version. In particular the idea developed by critics such as Robin Wood (1985), Michael Ryan and Douglas Kellner (1988), among others, that certain 1970s American horror films possess politically radical qualities is heavily dependent on a sense of these films' detachment or distance from the commercial imperatives of popular entertainment markets. Hence a critical preference for low-budget productions such as *Sisters* (1973) and *The Texas Chain Saw Massacre* (1974), and a suspicion of, or disdain for, more obviously commercial productions, not least in the 1970s *The Exorcist* (1973), which, not coincidentally, was an adaptation of a bestselling horror novel. Looking at 1970s American horror cinema in terms of literary adaptations brings into view a different set of films from those customarily discussed in critical accounts of the period, and also affords an opportunity to address from new perspectives some already accepted horror "classics." The overall effect will be to give a clearer picture of—to borrow Cook's term—the "mainstreaming" of horror during the late 1960s and 1970s. However, in order to pin down what exactly changes in the relationships between horror cinema and literature from the late 1960s onwards, one has to attend first to the role of literature in the development of horror cinema in the decades leading up to that point.

Before *Rosemary's Baby*

It is customary for historians of horror cinema to acknowledge that the genre has non-cinematic roots or antecedents, and that these include Gothic or gothic-styled novels of the eighteenth, nineteenth, and early twentieth centuries. After all, when horror emerged in the early 1930s as a recognizable industrial category of American cinema, it did so with a series of Gothic adaptations—namely *Dracula*, *Frankenstein*, and *Dr. Jekyll and Mr. Hyde* (all 1931), with *Island of Lost Souls* (1932), an adaptation of H. G. Wells' *The Island of Dr. Moreau* (1896), and *Murders in the Rue Morgue* (1932), from an 1841 short story by Edgar Allan Poe, appearing shortly thereafter. However, any categorization of Gothic that encompasses such a wide range of literary and indeed filmic texts is, to put it mildly, loose and imprecise, and one has to question ultimately how useful it is to an explanation of why and how films were made in the form that they were. It is certainly the case that these films tended to operate at some distance from their literary originators in terms of their faithfulness to story, character, or theme, with *Dracula* and *Frankenstein* in particular drawing more upon theatrical adaptations than they did upon Bram Stoker's *Dracula* (1897) or Mary Shelley's *Frankenstein* (1818) (see Skal, 2004). It follows that the economics of horror production during this early period of its existence were aligned more to theater and indeed to earlier silent film versions of various Gothic tales than they were to any literary notion of commercial value so far as identifying these tales as properties worthy of investment was concerned.

American horror cinema of the 1930s and 1940s continued to refer back to "gothic" novels and stories, not just in the sequels to *Dracula* and *Frankenstein* that appeared from 1935 onwards but also via some more prestigious adaptations—including another version of *Dr. Jekyll and Mr. Hyde* (1941), Arthur Lubin's 1943 adaptation of Gaston LeRoux's *Phantom of the Opera* (1910), and Arthur Lewin's 1945 version of Oscar Wilde's *The Picture of Dorian Gray* (1890), as well as, if one considers them horror films, *The Hunchback of Notre Dame* (1939) from Victor Hugo's 1831 novel, and *The Hound of the Baskervilles* (1939) from Arthur Conan Doyle's 1902 story.[1] Indeed, the forging of connections with venerable authors such as Hugo

---

[1] During the silent era of American cinema, versions of some of these novels were also produced, including four versions of *Dr. Jekyll and Mr. Hyde*, *The Hunchback of Notre Dame* (1923), and *The Phantom of the Opera* (1925), with the latter two featuring proto-horror star Lon Chaney. These, like various theatrical adaptations, may be seen both as a further filter between horror films of the 1930s and 1940s and their literary antecedents, and as helping to establish a cinematic market for the grotesque which later horror films would enthusiastically address and exploit.

and Wilde, and the traditional literary prestige that came with them, became in this context part of a strategy for marking certain films as upmarket "A" pictures, although, as Mark Jancovich (2010) has noted of the critical reception of both *The Phantom of the Opera* and *The Picture of Dorian Gray*, this could be interpreted as pretentiousness.

But what of the relationship, if there was in fact any, between American horror cinema and a more contemporary literary market? Here, it seems, there is little evidence of any sustained connection until the late 1960s. Prior to that date there are isolated examples of horror adaptations of contemporary or near contemporary novels. For example, *Mad Love* (1935) draws upon French author Maurice Renard's novel *The Hands of Orlac* (1920), and *The Old Dark House* (1932) is based on J. B. Priestley's 1927 English novel *Benighted*. The obscure *Undying Monster* (AKA *The Hammond Mystery*) (1942) is a version of an equally obscure 1922 novel (not published in the United States until 1936) by the English author Jesse Douglas Kerruish, and the psychological thriller *The Spiral Staircase* (1945), identified by some critics as a horror film (see Snelson, 2009), was inspired by another English novel, Ethel Lina White's *Some Must Watch* (1933, published in the United States in 1941). For American source material, one looks in the 1940s to *Conjure Wife*, Fritz Leiber's 1943 novel of witchcraft on campus, which was adapted into *Weird Woman* (1944) as part of the "Inner Sanctum" series of films, Cornell Woolrich's 1942 novel *Black Alibi*, which was filmed as the Val Lewton production *The Leopard Man* (1943), and, again if one thinks of it as at least in part a horror film, *Invasion of the Body Snatchers* (1956), which was based on Jack Finney's 1954 novel.[2] Of course, there is also Alfred Hitchcock's 1960 adaptation of Robert Bloch's 1959 novel *Psycho*—with the film version widely seen as one of the founding texts of modern horror cinema—and Robert Wise's *The Haunting* (1964) from Shirley Jackson's 1959 novel *The Haunting of Hill House*.[3]

It is hard to find any overall shape or structure to what appears to be a piecemeal, disorganized, and opportunistic set of literary appropriations running from the 1930s through to the early 1960s. Critically well-regarded works such as *The Haunting of Hill House* mingle with the pulpier outputs of Bloch, Finney, Leiber, and Woolrich and an eclectic mixture of non-American sources. There is a preference for psychological and crime-based stories—and

---

[2] *Conjure Wife* later received its definitive screen adaptation in the British horror production *Night of the Eagle* (1962), which was written by distinguished American fantasy authors Richard Matheson and Charles Beaumont.
[3] One should also add Roger Corman's *The Haunted Palace* (1963) which, although marketed as part of Corman's cycle of Poe adaptations and with a title taken from a Poe poem, is actually a rendition of H. P. Lovecraft's 1927 short novel *The Case of Charles Dexter Ward*.

indeed thinking of *The Leopard Man* and *The Spiral Staircase* as horror/crime thrillers extends some traditional understandings of the nature of 1940s American horror—but supernatural elements are present as well. However, by the late 1960s a more focused and organized relationship between horror literature and horror cinema was beginning to emerge.

Rosemary's Baby and after

> *Unrevised proofs. Confidential. Please do not quote for publication until verified with finished book. ROSEMARY'S BABY a novel by IRA LEVIN* [...] *"Who the hell put these galley proofs on my desk?" I asked Lisa, my secretary. Little did I know at the time that the word "hell" was most appropriate.*
> (William Castle [horror film producer],1982, p. 185; capitalization in original)

The year 1968 is a key year in just about every published history of American horror cinema. It is the year of both the low-budget independent production *Night of the Living Dead* and the glossy high-end Paramount production *Rosemary's Baby*, which together have often been seen as offering confirmation that the iconoclastic and genuinely disturbing horror cinema first intimated by Hitchcock's *Psycho* had finally arrived in force. Each film shares a nihilistic quality, with the representatives of good depicted as helpless in the face of monstrous or evil onslaughts (for exemplary discussions of horror history in these terms, see Pinedo, 1997; Tudor, 1989). Despite this, *Night of the Living Dead* has received far more critical attention as a landmark in the development of American horror cinema, while *Rosemary's Baby* has generally been seen in the context of its director Roman Polanski's internationally based authorship. Its high production values and possibly the fact that it had a non-American director sit uneasily with the aforementioned critical privileging of lower budgeted horror films of the late 1960s and 1970s in terms of authenticity and social engagement. That *Rosemary's Baby* was also an adaptation of a bestselling novel has probably not helped its status in this regard, although, from a perspective less preoccupied with horror's political and ideological credentials, the fact of that adaptation occurring at this particular moment in the genre's history becomes rather important.

Indeed, it could be argued that 1967 was as much a formative year for the new American horror of the 1970s as 1968, primarily because it saw the publication of Ira Levin's novel *Rosemary's Baby*. This was a significant event for a number of reasons, not least to do with the novel's contribution in terms of its themes and ideas to the development of modern American horror both in literature and film. It is certainly the case that historical and critical accounts of horror cinema that focus too narrowly on the films themselves as originating texts can sometimes overestimate how original some horror films, and not just literary adaptations, actually are, and consequently miss their appropriations of ideas generated elsewhere in the culture. Mark Jancovich has made this point in relation to Robert Bloch's novel *Psycho*, which, massively overshadowed by Hitchcock's film version, nevertheless comprises, according to Jancovich, "a significant contribution" (1996, p. 253). So far as American horror in the late 1960s and 1970s is concerned, the possession theme generally seen as central to horror cinema during this period was initiated within contemporaneous horror literature, with many possession-based movies, among them Polanski's *Rosemary's Baby*, turning out to be adaptations of contemporary novels.

Second, and more pertinently for this chapter, is the fact that, as John Sutherland has pointed out, *Rosemary's Baby* was the first supernatural novel to feature on any US postwar list of top ten novels of the year (2012, p. 60), although it was by no means the last. Indeed, its commercial success was widely seen as helping to inaugurate a more central role for horror novels in the market for popular literature than had ever been the case before for the genre, with this clinched in 1971 by the extraordinary commercial success enjoyed by William Peter Blatty's *The Exorcist*. Well into the 1970s, reviews of horror novels would invoke Levin's *Rosemary's Baby* as a generic exemplar, in so doing making the obvious connection between Rosemary's giving birth to the Antichrist and the novel itself generating numerous literary progeny. Thus the *Chicago Tribune* review of Thomas Tryon's *The Other* and Blatty's *The Exorcist*, both of which became bestsellers and both of which were subsequently filmed, begins, "A fertile creature, Rosemary. Not only did she give birth to that infamous offspring of the devil, she also has been the spiritual mother of dozens of other diabolical horror novels" (Blades, 1971, p. 15), while two years later in a *New York Times* review of Tryon's *Harvest Home* (later filmed as a television mini-series) one finds similar sentiments: "Rosemary had a baby. She also hatched the occult novel's current incarnation" (Walker, 1973, p. 21). Fred Mustard Stewart's 1969 occult possession novel *The Mephisto Waltz* (filmed in 1971) "is apt to turn on millions who liked *Rosemary's Baby*" (Petersen, 1970, p. M13), although for the *Boston Globe* reviewer, "Rosemary's Second child this ain't" (McLean, 1969, p. 26). The *New York Times* review of Blatty's *The Exorcist* begins with references to Levin's *Rosemary Baby* and Stewart's *The Mephisto Waltz* (Callendar, 1971, p. BR47), while, in an ongoing chain of associations, *Rosemary's Baby* and *The Exorcist* are both referenced in the *Washington Post* review of

Robert Marasco's 1973 horror novel *Burnt Offerings* (which itself was filmed) (Murray, 1973, p. C6).

Finally, the screen rights for *Rosemary's Baby* were purchased by producer William Castle prior to its publication, with the subsequent film released a mere year after the novel's first appearance. This method of securing screen rights was not uncommon in the film industry but rarely was it as speedily accomplished as it was with *Rosemary's Baby*. Not long afterwards, film executives were not even waiting for the galley proofs of forthcoming novels but were instead purchasing screen rights on the basis of plot outlines and a few sample chapters. Famously, this was how Paramount, the studio that oversaw the production of the film version of *Rosemary's Baby*, secured the rights to Mario Puzo's blockbusting 1969 gangster novel *The Godfather*.

The context for this was an increasing emphasis in the American film industry from the late 1960s onwards on projects with "pre-sold" elements. In large part this came out of the industry's reaction to a series of high-profile big-budget disappointments, including *Doctor Doolittle* (1967), *Hello Dolly!* (1969), and *Tora! Tora! Tora!* (1970), and an accompanying concern about its product becoming disconnected from the tastes of popular audiences. Cook cites a 1967 report on the American film industry's marketing strategies commissioned by the Motion Picture Association of America "which concluded that pre-release publicity 'seems unable to create extensive public awareness' for movies without 'a tie-in with a very familiar book or play or music'" (Cook, 2000, p. 27). The forging of connections between different sectors of the entertainment industry was further facilitated in the 1970s by the increasingly conglomerate nature of that industry, with film companies and publishing houses often located within the same corporate structures. In addition, as the film producer Robert Lowenheim pointed out in 1977, a reduction in the number of films being produced by the Hollywood majors meant that films were generally staying in theaters for longer periods and that this was generating more sustained opportunities for reciprocal cross-media word-of-mouth business: "Many an earlier book tie-in was over before it could ignite. [...] Today, every movie creates its own market. Correspondingly, every book tied in with a film does much the same thing" (quoted in Mahoney, 1977, p. 11.) As Cleo Coy, buyer for a chain of bookstores, put it more bluntly in 1972, "Movies actually get people to read. When *Rosemary's Baby* was released, we just couldn't keep the novel in stock" (quoted in Kneeland, 1972, p. B24).

The burgeoning popularity of horror novels after *Rosemary's Baby*, and the commercial success of the film as well, meant that, unsurprisingly, the genre became caught up in this new way of conducting business, with turnaround from novel to film sometimes taking only a year. The most visible outcome was a substantial increase in the number of horror-related novel-to-film projects that appeared between the late 1960s and early 1980s compared with previous decades, with the number of adaptations decreasing thereafter. These adaptations are listed below, along with their directors, followed by the novels' years of publications and their authors. As will be shown, the presence here of directors and authors who were not usually associated with horror is indicative of changes in the way the genre operated. For the few instances where the film's title is different from the title of the novel upon which it is based, the original title has also been included.

1968 *Rosemary's Baby*, Roman Polanski; novel, Ira Levin 1967
1971 *The Mephisto Waltz*, Paul Wendkos; novel, Fred Mustard Stewart 1969
1971 *The Omega Man*, Boris Sagal; novel (*I Am Legend*), Richard Matheson 1954
1971 *Willard*, Daniel Mann; novel (*Ratman's Notebooks*), Stephen Gilbert 1969
1972 *The Other*, Robert Mulligan; novel, Thomas Tryon 1971
1973 *The Exorcist*, William Friedkin; novel, William Peter Blatty 1971
1973 *The Legend of Hell House*, John Hough; novel (*Hell House*), Richard Matheson 1971
1973 *The Possession of Joel Delaney*, Waris Hussein; novel, Ramona Stewart 1970
1975 *Bug*, Jeannot Szwarc; novel (*The Hephaestus Plague*), Thomas Page 1973
1975 *Jaws*, Steven Spielberg; novel, Peter Benchley 1974
1975 *The Reincarnation of Peter Proud*, J. Lee Thompson; novel, Max Ehrlich 1973
1975 *The Stepford Wives*, Bryan Forbes; novel, Ira Levin 1972
1976 *Burnt Offerings*, Dan Curtis; novel, Robert Marasco 1973
1976 *Carrie*, Brian De Palma; novel, Stephen King 1974
1976 *The Little Girl who Lives down the Lane*, Nicolas Gessner; novel, Laird Koenig 1974
1977 *Audrey Rose*, Robert Wise; novel, Frank de Felitta 1975
1977 *Demon Seed*, Donald Cammell; novel, Dean Koontz 1973
1977 *Full Circle*, Richard Loncraine; novel, Peter Straub 1975
1977 *The Island of Dr. Moreau*, Don Taylor; novel, H. G. Wells 1896
1977 *The Sentinel*, Michael Winner; novel, Jeffrey Konvitz 1974
1978 *Coma*, Michael Crichton; novel, Robin Cook 1977
1978 *The Fury*, Brian De Palma; novel, John Farris 1976
1978 *Invasion of the Body Snatchers*, Philip Kaufman; novel (*The Body Snatchers*), Jack Finney 1954

1978 *Magic*, Richard Attenborough; novel, William Goldman 1976
1978 *The Manitou*, William Girdler; novel, Graham Masterton 1975
1978 *The Swarm*, Irwin Allen; novel, Arthur Herzog 1974
1979 *The Amityville Horror*, Stuart Rosenberg; book, Jay Anson 1977
1979 *Dracula*, John Badham; novel, Bram Stoker 1897
1979 *Nightwing*, Arthur Hiller; novel, Martin Cruz Smith 1977
1980 *The Shining*, Stanley Kubrick; novel, Stephen King 1977
1981 *Ghost Story*, John Irvin; novel, Peter Straub 1979
1981 *The Howling*, Joe Dante; novel, Gary Brandner 1977
1981 *Wolfen*, Michael Wadleigh; novel, Whitley Streiber 1978
1982 *The Entity*, Sidney J. Furie; novel, Frank de Felitta 1978
1982 *Incubus*, John Hough; novel, Ray Russell 1976
1982 *The Thing*, John Carpenter; novella (*Who Goes There?*), John W. Campbell 1938

The first point to note about this list is its random and somewhat chaotic quality. In this respect, it arguably reflects the messy and contingent nature of genre production itself, which rarely proceeds in an ordered and disciplined fashion or in terms of the delimited categorizations bestowed upon it by various genre theorists. As one aspect of this, some of these titles may and have been seen in terms other than horror. *The Omega Man* and *Invasion of the Body Snatchers* have often been viewed as science fiction, *Jaws* and *Coma* as thrillers, and *The Swarm* as a disaster film (in every sense of that term), although all contain elements pertinent to horror, especially in the case of *Jaws* and *Coma*. Even before one starts thinking about the actual subject matter of these films/novels, and the extent to which they might have anything in common, one also has to acknowledge that there are different kinds of adaptation at work here. Some map readily onto the industrial changes discussed above, while others seem to refer back to earlier ways of conducting business between literature and cinema, although usually one can trace connections with contemporary market-defined contexts. For instance, *Invasion of the Body Snatchers* and director John Carpenter's version of *The Thing* may best be seen not as adaptations of novels at all but rather as remakes of previous film versions, with their self-conscious allusions to those versions a more general feature of genre production during the 1970s—although Carpenter's film does recover from the literary source the concept of the shape-shifting alien that had not featured in the 1950s version of the tale (see Carroll, 1982). By contrast, *The Island of Dr. Moreau* and the 1979 version of *Dracula*, which were rare period-set dramas in a decade where contemporary settings predominated, function more as throwbacks to older forms of adaptation, with *Dracula* drawing its inspiration from a Broadway revival of the play that had also inspired the 1931 version of *Dracula*.

For all this, there is a sense here of a newly focused 1970s market for horror that offered opportunities both for established writers and new ones so far as particular kinds of horror fiction were concerned. Take the case of Richard Matheson, who appears twice on the list in relation to *The Omega Man* and *The Legend of Hell House* but who may initially seem distant from some of the changes taking place in the 1970s American film industry, not least because he was working mainly in television at that time. Matheson is now considered one of America's leading fantasy authors, with in particular his 1954 novel *I Am Legend* both a recognized classic and an acknowledged influence on Romero's *Night of the Living Dead* (see Jancovich, 1996). However, the status of that novel in the popular market in the early 1970s was clearly insufficient for it to merit the kind of treatment offered to the bestselling likes of *The Exorcist*, *The Other*, or *Audrey Rose*. *The Omega Man* unceremoniously drops Matheson's original title along with the novel's references to vampires, with the screen credit merely indicating that it was "based on a novel by Richard Matheson." This was presumably to align the film with a cycle of dystopic science fiction films that included *Planet of the Apes* (1968) and *Beneath the Planet of the Apes* (1970), both of which featured Charlton Heston, the star of *The Omega Man*. Reviewers of *The Omega Man* also connected it to the similarly disease-centered *The Andromeda Strain* (1971). No one compared the film to Matheson's novel, however.[4]

The Legend of Hell House is a yet more egregious inclusion on the list, not because it is not a horror film—it clearly is—but rather because it is not an American horror film. It is in fact a British production, albeit featuring a screenplay by Matheson himself. Here it is the novel itself that is significant, as it is the only Matheson novel that may be considered as "out-and-out" horror and one that had been very much molded for the new 1970s horror market. By contrast, *I Am Legend* hovered between the worlds of science fiction and horror. To this end, *Hell House* was more explicit in its depiction of sex, violence, and depravity than anything else written by the author, to the extent that some of this content had to be toned down for the film version. In this regard at least, Matheson, for all his virtuosity and his perceived importance in genre history, was caught up in, and his status defined by,

---

[4]The title *I Am Legend* is a literary conceit which has proved hard to translate into cinematic terms. When Matheson himself wrote an adaptation of the novel for Hammer Films in the late 1950s—which remained unproduced due to pressure from British and American censors—he retitled it *The Night Creatures*. The 1964 adaptation was entitled *The Last Man on Earth*, while the 2007 version, directed by Francis Lawrence, retained the novel's title but struggled to explain it (see also Hutchings, 2008).

specific market forces. As someone who was also in effect a jobbing writer, he clearly made some effort to engage with shifts in the way that the horror market operated.

During this period, other writers also turned to particular kinds of horror literature after working in other areas. Bestselling examples included Frank De Felitta, authoring *Audrey Rose* and *The Entity* after a career as a television script writer, Peter Straub, who, after some attempts at literary fiction focused on popular ghost stories adapted into *Ghost Story* and the Canadian-UK coproduction *Full Circle*, and William Peter Blatty, who, before *The Exorcist*, was best known as a comedy writer whose credits included the Inspector Clouseau movie *A Shot in the Dark* (1964). Stephen King was the most spectacular example of a new 1970s horror author who maintained an allegiance to the genre throughout his subsequent career, while other writers passed through the genre on their way to other things; for example, William Goldman and Martin Cruz Smith. The influence of certain writers, and especially the more bestselling ones, on the film/novel tie-ins was further evident in their adapting their own novels for the screen—including *The Other*, *The Exorcist*, *Bug*, *Jaws*, *The Reincarnation of Peter Proud*, *Audrey Rose*, *The Fury*, and *Magic*—and, in a few instances where they acquired a producer role as well, most notably Blatty on *The Exorcist* and De Felitta on *Audrey Rose*.

The directors who were involved in bringing these adaptations to the screen were also a diverse bunch so far as their career trajectories were concerned, and therein lies another possible reason why so many of these films have figured little in critical discussions of 1970s American horror cinema. There is a smattering of what may be termed horror auteurs on the list, directors who have developed a reputation for their horror work, notably John Carpenter whose *The Thing*, as previously noted, is more of a remake than an adaptation. Also present are Joe Dante, Brian De Palma—whose *Carrie* and *The Fury* marked his accession to a commercial mainstream after the more experimental phase of his career—and to a lesser extent the ultra-low-budget specialists William Girdler and Dan Curtis, although Curtis is better known for his television horror work.

However, there were also a significant number of directors who were not known at all for their association with horror, passing through the genre at a time when it had, in terms of novel/film tie-ins at least, "mainstreamed," and indeed their temporary presence within it was a sign of this change in its status. Thus previous credits for Daniel Mann, the director of *Willard*, included an Oscar-winning Elizabeth Taylor vehicle *Butterfield 8* (1960) and the comedy *Our Man Flint* (1966), Robert Mulligan, the director of *The Other*, was probably best known for *To Kill a Mockingbird* (1962), while Arthur Hiller came to *Nightwing* as the director of *Love Story* (1970). Another aspect of this, and a particularly noticeable feature of the adaptation list, is the presence of several British directors—among them Bryan Forbes, John Hough, John Irvin, J. Lee Thompson, and Michael Winner, along with Richard Attenborough, for whom *Magic* was a follow-up to his blockbuster war film *A Bridge Too Far* (1977). This should not be surprising; there were a lot of British film directors working on major Hollywood genre productions during the 1970s; for example, John Guillermin on *The Towering Inferno* (1974) and Michael Anderson on *Logan's Run* (1976). Yet, their presence in the horror genre, more than any other genre, can present problems for any positive critical evaluation of their work.

A constant in critical writing on 1970s American horror cinema is that it connected with, and expressed, nationally specific tensions and traumas in ways that were unusually disturbing and potentially socially critical (for recent examples of this approach see Lowenstein, 2005; Blake, 2008). The marginality of specialist horror directors in the 1970s field of adaptation, and the preponderance there of not just "mainstream" directors but also non-American filmmakers, potentially diminishes what for some is clearly a vital connection between films and their various contexts. The genre as manifested in these adaptations may indeed be viewed as enshrouded both in commercial opportunism and, for some of the bigger budgeted projects, in a meretricious approach to generic subject matter that compares unfavorably with the more disturbing and cutting-edge practices evident in lower budgeted horrors. In this regard, the "mainstreaming" of horror gets figured as a negative process. What then is the value, if any, of these horror adaptations?

Evaluating horror novel/film tie-ins: The case of *Audrey Rose*

In some ways, *Audrey Rose* is a locus classicus of the 1970s horror film/novel tie-in. Screen rights for the bestselling novel were sold prior to its publication, and the novelist Frank De Felitta scripted and produced the resulting film. The film's director Robert Wise did have some form as a horror filmmaker—he had worked with noted 1940s horror producer Val Lewton and had also directed *The Haunting*—but his eclectic credits also included musicals (notably *West Side Story* [1961] and *The Sound of Music* [1965]), thrillers, war movies, disaster movies, and science fiction films. Moreover, he was 63 years old at the time of *Audrey Rose*'s production and a Hollywood establishment insider at a time when the values of that establishment were being challenged by younger and more independently minded filmmakers. Accordingly, the film version of *Audrey Rose* is tasteful, conventional in form, and restrained, not qualities often associated with American horror cinema at its critically valorized best, not in fact cutting-edge at all. Although reviews at the time compared it to *The Exorcist*, they acknowledged that *Audrey Rose* did not feature the controversial and confrontational imagery of that earlier film. Perhaps because of this, *Audrey Rose* has rarely been discussed in critical accounts of 1970s horror cinema.

Audrey Rose also exemplified the novel/film tie-in in its most tightly constructed form, to the extent that a *New York Times* article from 1977 held it up as a state-of-the-art project so far as the intricacies of its packaging were concerned. It is worth quoting the details of the deal at some length to give a sense of how entwined novels and films could become at this time.

> Howard Kaminsky, president and publisher of Warner Books, put up a sizeable advance for paperback rights to the Frank DeFelitta novel and wanted to back the printing with a campaign that could cost up to $200,000. Unable to justify the expenditure, Kaminsky went to producer Joe Wizan and United Artists, asking them to help finance the promotional costs. U.A. invested $75,000 but on the condition that it be repaid through a 2½ per cent royalty after a certain number of copies of the book had been sold. Additionally, after the $75,000 is repaid, U.A. is to receive up to an additional $37,500, a 50 per cent profit on its investment.
> (Mahoney, 1977, p. 12)

Caught between the conventionality of its approach and its innovative financing, what kind of horror does *Audrey Rose* offer?

Essentially it is a possession story with a reincarnation theme, where a little girl is possessed by the spirit of a previous incarnation. This chapter has already noted that possession, including occult, demonic, and psychological possession, was a distinctive strand in American horror literature of the late 1960s and 1970s, with this shading into the haunted house format where the house in some way possesses its occupants. Examples include *Rosemary's Baby*, *The Mephisto Waltz*, *The Other*, *The Possession of Joel Delaney*, *The Exorcist*, *The Reincarnation of Peter Proud*, *Burnt Offerings*, *Audrey Rose*, *The Manitou*, *Magic*, and *The Amityville Horror*. It is striking how many of these novels are organized mainly or entirely around the perspectives of female characters, with this being particularly the case for *Rosemary's Baby*, *The Mephisto Waltz*, *The Possession of Joel Delaney*, *The Exorcist* (more so than the film), and *Audrey Rose*. A possible factor behind this focus on the female experience within a domestic and familial context was the general belief in the publishing industry at this time that women bought more books than men. In fact, the novel *Audrey Rose* was explicitly marketed to women readers, and was received in those terms, with one reviewer labeling it "Women's Fiction" (Kosek, 1975, p. F1). Both the novel and film versions of *Audrey Rose* are structured around the journey of the "possessed" girl's mother from skepticism to a belief in reincarnation. In this sense, she becomes our representative in the narrative, which makes her comparable to the mother in *The Exorcist* as she gradually comes to believe in demonic possession as an explanation for her daughter's condition.

A lot has been said in horror criticism about the ways in which the slasher films of the late 1970s and 1980s, for all their problematic sexual politics, transformed the nature of horror through their promotion of images of female heroism via the figure of—to use Carol J. Clover's term—"the Final Girl," which is the teenage girl or young woman who fights back against, and ultimately defeats, the killer (1992). Yet here, in some of these film/novel combinations, women take center stage too. They tend to be older, sometimes wealthier, often mothers, and not defined through the physical violence associated with the Final Girl. Instead, they operate in relation to more melodramatic scenarios in which their suffering derives from intense emotional investments with partners, with siblings, and with children. In this regard, they represent a distinctive new presence within the American horror genre, albeit one that has rarely registered in critical discussions of the period and which has not yet received the attention that it possibly merits.

Conclusion

Richard Nowell (2011) has explored the rise of the slasher film and the way in which it orientated horror firmly to teenage audiences. Here is the most plausible explanation for why horror film/novel tie-ins diminished in number from the early 1980s onwards, as the genre moved away from the kind of "mainstreaming" that was evident during the 1970s towards a more sectional notion of the audience. It is interesting that Nowell refers to the film version of *Audrey Rose* as "adult-centered," which it certainly was in comparison with the slasher likes of *Halloween* (1978) and *Friday the 13th* (1980) (ibid., p. 91). *Audrey Rose* may in fact be seen as the product of a moment in American horror history when horror, at least in part, operated in much the same way as any other mainstream genre as far as its financing and its marketing, and indeed its potential audiences, were concerned. Achieving bestseller and top box office status meant reaching out to audiences that previously had not engaged with the genre. But within this practice there was nuance, and in this regard *Audrey Rose*, and some other films of its type, offered something different. Not all novel/film ties were like this, but simply because those tie-ins necessarily foregrounded the commerce of horror does not automatically lessen their contribution to the development of the genre.

Since the 1980s, American horror cinema has returned sporadically to the bestseller list, often with projects that in 1970s style reach out to audiences beyond the youth market, with *The Silence of the Lambs* (1991) perhaps the most successful example of this strategy. More recently, young adult fiction has been an inspiration with the *Twilight* (2008–12) series of films. This is where the genre most visibly "mainstreams" and begins to resemble other genres. From some critical perspectives, the overt commercialism this entails is a problem. A fetishization of the marginal that is evident in some cult-based approaches to horror and exploitation cinema also entails a strongly negative attitude to anything that looks even vaguely mainstream. Yet, this strand of horror—which is horror for audiences who are not necessarily devotees or fans of the horror genre as a whole—is an important element in the ongoing development of horror, and should not be ignored or downgraded. Horror novel/film tie-ins from the 1970s arguably offered qualities that were not apparent elsewhere in the American version of the genre at the time, and are worthy of consideration in that regard alone as part of an inclusive approach. However, looking at these tie-ins also draws our attention to broader issues about how we understand the relationship between the commercial and cultural aspects of the horror genre, and how this relationship gets written into, or in the case of the 1970s, out of, horror histories.

References

Blades, J. (1971), "Books Today—Rosemary's Babies," *Chicago Tribune*, June 4, p. 15.
Blake, L. (2008), *The Wounds of Nations: Horror Cinema, Historical Trauma and National Identity*, Manchester: Manchester University Press.
Callendar, N. (1971), "Criminals at Large," *New York Times*, June 6, p. BR47.
Carroll, N. (1982), "The Future of Allusion: Hollywood in the Seventies (and Beyond)," *October*, 20: 51–81.
Castle, W. (1992), *Step Right Up! I'm Going to Scare the Pants off America: Memoirs of a B-Movie Mogul*, New York: Pharos Books.
Clover, C. J. (1992), *Men, Women and Chainsaws: Gender in the Modern Horror Film*, London: BFI.
Cook, D. A. (2000), *Lost Illusions: American Cinema in the Shadow of Watergate and Vietnam 1970–1979*, Berkeley and Los Angeles: University of California Press.

Hutchings, P. (2008), "American Vampires in Britain: Richard Matheson's *I Am Legend* and Hammer's *The Night Creatures*," in D. North (ed.), *Sights Unseen: Unfinished British Films*, Newcastle: Cambridge Scholars Press.
Jancovich, M. (1996), *Rational Fears: American Horror in the 1950s*, Manchester: Manchester University Press.
—(2010), "'Two Ways of Looking': The Critical Reception of 1940s Horror," *Cinema Journal*, 49.3: 45–66.
Kneeland, P. (1972), "Boston Globe Book Festival: He Never Planned to Sell Books," *Boston Globe*, August 27, p. B24.
Kosek, S. (1975), "Three Novels (2 Hits, 1 Miss) in Competition with Television," *Chicago Tribune*, December 21, p. F1.
Lowenstein, A. (2005), *Shocking Representation: Historical Trauma, National Cinema, and the Modern Horror Film*, New York: Columbia University Press.
Mahoney, J. (1977), "Book and Movie Tie-ins – Scenes from a Marriage of Convenience," *New York Times*, March 13, pp. 1, 11–12.
McLean, R. (1969), "Book of the Day: 'Faust' Furious Fable Treats Terror Tautly," *Boston Globe*, April 24, p. 26.
Murray, M. (1973), "Thriller-chiller Views of Evil," *The Washington Post*, February 13, p. C6.
Nichols, B. (1985), *Movies and Methods – Volume 2*, Berkeley: University of California Press.
Nowell, R. (2011), *Blood Money: A History of the First Teen Slasher Film Cycle*, New York: Continuum.
Petersen, C. (1970), "Paperbacks," *Chicago Tribune*, March 29, p. M13.
Pinedo, I. C. (1997), *Recreational Terror*, New York: State University of New York Press.
Ryan, M. and Kellner, D. (1988), *Camera Politics: The Politics and Ideology of Contemporary Hollywood Film*, Bloomington and Indianapolis: Indiana University Press.
Skal, D. J. (2004), *Hollywood Gothic: The Tangled Web of Dracula from Novel to Stage to Screen*, New York: Faber.
Snelson, T. (2009), "'From Grade B thrillers to Deluxe Chillers': Prestige Horror, Female Audiences, and Allegories of Spectatorship in *The Spiral Staircase* (1946)," *New Review of Film and Television Studies*, 7.2: 173–88.
Sutherland, J. (2012), *Bestsellers: Popular Fiction of the 1970s*, London: Routledge.
Tudor, A. (1989), *Monsters and Mad Scientists: A Cultural History of the Horror Movie*, Oxford: Blackwell.
Walker, G. (1973), "Books of the Times—Sons of Rosemary's Baby," *New York Times*, October 6, p. 21.
Wood, R. (1985), "An Introduction to the American Horror Film," in B. Nichols (ed.) *Movies and Methods – Volume 2*, Berkeley: University of California Press.

4

Risen from the Vaults

Recent Horror Film Remakes and the American Film Industry

Kevin Heffernan

The year 2003 will likely be remembered as the Year of the Zombie; American companies were developing several movies which had their origins in George Romero's *Night of the Living Dead* (1968), including *Resident Evil: Apocalypsa* and Universal Pictures' remake of Romero's own *Dawn of the Dead* (1978). In response to this development, Jonathan Bing of the trade paper *Variety* lamented that "[t]he zombie genre is an apt metaphor for an industry that perpetually goes back to the vaults to cannibalize its past when it runs short on ideas" (Bing, 2003a, p. 5). But the horror remake would become one of the dominant trends in late twentieth- and early twenty-first-century American cinema. At one end of the budgetary spectrum, the companies behind films such as *The Haunting* (1999) and *The Stepford Wives* (2004) paired high production values with major Hollywood stars in order to contemporize box office successes and well-loved films. Moreover, in horror's traditional home at the lower end of this scale, above-the-line talent, such as the directors Michael Bay, Sam Raimi, and Robert Zemeckis, have formed companies to produce genre pictures that feature television stars, which are helmed by first-time directors and booked into theaters during the comparatively slow fall and spring seasons. Dreamworks' *The Ring* (2002) and New Line Cinema's *The Texas Chainsaw*

Massacre (2003) are important examples of this trend that I examine in the first section of this chapter.

Furthermore, and as the second section of the chapter shows, the years leading up to this period also saw American film companies take an unprecedented interest in the popular cinemas of East Asia. They began to hire stars and production personnel from Hong Kong, Taiwan, and Japan in an effort to craft films that would also be marketable and appealing in Asia, one of Hollywood's most important overseas markets. This trend, combined with the American film industry's propensity to remake and rework earlier hits, led to a spate of US remakes of East Asian horror films that I call the J-horror remake cycle. Dreamworks' *The Ring* and its sequel *The Ring Two* (2005) exemplify these attempts to accommodate an increasingly internationalized audience and to respond to changing generic norms. The J-horror remake cycle also brings to light a number of important exchanges between the film industries of the United States and East Asia.

The remakes that bracketed the millennium represent an important transitional period in American horror cinema. Where the baroque and parodic inflections of the teen slasher subgenre as exemplified by the *Scream* films (1996–2000) were already coming to an end due to diminishing returns, the so-called torture porn cycle would not begin until after the solid performances of *Saw* (2004) and *Hostel* (2005). In fact, the most commercially successful horror film of this entire period was *The Sixth Sense* (1999), in which writer-director M. Night Shyamalan abjured violence and shock in favor of suspense, dread, and narrative experimentation. The horror remake cycle, which peaked during the years 1999 to 2005, may be seen as a response to both the waning of the teen slasher film cycle and to the more allusive, family-based psychological horror of *The Sixth Sense*. Films from Hollywood's past and from East Asia provided templates in which filmmakers could explore both psychological and visceral modes of horror. Far from signaling a mannered or moribund phase of the genre, these horror remakes display tremendous suppleness and ingenuity in their deployment of motifs drawn from both the original movies and contemporaneous horror films.

Modernizing modern American horror

Where they historically occupied fallow periods of the annual release schedule (see Heffernan, 2004), in the late twentieth and early twenty-first centuries, horror films that were made on generous budgets, and boasting intricate special effects, major stars, and recognized auteurs, were released on large numbers of screens in the peak summer and holiday seasons, and were backed by huge advertising pushes. The most successful examples include *Invasion of the Body Snatchers* (1978), *The Fly* (1986), *The Haunting* (1999), and 2004's *The Stepford Wives*.

The penultimate of these films is a remake of Robert Wise's 1963 ghost story of the same name. The original film, which was marketed as both a horror film and a prestige adaptation of Shirley Jackson's 1959 novel *The Haunting of Hill House*, starred Julie Harris as Eleanor, an unmarried, emotionally dependent woman who had cared for her bedridden mother for eleven years, before the old woman's death. Boarding with her sister's family, Eleanor is chosen by Dr. Markway (Richard Johnson) to join a group of people who will spend a night in the supposedly haunted Hill House as part of an investigation into the paranormal. As the night progresses, Eleanor is drawn further and further into the spirit world of the house, finding in the ghosts who reside there (and they in her) a retelling of her own miserable family history. During the conclusion of the film, she drives a car into the house's gates and dies, thereby replaying the death of the young wife of the house's first owner, Hugh Crain, and joining her new family: the unhappy ghosts of Hill House.

The 1963 film *The Haunting* would seem a poor candidate for the late twentieth-century effects-laden horror treatment. Apart from a scene in which a door buckles and bends under the force of an unseen ghost, its makers had eschewed on-screen violence of any kind. Its portrayal of the spirit world as a projection of human fears, desires, and resentments makes *The Haunting* appear like a throwback to Val Lewton's RKO films such as *Cat People* (1942), *The Leopard Man* (1943), and *The Body Snatcher* (1945). The angry, lonely, frustrated Eleanor first pursues Dr. Markway, whom she does not realize is married, and is then herself pursued by Theodora. It is only after these faltering attempts at human contact have failed that Eleanor slowly appreciates that her own life is replaying that of Hugh Crain's spinster daughter Abigail, that of her paid companion from the village who committed suicide, and finally that of a young wife who died in a carriage accident shortly after the house was built. In addition to this circumspect presentation of the supernatural, *The Haunting* was shot in Wellesian black-and-white chiaroscuro deep focus, and its soundtrack makes extensive use of diegetic voice-over narration and internal monologues—two stylistic devices that have tended to be used for ironic, and even parodic, effect in recent American cinema.

Older horror fans, or at least those who read *Variety*, would therefore have been quite surprised in 1998 to learn that the action director Jan De Bont was attached to Dreamworks' $80 million remake of *The Haunting* (*Variety*, 1998a, p. 1). De Bont, who had been the cinematographer on both *Die Hard* (1988) and *The Hunt for Red October* (1990), and had directed the special effects-laden action pictures *Speed* (1994) and *Twister* (1996), seemed an odd choice to remake a four-character chamber piece in which a supernatural presence remained very much off-screen. For the remake, the filmmakers cast in the lead role of Eleanor the versatile and accomplished Lili Taylor, an actress who had drawn praise for her performances in indie fare such as *I Shot Andy Warhol* (1995), in which she played Warhol's would-be assassin Valerie Solanis (*Variety*, 1998b, p. 5). The filmmakers signed Catherine Zeta-Jones, who had become an A-lister following her appearance in *The Mask of Zorro* (1998), for the once-lesbian now-bisexual Theo. Giving *The Haunting* a measure of gravitas was Liam Neeson—Oscar Schindler himself—as Dr. David Marrow.

In contrast to their understated inspiration, but like Hollywood remakes across a range of genres, *The Haunting* emphasized production values and filmmaking technology. The film's effects designer Phil Tippet told the press that "[o]ur challenge was to create the character of the house. [...] There are different kinds of effects going on here. Very common objects—curtains, furniture, gusts of wind, condensation—all play a role" (quoted in Levine, 1999, Special Section). Reworkings of key moments in the original film are all played out in production designer Eugenio Zanetti's spectacularly realized architectural space: the speech of Mrs. Dudley, who warns Eleanor and Theo that no one from the village will come to their aid after sundown, is repeated verbatim from the 1963 film in a cavernous room using all of the 2.35 frame; the spirits write a note to Eleanor on the walls of the mansion and across a foreboding portrait of the evil patriarch Hugh Crain, and Eleanor is trapped on a rickety spiral staircase from which one of the house's victims committed suicide.

Even more crucial than the elaborate production design and digital effects, however, is the film's sound design. Where the makers of the original version of *The Haunting* used the camera to follow mysterious sounds as they moved through the house, the new film's sound designer Gary Rydstrom employed directional theater sound to create spaces that are both off-screen and otherworldly (Sullivan, 1999, p. 19). Groaning pipes, moving doors, creaking floors, and whistling wind are manipulated through a bewildering array of blending and altering effects. "You're not quite sure what they are," Rydstrom told the press; "It could be wind or it could be somebody breathing, you're not quite sure what it is. [...] Later, the house itself becomes almost a character in its own right. It comes alive, and is inhabited by this ghost, so the sounds start to sound organic" (Cohen, 1999, Special Report).

Since at least *Halloween* (1978), *Alien* (1979), and *The Terminator* (1984), the largely static characters who populate horror films have often been set off against a female protagonist, whose development from passive victim to resourceful heroine provides much of the human drama in such movies.

One of the strategies the filmmakers use to "upscale" *The Haunting* is to display the complex virtuosity of Taylor's performance as a young woman who comes to realize that she is a participant, rather than an observer, in the tragic supernatural drama of the house. To this end, David Self's screenplay offers a new back-story of Hill House itself. Instead of the festering family resentments, isolation, jealousy, and sexual repression of the 1963 version, we have the industrialist Hugh Crain, a man who, in a vain attempt to compensate for a cold and unsatisfying marriage, kidnaps children from sweatshops and imprisons them in his house; when the children died, they were incinerated in the fireplace, and it is their spirits who call out to Eleanor as she explores both the house and its past. Where the 1963 version of Eleanor found an affinity with the ghosts in her own wretched family life, the 1999 Eleanor is revealed to be a descendant of the Crains, one who has been summoned to the house by the restless spirits. Her joining of the spirits in death at the end of the film becomes a sacrifice of her body to release their trapped souls to heaven. In this way, the filmmakers behind *The Haunting* adapt its female protagonist to the conventions of late twentieth-century horror, showcase the acting skills of name stars and a talented female lead, and display state-of-the-art sound design and special effects. These elements are characteristic of the horror remakes of this period that occupy the upper end of the budget spectrum.

Around Halloween 1999—just a few months after the global box office success of *The Haunting* (see Hindes, 1999, p. 1; Klady, 1999, p. 12; Cahill, 1999, p. 452)—baby boomer horror fans were confronted with television advertisements for another familiar haunted house tale: Warner Bros.' hi-tech remake of William Castle's *House on Haunted Hill* (1959). Castle, who died in 1997, had been the premier barker and gimmick schlockmeister of the 1950s and 1960s. His cheaply made and highly derivative films also included *Macabre* (1957), *The Tingler* (1959), *Homicidal* (1961), and *13 Ghosts* (1963); these too seemed to be among the least likely candidates for glossy, effects-laden Hollywood remakes. Yet, the successful producer Joel Silver and the equally successful director Robert Zemeckis launched their production company, Dark Castle, with *House on Haunted Hill*, and followed it two years later with a remake of *13 Ghosts*. In what seemed an astonishing non sequitur, Silver told *Variety* that "[w]e will invoke the spirit of William Castle, but our pictures will be cool and smart" (quoted in Carver, 1999, p. 16). The new *House on Haunted Hill* was budgeted at $25 million and drew together an ensemble cast of television stars and Hollywood supporting players (Harris and Lyons, 2001, p. 1). For the role of a cuckolded millionaire who summons the other characters to the supposedly haunted house with the promise of a $1 million reward—a character originally played by Vincent Price—the filmmakers cast Australian actor Geoffrey Rush, winner of the Best Actor

Oscar in 1997 for *Shine*. Furthermore, *Saturday Night Live* player Chris Kattan inherits Elisha Cook's role as Watson Pritchard, owner of the house and keeper of its secrets.

Silver and Zemeckis recognized that Dimension Films' *Scream* series had enjoyed consistent box office success in the late 1990s and the year 2000, and that the $15 to $40 million budgets on which these films were made promised equally impressive returns for similarly priced fare, based on a high cost-to-profit ratio. Dimension was the genre production division of Miramax Films (see Wee, Chapter 9, this volume). It specialized in $20 million horror and action films, emphasized brand recognition, and targeted niche audiences in the slow fall and winter seasons. Dark Castle exemplified the kind of outfit that dominated the production of horror remakes over the coming years. In its second Castle remake, *Thir13en Ghosts*, the company added the final element to what would become the prevailing production model when it recruited Steve Beck, a first-time director who had previously worked on TV and music videos. Thereafter, Zack Snyder made his debut with *Dawn of the Dead* (2004), Andrew Douglas with *The Amityville Horror* (2005), and Jaume Collet-Sera with *House of Wax* (2005). Such films also enabled several overseas directors to make their Hollywood bows. In addition to Hideo Nakata and Takashi Shimizu's contributions to the J-horror remake cycle (discussed below), the Brazilian filmmaker Walter Salles directed Touchstone Pictures' *Dark Water* (2005), and the Paris-born director Alexandre Aja—the man behind the French home-invasion thriller *Haute Tension* (2003)—wrote and directed Fox-Searchlight's 2006 remake of the 1977 Wes Craven film *The Hills Have Eyes*.

Many of the features that came to characterize this cycle of remakes may be found in New Line Cinema and Platinum Dunes' 2003 version of the 1974 film *The Texas Chainsaw Massacre*. This project followed the pattern established by Dark Castle's *House on Haunted Hill*. It was produced for distributor New Line by Platinum Dunes, a company established by director Michael Bay, Brad Fuller, and Andrew Form to produce modestly budgeted genre pictures that would be helmed by directors with a track record in music video and television commercials (Fleming, 2003a, p. 5). Moreover, the film was financed by Radar Pictures, which was set up by the record company executive and Hollywood producer Ted Field, and which had enjoyed box office hits like *Revenge of the Nerds* (1984), *Three Men and a Baby* (1987), and *Bill & Ted's Excellent Adventure* (1989) (LaPorte, 2004, p. 1). Radar supplied *The Texas Chainsaw Massacre*'s $9.5 million budget; modest by contemporary standards but about fifty times the reported $174,000 cost of the original film (Higgins, 2003, p. 63; Fleming, 2003b, p. 1). Screenwriting duties fell to newcomer Scott Kosar, and television commercial director Marcus Nispel made his feature film directing debut (Harris, 2002, p. 1).

Because the ubiquity of cell phones in 2003 would have rendered the threatened characters' isolation from each other dramatically implausible, Nispal's film was, like its model, set in the mid-1970s. But gone from the remake is the powerful element of Watergate-era social and political satire that had suffused screenwriter Kim Henkel and director Tobe Hooper's 1974 approach to the material. The wider depoliticization of horror motifs in the remake cycle was noticed by Larry Cohen, writer and director of dozens of 1970s and 1980s exploitation films, including *It's Alive* (1974), who told *Variety* "[h]orror movies used to be about something—Vietnam, the sexual revolution, morality, relationships. Now they're just scare-the-pants-off-you movies" (quoted in Bing, 2003b, p. 8). Still, the commercial success that was made possible by Platinum Dunes' model for financing and reimagining source material was evidence that the horror remake would flourish at the lower end of the budgetary scale. There, suggests New Line's president of production Toby Emmerich, such a project is "not cast-dependent, it's read-to-go, and it's the kind of picture you can make for a price, and one on which [the production company is] willing to bet on with us. Plus, it seems like it's franchisable" (quoted in Brodesser and Lyons, 2001, p. 1). Platinum Dunes, for example, continued its policy of producing horror remakes by developing a new version of *The Amityville Horror* (1979) in 2005 and of *The Hitcher* (1986) in the following year (Fleming, 2005, p. 1).

Another key trend in the early twenty-first century was a cycle of American remakes of recent Japanese horror pictures that included Dreamworks' 2002 film *The Ring*, as well as Sony Pictures' *The Grudge* (2004), Paramount's *The Eye* (2006), Fox's *Shutter* (2007), and Dreamworks' *The Uninvited* (2009).

Hollywood and the remaking of contemporary Asian horror

In the late 1990s and early 2000s, Hollywood placed increased importance on its major international markets. This strategy underwrote the assembly of globally marketable and appealing calculated blockbusters such as *Titanic* (1997), *The Matrix* (1999), *Monsters, Inc.* (2001), and *Spider-Man* (2002), its heavy investment in theater construction in Europe, Japan, and Taiwan, and its recruitment of Asian stars such as Takeshi Kitano, Jackie Chan, Jet Li, Michelle Yeoh, and Chow Yun-Fat (see Groves, 1995, p. 55; Groves, 1997, p. 37; *Variety*, 1996, p. 20; Groves, 1996, p. 39; Groves, 2002, p. 12). Moreover, the directors John Woo and Stanley Tong, the martial arts choreographer

Yuen Woo-Ping, and others were enlisted to re-energize the Hollywood action film by injecting it with style and adrenaline. At the same time, Washington was pressurizing South Korea to 'open up' its markets to American products by such means as the elimination of a Screen Quota Law that many in the Seoul movie center of Chungmuro believed to be crucial to the survival of local filmmaking (Sullivan, 1999, p. 93; Alford, 1999, p. 34). These moves at the levels of film production, distribution, and exhibition were all engineered to increase the box office returns of major studio releases in several of East Asia's most lucrative markets.

Mindful of their international audience, and committed to repeating successful textual formulae, Hollywood companies continued to acquire Asian properties with a view to remaking them. Andrew Lau and Alan Mak's *Infernal Affairs* (2002) was bought by Warner Bros. to be remade as *The Departed*, Miramax remade Mitayuki Suo's *Shall We Dance?* (1996) in 2004, and, at Paramount, Tom Cruise's production company, Cruise Wagner, bought the rights to remake the Pang Brothers' supernatural thriller *The Eye* (2002) (*Variety*, 2003, p. 14). Hollywood companies could therefore target a series of remakes of popular Asian movies to the growing audiences of East Asia, as well as to their so-called domestic base of North America. Moreover, the horror remakes' medium budgets of $15 to $30 million, and their PG-13 ratings, both minimized risk and provided a safety net in the form of appeal to the American youth market.

An assessment of the key commercial and creative personnel behind the 2002 American remake of the Japanese horror picture *Ringu* (1998), *The Ring*, helps us to understand the role that the J-horror remake cycle played with respect to broader trends in Hollywood's production and marketing of medium-budget genre films. In 2001, this project was greenlighted by Dreamworks, with Roy Lee and Michael Macari sharing an executive producer credit for serving as intermediaries between Japanese distributor Asmik Ace and Dreamworks. Lee, a Korean-American consultant, who later described himself as Hollywood's perfect go-between with Asia, soon formed Vertigo Entertainment to propose projects to Hollywood companies. Miramax paid Vertigo's overheads in exchange for first option on its properties. Lee then negotiated the sale of the rights to remake three South Korean box office hits: *My Wife is a Gangster* (2001) (rights bought by Miramax), *My Sassy Girl* (2001) (rights bought by Warner Bros.), and *Married to the Mafia* (2002) (rights bought by Dreamworks). *The New Yorker* journalist Tad Friend described this process in the following way:

> Lee's Asian initiative enables Hollywood, in effect, to test fully realized cinematic ideas in front of millions of people, and then go forward with

remakes of movies that are already proven hits. Everyone benefits: Asian studios get a windfall; American studios get a buffet of market-tested ideas; and Lee gets a producer's fee in the range of three hundred thousand dollars whenever one of his remakes goes into production.

(Quoted in Friend, 2003; for an interview with Lee and his account of this process see Heianna, 2005)

Lee and his associates shepherded projects through this process across the duration of the J-horror remake cycle. Vertigo was involved as a company in, and Lee's name would appear as a producer or executive producer on, among others, *The Grudge*, *Ring 2*, and *The Eye*.

Ringu's producer Taka Ichise was brought to Hollywood to supervise Dreamworks' *Ring* remake. The company tapped Ehren Kruger, who had written *Scream 3* (2000) for Dimension, to write the screenplay for *The Ring*. Kruger was attractive because the *Scream* films—with their knowing deployment of slasher film clichés and appealing young casts drawn from prime-time television—had dominated horror ticket sales around the millennium. *The Ring* was directed by Gore Verbinski, who had helmed the hit Julia Roberts action-comedy *The Mexican* (2001), and the English actress Naomi Watts continued her string of American characters in the lead role of the journalist Rachel Keller. Like those behind its Japanese inspiration, the makers of *The Ring* downplayed physical horror in favor of suspense and dread; most of the terror in *The Ring* derives from family cruelty, loss, grief, and rage in a series of sub-plots which coalesce around the central horror plot of a haunted videotape which results in the death of everyone who watches it. *The Ring* was a major box office hit. It performed well in East Asia, where its $14 million haul in Japan almost doubled that of the original (*Screen Daily*, 2002a, 2002b). Having grossed almost $250 million worldwide, it remains at the time of writing the most financially successful horror remake in history (see Box Office Mojo, 2013). The film's success made a sequel almost inevitable. In keeping with the now-established practice of using these modest horror pictures for the Hollywood debuts of international directors, in March 2005, *The Ring Two*, which was directed by Hideo Nakata—the man behind the original films—was released theatrically. The haunted videotape of the first film drops out of the narrative after 20 minutes, and the film focuses instead on Rachel's efforts to exorcise the vengeful Samara's possession of Aiden in a story that is almost obsessively concerned with infanticide. The intertwined motifs of demonic possession and the monstrous child—Aidan's possession is always signaled by a dull "I'm here, Mommy"—is emblematic of one of the dominant narrative trends of the contemporary American horror film, with the late 1990s witnessing the proliferation of these motifs in horror hits such as *The Sixth Sense*, the US theatrical rerelease of *The Exorcist* in the year 2000, and *The Others* (2001); like these films, *The Ring Two* is told largely from the point of view of the mother, and, in keeping with many of its predecessors, forgoes graphic violence in favor of the primal terrors of familial loss and violence.

Although some fans and critics have complained that the PG-13 ratings of the J-horror remakes are a sign of horror filmmakers' pusillanimity in the face of the disdain of the Motion Picture Association of America's certification office CARA, the films' downplaying of graphic mayhem in favor of psychological and family anxiety is one of the most distinctive ways in which they were addressed to a female audience. The courting of female youth has been a key component of horror film production and promotion at least since the first teenage slasher film cycle of the early 1980s (Nowell, 2011). During the theatrical release of *The Ring Two*, the *USA Today* newspaper printed a long article on distributors pitching horror films to teenage girls: "A survey by the consumer research firm OTX shows that 16% of women are likely to see a horror movie if it looks scary without being gory," wrote correspondent Scott Bowles (2005). "About 2% of the female respondents said they were drawn to a film primarily for its gore. By contrast, about 11% of males said they were likely to see a horror movie that looks scary but not gory, and 6% said graphic violence was a key draw for a horror film" (ibid.). The young female audience was believed by the film industry to have made up over 60 percent of the American horror film audience in 2004 and 2005. The same article quoted Tom Sherak of Revolution Pictures opining the fact that this audience's attending horror movies in groups had "almost become a rite of passage. [...] They'll go four or five together to see a movie as a group and scream at the screen. It's a safe way to explore fear" (quoted in ibid.). Ghost House Pictures head Sam Raimi, who was himself criticized for the perceived misogyny of his breakthrough film *The Evil Dead* (1981), saw a direct connection between the Asian approach to horror and an appeal to female audiences:

> Things move in cycles, and right now the cycle is toward less ugly horror. Asian horror deals with ghosts and goblins and witches, not serial killers. It's a little more spiritual, a little different from what audiences are used to. And that's what the kids want; a story they know told in a new way.
> (Bowles, 2005)[1]

---

[1] Ghost House, a genre producer run by Raimi, Rob Tappert, and sales agent Sentator International, is typical of the companies that were inspired by Dimension Pictures' success. After 1999, it specialized in horror films, including a remake of Takashi Shimizu's *Ju-On* (2002), released in 2004.

The three biggest hits of the J-horror remake cycle—*The Ring*, *The Ring Two*, and *The Grudge*—bear all the hallmarks of having been carefully constructed to serve such ends. First, none of the films cast their female leads in damsel-in-distress roles, where male characters would act as their protectors. For example, the men in *The Ring* and *The Grudge*—husband Noah and boyfriend Doug—are periodically helpful to the heroines, but Rachel's friend Nick in *Ring Two* is an active impediment. In addition, two of the films contain deposed patriarchs—the suicidal Professor Pullman in *The Grudge*, and both Richard and Noah in *The Ring*. *The Ring Two* writes the patriarchs completely out of the narrative. Both Samara and Aidan are struggled over by their birth mothers and by social institutions that are cast explicitly as feminine: a hospital in the form of the female psychiatrist Dr. Temple and the home for unwed mothers, exemplified by the nuns, where Evelyn had attempted to drown the infant Samara. Finally, the makers of *The Grudge* activate one of the oldest conventions of the horror genre by contrasting the parallel investigations of a curious woman protagonist, and a male detective who, in spite of being backed by the state, lacks the empathic qualities that enable his female counterpart to probe deeper into the mystery. But it is *The Ring Two* that pushes this feminization of generic conventions the furthest. In this film, the traditional phallic imagery of horror—knives and other weapons, objects bursting in from off-screen space, the mutation of the act of copulation into violence and horror—is replaced by hataeric and vaginal imagery, including the deep well out of which Rachel must flee, the torrent of water that is unleashed twice in the bathroom, and the drowning of Samara and Aidan, both of which replay the sacrament of baptism: patriarchal religion's appropriation of the rituals and experiences surrounding childbirth. A horror film that is angled to teenage girls and young women on a protagonist who is struggling with voices that tell her to murder her son, and which is resolved first by her own ritual suicide and then by her casting a ghost child into a well while hissing, "I'm not your fucking mother!", represents, I would suggest, a significant reimagining of the landscape of American horror.

Conclusion

The J-horror remakes have a family resemblance to both the remakes of Hollywood's own horror films and a contemporaneous cycle of remakes of Asian movies from across a range of genres that included the action films mentioned above. They were financed by many of the same companies, they deploy motifs and narrative strategies in similar ways, and together they represent the most high-profile instance of a nominally American horror cinema that proliferated between the baroque or 'postmodern' *Scream* films and the later return to graphic violence, evisceration, and suffering in *Saw*, *Hostel*, and the cycle of so-called torture porn films that they initiated. In the case of the J-horror remakes, budgets that are admittedly modest by Hollywood standards nevertheless dwarf those of their Japanese, Korean, and Hong Kong counterparts. Audiences in these East Asian markets are thus happy to buy a ticket to enter a gleaming new multiplex theater to watch Hollywood's versions of stories they already know well. Meanwhile, remakes of American horror films offered above-the-line US-based industry players an opportunity to move into the lucrative field of motion picture financing via the bankrolling of films that boasted a potentially enormous profit-to-cost ratio. These films also served as a training ground for directors and on-screen talent looking to make the transition from the small to the big screen, or who were making their Hollywood debuts after having enjoyed successful careers overseas. Because of the success of these patterns in film financing and international distribution, horror remakes coalesced into a recognizable genre, with a characteristic mode of production, a distinctive approach to generic norms, and a successful distribution strategy. Horror remakes aped the successful financing and distribution of the *Scream* films. After the successful remake production trend proliferated in the mid-2000s, it developed into different strands such as remakes of the late 1970s and early 1980s teen slashers, including *Halloween* (2007 [1978]) and *Friday the 13th* (2009 [1980]), and 1970s prestige horror films such as *The Omen* (2005 [1976]) and *The Amityville Horror* (2005 [1979]), before dissipating by the end of the decade. Far from "cannibalizing the past," this trend was vitally engaged in both a changing movie marketplace and long-term changes in the horror genre.

References

Alford, C. (1999), "Goliath Balks at David's Quotas," *Variety*, August 9–15, p. 34.
Bing, J. (2003a), "Hip to be Ghoul," *Variety*, June 23, p. 5.
—(2003b), "Auds have Hankering for Horror," *Variety*, December 1, p. 8.
Bowles, S. (2005), "Girls just Wanna Scream: Horror Movies Rule with Trembling Teenagers," *USA Today*, March 11. Available online at http://usatoday30.usatoday.com/life/movies/news/2005-03-10-women-horror-films_x.htm (accessed August 15, 2013).
Box Office Mojo (2013), "The Ring." Available online at http://www.boxofficemojo.com/movies/?id=ring.htm (accessed August 12, 2013).
Brodesser, C. and Lyons, C. (2001), "'Final' Duo Fill a Double Bill," *Variety*, September 7, p. 1.
Cahill, P. (1999), "'Haunting' Scares Big Auds O'Seas," *Variety*, September 29, p. 452.

Carver, B. (1999), "New Duo in the 'House,'" *Variety*, January 18, p. 16.
Cohen, D. S. (1999), "Groans and Growls take Center Stage in 'Haunting,'" April 22, Special Report.
Fleming, M. (2003a), "New 'Horror' Haunts," *Variety*, October 24, p. 5.
—(2003b), "Dimension Mines Deal with Platinum Shingle," *Variety*, November 4, p. 1.
—(2005), "Platinum Rides 'Hitcher' Redo," *Variety*, April 18, p. 1.
Friend, T. (2003), "Remake Man," *New Yorker*, June 2. Available online at http://www.newyorker.com/fact/content/?030602fa_fact (accessed August 12, 2013).
Groves, D. (1995), "Competition in Asia's Multiplex Biz Heats Up," *Variety*, January 23, p. 55.
—(1996), "Asia's Exhibition Boom; Confab Finds Film Biz Focus," *Variety*, January 29 to February 4, p. 39.
—(1997), "H'w'd Hits Gold; Confab Finds Asia-Pacific in Growth Mode," *Variety*, January 27 to February 2, p. 37.
—(2002), "Day-and-date Strategy Spins 'Spidey' Success," *Variety*, May 13–19, p. 12.
Harris, D. (2002), "Radar Revs 'Chainsaw,'" *Variety*, January 31, p. 1.
Harris, D. and Lyons, C. (2001), "Strouse Enters Castle to Pen 'Macabre,'" *Variety*, April 6, p. 1.
Heffernan, K. (2004), *Ghouls, Gimmicks, and Gold: Horror Films and the American Movie Business, 1952–1968*, Durham, NC: Duke University Press.
Heianna, S. (2005), "Interview with Roy Lee, Matchmaker of the Macabre *Kateigaho*." Available online at http://int.kateigaho.com/win05/horror-lee.html (accessed August 12, 2013).
Higgins, B. (2003), "Slaughtering the Past," *Variety*, October 20, p. 63.
Hindes, A. (1999), "All's Right at Fright Sights: D'Works' 'Haunting' Houses $33 mil; 'Blair' Scares Life into B.O.," *Variety*, July 26, p. 1.
Klady, L. (1999), "'Haunting' Scares up Strong B.O.," *Variety*, August 2, p. 12.
LaPorte, N. (2004), "Eclectic Pix on the Radar," *Variety*, September 21, p. 1.
Levine, S. (1999), "'The Haunting,'" *Variety*, May 14, Special Section.
Nowell, R. (2011), *Blood Money: A History of the First Teen Slasher Cycle*, New York: Continuum.
Screen Daily (2002a), "Triple Whammy as *Gangs*, *Ring*, and *8 Mile* Pass the $100m Mark," October 21. Available online at http://www.screendaily.com/triple-whammy-as-gangs-ring-and-8-mile-pass-the-100m-mark/4012718.article (accessed August 15, 2013).
—(2002b), "US Remake of *The Ring* Outperforms Original in Japan," November 19. Available online at http://www.screendaily.com/us-remake-of-the-ring-outperforms-original-in-japan/4011297.article (accessed August 15, 2013).
Sullivan, M. (1999), "Quest for Survival," *Variety*, June 25, p. 93.
Variety (1996), "UA Back to Malaysia," February 20, p. 20.
—(1998a), "De Bont Haunts 'House,'" August 11, p. 1.
—(1998b), "Indie Fave Taylor Tapped for Dreamworks 'House,'" September 28, p. 5.
—(2003), "Overseas Options: Remake Wranglers Mine Asia, South America," July 21, p. 14.

5

Monster Factory

International Dynamics of the Australian Horror Movie Industry

Mark David Ryan

From the early to mid 2000s, the Australian horror film production sector achieved growth and prosperity of a kind not seen since its heyday in the 1980s. Australian horror films can be traced back to the early 1970s when they experienced a measure of commercial success. However, throughout the twenty-first century, Australian horror gained levels of international recognition that have surpassed the cult status enjoyed by some of the films in the 1970s and 1980s (see Hartley, 2008). In recent years, Australia has emerged as a significant producer of breakout, cult, and solid B-grade horror films which have circulated in markets worldwide. The increased visibility of Australian horror is also partly attributable to the rediscovery of the nation's 1970s and 1980s genre picture heritage, which is known in the popular vernacular as "Ozploitation", thanks to the documentary *Not Quite Hollywood: The Wild, Untold Story of Ozploitation!*, and to the endorsement this film received from none other than leading auteur Quentin Tarantino.

While the annual horror output of the Australian film industry pales in comparison to that of other Anglophone nations like the United States, Great Britain, and Canada, it has produced several significant titles that have performed well at the international box office over the past decade and a half. The low-budget slasher film *Wolf Creek* (2005), for example, grossed over US$50 million in theatrical and ancillary markets on a budget of AU$1.4 million (circa US$1.25 million), and the futuristic vampire movie *Daybreakers* (2009) generated over US$51 million at the global box office. What is more, in 2012 the 3D shark film *Bait* became something of a sleeper hit when it made over US$33 million worldwide, despite not receiving a US theatrical release. The breakout hit *Saw* (2004), which was filmed in the United States after failing to secure Australian sources of finance, was initially developed in Australia by the Melbourne-based filmmakers Leigh Whannell and James Wan. As Tim Kroenert has observed, "If the Australian film industry dropped the ball by allowing the *Saw* horror franchise to slip through its fingers, it was a mistake they [sic] weren't going to make twice" (2007, p. 28). Australia has also produced numerous movies that have achieved a measure of cult status on platforms such as home video and pay-TV, and online. Examples of these films include *Black Water*, *Rogue*, *Storm Warning* (all 2007), the UK/Australian co-production *Triangle*, *The Loved Ones* (both 2009), *The Reef* (2010), and *The Tunnel* (2011).

Australian horror's recent successes have been driven by one of its distinguishing features: its international dimensions. As this chapter argues, the Australian horror film production sector is an export-oriented industry that relies heavily on international partnerships and pre-sales (the sale of distribution rights prior to a film's completion), and on its relationships with overseas distributors. Yet these traits vary from film to film, since the sector comprises several distinct domains of production activity, from guerrilla films destined for niche video markets like specialist cult video stores and online mail-order websites to high(er)-end pictures made for theatrical markets. Furthermore, the content and style of Australian horror movies has often been tailored for export. While some horror filmmakers have sought to play up the Australianness of their product, others have attempted to pass off their films as American or as placeless films effaced of national reference points.[1]

---

[1] This chapter uses the term "independent" to refer to films that are not bankrolled by the Hollywood companies. Rather, they are financed either wholly by private investors or by a combination of private investment and public subsidy. Another key point of clarification concerns production budgets. The average Australian feature film budget is approximately AU$7 million (circa US$6.3 million). As a guide, low-budget filmmaking typically accounts for movies budgeted at AU$1 million to AU$15 million (circa US$900,000 to US$13.5 million), mid-range films AU$15 million to AU$50 million (circa US$13.5 million to US$45 million), while a big-budget film can cost between AU$50 million and AU$100 million (circa US$45 million to US$90 million). Big-budget movies are almost always financed primarily by Hollywood companies, and comprise a small proportion of Australian output.

The history and cultural status of Australian horror movies

Since the 1970s, horror has occupied a marginal position within the Australian film industry. A production system that is sustained largely by government subsidy, the industry has been underwritten by cultural policy objectives that were partly intended to foster the "representation and preservation of Australian culture, character and identity" (Mayer, 1999, p. 13). In response, the most celebrated Australian films have tended to focus on "authentic" representations of national identity and have told stories that emphasize "Australianness" (O'Regan, 1996; Moran and Vieth, 2006; Routt, 1999; Mayer, 1999). This practice has also seen the prioritization of a "quality" cinema that is aligned with the sensibilities of, and which borrows from, European art cinema and American indie cinema, in order to offer an alternative to forms of filmmaking that some associate with Hollywood, and in particular the action, fantasy, science-fiction genres. As Geoff Mayer has argued, until quite recently, the Australian film industry's long-standing refusal to "recognise [...] generic status" amounted to an attempt to differentiate "itself from Hollywood, which has always been interested in refining and developing specific film genres" (1999, p. 178).

Since 2007, however, policy shifts have encouraged the Australian film industry to put commercial considerations first, by making films that are more likely to reach a wide audience (Ryan, 2012). For example, the "Producer Offset" was introduced to stimulate Australian production by offering producers a 40 percent rebate on eligible film expenditure.[2] As a consequence, much as it did in the 1980s, the industry turned to medium- to high-budget genre films such as the science fiction movie *Knowing* (2009) and the action film *Killer Elite* (2011) (ibid.). This development also spurred the production of horror and other forms of genre filmmaking that were already on the rise in the mid-2000s following the relative commercial success of *Saw*, *Wolf Creek*, and others.

A local horror movie tradition emerged during the New Wave of Australian cinema in the early 1970s. The New Wave, which lasted from 1970 to 1988, came about following the introduction of a range of government initiatives that were intended to energize domestic film production, including a commitment to state sponsorship and the establishment of supportive institutions like the

---

[2]Eligibility for the Producer Offset is assessed on whether a film meets criteria defining "Australian content" and provisions regarding domestic production/post-production expenditure (see Screen Australia, 2013d).

Australia Film Development Corporation and the Australian Film, Television and Radio School. Such steps reversed a precipitous decline in Australian feature filmmaking that had taken place in the 1960s. *Night of Fear* (1972)—a story about a mute hermit who terrorizes a woman who has stumbled onto his property—was Australia's first horror film. Several more quirky titles were to flow, including the horror Western *Inn of the Damned* (1975), the internationally known tale of a comatose telekinetic patient *Patrick* (1978), and the vampire movie *Thirst* (1979).

In addition to seeing the rise to prominence of critically acclaimed showcases of national identity such as *Sunday too far Away* (1975), *My Brilliant Career* (1979), and *"Breaker" Morant* (1980), the 1970s and 1980s also witnessed Australian horror films proliferate as part of a broader upsurge in low-budget genre films that would come to be known as "Ozploitation". These films included locally shot action movies, road movies, sexploitation pictures, and "ocker" comedies that relied heavily on Australian slang (see O'Regan, 1989). Among the better known horror films from this period were *Razorback* (1984), the tale of a small outback community being assaulted by a giant man-eating boar, and *The Marsupials: Howling III* (1987), a story about marsupial werewolves from the outback attempting to integrate into urban society. Most of the Australian horror films made during this period were B-movies insofar as they were aimed at drive-ins or were expected to receive a limited theatrical run before being released on home video.

Production declined by 50 percent in the 1990s, during which time a mere 20 horror films were made in Australia (see Ryan, 2010; see also Table 5.1). Only two of these projects—the slasher film *Bloodmoon* (1990) and the splatter movie *Body Melt* (1993)—were distributed theatrically in Australia, and both failed dismally at the box office. The remainder either underperformed on home video or remained unreleased. A key factor in this decline was the decision by the government in 1988 to wind down the 10BA tax incentive, from its peak as a 150 percent tax write-off between 1981 and 1988 to a 100 percent write-off by 2002. Thereafter, national funding bodies such as the Australian Film Commission and the Film Finance Corporation became the principal financiers of Australian feature films.[3] As these institutions prioritized support for what they deemed to be "authentic cultural stories" or comparatively prestigious art cinema destined for the international film festival circuit, horror and Ozploitation generally became marginalized within this public funding environment. Conversely, Australian horror boomed

---

[3] The Australian Film Commission (1975–2008) and the Film Finance Corporation (1988–2008) became Screen Australia in 2008.

Table 5.1 Australian horror film production by decade

Decade	No. of Films	Average per Annum	Comparison to Previous Decade	Expenditure per Annum (AU$m)	Average Budget per Annum (AU$m)
1970s	20	2	–	n/a	n/a
1980s	48	4	+28	n/a	n/a
1990s	19	2	–29	15 (est.)	1.5
2000–2008	62	8	+43	107.5	15.8

Source: Adapted from Ryan (2010).

during the 2000s, when production tripled.[4] Some of these new films broke out internationally by either performing well in overseas markets or receiving the "buzz" and press coverage that can accompany films received as cult artifacts.

The increasing internationalization of the Australian film industry during the 1990s gave rise to growth in international participation, partnerships, and co-productions in the twenty-first century (Reid, 1999). By the turn of the century, Australian producers turned once again to horror in an attempt to target international markets and the relatively high margins of return that could be earned from low-budget horror productions. The growth of Australian horror production was also fueled by the rise of low-cost digital video as a shooting gauge, the opening up of online video markets, strong global demand for horror fare during the early to late 2000s, and the expansion of DVD markets (see Ryan, 2009). Additional factors included a growing demand among major international distributors for new horror product (Church, 2006).

---

[4] The horror film production boom of the 2000s was not unique to Australia. On the contrary, this was a broader international development which saw the output of such diverse national film industries as those in Japan, Korea, Turkey, India, and Norway grow strongly during this period. An early study of horror production outside the US and the UK argued that this shift was a product of a "decline of rigid national boundaries, and the trans-cultural phenomenon affecting virtually all sectors of cinema," as well as the rise of online distribution opportunities and easier access to non-Anglophone horror films (Schneider and Williams, 2005, p. 3).

Production and distribution

In contrast to the US and the UK, where horror film production has been driven by powerful production companies and financier-distributors such as Hammer Film Productions, Lionsgate, and Twisted Pictures, Australian horror has been produced by independent filmmakers, small firms, and emerging filmmakers who "dabble[d] in horror from time to time" (Hood, 1994, p. 10). Three distinct models of production have come to characterize the sector since the early to mid-2000s: higher-end films backed by international capital and major distributors; low- to medium-budget independent productions; and guerrilla filmmaking.

Following the breakout success of *Wolf Creek* in 2005, major international distributors took more of an interest in Australia as a potential source of independently produced films, and large-scale co-productions became commonplace by the end of the decade. For instance, the US-based Weinstein Company greenlighted director Greg McLean's follow-up to *Wolf Creek*, the AU$28 million (circa US$25.2 million) killer crocodile film *Rogue*. Similarly, in 2009 the major American independent financier-distributor Lionsgate bankrolled the Spierig Brothers' follow-up to their low-budget zombie picture *Undead* (2003): the AU$25 million (circa US$22.5 million) vampire film *Daybreakers*. Several relatively big-budget co-productions also took place after 2007 when the Producer Offset became the primary funding mechanism for local productions. The AU$18 million (circa US$16.2 million) 2009 film *Triangle* was, for example, backed by Icon Entertainment International and financed by Australian and British capital. As noted above, internationally financed horror movies—and some co-productions—have medium budgets—relative, that is, to the production costs of Australian films. Such pictures are typically helmed by emerging filmmakers, or those with a track record in Australian-made genre pictures. Generally boasting high production values, they tend to feature B-list stars such as Ethan Hawke and Sam Neill, who appeared in *Daybreakers*, or Michael Vartan and Radha Mitchell, who headlined *Rogue*. With the backing of powerful international distributors, these films are usually the recipients of quite costly marketing campaigns and theatrical releases around the world.

Low-budget independently made films, contemporary examples of which include *Wolf Creek*, *Undead*, *The Reef*, *Black Water*, *Needle*, and *Primal* (both 2010), have been a staple of Australian horror film production. The commercial viability of projects such as these was summed up by one producer who claimed that they offer "the simplest model you can have—make it cheap as you can, sell it for as much as you can" (Ford, 2008). In other words, production companies aim to maximize profit by crafting such films as inexpensively as possible, before selling off the rights for the picture to distributors in as many international territories as they can. A case in point is *Black Water*, which had already recouped its AU$1.2 million (circa US$ 1.1 million) budget from international pre-sales before it flopped at box offices around the world (Robertson, 2008), thereby generating profits for its producers and investors in spite of its underwhelming ticket sales (see Table 5.2). Low-budget Australian horror is produced for between AU$1 million and AU$7 million (circa US$900,000 to US$6.3 million) and is largely financed with private capital, direct subsidies provided by governmental agencies (Screen Australia will, for example, invest directly in an individual film), or indirect government benefits such as tax breaks and production rebates, including the Producer Offset. Less glossy than their high-end counterparts, such films generally feature largely unknown actors or those who are looking to move into feature films after making a name for themselves in television. While the filmmakers behind these low-budget efforts target a theatrical release, there is no guarantee that they will be distributed at all. Most of the low-budget fare that does in fact enter into circulation does so by virtue of the negative pick deals that see distributors purchase completed films. Many are, however, limited to a direct-to-DVD release.

Guerrilla production is driven by very different forces. Films such as *Reign in Darkness* (2002), *I Know how many Runs You Scored Last Summer* (2008), *Family Demons* (2009), and *The Killbillies* (2012) largely fly beneath the radars of most audiences, are by and large unaffected by policy initiatives, and are seldom the subject of industry discussion. Although some aspects of guerrilla production vary from country to country, such pictures may be regarded as do-it-yourself filmmaking in the sense that they are produced on miniscule budgets and are driven by an ethos that amounts to "don't stand around thinking about it—do it" (Reid, 1999, p. 34). In this respect, what may be thought of as the low end of Australian horror production "is characterised by filmmakers who self-finance [...] shooting guerrilla style and working with crews drawn from a combination of film-school dropouts, enthusiastic amateurs and professionals honing their trade between gigs" (Sargeant, 2011, p. 90). These projects are typically budgeted at between AU$1,000 and AU$100,000 (circa US$900 to US$90,000), and are usually shot on digital video. Even though they often secure international distribution deals, Australian guerrilla films rarely make it onto theater screens. Most of these underground films are instead released direct-to-video, sold through online mail-order services, or offered on a pay-per-download basis by websites that bill themselves as specialists in cult and indie cinema. Most of Australia's low-end horror films are also the subject of negative pickup deals. As such, filmmakers often "cater to distributors' preferences from [...]

inception if they hope to be seen by an international audience, which usually means ramping up the exploitation and gore" (Lobato and Ryan, 2011, p. 196). In terms of commercial performances, *Reign in Darkness* is a standout example. Produced for AU$49,000 (circa US$44.000), this film was sold to over 27 countries, where by 2003 it had managed to amass for distributors AU$4 million (circa US$3.6 million) from DVD sales and rentals (Dolen, 2003, p. 2003).

Structural barriers and the marketplace

The size of the Australian market provides a major impediment to the commercial performances of domestically produced horror movies. Australia's population currently stands at a mere 23 million inhabitants. By contrast, some 330 million people live in the United States. Accordingly, most Australian films struggle to recoup their production costs in the domestic market alone (O'Regan, 1996; Harris, 2007). The limited appeal of horror among Australian audiences ultimately ensures that films of this type find themselves competing for a thin slice of an already small pie. From the limited data available, no horror film appears among the 50 top-grossing pictures in the history of the Australian market (Screen Australia, 2013a). More importantly, a mere 46 horror films from a total of 1,050 (or 4 percent) feature on the lists of annual top-grossing films for the years 1992 to 2012 (Screen Australia, 2013b).

Even high-profile non-Australian horror films that perform well in other theatrical markets have a tendency to underperform in Australia due in no small part to the genre's limited fan base in that country. The science fiction horror film *Prometheus* was the highest-grossing horror movie at the Australian box office in 2012, but it generated only AU$18.7 million (circa US$16.8 million) or 4.5 percent of its worldwide theatrical returns in that market (see Table 5.3). Of the remaining four horror films that earned over US$100 million in worldwide ticket sales that year, *Paranormal Activity 4* generated AU$7.8 million (circa US$7 million), which represented 5.5 percent of its theatrical gross, *Abraham Lincoln: Vampire Hunter* AU$2.5 million (circa US$2.25 million) (2 percent), and *The Devil Inside* AU$1.6 million (circa US$1.4 million), (1.5 percent). *The Possession* failed to secure an Australian release in spite of the fact that it generated over US$84 million worldwide, and *The Cabin in the Woods* (2012), which had initially been relegated to a direct-to-DVD release in Australia, made a pitiful AU$263,084 (circa US$236,700) when it was released on seven screens following calls from a vocal minority of fans.

Table 5.2   Horror films at the Australian box office, 2012

Film	Budget (US$m)	Australian Theatrical Gross		Worldwide Theatrical Gross (US$m)
		AU$m	circa US$m	
Prometheus	130	18.7	16.8	403.3
Paranormal Activity 4	5	7.8	7	140.7
Abraham Lincoln: Vampire Hunter	69	2.5	2.25	116.4
The Devil Inside	11	1.6	1.44	101.3
The Possession	14	n/a	n/a	84.4
The Cabin in the Woods	n/a	0.263	0.237	66.4
House at the End of the Street	10	n/a	n/a	39.4
Chernobyl Diaries	n/a	n/a	n/a	37.1
Silent Hill: Revelation 3D	20	n/a	n/a	52.3
Silent House	n/a	n/a	n/a	13.1
Totals	259	30.86	27.72	

Source: Nash Information Services, 2013: www.boxofficemojo.com.

The commercial potential of the Australian horror film market is further tempered by culturally specific factors that undermine the appeal of locally produced fare. At the heart of this issue is the notion of "cultural cringe." This concept was initially developed by the Australian literary critic Arthur Phillips (1950) to illuminate a social phenomenon wherein Australians tend to view local cultural works as inferior to those from other countries. The term refers to the idea that local audiences physically "cringe" in revulsion of, or in embarrassment at, local forms of cultural expression. Before the 1970s New Wave, this included "a cringing embarrassment" towards the onscreen representation of the Australian "accent, syntax and vocabulary" (Cao, 2012, p. 243). It has been suggested that cultural cringe resulted from Australia's heritage as a former British colony, the dominance of US—and to lesser extent British—cultural imports in the local market, and a perceived dearth of "authentic" Australian culture (for a discussion of how the construction and representation of Australian identity has been "caught between the British Empire and the American Empire" see Cao 2012, p. 239). In a similar vein, Australian-made films have been seen domestically as mundane cinema that is found wanting when compared to Hollywood (O'Regan, 1996, p. 121). Whereas some non-Australian audiences fetishize them as an exotic Other, Australian films are often seen by the country's distributors, exhibitors, and moviegoers as disposable. Although cultural cringe has affected the domestic reception of Australian cinema as a whole, it was directed with particular veracity towards the Ozploitation movies of the 1970s and 1980s; both critics and audiences tended to distinguish such films from Australian stories and quality cinema by dismissing them as trite approximations of American forms of storytelling (see T. Ryan, 2008).

Unless they develop a high profile internationally, Australian horror films are likely to struggle at the domestic box office. Since 2005, only four horror films—*Wolf Creek*, *Rogue*, *Daybreakers*, and *Bait*—generated more than AU$1 million (circa US$900,000) at the Australian box office. Domestic box office receipts represent a small fraction of gross theatrical revenue. For example, the Australian market accounted for only AU$2.5 million (circa US$2.25 million) of *Daybreakers*' US$51 million worldwide theatrical returns, and a mere AU$1 million (circa US$900,000) of *Bait*'s US$33 million haul

Table 5.3 Recent Australian horror films at the box office

Film	Year of Release	Budget (AU$m)	Australian Theatrical Gross		Worldwide Theatrical Gross (US$m)
			AU$m	circa US$m	
Daybreakers	2009	25	2.4	2.2	51
Bait	2012	20	1	0.9	33
Wolf Creek	2005	1.4	6	5.4	27
Rogue	2007	28	1.8	1.6	4.6
Triangle	2009	18	0.011	0.01	1.3
Black Water	2007	1.2	0.112	0.1	0.637
The Reef	2011	3.8	0.124	0.11	0.305
Totals		102.4	11.4	10.3	118.1

Source: Sources: Australian box office: Screen Australia, 2013c; Budget: www.imbd.com (see Lightfoot (2007) for *Rogue*; Total Int. box-office: www.boxofficemojo.com.

(see Table 5.2). As one commentator suggested, "[l]et's face it: Australians don't tend to go out to see horror films. Especially Australian horror films" (Kroenert, 2010, p. 10). Greg McLean, the writer-director-producer of *Wolf Creek*—the only Australian horror film to fare well domestically during this period—has suggested that such fare must "play overseas first before it plays properly here" (McLean, 2007). In McLean's eyes, *Wolf Creek* became a hit in Australia "because it [was a success] overseas" and as a result "people in Australia were desperate to see it" (ibid.). This reliance on overseas markets, and hence international distributors and audiences, has influenced the style and content of Australian horror films.

Textual strategies: Australianness, faux-American horror, and placeless horror

Two primary tendencies characterize the content of recent Australian horror films: showcasing "Australianness," and developing a faux-American or "placeless" textual identity.

In a global marketplace that is often seen to be saturated with clichéd, formulaic horror films, cultural specificity or national branding can provide a measure of product differentiation in English-speaking territories, while lending such fare an air of the exotic in others. Consequently, many Australian horror films have traded in what might be termed an "Australian style" or an Australian "accent." While the content of Australian horror films is often influenced by international cycles of films, their makers have tended to eschew gothic standards such as vampires, werewolves, and supernatural ghosts, and their associated tropes—dark crypts, haunted houses, graveyards, and the like. Rather, from older films such as *Razorback*, *Picnic at Hanging Rock* (1975), and *Howling III: The Marsupials* to recent efforts like *Wolf Creek*, *Rogue*, *Black Water*, and *Primal*, the lion's share of recognizably Australian titles have been dominated by backwoods settings and crazed animals. An overarching theme of horror movies that trade in their Australianness is the struggle for survival in an inhospitable and dangerous landscape.

These films utilize Australian tropes, social and cultural themes, and character types. A much-used trope is the elevation of landscape from a mere backdrop for narrative action to something akin to the status of a character in its own right. In terms of their thematic terrain, such films often consider the dark side of "mateship" (a term that refers to the celebration of masculine values and male–male friendships), entrapment and isolation in rural locales, and the validity of national stereotypes such as the good-natured larrikin character type. These features are exemplified by *Wolf Creek*, in which the mad slasher Mick Taylor amounts to a maniacal version of the character of Mick Dundee from *Crocodile Dundee* (1986). Taylor is both a laconic, rugged, larrikin bushman in the mold of the stereotypical Australian male that was popularized in classic works of Australian literature such as those written by Banjo Patterson and Henry Lawson, and a serial murderer who preys on unsuspecting backpackers. The film subverts the stereotypical image of the good-natured, rough-hewn Aussie outback type to present a negative image of the Australian bushman. Until quite recently, the vast majority of Australian horror films were set in the Australian outback. This practice led to the showcasing of Australia's unique flora and fauna. For example, *Razorback* thematizes the dangerous implications of ravaging the land for commercial gain, in this case opal mining and kangaroo shooting, and its cinematography showcases the ethereal colors of the outback. With its red desert, rusted shanties, and car shells hanging from twisted Eucalyptus trees, *Razorback* is reminiscent of the post-apocalyptic wasteland of *The Road Warrior* (1981).

By contrast, some Australian-based filmmakers have attempted to increase the international appeal of their films by stripping them of Australian national reference points. As Susan Dermody and Elizabeth Jacka (1988, p. 48) have observed of Ozploitation movies from the 1970s and 1980s,

> Trans-national "genre" films [...] were products consciously designed for easy recognition in specific overseas markets. These packages were intended for marketing in terms easily understood by film-buyers. [...] they had to be emptied of all reference and relationship to the site of production; they had to belong to a transnational American-derived, moneyed cultural limbo.

Filmmakers who employ this model often suggest that such practice is driven by fears of "cultural discount." They posit that overseas audiences struggle to understand Australian accents, dialects, and cultural quirks, and that Australian humor is lost on them. Their fears do not seem to be wholly unfounded. For example, although the comedy *Kenny* was the highest-grossing Australian movie at the domestic box office in 2006—earning over AU$7.7 million (circa US$6.9 million)—it generated limited interest among international distributors, and failed dismally in the United States, where paradoxically it was screened with subtitles after test audiences had found the dialogue incomprehensible.

The concern that cultural discount will undermine the international appeal of films which foreground Australian reference points has exerted an influence on the content of some Australian horror films. Above all others, it is the targeting of the US market that has had the greatest influence on the style and subject matter of Australian-produced horror. In the words of Robert Hood, numerous titles have been made "with more than an eye on America's large lucrative audience" (1994, p. 1). For example, the filmmakers behind *Needle*, *Reign in Darkness*, *Feed* (2005), and *The Gates of Hell* (2008), among others, attempted to produce films that would be perceived as American films by having Australian actors play American characters in storylines that unfolded either fully in the United States or sometimes in both the United States and Australia. Furthermore, the makers of the crime/psychological horror film *Feed* tried to pass off Australian locations as American settings. Other filmmakers have attempted to contrive films with a non-culturally specific or placeless identity. For example, the sci-fi horror film *Subterano* (2003) is set in an unspecified futuristic cityscape, wherein characters played by Australian actors speak with a combination of mild-Australian and British accents. A less clear-cut example is *Triangle*, a story loosely based on the mysterious disappearances that have plagued the Bermuda Triangle. In this film, Australian actors play what can only be assumed to be American characters, as they speak with American accents. Yet, the suburban streets that appear in the opening scenes of this film are quite clearly Australian, and a shot of a billboard advertising "The Sunshine State" could just as easily be referring to the Australian state of Queensland—where *Triangle* was in fact shot—as the American state of Florida; the protagonists are picked up by a ship that is registered in Miami after their own yacht has capsized. Ultimately, however, the setting of this film is never made clear. As the critic Sandra Hall explained, *Triangle* was "originally set [...] off the coast of Florida [...] but, as things have turned out, we're left to make up our own minds as to where [...] we are" (2010). Having reached a peak in the 1980s, when films such as *Harlequin* (1980) were released, Australian-made placeless horror has been less common than faux-American titles during the past decade and a half.

The influence distribution strategies exert upon the content of Australian horror films is exemplified by the case of the Australian-Singaporean co-production *Bait*. This tale of tsunami survivors menaced by sharks in a flooded supermarket was tailored not for the US market but for Chinese audiences. In order to increase the film's chances of faring well in that country, Chinese investors required the shooting of new scenes that focused on Asian characters and their back stories, and called for the dialogue of some Australian characters to be dubbed by actors speaking mid-Atlantic English (see Quin, 2012). As such, two versions of the film were produced: one for the Chinese market and one for the rest of the world. This strategy is all the more significant if we consider the fact that this movie's most successful market was by a significant margin China. Of its total box office takings of AU$33 million (circa US$29.7 million), *Bait* earned almost US$25 million in its first three weeks of release in that country (*Screen Daily*, 2012).

With Australian horror films increasingly integrated into globalized systems of production and circulation, the pressure grows for them to perform well overseas. Yet, in the context of rising production budgets, the need to capture Australian audiences remains fundamentally important, not least to justify the sizable investment of public money into high-end projects. A failsafe way of fulfilling these objectives has nevertheless remained elusive. Whereas some of Australia's horror films could be accused of perpetuating national stereotypes in an effort to pander to overseas markets, others may be said to have abandoned vernacular storytelling on the back of the misguided belief that international audiences will be incapable of telling an American film from an Australian film in American clothing.

References

Cao, B. (2012), "Beyond Empire: Australian Cinematic Identity in the Twenty-first Century," *Studies in Australasian Cinema*, 6.3: 239–50.
Church, D. (2006), "Scream and Scream Again: Return of the Return of the Repressed: Notes on the American Horror Film (1991-2006)," *Offscreen.com*. Available online at http://www.offscreen.com/biblio/phile/essays/return_of_the_repressed (accessed March 27, 2008).
Dermody, S. and Jacka, E. (1988), *The Screening of Australia: Anatomy of a National Cinema, Vol. 2*, Sydney: Currency Press.
Dolen, K. (2003), "DIY: May the 4th be with You," *IF*, 52, pp. 32–4.
Ford, P. (2008), Interview with author, February 11.
Hall, S. (2010), "Triangle," *Sydney Morning Herald*, April 24. Available online at http://www.smh.com.au/entertainment/movies/triangle-20100423-tiv7.html (accessed July 5, 2013).
Harris, R. (2007), *Film in the Age of Digital Distribution: The Challenge for Australian Content*, Platform Paper No. 12, Currency House, Sydney.
Hartley, M. (2008), *Not Quite Hollywood*, Madman Entertainment.
Hood, R. (1994), "Killer Koalas: Australian (and New Zealand) Horror Films: A History," in Bob Morrish (ed.) *The Scream Factory*, June/July. Available online at http://www.tabula-rasa.info/AusHorror/OzHorrorFilms1.html (accessed April 28, 2008).
Kroenert, T. (2007), "Reign of Terror," *Inside Film*, 101, pp. 28–9.
—(2010), "The Rocky Horror Picture No-show," *Inside Film*, 135, pp. 10, 15.
Lightfoot, D. (2007), Interview with author, September 25.
Lobato, R. and Ryan, M. D. (2011), "Rethinking Genre Studies through

Distribution Analysis: Issues in International Horror Movie Circuits," *New Review of Film and Television Studies*, 9.2: 188–203.

McFarlane, B., Mayer, G., and Bertrand, I. (eds) (1999), *The Oxford Companion to Australian Film*, Oxford: Oxford University Press.

McLean, G. (2007), Interview with author, September 25.

Maher, S. (1999), *The Internationalisation of Australian Film and Television Through the 1990s*, Woolloomooloo: Australian Film Commission.

Mayer, G. (1999), "Genre, Post-World War II," in B. McFarlane, G. Mayer, and I. Bertrand (eds) *The Oxford Companion to Australian Film*, Oxford: Oxford University Press.

Moran, A. and O'Regan, T. (eds) (1989), *The Australian Screen*, Ringwood, VIC: Penguin Books.

Moran, A. and Vieth, E. (2006), *Film in Australia: An Introduction*, Cambridge: Cambridge University Press.

Nash Information Services (2013), "Box Office Performance for Horror Movies in 2012." Available online at http://www.the-numbers.com/market/2012/genre/Horror (accessed May 18, 2013).

O'Regan, T. (1989), "Cinema Oz: The Ocker Films," in A. Moran and T. O'Regan (eds) *The Australian Screen*, Ringwood, VIC: Penguin Books.

—(1996), *Australian National Cinema*, London: Routledge.

Phillips, A. (1950), "The Cultural Cringe", *Meanjin*, 9.4 (summer): 299–302. Available online at http://search.informit.com.au/documentSummary;dn=692761906212773;res=IELLCC (accessed April 15, 2013).

Quin, K. (2012), "Sinking our Teeth into China," *Sydney Morning Herald*, October 30. Available online at http://www.smh.com.au/entertainment/movies/sinking-our-teeth-into-china-20121024-285n9.html (accessed February 26, 2013).

Reid, M. (1999), *More Long Shots: Australian Cinema Successes in the 90s*, Woolloomooloo: Australian Film Commission.

Robertson, M. (2008), Interview with author, February 15.

Routt, W. D. (1999), "Genre, Pre-World War II," in B. McFarlane, G. Mayer, and I. Bertrand (eds) *The Oxford Companion to Australian Film*, Oxford: Oxford University Press.

Ryan, M. D. (2009), "Whither Culture? Australian Horror Films and the Limitations of Cultural Policy," *Media International Australia: Incorporating Culture and Policy*, 133: 43–55.

—(2010), "Australian Cinema's Dark Sun: The Boom in Australian Horror Film Production," *Studies in Australasian Cinema*, 4.1: 23–41.

—(2012), "A Silver Bullet for Australian Cinema? Genre Movies and the Audience Debate," *Studies in Australasian Cinema*, 6.2: 141–57.

Ryan, T. (2008), "Tom Ryan in Conversation with Mark Hartley about Not Quite Hollywood," *The Monthly Online: Australian Politics, Society and Culture*. Available online at http://www.themonthly.com.au/tm/node/1164 (accessed January 10, 2012).

Sargeant, J. (2011), "Notes from the Underground: Guerrilla Filmmaking in Australia," *Metro Magazine*, 168: 90–2.

Schneider, S. J. and Williams, T. (eds) (2005), *Horror International*, Detroit: Wayne State University Press.

Screen Australia (2013a), *Top 50 films in Australia of all Time, Ranked by Total Reported Gross Australian Box Office as at February 2013*, Woolloomooloo: Screen Australia. Available online at http://www.screenaustralia.gov.au/research/statistics/wctopalltime.aspx (accessed June 20, 2013).

—(2013b), *Top 50 films in Australia Each Year since 1992, Ranked by Reported Gross Australian Box Office as at 31 December Each Year*, Woolloomooloo: Screen Australia. Available online at http://www.screenaustralia.gov.au/research/statistics/wctopfilms.aspx (accessed June 22, 2013).

—(2013c), *Australian Content: Box Office: Australia: Top 5 Each Year Since 1988*, Woolloomooloo: Screen Australia. Available online at http://www.screenaustralia.gov.au/research/statistics/mrboxausttop5.aspx (accessed June 17, 2013).

—(2013d), *Producer Offset*. Available online at http://www.screenaustralia.gov.au/producer_offset/ (accessed June 17, 2013).

Screen Daily (2012), "China Box Office Monthly Round-up: *Bait 3D* Makes Surprise Attack," *Screendaily.com*, November 15. Available online at http://www.screendaily.com/china-box-office-monthly-round-up-bait-3d-makes-surprise-attack/5048999.article (accessed February 24, 2013).

PART TWO

Film Content, Style, and Themes

6

"Bad Medicine"

The Psychiatric Profession's Interventions into the Business of Postwar Horror

Tim Snelson

Janet Bergstrom and others have highlighted the parallel and occasionally intersecting histories of the psychological sciences and cinema, both of which may be seen as aspects of modernity that struggled across the twentieth century to gain popular recognition and respectability (1999). The convergence of psychiatry and cinema manifested at a more prosaic level soon after World War II, when in 1946 a discursive struggle erupted over how Hollywood should utilize psychological discourses in a responsible manner. At this time, several renowned psychiatrists and social scientists attempted to influence the ways in which Hollywood depicted their respective professions. As this chapter argues, the testimony of these scientific professionals initiated a representational shift, wherein the mad psychiatrists of wartime horror were superseded by psychological scientists. The unbalanced, exploitative, and sometimes murderous doctors of such films as *Cat People* (1942), *Calling Dr. Death*, *The Seventh Victim* (both 1943), and *Strange Illusion* (1945) would ultimately give way to benevolent psychiatric professionals in pictures like *The Dark Mirror* (1946), *Possessed* (1947), and *The Snake Pit* (1948).

Accordingly, this chapter begins by shedding light on the social conditions that precipitated the shifting representation in horror cinema of the psychiatrist/psychologist, two distinct professions that tended to be conflated into a single figure on the silver screen. I focus on the outcry that took place over Twentieth Century-Fox's *Shock* (1946); a horror film that was seen as doing a major disservice to psychiatry at a time when the profession was seeking to gain greater levels of public acceptance, and was hoping for increased government funding to treat returning war veterans. Experts and cultural guardians from the fields of psychiatry, social psychology, and film criticism would exert a meaningful influence over Hollywood's horror film content in the immediate postwar period—a situation that is evinced by the films themselves and by the publicity materials that accompanied their release. The chapter moves on to explain how Hollywood bowed to such pressures, by incorporating into horror films the more accurate and positive depictions of psychological professionals and practices that claims-makers were demanding.[1] Judged against criteria of aesthetic realism and social relevance, which were favored by middlebrow critics such as Bosley Crowther of the *New York Times* (see Klinger, 1994), horror films like *The Dark Mirror* and *The Snake Pit* were seen as antidotes to the sensationalism and negative influence of wartime fare like *Shock*.

Previous studies have tended primarily to focus on the representation of psychiatry in classical Hollywood films, or have employed psychoanalytic theory to analyze this content. Such tendencies are exemplified by the influential *Psychiatry and Cinema* (1999), in which the psychiatrist Glen Gabbard and his brother Krin, a Film Studies scholar, employ both of these approaches in separate sections of a single book. In contrast, few studies have focused on the manner in which psychiatrists and psychologists precipitated Hollywood's recalibration of its representational strategies. As Michel Foucault has demonstrated—and as this chapter shows by example—discourse is not only constraining but can also be productive and enabling (1989).

The horrors of war: The aggressive fem hero and the mad psychiatrist

In order better to understand the ways in which discourses pertaining to psychology and psychiatry shaped the content of Hollywood's postwar horror films, it is helpful to illuminate how these discursive interventions unfolded alongside other important societal trends of the period.

---

[1] Mark Jancovich (2012) has detailed the shifting critical discourses that surrounded "psychological themes" across the 1940s, as they came increasingly to be valued by virtue of their association with notions of realism.

With the moral certainties of wartime diminished, American society was increasingly exposed to scientists—especially psychologists—who were presented as cultural and moral authorities that, in the words of William Graebner, could "ground and anchor values, or at least [help the public] function more effectively within the milieu of contingency" (1998, p. 27). Popular magazines, radio shows, marketing campaigns, and self-help literature all embraced Pop-Freudian psychoanalysis as an exciting and authoritative way of explaining human behavior and interaction. For example, numerous magazines paraphrased, or reprinted excerpts of, the 1947 book *Modern Women: The Lost Sex*, which had used a simplified version of Freudian psychoanalysis to argue for a return to prewar gender roles. Its authors Ferdinand Lundberg and Marynia Farnham argued that, during World War II, feminists had prompted women to suppress their "true instincts" in favor of adopting flawed versions of male traits; a process that involved the repression of their nurturing roles. Lundberg and Farnham bemoaned the loss of the "old-time concepts of the 'good' and the 'bad' woman," which, they suggested, "had the merit of resting at least on generally factual physical, psychological and social differentiation of sexual function" (1947, p. 203). These writers advocated a government-backed program designed to restore prestige to the sexually ordained roles of the wife and the mother.

Journalists writing about media also looked to psychology to provide a corrective to the gender confusion that was said to have emerged during wartime. This tendency is exemplified by an article printed in an August 1945 issue of the trade paper *Variety* under the title "Chicago Psychiatrist Traces Aggressive Girls to Pix Not-So-He-Men" (pp. 1, 16). The article cited an unnamed professor of psychology who observed that a University of Chicago Report offered indisputable evidence that "American women have become more aggressive during World War II," in large part, he proposed, due to the proliferation on the big screen of "fem heroes" and "not-so-he-men" (*Variety*, 1945, p. 1). The professor complained that "aggressive is the only word that can be used to describe the modern American female" (ibid.). This research, or at least *Variety*'s selective reporting of it, posited a direct effects model of media influence. It implied that onscreen messages about gender roles and power relations were capable of determining the behavior of young American women.

The type of aggressive "fem hero" that so disheartened this anonymous psychology professor was to be found most prominently in B-horror and murder-mysteries that both Universal and RKO produced during World War II. These films portrayed women as stepping out from their hitherto marginal positions as love interests and victims, by taking up the central roles of monsters and investigators which had previously been assigned to male characters (see Snelson, 2014).[2] What is more, such films typically articulated a suspicion of psychology, especially the figure of the psychiatrist who, as Dana Polan has suggested (1986, p. 179), often approximated mad scientists inasmuch as both types of character were portrayed as "equal violators of the rules of normality." Polan was referring specifically to Universal's *Captive Wild Woman* (1943). In this film, the psychiatrist and geneticist Dr. Sigmund Walters (John Carradine) transfers a female hysteria patient's "unusual amount of sex hormones" to a circus ape in the hope of creating a new master race.

The makers of *Captive Wild Woman* literalized a series of metaphorical accounts of female patients that appeared in Freud's early studies. In these accounts, women's bodies become what Peter Stallybrass and Allon White described as a "battleground in the hysterical repression of the grotesque form" (1986, p. 184). Stallybrass and White detail how the repression of female sexual desire, in conjunction with a lack of everyday terminology with which to discuss the female body, led Freud's female subjects to invoke the circus and the carnivalesque as a way of expressing their feelings about this issue in a manner free of the rhetoric of disgust (ibid., p. 187). Through the nervous and neurotic character of Dorothy Colman (Martha MacVicar), *Captive Wild Woman* enacts the link between the repression of female sexual desire and the eruption into everyday life of circus terrors. When he diagnoses Dorothy with a "rare case of follicular cyst which induces secretions of unusual amounts of sex hormones," Dr. Walters echoes the explanatory discourse that Freud employed when he attributed the neuroses of a patient named Dora to an "abnormal secretion of the mucous membrane of the vagina [that] is looked upon as a source of disgust" (Freud, 1966, p. 103). By transferring these secretions to a circus ape that becomes "a human form of animal instinct," as the film describes it, Walters enacts a Freudian reversal. He transposes the sexual hysteria that he himself has diagnosed back into the metaphorical terms of the circus and the freak show that were used by Freud's patients. The film erases the distinction between the circus and the surgery by cutting between these two otherwise antithetical locations, while at the same time linking them by way of a dialogue overlap which showcases a form of carnival barking that applies to both situations: "you are about to see what no human has seen before." In *Captive Wild Woman*, Walters' scientific methods amount to a form of diabolical showmanship that is enacted on the female body.

---

[2] *Cat People* provides another high-profile case of a wartime picture that featured both a female monster/investigator and a horrific psychiatrist. In this film, the psychiatrist Dr. Judd is presented as an unscrupulous character who exploits his profession to fulfill an unhealthy desire for power and sex, which is directed lasciviously at Irena, the titular cat person.

The psychiatrist of *Captive Wild Woman* is linked not only to Freudian science but also to Nazi science; this in spite of its makers' efforts to condemn the megalomaniacal Dr. Walters by aligning him to the German National Socialist Party, most explicitly by his use of "master race" rhetoric. Such themes were criticized by the liberal New York newspaper *PM*, which attacked both *Captive Wild Woman* and its 1944 sequel *Jungle Woman* for endorsing "Nazi race theories" (McManus, 1944 [1944], p. 303).[3] These race theories, which tied sexual instinct to heredity—and hence also with eugenics and various forms of racism—drew upon the perversion-heredity-degenerescence system in a manner that Foucault has since suggested was rigorously opposed by Freud himself (Foucault, 1998, p. 119). This conflation of ideas was seen to be "morbid and neurotic – as [...] in some pre-Nazi German films" (Crowther, 1943, p. xi). Quite understandably, the critics who voiced such positions were concerned with the implications of *Captive Wild Woman*'s racial politics and theories, as well as by its general luridness, rather than its representation of a psychiatrist and of the psychological sciences.

Postwar horror: Traumatized veterans and psychophobic audiences

After World War II, Hollywood companies found it increasingly difficult to rationalize the production of lurid horror pictures in the vein of *Captive Wild Woman*. The Hays office and film critics somewhat paradoxically attacked these films both for their gruesomeness and their ineffectuality. Thus, a writer at the *Hollywood Reporter* condemned *The Spider Woman Strikes Back* (1946)—one of the final films of the Universal horror cycle—for being out of touch with a contemporary audience's capacity to endure depictions of horror and death (1946, p. 3). The critic in question stated that the producers of this film should have been aware of the fact that "the public ha[d] gained a familiarity with wartime blood banks that removes a large share of the horror of such mild blood-letting" (ibid., p. 3). Despite its supposed restraint and failure to provoke audience horror, *The Spider Woman Strikes Back* encountered difficulties receiving approval from the Motion Picture Association of America (hereafter MPAA), the industry organization that was responsible for determining whether a script was deemed acceptable under the terms of the Production Code. The film was refused a seal on the grounds that it employed

---

[3] *Captive Wild Woman* was also challenged in at least one letter to the Bureau of Motion Pictures, which nevertheless refused officially to condemn the movie (see Myers, 1998, p. 118).

"extremely gruesome angles" of transfusion scenes and the suggestion that the carnivorous plants were being fed the bodies of the various girls, which, according to Joseph Breen of the MPAA, would "undoubtedly prove objectionable to audiences generally" (1945).

The most pressing postwar concern over Hollywood's horror output related to the perceived thoughtlessness with which the psychiatric profession was being represented on the screen, as well as the manner in which psychological themes appeared to be articulated by such fare. MGM's *Bewitched* (1945), which dramatized a supposed case of "schizophrenia" that had been triggered by supernatural possession, proved especially problematic for New York reviewers, because it was deemed to blur generic boundaries between horror and psychological drama. For example, Wanda Hale of the *Daily News* dismissed this picture as "morbid and unpleasant, and, to me a little ridiculous" on account of seeing it as "a sort of feminine counterpart of Jekyll and Hyde," and thus as a straight horror film (1945 [1945], p. 250).[4] Conversely, other reviewers saw *Bewitched* as a problem precisely because they believed that its makers were aspiring to fashion something more than just a straight horror film, due to their apparent efforts seriously to engage with psychological issues. "There ought to be a law about movies like [this...]," a reviewer writing for *PM* suggested, "[i]f you saw *Bewitched* at your local creep house, with Dr Karloff skulking around [...] you could just file it and forget it along with the year's crop of Draculas and stuff" (McManus, 1945 [1945], p. 249). This reviewer concluded, however, by lamenting that "in full top-budget regalia [...] you have a right to expect a certain clinical validity" (ibid.).

The backlash against the type of representation on show in *Bewitched* reached an apotheosis during the outcry over Twentieth Century-Fox's 1946 film *Shock*. In this film, a psychiatrist, Dr. Cross (Vincent Price), murders his wife before attempting to use hypnotic suggestion to drive insane the only witness: Janet, the nervous wife of a recently returned prisoner of war. Cross tries to kill Janet by administering a lethal dose of insulin as he gives her shock treatment. The scene plays out in such a way as to encourage audience horror, with superimposition used to juxtapose a close-up of Janet's pained, distressed face, and a rapid montage of injections, surgical apparatus, records of increasing doses, and calendar pages. The intense disorientation that this scene was clearly designed to induce is enhanced further by the eerie musical score which is built around the swelling drone

---

[4] Siegfried Kracauer's 1946 essay on the "Hollywood Terror Film" also questioned the secularization of postwar horror, suggesting that atypical levels of realism and sadism were a by-product of the war, and a cause for concern.

of a Theremin—a musical instrument that was used regularly at this time on the soundtracks of psychological horror films. In the final minutes of *Shock*, Dr. Cross sees the error of his ways. He strangles his nurse-cum-lover, who had intended to proceed with the plan, and saves Janet by injecting her with adrenalin. He then quite literally hangs up his doctor's coat and gives himself up to the police. This conciliatory gesture was seen by film critics and psychological scientists as having failed to offset the material that had gone before it.

In New York, more than anywhere else, the middlebrow press was quick to condemn the film as causing damage to the psychiatric profession. In a *New York Times* review entitled "Bad Medicine," Bosley Crowther condescended that, although horror films could usually be "quietly dismissed," *Shock* amounted to nothing short of a "social disservice at this time," adding that the film "should excite the critical observer to protest in no uncertain terms" (1946a, p. 20). Crowther feared that a film like *Shock* could induce a distrust of the psychiatric profession among potential patients and their relatives, a concern that he felt was compounded by the fact that the "treatment of nervous disorders is being practiced today upon thousands of men who suffered shock of one sort or another in the war" (ibid.). Crowther went on to attack both the film's producer Aubrey Schenck and its distributor Twentieth Century-Fox, using the term "deplorable" to lambast the decision to make and release such a picture (ibid.).

John McManus of *PM* went even further than his colleague at the *New York Times* when, the day after Crowther's review was published, he suggested that *Shock* had made him "not only physically ill, but almost tearfully angry and deeply ashamed for the studio" (1946 [1946], p. 627). McManus supported his four-column polemic with statistics on the number of soldiers who had been discharged or rejected from the army on the grounds that they were suffering from mental and emotional disorders. He called for a team of medics to assess *Shock*, and, if it turned out that they shared his views on its harmful nature, to appeal to Darryl F. Zanuck to "yank it off the screen and burn it" (ibid.). If Zanuck refused, McManus implored the medical experts to "go after it in the courts, as a menace to public health and welfare" (ibid.).

The New York press continually denounced *Shock* as emblematic of Hollywood's generally irresponsible handling of psychological themes. One week after his first attack on the film, Crowther wrote a much longer polemic (1946b). He argued that *Shock* was representative of a cycle of what he called psychological pictures, all of which fostered among an already skeptical public a phobia of psychology generally and of insulin shock therapy in particular, by making standard treatments appear to be "deliberately evil practices" (ibid.).

Crowther cited a contemporaneous article from the *Hollywood Quarterly* in which a Professor Franklin Fearing of the University of California had bemoaned Hollywood's representation of the psychological sciences, as well as its overuse of amnesia as a plot device, which, suggested Fearing, "occurs about as often as toothache, according to these films" (ibid.). In that article, Fearing suggested that psychological conditions are ideal plot devices for melodramas and mystery thrillers, because "the layman," as he called the general public, already viewed such conditions with a "curious mixture of fascination and horror" (Fearing, 1946, p. 154). Fearing nevertheless encouraged Hollywood to complement its need to entertain audiences with a greater degree of discrimination when it came to mobilizing material related to psychopathology, which he suggested ought best serve "justifiable aesthetic, social or educational ends" (ibid., p. 155).

Less generous than Fearing, Crowther derided the horror pictures as simultaneously standardized and sensationalized, while also attacking their producers—in particular Twentieth Century-Fox—for their commercial exploitation of a "witless" public (1946b, p. xi). He went on to suggest that a series of documentaries that had been recently produced by the US Army promised to offer a much-needed riposte that would showcase the benefits of this new and misunderstood science. Singled out for praise was John Huston's *Let There Be Light* (1946), a documentary about servicemen undergoing successful psychological treatment that had been screened at New York City's Museum of Modern Art. Here, Crowther invoked a politics of taste by contrasting the passive consumers of supposedly standardized horror against what he saw as the refined tastes and social engagement of the connoisseurs who visited this prestigious location.

Following Crowther's campaign against *Shock*, the *New York Times* persuaded Dr. Manfred Sakel—an internationally renowned neurophysiologist and psychiatrist, and the pioneer of insulin shock therapy—to attend a screening of the film at New York City's Rialto, an infamous grindhouse theater (Weiler, 1946, p. 51; for more on the Rialto and its audiences see Snelson and Jancovich, 2011). Sakel concluded that the film did indeed do damage to psychiatry. "Having the psychiatrist attempt to hypnotize a patient," he lamented, "puts the science into the realm of demonology" (ibid.). Sakel suggested that Hollywood could exert a positive influence on the "more than 600,000 mental cases in institutions in America today by studying the problem as it really is" (quoted in Weiler, 1946, p. 51). Perhaps in response to Sakel's objections, as well as to the protests of medical bodies such as the New York Society for Clinical Psychiatry, the New York Academy of Medicine, and the American Psychiatric Association, censors in Canada deleted all references to insulin shock treatment from the prints of the film that were set to be circulated in their country (AFI, 1971, p. 2169).[5]

The following week, the *New York Times* reported that Dr. Lawrence Kubie, a practicing psychiatrist and neurologist at the New York Neurological Institute, had called for a commission of qualified psychiatrists to study the effects on mass audiences of such films as "horror pictures with strong neurotic impact" (Weiler, 1946, p. 8). This report also called for producers to seek advice from qualified independent psychiatrists when making films that tackled psychiatric subjects (ibid.). Kubie highlighted the screen industry's responsibility to the six million Americans who would need psychiatric treatment in the future, calling for Hollywood to fund research into the psychological effects of its products, and to pay fees to the psychiatrists whom they would employ as consultants during the production of their films (ibid.) Social psychologists, including the aforementioned UCLA professor Frederic Fearing, would go on to challenge Kubie's assertions that psychiatrists should conduct research for, and serve as consultants to, Hollywood, claiming that social psychology was better suited to shedding new light on the influence of the media (Fearing, 1947).

While the furor over *Shock* had begun to subside by late April 1946, the American media continued to alert the public and the medical profession to the dangers of "Hollywood's current series of easy lessons in psychiatry" (*Time*, 1946). For example, in an October issue of the *New York Times*, Dr. Carl Binger, an Assistant Professor of Clinical Psychology at Cornell University, warned against scientific misinformation being spread by what he described as "the sensation seekers in Hollywood" (*New York Times*, 1946c). He honed in on a spate of "far-fetched psychiatric films," which he suggested effectively laid down the gauntlet to psychiatrists to push for more accurate cinematic representations of their profession and its practices (ibid.).

---

[5] It may appear surprising that a respected scientist like Sakel would invest his time and energy into investigating such low cultural artifacts as *Shock* and the Rialto. The following month Sakel's interest in the popular perception of his practices was highlighted when the *New York Times* printed his urgent request for government funding to support a new institute for insulin therapy, and for greater numbers of trained physicians to administer it. He claimed that his methods offered the greatest promise for the recovery of America's psychologically damaged servicemen, who Sakel claimed represented between 30 and 40 percent of the country's war casualties (*New York Times*, 1946a, p. 29). For more on Sakel and the history of the largely discredited psychiatric practice of insulin therapy see Blythe Doroshow, 2007, pp. 213–43.

Let there be light: Social realism and serious psychological treatments

On October 18, 1946, some seven months after *Shock* had prompted calls for positive representations of the psychiatric profession, Universal-International opened *The Dark Mirror* in New York City. Although it went into production before the aforementioned controversy broke, the promotional strategies and critical reception of *The Dark Mirror* were certainly influenced by the debates surrounding *Shock* ("*The Dark Mirror* Call Sheets").

The Dark Mirror was both framed and received as a serious portrayal of psychiatry, in which a psychologist and his psychological procedures are presented as redemptive. The film showcased an innovative split-screen technique to allow Olivia De Havilland to play identical twin sisters, Ruth and Terry, one of whom is a murderer. Although eyewitness accounts place one of the twins at a murder scene, the pair refuse to reveal the identity of the guilty party, thereby obstructing police efforts to apprehend and prosecute the culprit. The psychiatrist Dr. Scott Elliot (Lew Ayres) ultimately reveals that Terry is guilty, thanks to his use of psychiatric and scientific methods, including Rorschach tests, a polygraph machine, and exercises in free association. By freeing Ruth from her dark double, Elliot effectively reinscribes the good/bad woman distinction, the loss of which Lundberg and Farnham had so vehemently lamented. Furthermore, Ruth is now free to begin a relationship with Dr. Elliot, safe in the knowledge that he had always thought of her as "so much more beautiful than her sister." In the light of his professional and personal triumphs, this turn of events restores gendered power relations and commits the dark and mysterious side of the female psyche to an asylum, where it can be examined, categorized, and contained.

The American media explicitly linked *The Dark Mirror* to the outcry over Hollywood's duty to represent science and medicine responsibly. Thus, a *New York Times* writer noted: "luckily Lew Ayres [who played Dr. Elliot] has returned from the Army Service to rescue medical practice, this time as a psychiatrist" (TMP, 1946). Significantly, the press book which accompanied the release of *The Dark Mirror* encouraged journalists to spread the word that Ayres had ended a four-year hiatus from Hollywood films because he believed that the psychiatric profession would be central to postwar social reconstruction efforts, both nationally and internationally. Ayres, this studio-produced document went on to explain, had himself returned from the horrors of war furnished with a new set of values and boasting a reaffirmed faith that "his life work of entertainment [was] eminently worthwhile" (Universal-International, 1946, p. 9). Ayres was presented as a man who believed firmly that psychiatry held the answers to a contingent and uncertain postwar world, and that it was Hollywood's responsibility to dramatize this position. Journalists also praised *The Dark Mirror* for its scientific accuracy, and for the cinematic realism they saw resulting therefrom. A writer at the *Los Angeles Times* suggested that the film was "closer to being psychological than most pictures thus labeled," adding that the "psychoanalysis it goes in for [...] makes credible the premise of the film, which on analysis, must be regarded as fantastic" (Schallert, 1946).

Universal-International sought to differentiate *The Dark Mirror* from the aforementioned "orthodox" horror pictures by stressing that the film "derives all its tensely developed dramatic values solely from the brain, and by a scientifically tested method of procedure" (1946, p. 6). The company's press book went into great detail about ambivalent psychoneurosis, the condition from which Terry suffered (ibid., p. 9). It attributed theories about this condition to Carl Jung, who, it went on to explain, had learned psychoanalysis from Sigmund Freud. Universal-International therefore invoked the authority of the most venerated experts in the field in order to confirm the sound scientific basis of *The Dark Mirror* (ibid., p. 8). The company also stressed that *The Dark Mirror* was built on cutting-edge empirical "scientific aspects," by highlighting the fact that the film's writer-producer Nunnally Johnson had "kept a psychology expert at his elbow all the while he was producing the screenplay," and that the Federal Bureau of Investigation (FBI) had verified the scientific data upon which the film's makers had drawn (ibid.).

In the wake of the controversy over *Shock*, Universal-International was at pains to anchor the realism and social relevance of *The Dark Mirror* to the expertise of professional psychiatrists and psychologists, and to the authority of established psychological discourse. Universal-International's attempts to avoid the type of controversy that had previously engulfed *Shock* also saw psychology appropriated as an explanatory framework that could be used not only to account for the development of *The Dark Mirror*, but its consumption as well. Accordingly, Siodmak explained that "audiences love a picture like *The Dark Mirror* because it affords what psychoanalysts call a psychic renovating" (Universal-International, 1946, p. 8). The strategy of bringing all aspects of *The Dark Mirror* under the rubric of psychological science, including even its purportedly positive influence on audiences, is indicative of the representational shift away from the cynical and at times gruesome depictions of psychiatrists and psychological practices that characterized wartime horror cinema.

The horror films that went into production after the ebbing of the *Shock* controversy evinced Hollywood's newfound commitment to responsible depictions of psychiatry. A case in point was the 1947 film *Possessed*, in which

Joan Crawford stars as a schizophrenic undergoing psychiatric treatment. The *New York Times* praised this film on the grounds that it demonstrated integrity and authenticity in terms of its representation of the condition and its treatment (Crowther, 1947a, p. 25). Once again, writers at the newspaper lauded the manner in which montage and special effects were used to visualize a character's mental state. The "unqualified realism" generated by such techniques, it was suggested, enabled "the audience [to] actually participate in the mental confusion pictured on the screen" (Spiro, 1946, p. 3). The paper stressed that the director of *Possessed*, Curtis Bernhardt, had read over 30 books about mental disorders, that he had conducted extensive preproduction research at a Los Angeles psychiatric ward, and that he had employed a professor of psychology at the University of Southern California and the Head of Neurology at New York University as technical advisor and consultant respectively (ibid.).

The postwar shift in content would also become a key talking point in the *New York Times*' reception of *The Snake Pit* (1948). In this case it is clear that Hollywood's efforts to appease scientific and cultural elites were not without consequence, as a new set of concerns emerged about the implications of revealing information on the psychiatric profession to the general public. The first Twentieth Century-Fox film to foreground this material since the outcry over *Shock*, *The Snake Pit* adopted ambivalent positions towards psychiatric procedures and institutions. Although the film ultimately appeared to validate the treatment administered by its sympathetic psychiatrist Dr. Kik (Leo Gen), it also portrayed its protagonist's return to sanity as a fraught and difficult experience. The protagonist's encounter with electro-shock therapy (ECT)—as well as her time in an overcrowded, oppressive, and poorly run sanitarium— are portrayed as harrowing events. Accordingly, Crowther commended Twentieth Century-Fox for dealing with this material in a responsible fashion (Crowther, 1947b, p. 29). In much the same way as he had done in response to *Possessed*, this critic championed a sense of "faithful realism" that he saw being showcased by *The Snake Pit* (ibid.). Crowther put this down to the filmmakers' commitment to "Freudian explanation," and to the steps they had taken to allow viewers to empathize both with psychotic episodes and such treatments as ECT, hydrotherapy, and narcosynthesis (ibid.).[6]

The generally positive response that *The Snake Pit* initially enjoyed soon gave way to concern over its suitability for general consumption. Ten days

---

[6]Although Crowther praised Alfred Hitchcock's *Spellbound* (1945) for its suspense and technical artistry, he stressed that "we are told by studious people that the psychology in the film is not much more reliable than that practiced in *Lady in the Dark* [1944]" (1945, p. 45). The representational and formal strategies used in *Possessed* and *The Snake Pit* were therefore seen to serve different ends.

after having championed the film, Crowther would begin to ask whether such a hard-hitting picture should in fact be shown at a "mass appeal theatre" like Times Square's Rialto (Crowther, 1947c, p. xi). While maintaining that Twentieth Century-Fox deserved credit for paying "reparation for a previous fright called *Shock*," he had started to question the implications of allowing such a "precarious picture to shoot at a crowd of innocent movie-goers of all ages, dispositions and states of mind" (ibid.). Crowther instead proposed that it was more appropriate to screen *The Snake Pit* on a bill of "better class pictures to which more discriminating patrons would be drawn" (ibid., p. xi). Even though Hollywood, and Twentieth Century-Fox in particular, was adjudged to have responded conscientiously to the calls of psychological scientists and critics, it found itself the subject of new forms of scrutiny from a self-ordained "high standards critic" like Bosley Crowther (ibid.). Once more, a clear politics of taste was in operation, as Crowther sought not only to position himself as a protector of the vulnerable masses, but also to insulate sophisticated consumers from suggestions that they, by virtue of their consumption of films like *The Snake Pit*, were imbricated within this most lowly of audiences.

Conclusion

This chapter has argued that the content of Hollywood's postwar horror films was shaped in response to claims emanating from the popular media, as well as from academic, professional, and medical organizations, all of which competed to assert their power in various established and emergent fields. The chapter has detailed how a seemingly inconsequential horror film like *Shock* could become a key transfer point in debates over Hollywood's roles after World War II; debates that involved the contributions of diverse stakeholders who possessed both diverging and similar interests. Psychiatrists and psychologists were concerned about the public perception of their professions, as well as state and private research funding. Film critics, on the other hand, sought to assert their authority as moral and cultural guardians, and to protect the expertise that underwrote their sense of authority. The business of postwar horror cinema was therefore shaped not only by the will of creative talent, of industrialists, and by audiences' viewing choices, but by a variety of competing and converging claims-makers, all scrambling for territory in the contested environment of postwar America.

References

AFI (1971), *The American Film Institute Catalog of Motion Pictures Produced in the United States*, Berkeley and Los Angeles: University of California Press.
Bergstrom, J. (ed.) (1999), *Endless Night: Cinema and Psychoanalysis. Parallel Histories*, Berkeley and Los Angeles: University of California Press.
Blythe Doroshow, D. (2007), "Performing a Cure for Schizophrenia: Insulin Coma Therapy on the Wards," *Journal of History of Medicine and Allied Science*, 62.2: 213–43.
Breen, J. L. (1945), Letter to Maurice Pivar, "re: script dated May 8th 1945," May 14, 1945. MPAA files, Margaret Herrick Library, California.
Crowther, B. (1943), "Old Black Magic," *New York Times*, June 13, p. xi.
—(1945), "Hitchcock Marches On," *New York Times*. November 11, p. 45.
—(1946a), "Bad Medicine," *New York Times*, March 9, p. 20.
—(1946b), "Hitting a Nerve: Shock is a Painful Example of Distortions of Psychopathology," *New York Times*, March 17, p. xi.
—(1947a), "'Possessed', Psychological Film with Joan Crawford as the Star," *New York Times*, May 30, p. 25.
—(1947b), "'Snake Pit' Study of Mental Ills Based on Mary Jane War's Novel, Opens at Rivoli," *New York Times*, November 5, p. 29.
—(1947c), "'The Snake Pit': Question of Exhibition Raised By New Film," *New York Times*, November 14, p. xi.
Fearing, F. (1946), "The Screen Discovers Psychiatry," *Hollywood Quarterly*, 1/2: 154–8.
—(1947), "Psychology and the Films," *Hollywood Quarterly*, 2.2: 118–21.
Foucault, M. (1989), *The Archaeology of Knowledge*, London: Routledge.
—(1998), *The Will to Knowledge: The History of Sexuality: 1*, London: Penguin.
Freud, S. (1966), *Dora: An Analysis of a Case of Hysteria*, trans. D. Bryan, New York: Macmillan.
Gabbard, G. and Gabbard, K. (1999), *Psychiatry and the Cinema*, Washington, DC and London: American Psychiatric Press.
Graebner, W. (1998), *The Age of Doubt: American Thought and Culture in the 1940s*, Illinois: Waveland Press.
Hale, W. (1945 [1945]), "'Bewitched' Strange Film, At Criterion," in *New York Motion Picture Critics' Reviews*, New York: New York Theater Critics' Reviews.
Hollywood Reporter (1946), "The Spider Woman Strikes Back," March 13, p. 3.
Jancovich, M. (2012), "'Terrifyingly Real': Psychology, Realism and Generic Transformation in the Demise of the 1940s Horror Cycle," *European Journal of American Culture*, 31.1: 25–39.
Klinger, B. (1994), *Melodrama and Meaning: History, Culture and the Films of Douglas Sirk*, Bloomington: Indiana University Press.
Kracauer, S. (1946), "Hollywood Terror Films: Do They Reflect an American State of Mind?," *Commentary*, 2: 132–6.
Lundberg, F. and Farnham, M. (1947), *Modern Women: The Lost Sex*, New York: The Universal Library.
McManus, J. T. (1944 [1944]), "Jungle Woman," in *New York Motion Picture Critics' Reviews*, New York: New York Theater Critics' Reviews.

—(1945 [1945]), "Oboler Bothers and Bewilders," in *New York Motion Picture Critics' Reviews*, New York: New York Theater Critics' Reviews.
—(1946 [1946]), "A Film to be Shocked About," in *New York Motion Picture Critics' Reviews*, New York: New York Theater Critics' Reviews.
Myers, J. (1998), *The Bureau of Motion Pictures and Its Influence on Film Content during World War II: The Reasons for Its Failure*, New York: Edwin Mellen Press.
New York Times (1946a), "Ill Veteran's Need for Insulin Noted," April 18, p. 29.
—(1946b), "Psychiatric Study by Movies is Urged," April 24, p. 8.
—(1946c), "Radio 'Plugs' Held Harm to Medicine; Misinformation Spread also by 'Sensation Seekers', Mental Hygiene Group is Told," October 31, p. 36.
Polan, D. (1986), *Power and Paranoia: History, Narrative and the American Cinema, 1940–1950*, New York: Columbia University Press.
Schallert, E. (1946), "'Dark Mirror' Sinister Sister Tale," *Los Angeles Times*, November 7, p. 21.
Snelson, T. (2014), *Phantom Ladies: Hollywood Horror and the Home Front*, New York: Rutgers University Press.
Snelson, T. and Jancovich, M. (2011), "'No Hits, No Runs, Just Terrors': Exhibition, Cultural Distinctions and Cult Audiences at the Rialto Cinema in the 1930s and 1940s," in D. Biltereyst, R. Maltby, and P. Meers (eds) *The New Cinema History*, Malden, MD: Blackwell.
Spiro, J. D. (1946), "Hollywood and Politics," *New York Times*, September 22, pp. X1, X3.
Stallybrass, P. and White, A. (1986), *The Politics and Poetics of Transgression*, Ithaca, NY: Cornell University Press.
"*The Dark Mirror*" Call Sheets, Duncan Cramer Papers, Box 1-f.5. Margaret Herrick Library, Los Angeles, CA.
Time (1946), "The New Pictures," September 16. Available online at http://www.time.com/time/magazine/article/0,9171,855545,00.html (accessed July 22, 2013).
TMP (1946), "'Dark Mirror' New Mystery at Criterion," *New York Times*, October 19, p. 25.
Universal-International (1946), *The Dark Mirror* press book.
Variety (1945), "Chicago Psychiatrist Traces Aggressive Girls to Pix' Not-So-He-Men," August 29, pp. 1, 16.
Weiler, A. H. (1946), "By Way of Report," *New York Times*, March 24, p. 51.

7

Horror Film Atmosphere as Anti-narrative (and Vice Versa)

Robert Spadoni

> *It's a perfect night for mystery and horror.*
> *The air itself is filled with monsters.*
> MARY SHELLEY, *THE BRIDE OF FRANKENSTEIN* (1935)

Horror films, particularly those made before 1960, are often praised for their atmosphere, a word that comes up constantly in reviews and academic writing on these and many other sorts of film. Far less common have been attempts to define what is meant by this term. And yet some filmmakers seem to understand, intuitively perhaps, just what to do to enhance the aesthetic, and, they hope, economic power of their productions. They make memorably atmospheric films, but how do they achieve this?

A basic way to explore this question is to regard an "atmospheric film" as a system, and to ask how the parts of that system relate to each other. In this spirit, this chapter explores a possible relationship between horror film atmosphere and narrative, which is, succinctly put, that less of one can mean more of the other. I will suggest that this push-pull dynamic has long been grasped by critics and others writing about horror as well as other types of film; I will briefly consider some implications of this dynamic; and finally I will turn to a 1960 British horror film, *The City of the Dead* (US title: *Horror Hotel*). This film's curiously bifurcated structure affords us a chance to observe how the different sorts of narrative that can be concentrated within, and distributed across, a film's formal make-up can yield predictably different atmospheric results.

A seesaw

> Some of these accounts are hardly stories at all, but rather studies in elusive impressions and half-remembered snatches of dream. Plot is everywhere negligible, and atmosphere reigns untrammeled.
> (Lovecraft, 2000, p. 67, on short stories by Algernon Blackwood).

A long-standing tendency in critical writing on horror films is to find some films succeeding, as films, on the strength of their atmospheres alone. Of *The Old Dark House* (1932), one writer notes that "the plot of *House* is not an important element in the film. Instead, the significant points are its mood and atmosphere" (Ellis, 1980, p. 137). More recently, another finds that "the story holds a few surprises, but what makes 'Let Me In' [2010] so eerily fascinating is the mood it creates" (Scott, 2010).[1] Such comments suggest that a sufficiently atmospheric film can be critically well received despite any narrative deficiencies it may possess.

A stronger claim, running alongside this trend, is that atmosphere can not only make up for a weak narrative but thrive in the vacuum created by its diminished force. When a plot's gears mesh tightly, an atmospheric spell may quickly be broken, as when, in *Castle in Flanders* (1936), "the ambiguous atmosphere is admirably maintained: it is when the hero turns out not to be a ghost at all that we lose interest and the film reality" (Greene, 1995 [1937], p. 219). Explanation can be bad for atmosphere. Backstories, and other means of filling gaps that would make a character's motivations or nature less mysterious, can cause an atmosphere to dissipate. By this thinking, *Halloween* (1978) goes right where *Psycho* (1960) goes wrong: "If there is an overexplained logic to Norman Bates' crimes, an earlier scenario that motivated his pathological violence (a thread continued in most slasher movies), such basic information is almost entirely lacking in *Halloween*, adding to its atmosphere of encroaching doom" (Worland, 2007, p. 232).

The collective hunch that is implicitly expressed by these comments is that atmosphere can gather and thicken in the textual spaces opened up by sparse storytelling. If this proposition seems intuitively correct, can we formulate it more explicitly? I suggest that one way to do so is to use what we know

---

[1] In this chapter, I treat "mood" and "atmosphere" as synonyms, as writers frequently use these terms interchangeably.

about narrative, which has been well described in Film Studies literature, in order to explore the much more nebulous thing we call atmosphere.

Such a strategy may lead us to hypothesize that atmosphere and narrative are animated by antipodal energies. Narrative represents a force of rationality within a film; to varying degrees, this formal subsystem clearly delineates space and time, and forges causal links that bind a film's elements together. Atmosphere, at least as some understand it, consists of something altogether different. Insight into its nature can be gained by looking outside Film Studies. For example, the architect and architecture theorist Mark Wigley (1998, p. 27) writes:

> those who embrace effect cannot approach atmosphere directly—cannot point to it, cannot teach it. Atmosphere escapes the discourse about it. By definition, it lacks definition. It is precisely that which escapes analysis. Any specific proposal for constructing atmosphere, no matter how changeable or indeterminate, is no longer atmospheric. […] Atmosphere may be the core of architecture but it is a core that cannot simply be addressed or controlled.[2]

Wigley's words resonate with an idea expressed by Julian Hanich when he writes:

> materialist accounts of the natural sciences […] reject everything that is not recordable: what cannot be measured does not exist. Many rejections of phenomenological descriptions must therefore be ascribed to such limitations. This certainly goes for vital cinematic phenomena such as brooding atmospheres.
>
> (Hanich, 2010, p. 47)

Both Wigley and Hanich address a thorny problem, which is how to go about rationally describing something that itself may be irrational. They also suggest that atmosphere and narrative can be set in opposition to each other. The two are mutually supportive but their relationship is not, as has often been suggested, one mainly of first and second tiers within a film's formal system, with narrative on top (see e.g. Hanich, 2010, pp. 170–1; for a refutation see Spadoni, forthcoming). Going further, we may surmise that the two can exist in a film in a kind of inverse relationship, meaning again that more of one will mean less of the other.

---

[2] Gernot Böhme notes that "atmospheres have something irrational about them, in a literal sense: something inexpressible" (2012, p. 2; see also Böhme, 1993, p. 113).

To make such a claim is to risk oversimplification, and it seems to ignore the fact that every film narrative exudes its own kind of atmosphere (on narrative's contributions to horror film atmosphere see Spadoni, forthcoming). Thus let me stress that I am only describing one possible relationship between these two aspects of a film, albeit an important one for understanding many pre-modern horror films, as I hope to show. I propose that one way to explore this hypothesis is to consider some implications that would follow from it.

Three implications

"The great clump of trees looked like a tomb in which my house was buried" – thus we are introduced at the start into the tale's sepulchral atmosphere.
(Todorov (1975 [1970], p. 81) on a Guy de Maupassant short story)

One implication is that a filmmaker wishing to create a strong atmosphere will lay importance on a film's beginning. If we take the beginning of a film to be its title screen, what may immediately come to mind are all those screens in which the title is carved on a rough plank of wood, or rises out of a swamp, or is written on sand, or forms out of smoke. Reflecting on what critics often mean by atmosphere brings us quickly to considerations of fogbound London streets, or the particular sounds of a carnival that a film gets exactly right, or, less tangibly, the feel of a certain historical period that a film captures perfectly. Atmosphere is in the air, spread out. It inhabits the details surrounding—and, less often recognized by critics and other writers—constituting the action. It is the texture of the world a film creates. A film that etches its title into something as tactile as sand or wood is setting up its atmosphere from the outset, as this writer understands: "In *The Cat and the Canary* [1939], a Gothic atmosphere is established from the film's opening, where cobwebs are brushed away to reveal the credits" (Conrich, 2004, p. 48).

It is not difficult to find writers who would agree that a film's beginning is an especially opportune place to attend to atmosphere. An atmosphere may even be established before a film begins. A guide to silent film musical accompaniment notes that "sometimes a carefully prepared number which embodies the general atmosphere or dominant emotion of the play ushers in the picture" (Beynon, 1921, p. 74). Another example is illustrated by *The Golem* (1920), which, as the *Motion Picture News* reported, was "presented with an atmospheric prologue, in which seven singers render 'Eli! Eli!' with fantastic stage setting of ancient Jewish period" (Altman, 2004, p. 381). Here, what from a narrative standpoint is a form of "excess" becomes permissible when it begins a film and when it functions to create atmosphere.

Edging into the start of the film proper, we come to those atmospheric film titles and to other sorts of introductory text. Another guide, this time for screenwriters, offers the following advice for composing titles: "Restrict the average title to about twenty words—fewer is generally better, except in the case of introductory or prologue titles in which the atmosphere of an entire picture is being presented" (Gale, 1936, p. 24). Another form of excusable excess thus occupies a similar place and serves a similar purpose. And, of course, once a film begins, the real work of building atmosphere gets underway. A writer notes that the opening of *Murders in the Rue Morgue* (1932) "provides lots of atmosphere right in the beginning before digging into the exposition and main plot" (Lennig, 2003, p. 153).[3]

From our perspective, it makes sense for a beginning to be a place to lay on the atmosphere especially heavily because it is here that the imprint of the narrative on a film will be at its faintest. In a film's first moments we rarely know the characters' names, their goals, or the obstacles to their goals, and few or no patterns of development will have begun to be elaborated. The story's grip on the film has not yet tightened. This creates an opportunity, a gap that a filmmaker can fill with atmosphere. And, once established with bold strokes, an atmosphere can then spread across a film, and a filmmaker can return to it later, either to pump it up again or to alter it—but the outset is a crucial place to begin the work.

A second implication brings us back to those letters carved on planks of wood, and to the painted swamps and Parisian rooftops making up the backgrounds of film titles. This is the importance of background and environment for creating atmosphere. (On cinema in relation to weather and environment, including weather as "atmosphere" see Hanich, 2010, pp. 170–2; McKim, 2013.) This may be more intuitively obvious than my claims about a film's beginning, but look at how these two implications interweave in most films. It is standard for a classical Hollywood film to begin a scene with an establishing shot. What is being established? These shots show the space wherein the ensuing action, and subsequent closer views—medium shots, close-ups, and so on—will unfold. But an establishing shot also shows us a space, and a space can carry a stronger whiff of atmosphere than the tighter framings that typically come later in a scene. And so this fixture of classical scene construction works also to establish atmosphere.

---

[3]The importance of beginnings for establishing atmosphere is noted by Greg M. Smith, who advises critics "to pay close attention to the way that emotion cues act together to create mood at the beginning of a film" (2003, pp. 43–4).

One is likely to see more space not just at the starts of scenes but at the starts of films. Extreme long shots often take us into a film's world. We get sweeping shots of the environment, and it is here—in these wide shots, where a film is not unspooling a tight narrative or negotiating a hairpin plot turn—that atmosphere rushes in. The tendency to exploit, simultaneously, these two atmospherically privileged aspects of a text pre-dates cinema. This section's epigraph attests to this, as does a nineteenth-century magic lantern show in which "the first projection that the audience saw [...] was a lightning-filled sky" (Barber, 1989, p. 77).

Of course, a filmmaker may place emphasis on the environment at other points in the film as well. The filmmaker Alberto Cavalcanti wrote: "I have a bit of dog-barking in my sound library which I sometimes stick into the track when I wish to suggest the open air, and a pleasant, gay atmosphere" (1985, p. 108). At the climax of *Frankenstein* (1931), "even so apparently innocent a structure as a windmill lends itself to the unrelieved gloom of atmosphere. It stands gaunt and alone on a high, barren hill against a backdrop of scudding clouds" (Douglas, 1966, p. 124). And, in *Psycho*, "the plush rooms contain conspicuous carpets that contribute to the hushed, smothering atmosphere of the house, which is crammed with furniture and objects" (Jacobs, 2007, p. 129). Environment is background. Characters, for the most part, occupy a film's foreground, and they move the narrative along. Foreground/background thus meshes with narrative/atmosphere as mutually supportive but contrasting entities within a film's formal system.

A third implication brings us to particular films and their makers. All films have beginnings. Most, I would argue, have atmospheric beginnings. And all films have backgrounds. But some films are more atmospheric than others, and some of these have attenuated narratives. Take *Vampyr* (1932), a film that thwarts narrative comprehension at every turn, and not by being convoluted or too fast-paced to follow. Things move slowly, and yet the viewer is frequently lost. If this misty ghost tale is not atmospheric, then no film is. A writer notes that, with it, the director Carl Theodor Dreyer "did not lay much emphasis on the actual tale," and that even the scene of the vampire's staking "is not made the dramatic climax, hardly even a release" (Neergaard, 1950, p. 27).

Also distinctive among horror films, but less esoteric than *Vampyr*, is Val Lewton's horror cycle of the 1940s. These films, again, are atmospheric if any films are—and their narratives have also been much remarked upon. For example, the films "stressed mood and atmosphere rather than star, story value, or special effects" (Schatz, 1997, p. 232). *Cat People* (1942) has been compared to director Paul Schrader's 1982 remake in the following way: "Lewton's film, like all of his outstanding horror pictures at RKO, emphasized mystery, implication, and atmosphere. By contrast, Schrader played up sex and explicit violence, attributes that overly literalized the ambiguities and narrative mystery of Lewton's original production" (Prince, 2000, p. 301). Schrader explains and shows more, and his film is a more arid production than the original.

Lewton's films foreground their environments and make their narratives less explicit at the same time. *Leopard Man* (1943), Manny Farber wrote, gives "the creepy impression that human beings and 'things' are interchangeable and almost synonymous and that both are pawns of a bizarre and terrible destiny" (1998 [1951], p. 49). In that film's most famous sequence, a young woman tries to get inside the safety of her home but is mauled to death by a leopard instead. We do not see the violence. In characteristic Lewton fashion, it is only suggested by the frantically moving door latch, the sounds of her pleading and screaming, the door palpitating once in its frame while scratching noises are heard, and finally blood pooling under the door. Of this sequence, Farber wrote that "all the psychological effects—fear and so on—were transformed by [its director Jacques] Tourneur into nonhuman components of the picture" (ibid., p. 50). Farber is describing the importance of *things* in the Lewton universe. This is tied to what people often mean when they celebrate a Lewton film's atmosphere. Instead of seeing the act, we see only effects and traces of it, such as shadows, sounds, or a torn garment. Actions become less concrete when they are projected onto the environment. And a film's environment is atmospheric. These become characteristic attributes of Lewton's films, of Tourneur's films, and perhaps never more potently than when the two collaborated.

One such collaboration, and another pinnacle of horror film atmosphere, is *I Walked with a Zombie* (1943). This film, writes Chris Fujiwara (1998, pp. 86–7), takes

> elliptical, oblique narrative procedures to astonishing extremes. The dialogue is almost nothing but a commentary on past events, obsessively revising itself, finally giving up the struggle to explain and surrendering to a mute acceptance of the inexplicable. We watch the slow, atmospheric, lovingly detailed scenes with delight and fascination, realizing at the end that we have seen nothing but the traces of a conflict decided in advance.

Fujiwara also writes that "the opening image of Betsy and Carrefour (the guardian of the crossroads) walking along a shoreline will prove not to have a place in the narrative" (ibid., p. 88). Here, we have a beginning—tiny silhouetted figures beneath a sky that dominates the frame—showing us something that never happens in the film proper. It serves no narrative purpose, only an atmospheric one. Another critic writes of a famous sequence in the film:

> Even the highly atmospheric walk through the cane fields seems almost an exercise in deception, since we are led to believe, by Betsy's loss of the "voodoo badge" needed to pass by Carrefour, by the recurring images of death and decay, and by the eerie sound effects, that this journey is indeed hazard filled; however, nothing happens.
>
> (Telotte, 1985, p. 52)

Nothing happens, and yet this sequence, in which the wind loudly and insistently whips through the setting, performs a vital function. Finally, of Lewton's films, Mark Robson, who directed *The Seventh Victim* (1943) and other entries in the cycle, said:

> These were unstructured works. Unstructured in the sense that character conflicts between protagonist and antagonist were diffuse. I think that this added to the charm of those films. In ways they broke many of the rules of story telling. They're almost film novels. Their form is different from any films of that period or since—they're much freer. They follow very few dramaturgical rules.
>
> (quoted in Peary, 1973, p. 37)

I would argue that some of this diffuseness owes to the hallmark Lewton transposition, noted by Farber, of actions onto things and the environment. It is here that we can turn to the greatest theorist of atmosphere that we have, namely German philosopher Gernot Böhme, who wrote:

> tone and emanation—in my terminology, *ekstases*—determine the atmosphere radiated by things. They are therefore the way in which things are felt to be present in space. This gives us a further definition of atmosphere: it is the felt presence of something or someone in space.
>
> (2012, p. 8; italics in original)

An artist who can make things "radiate" with "felt presence" in an especially intense fashion will produce an atmospheric film. Asking how creative practitioners such as Lewton and Tourneur de-emphasize the human within the environment, the foreground against the background, and the narrative against the atmosphere may help us to explore with greater concreteness what is meant by that intangible thing atmosphere, and to consider why some films, more than others, brim with this elusive aesthetic air.

The City of the Dead

> I feel I need some first-hand research. I want to get the atmosphere.
> (Nan Barlow, *The City of the Dead*)

Not as well known as Lewton's films, but often compared to them (see e.g. Pirie, 1973, p. 111; Newman, 2002, p. 54), is *The City of the Dead*. This film has also been compared to works by H. P. Lovecraft (see e.g. Hardy, 1986, p. 129; Hunt, 2002, p. 83), who called atmosphere "the all-important thing" (2000, p. 23). The film has been called atmospheric by almost everyone who has written about it. A pair of authors labels it "one of the most atmospheric chillers of the decade" (Clark and Senn, 2011, p. 26), another "one of the most atmospheric horror films ever" (Johnson and Miller, 2004, p. 96). In this film, undergraduate Nan Barlow travels to an old Massachusetts town, Whitewood, in order to research witchcraft. Unbeknown to her, the town harbors a group of undead devil worshipers led by Elizabeth Selwyn, who was burned at the stake in 1692, but not before she had made a pact with the devil to go on serving him in return for his protection. Her service, assisted by acolyte Jethrow Keane, involves human sacrifice, and Nan becomes the next victim. When Nan fails to return from the trip, her brother Dick and boyfriend Bill go in search of her, eventually rescuing Selwyn's next intended sacrifice and sending the witch into perdition.

Critics find *The City of the Dead* possessing, to pronounced degrees, attributes I see characterizing some atmospheric films. One is that its narrative is notably underdeveloped. The film has a "simple yet involving script" ("City of the Dead", 2003, p. 87); is "repetitive and short on complexity" (Rigby, 2000, p. 68); and is marked by "eccentric minimalism" (Bansak, 1995, p. 506). Here is the best reflection on the film's narrative I have found:

> *The City of the Dead* is not a complicated movie. There is no psychological dimension to the developing horror. Instead, we get a story that is simply about light vs. dark. We don't know why Elizabeth Selwyn became attracted to witchcraft. We don't know the nature of her relationship with Jethrow Keane. We don't know why the townsfolk of Whitewood have become attracted to the dark forces. We don't know why Nan is attracted to occult studies. Ultimately, the movie offers a simplistic dichotomy of good/normal society [...] vs. the evil outsiders.
> (Johnson, 2002)

And yet, with all this pointing to the simple story, it is hard to a find a bad review of *The City of the Dead*. Even the following criticism of the film is, for our purposes, noteworthy: "In my opinion, there's too much atmosphere; I'd gladly trade some of it for something in the way of some good story twists or a couple of surprise revelations" (Sindelar, 2006).

A more common response is for critics to find the narrative playing a role in making the film as memorable as it is. For one critic, *The City of the Dead* is a "spare but harrowing scare tale" (Kane, 2002, p. M20), which "continually provides interest even when the scenes are otherwise pedestrian" (S. Harrison, 1995, p. 24). For another, "the uncomplicated plot is greatly enhanced by atmospheric black-and-white photography, taut direction, and some eerie performances" (Smith, 2000, p. 50). This film appears to benefit from the seesaw dynamic that I describe above: "Although cheaply made, studio-bound and short on complexity, the film has a beautifully eerie Lovecraftian atmosphere" (Hardy, 1986, p. 129).

In light of our implications, first, and least remarkably, the film begins in 1692 with a shot of a flaming brazier, while the party that has condemned Selwyn emerges from the far distance and marches into the foreground. Mist roils and swirls through every part of the frame. We thus have an opening that shows us the environment before it shows us any people.

More distinctive is the heavy presence of the setting one feels at many points in the film, an emphasis that is signaled by its original and its U.S. titles—*The City of the Dead* and *Horror Hotel*—both of which name places. Critics have picked up on how the film emphasizes this presence as something textural, appealing to the skin as much as to the eyes. Foremost in this regard is the fog, certainly a generic trait of the horror film but also, through its quantity and density, something that sets this film apart from others of its type.

The City of the Dead is a film in which the background refuses to stay in the background. An admirer finds that "so pervasive is the fog that it practically becomes an important character in the film" (Shinnick, 2002, p. 75). Director John Llewellyn Moxey recalled: "We tried to lay it in layers, not just in a mass on the floor like you often see it. By changing the heat on the guns that fired it, we found that we could lay it in layers. That worked very well" (Weaver, 1998, p. 257). One does get a sense that this fog—in this preternaturally still and decrepit town, constructed entirely indoors—was rolled onto the set in layers, like one carpet on top of another. One layer seems to bump and nudge against the next, as the mass refuses to rise and dissipate like any earthly fog. The mist is so soupy that, when Nan stops at a gas station, it collects around her car like liquid—and note how it sits on the roof of the station like snow (see Figure 7.1).

Many critics have tried their hand at characterizing this visual quality of *The City of the Dead*, and their choice of language exhibits a pattern. Whitewood is "saturated in fog and gloom" (Pirie, 1973, p. 111), "blanketed in a perpetual

HORROR FILM ATMOSPHERE AS ANTI-NARRATIVE

FIGURE 7.1 The City of the Dead. *Nan stops at a gas station to ask for directions.*

fog" (Clark and Senn, 2011, p. 216), and "shrouded in knee-high fog" (Hogan, 1996, p. 46). It is a place where "billows of white smoke (looking like clouds) snake across the ground" (Sipos, 2010, p. 137). Another writes that the settings are "swathed in more mist than all the other films in this survey put together" (Rigby, 2000, p. 67). Shrouds, blankets, snakes—this fog wraps and enfolds, appealing more emphatically to touch than the wispier stuff seen in other horror films.

The fog stops at the doorways leading to the town's interiors, but the insistent tactility of the settings does not. The lobby of the Raven's Inn, where Nan spends her last days, is alive with dark and dancing shadows thrown up by the fireplace (see Figure 7.2). The still image included here does not capture the manic movement of these shadows, and how they subsume everything, including Nan, into one frenetically crawling backdrop. Writers have also recognized these shadows and their excessive salience (see e.g. Johnson and Miller, 2004, p. 96; Rigby, 2000, p. 67).

Another setting is Nan's room at the inn (see Figure 7.3). It is not clear what these walls are made of—knotty wood, or perhaps this is outstandingly ugly and ineptly hung wallpaper. The uncertainty only makes me stare at these backgrounds more intently. The walls seem to me to be thickly coated with centuries of corrosion. It does not take much to envision rust and barnacles creeping over their surfaces. They are, at any rate, completely covered in roughness, bumps, and ridges.

FIGURE 7.2 *Nan steps into the lobby of the Raven's Inn.*

FIGURE 7.3 *Nan in her room at the inn*

Settings importune themselves on the action with their weird texturality and foregroundedness. Faces, which are more conventionally foregrounded, also prompt some critics to reach for language that evokes the sense of touch. Keane and a blind priest character have "shadow-etched faces" (Newman, 2002, p. 55); and Keane and Selywn have faces that look "almost as though sculpted in clay" (Johnson and Miller, 2004, p. 96). The voices of these characters, in particular Keane's, go a long way to extending this quality to the soundtrack. Regarding Nan, Keane intones, "He will be pleased," laying emphasis with his sonorous baritone on the word "he," and leaving little doubt as to who "he" is. This character has been called "sepulchral voiced" (Clark and Senn, 2011, p. 217), while another critic writes that actor Valentine Dyall "possessed a voice that sounded as though it originated at the bottom of a well instead of within a human diaphragm" (Hogan, 1996, p. 47). We are invited to think of deep, echoing places by a voice—an element that typically functions in a film as primarily a carrier of semantic meaning. We listen to the characters' words to gain story information about what happened, what is going to happen, and how the characters feel. But, as Johnson (quoted above) notes, this film does not bother much with such details. Instead, a voice's grain acts as a kind of special effect; we let Dyall's basso profundo pour over us, just as, when Nan is in the inn lobby, we listen to the too-loud crackling of the fire, and to the clock that does not just tick but creaks with an insistently aged and wooden timbre. This film appeals to our sense of touch not just through our eyes but through our ears as well.

Do these qualities contribute to the film's atmosphere? While the answer is obvious, I want to point out how effortlessly writers retool the language they use to describe the setting in order to describe something more abstract. The film is "knee-deep in New England creepiness" (Rigby, 2000, p. 67), with a "dry ice-shrouded Lovecraftian atmosphere" (Hunt, 2002, p. 83). It "brims with atmosphere and suspense" (Kane, 2002, p. M20), and is simultaneously "drenched in fog and smoke" and "dripping mood" ("City of the Dead", 2003, p. 87).

Fog churns through every part of Whitewood, and Whitewood dominates the story, but I would not argue that *The City of the Dead* is atmospherically homogeneous. Relevant here is an oft-made comparison to *Psycho* (see e.g. Weldon, 1983, p. 329; Hardy, 1986, p. 129; Johnson and Miller, 2004, p. 96). In both films, the central female protagonist is killed part-way through, after which a sibling and a lover come looking for her, eventually uncovering and thwarting the respective woman's murderer. These and other similarities have prompted some writers to view Moxey's film as an imitation of Hitchcock's, while others note that the production schedules of the two make the similarities a coincidence (on the films' production schedules, see Clark and Senn, 2011, p. 216). What matters for us is that these similarities point to the fact that *The City of the Dead* breaks neatly into two parts.

In each part, a different woman is imperiled, and we have many shots of the foggy town. A few writers have complained that, for example, "the entire second half of the movie is almost a complete repeat of the first" (McDaniel, 2006; see also e.g. B. Harrison, 1995, p. 74; Scheib, n.d.; Clark, n.d.).

However, I would argue that the differences outweigh the similarities, and that these differences can help us further to explore the inverse relationship that film atmosphere and narrative sometimes exhibit.

Critics, I was surprised to discover, do not explicitly reflect upon atmospheric differences between the two parts. This is possibly because, once established in the film's first half, the atmosphere percolates forward, all the way to the end. One critic, who finds that "Nan's drive into Whitewood is wonderfully atmospheric," then notes, of the film's second part, the "exciting, fiery ending of *The Witches*" (B. Harrison, 1995, p. 74). He echoes many others who praise the action-filled climax, for example:

> It's the graveyard ending which will blow you away. It has to be the most spectacular set-piece that 50s/60s British horror produced, and the film is worth sitting through for the last 10 minutes alone. Noble teenage sacrifice and dozens of exploding monks—does it get any better than that?
> ("City of the Dead", 2010; see also Weldon, 1983, p. 330; B. Harrison, 1995, p. 74; S. Harrison, 1995, p. 24; Svehla, 1995, p. 71; Cowan, 2008, p. 223)

Things happen in the film's second part: the ending delivers spectacular action.

The second half provides thrills, but it is, I submit, chiefly the first half that has earned *The City of the Dead* its reputation as an atmospheric film. If the second half feels to some like a virtual replay of the first, it is a replay in fast forward; the time spent in Whitewood is briefer, and the stillness that hangs over Nan's time there is largely absent. If, as I believe, the first half is more atmospheric than the second, we should be able to probe this claim by contrasting the narrative energies of the two parts.

When Nan is driving to Whitewood, her car sits in the soupy fog while hidden stagehands rock it back and forth to simulate a bumpy road. This simulation is not very convincing. The effect is of a stationary car rocking. The snatches of background that slip past appear as if they are moving more than the car does. Nan is not going anywhere. What is the distance between Nan's college and this town? The question seems meaningless, the journey imaginary. Moreover, the locations of Whitewood's few buildings, relative to each other, seem stable enough, but the geography of the town for Nan is not the same as it will be for Dick and Bill when it is their turn to navigate the space.

Time supplies another axis along which we can contrast the two halves. Keane tells Nan that the town is "off the beaten path. Few tourists come here. For Whitewood, time stands still." Time in Whitewood, in Nan's part of the story, is undifferentiated. Then is now is then. In the inn hangs a plaque that reads: "March 3rd, 1692—On this site was burned for witchcraft Elizabeth Selwyn." This spot is fixed in space, and, since Selwyn made her pact and issued her curse, it and Whitewood are fixed in time as well. We see working phones, but the town still seems to be unhooked from the grid of modern society. Its connection to its past overwhelms any to its present. Like the car that traverses the non-space that separates Whitewood from the twentieth century, time is unmoving.

This static sense of time is reinforced by the Black Mass ritual at which Nan is sacrificed. It occurs on Candlemas Eve, a holiday that the worshipers have appropriated for their own dark purposes. As a holiday, it carves out a time-space that re-creates the last Candlemas Eve, and the one before that, and so on. Days of remembrance are about a relationship to the past. These special days in the calendar are sectioned off from the ones preceding and following them. What is more, Selywn must wait until "the hour of thirteen" to plunge the dagger. The hour of thirteen is outside time.

I would label the temporality in this part of the film "atmospheric time," an emblem of which is the clock on the town church (see Figure 7.4). These hands do move, and show the proper time, as does the clock in the inn lobby. But like that clock's creaky ticking, on this face—again covered with what might be wood grain or stains, or both—we read not only information but also texture.

Narratives propel persons and objects through space and time. Their velocity shapes our sense of a plot's tautness and pacing. By this standard,

FIGURE 7.4 *The church in Whitewood.*

the first part of *The City of the Dead* has almost no tautness or pacing at all. This becomes clearer in a consideration of a third dimension of the film's narrative: causality. Here we can try to locate Nan's agency within the transpiring events. She possesses virtually none at all. She is never more than an obedient pawn, even when she thinks she is taking advantage of an opportunity to do firsthand research; her professor, Driscoll, turns out to be one of the undead townspeople, a follower of Selywn. A symptom of Nan's lack of narrative agency is the trapdoor in her room. There is no ring or handle on her side of the door, Selywn tells her, because there is only earth underneath. In truth, it is not yet time for her to open it. When that time comes, she hears a banging on her windowpane and sees the handle swinging there from a string. Nan descends and is murdered.

The second part of the film has a different feel than the first, for reasons we can describe concretely. A graphic match joins a shot of the plunging dagger to one of a knife cutting a birthday cake. We're back in the electrically lit brightness of the twentieth century, where we learn that Nan was expected at this party and that it has been over two weeks since Bill last received a letter from her. We thus have a good sense of how long it has been since Nan's death. We are back in time. Meanwhile, in Whitewood, Pat, a woman with whom Nan had conferred briefly, is concerned about her disappearance and starts looking into it. She greets someone from the sheriff's office, who is in town because Dick and Bill have filed a missing person's report. Thus is launched the theme of investigation that will turn the second half of the film into a search for clues and a hunt for the truth that will culminate in the exciting climax.

Pat comes to the college and shows Bill and Dick a sheet of Driscoll's stationery, on which he wrote Nan directions to Whitewood, and Nan's bracelet, which has been retrieved by the housekeeper at the inn. One clue leads to another, as the trio begin to retrace Nan's path. A narrative of what happened to her starts to come together.

The men take separate cars to Whitewood, and for each ride we get more of the unconvincing shots of cars rocking in the fog. But the rocking is less pronounced than in Nan's drive, and her ride was quieter; only a bit of jazz music was heard, while upbeat and even jaunty jazz plays when we watch the men. The music alters the mood of their journey through the mist. This deathly atmosphere does not swamp these characters; they are going to cut through it.

Moreover, the sequences of Dick and Bill driving make more extensive use than Nan's of through-the-windshield point-of-view shots. Through these, we share the gaze of these empowered male characters, to borrow from 1970s spectator theory; and these shots show us that the car really is moving through space. In Nan's sequence, we see only one such shot. It shows Keane standing at a crossroads, and the sight of him causes Nan to pull over: it arrests her forward motion. Bill proves harder to stop. He crashes his car when a fiery vision of Selwyn forces him off the road, but he continues on towards Whitewood and the film's climax.

Pat is selected as the next sacrifice, but Dick will rescue her at the last second. Thus, where the first half is one continuous descent, marked by inevitability, in which Nan is more or less sucked towards her doom, in the second Dick rushes towards the same spot where Nan died, and his intervention makes all the difference. Dick and Bill possess agency, and this is evident when Dick finds the same trapdoor that Nan went through. For him this door has a handle, and he lifts it with a hand that holds a gun (see Figure 7.5). Below, he finds Nan's necklace where, in her struggle, it was ripped from her neck. One clue leads to another. A trail leads towards climax and closure. When his flashlight fails, Dick holds up a cigarette lighter. Nothing is going to stop him. He and the story press forward. He walks where Nan had been dragged.

Dick brushes aside chains, cobwebs, and a spider as he penetrates the space, our sense of which changes after the men arrive in the town. Dick descends through the trapdoor, and later, with Pat, he exits through a crypt in the graveyard. The space of Whitewood has become legible, something that can be mapped. The space has become delineated by actions that slice through the formless fog.

FIGURE 7.5 *Dick, gun in hand, opens the trapdoor.*

Shooting his gun does not harm the worshipers, but Dick pushes past them, grabs Pat, and dashes out of the crypt. And, while Dick's gun was ineffective, the cross Bill holds up, when he learns that a cross's shadow will destroy the worshipers, becomes essentially a big gun which he aims, with explosive results. Agency is everywhere on display. Gone is the thick stillness and creeping dread that hung over the film's first part. The gain in narrative velocity and fire power corresponds with a palpable drop in atmosphere.

A question one might ask about this film, about more famous horror films like Lewton's, and about B-movies like *The Strangler of the Swamp* (1946), is whether their narrative simplicity constitutes a serendipitous flaw or whether it represents the filmmakers' intuitive grasp of what it takes to conjure atmosphere. Whatever one may conclude about *The City of the Dead*, its unusual structure allows us to see, in action, the zero-sum game that narrative and atmosphere sometimes play. Lastly, further research might consider what, if any, correlation may be found among films that critics, at the time or decades later, praised as atmospheric and those that perform well at the box office.

References

Altman, R. (2004), *Silent Film Sound*, New York: Columbia University Press.
Bansak, E. (1995), *Fearing the Dark: The Val Lewton Career*, Jefferson, NC: McFarland.
Barber, X. (1989), "Phantasmagorical Wonders: The Magic Lantern Ghost Show in Nineteenth-century America," *Film History*, 3.2: 73–86.
Beynon, G. (1921), *Musical Presentation of Motion Pictures*, Boston, MA: G. Schirmer.
Böhme, G. (1993), "Atmosphere as the Fundamental Concept of a New Aesthetics," *Thesis Eleven* 36: 113–26.
—(2012), "The Art of the Stage Set for an Aesthetics of Atmospheres," Keynote address, *Understanding Atmospheres: Culture, Materiality and the Texture of the In-between*.
Cavalcanti, A. (1985 [1939]), "Sound in Films," in E. Weis and J. Belton (eds) *Film Sound: Theory and Practice*, New York: Columbia University Press.
"City of the Dead" (2003), *Midnight Marquee*, 69–70, pp. 87–8.
—(2010), *British Horror Films*. Available online at http://www.britishhorrorfilms.co.uk/cityofthedead.shtml (accessed July 30, 2013).
Clark, G. (n.d.), "City of the Dead," *The Spinning Image*. Available online at http://www.thespinningimage.co.uk/cultfilms/displaycultfilm.asp?reviewid=1584&aff=13 (accessed July 30, 2013).
Clark, M. and Senn, B. (2011), *Sixties Shockers: A Critical Filmography of Horror Cinema, 1960–1969*, Jefferson, NC: McFarland.
Conference, March 16–17, Aarhus, DK: University of Aarhus, pp. 1–10.

Available online at http://www.cresson.archi.fr/PUBLI/pubCOLLOQUE/AMB8-confGBohme-eng.pdf (accessed July 30, 2013).

Conrich, I. (2004), "Before Sound: Universal, Silent Cinema, and the Last of the Horror-spectaculars," in S. Prince (ed.) *The Horror Film*, New Brunswick, NJ: Rutgers University Press.

Cowan, D. (2008), *Sacred Terror: Religion and Horror on the Silver Screen*, Waco, TX: Baylor University Press.

Douglas, D. (1966), *Horror!*, New York: Macmillan.

Ellis, R. (1980), *A Journey into Darkness: The Art of James Whale's Horror Films*, New York: Arno Press.

Farber, M. (1998 [1951]), "Val Newton," in *Negative Space: Manny Farber at the Movies*, New York: Da Capo.

Fujiwara, C. (1998), *Jacques Tourneur: The Cinema of Nightfall*, Baltimore, MD: Johns Hopkins University Press.

Gale, A. (1936), *How to Write a Movie*, New York: Brick Row Book Shop.

Greene, G. (1995 [1937]), "Night and Day," in D. Parkinson (ed.) *The Graham Greene Film Reader*, New York: Applause.

Hanich, J. (2010), *Cinematic Emotion in Horror Films and Thrillers: The Aesthetic Paradox of Pleasurable Fear*, New York: Routledge.

Hardy, P. (ed.) (1986), *The Overlook Film Encyclopedia: Horror*, Woodstock: Overlook.

Harrison, B. (1995), "Horror Hotel," *Monsterscene*, 5: 74.

Harrison, S. (1995), "Horror Hotel," *Fatal Visions*, 18: 24.

Hogan, D. (1996), "Horror Hotel," *Filmfax*, 57: 46–7.

Hunt, L. (2002), "Necromancy in the UK: Witchcraft and the Occult in British Horror," in S. Chibnall and J. Petley (eds) *British Horror Cinema*, London: BFI.

Jacobs, S. (2007), *The Wrong House: The Architecture of Alfred Hitchcock*, Rotterdam: 010 Publishers.

Johnson, G. (2002), "The City of the Dead," *Images: A Journal of Film and Popular Culture*, 10. Available online at http://www.imagesjournal.com/issue10/reviews/citydead (accessed July 30, 2013).

Johnson, T. and Miller, M. (2004), *The Christopher Lee Filmography: All Theatrical Releases, 1948–2003*, Jefferson, NC: McFarland.

Kane, J. (as "The Phantom of the Movies") (2002), "Viewers May Have Sleepless Night after Heroine Wanders into 'City'; More Chills Await with Horror Dozen; 'Apes' Set Complete," *Washington Post*, January 17, p. M20.

Lennig, A. (2003), *The Immortal Count: The Life and Films of Bela Lugosi*, Lexington: The University Press of Kentucky.

Lovecraft, H. P. (2000 [1927]), *Supernatural Horror in Literature*, New York: Hippocampus.

McDaniel, I. (2006), "The City of the Dead," *Horror Madness*. Available online at http://www.freewebs.com/horrormadness/reviews/movies/cityofthedead.html (accessed July 30, 2013).

McKim, K. (2013), *Cinema as Weather: Stylistic Screens and Atmospheric Change*, New York: Routledge.

Neergaard, E. (1950), *Carl Dreyer, A Director's Work*, London: BFI.

Newman, K. (2002), "The City of the Dead," *Video Watchdog*, 88, October: 53–6.

Peary, D. (1973), "Mark Robson Remembers RKO, Welles, and Val Lewton," *The Velvet Light Trap*, 10: 32–7.
Pirie, D. (1973), *Heritage of Horror: The English Gothic Cinema, 1946–1972*, New York: Equinox.
Prince, S. (2000), *A New Pot of Gold: Hollywood Under the Electronic Rainbow, 1980–1989*, Berkeley: University of California Press.
—(ed.) (2004), *The Horror Film*, New Brunswick, NJ: Rutgers University Press.
Rigby, J. (2000), *English Gothic: A Century of Horror Cinema*, London: Reynolds and Hearn.
Schatz, T. (1997), *Boom and Bust: American Cinema in the 1940s*, Berkeley: University of California Press.
Scheib, R. (n.d.), "City of the Dead," *Moria: Science Fiction, Horror and Fantasy Film Review*. Available online at http://0to5stars-moria.ca/horror/city-of-the-dead-1959-horror-hotel.htm (accessed July 30, 2013).
Scott, A. (2010), "Lonely Boy Finds Friend in Blood-crazing Pixie," *New York Times*, September 30. Available online at http://www.nytimes.com/2010/10/01/movies/01letmein.html (accessed July 30, 2013).
Shinnick, K. (2002), *Scarlett Street*, 44: 75.
Sindelar, D. (2006), "Horror Hotel, Fantastic Movie Musings and Ramblings!" Available online at http://www.scifilm.org/musing1701.html (accessed July 30, 2013).
Sipos, T. (2010), *Horror Film Aesthetics: Creating the Visual Language of Fear*, Jefferson, NC: McFarland.
Smith, G. (2000), *Uneasy Dreams: The Golden Age of British Horror Films, 1956–1976*, Jefferson, MD: McFarland.
—(2003), *Film Structure and the Emotion System*, Cambridge: Cambridge University Press.
Spadoni, R. (forthcoming), "Carl Dreyer's Corpse: Horror Film Atmosphere and Narrative," in H. Benshoff (ed.) *A Companion to the Horror Film*, Medford: Blackwell.
Svehla, G. (1995), "Horror Hotel," *Midnight Marquee*, 49: 71.
Telotte, J. (1985), *Dreams of Darkness: Fantasy and the Films of Val Lewton*, Urbana: University of Illinois Press.
Todorov, T. (1975 [1970]), *The Fantastic: A Structural Approach to a Literary Genre*, trans. R. Howard, Ithaca, NY: Cornell University Press.
Weaver, T. (1998), *Science Fiction and Fantasy Film Flashbacks*, Jefferson, NC: McFarland.
Weldon, M. (1983), *The Psychotronic Encyclopedia of Film*, New York: Ballantine.
Wigley, M. (1998), "The Architecture of Atmosphere," *Daidalos*, 68: 18–27.
Worland, R. (2007), *The Horror Film: An Introduction*, Malden, MA: Blackwell.

8

"A Kind of Bacall Quality"

Jamie Lee Curtis, Stardom, and Gentrifying Non-Hollywood Horror

Richard Nowell

In 1980, the American-based financier-distributor Avco Embassy Pictures drafted a biography of a starlet who had appeared in three of its films (1980a). Written for publicity purposes, this document described the 21-year-old Jamie Lee Curtis as "[o]ne of Hollywood's busiest young actresses" and a "statuesque beauty," and emphasized her presence in what the company deemed to be commercially successful and critically applauded horror films (ibid., p. 1). In so doing, the horror specialist of its day was framing Curtis as a conventionally attractive career woman who owed her success in tinsel town to scary movies.

Although the various facets of this star image were circulated widely in the late 1970s and early 1980s, Curtis has come to be seen as the quintessential American scream queen of her generation. The durability of her reputation is evinced by dialog from the 1996 teen slasher film *Scream*. "*The Fog*, *Terror Train*, *Prom Night*; how come Jamie Lee Curtis is in all of these movies?" wonders a female youth. "Because [...]," her friend replies, "she's the scream queen." Its longevity is illustrated by a recent biography entitled simply *Jamie Lee Curtis: Scream Queen*, the cover of which bears a rare publicity still of the actress actually screaming (Grove, 2010). It may seem reasonable to think of Curtis in this way, given the fact that at the start of her career she appeared in half a dozen horror films: *Halloween* (1978), *The Fog*, *Prom Night*, *Terror Train* (all 1980), *Halloween II*, and *Road Games* (both 1981). Yet, it is important to recognize that at this time the scream queen title was rarely used to frame this actress as a fear-struck target of celluloid evildoers. It was in fact one of several epithets that industry watchers and publicists employed to suggest her agency and achievement in front of the screen, rather than passivity and inaction on it (see Knoedelseder, 1980). Others, such as "queen of the [horror] genre," "queen of teenage horror movies," and "the biggest thing in horror movies," clearly emphasized this sense of professional achievement over fear and victimization (see e.g. Knoedelseder, 1980; Harmetz, 1980; Shewey, 1981, p. 35; Scott, 1981b).

Nevertheless, between late 1981 and the mid-1980s, marketing executives, talent agencies, journalists, and Curtis herself did much to cement her status as the premier cinematic damsel in distress of the late 1970s and early 1980s. They invoked this concept to suggest that Curtis' subsequent roles in non-horror projects such as the Telefilm *Death of a Centerfold: The Dorothy Stratten Story* (1981), and medium-budget comedies and dramas like *Trading Places* (1983), *Grandview U.S.A.* (1984), and *Perfect* (1985) were a sign of career development and upward mobility (see e.g. Scott, 1981b; Goldstein, 1984, pp. G1, G6). Invoking the low cultural status of cinematic representations of female victimization enabled interested parties to downgrade Curtis' previous activities, thereby making it easier to claim that she had moved on to bigger and better things. Curtis' reputation as a scream queen is pervasive and enduring, but it bypasses the multidimensionality and industrial functions of her early star persona.

Proclaiming Curtis to be a scream queen par excellence overlooks the majority of public-sphere discourse that contributed to her star persona. Such claims effectively reduce her persona to the shy high school student she played in *Halloween*, and to isolated moments of jeopardy in her other films.[1] However, if we consider the dynamic interplay of media texts—films, promotion, publicity, and commentary/criticism (Dyer, 1998, pp. 60–3)—that constitutes a star's persona, it is clear that the figure of Curtis which entered the American public sphere of the late 1970s and early 1980s was more multifaceted than the image of the damsel in distress suggests. As the second section of this chapter explains, Curtis' relationships to horror were characterized by a degree of nuance that her scream queen mantle elides;

---

[1] Studies have shown that the personae of performers that are associated with horror exceed their relationships to this genre. For example, Kate Egan has argued that the Polish-born Hammer star Ingrid Pitt embodied an authenticity based on her projection of unburdened sexuality and of determination, which derived from both her big screen roles and biographical legend (2013).

she was associated with two relatively innocuous forms of horror cinema: exceptionally prestigious films and unusually anodyne ones. Moreover, and as the third and fourth sections show, Curtis' star persona was also built on her affiliations to the institution of Hollywood, and to a philosophy-cum-lifestyle movement that the feminist media historian Hilary Radner has since dubbed "neo-feminism" (2011).

The notion of the scream queen also inadequately reflects the ways in which Curtis' early star persona operated as a source of symbolic, and ultimately economic, capital for both her paymasters and herself (see McDonald, 1998, pp. 194–9; McDonald, 2000, pp. 5–14). To overlook these issues is to risk underestimating the extent to which Curtis' persona was shaped by—and supported—a strategy that has underwritten the production and distribution of countless horror films: gentrification. As is elucidated in the first section of this chapter, I use this term to refer to the steps that industry personnel take during the pre-production, assembly, and dissemination of a film in an effort to elevate it above the perceived cultural standing of its constituent genre(s)—in this case of horror; or, to be exact, a historically and culturally situated reputation thereof. Accordingly, if we consider the industrial functions, as well as the structure, of star images, it soon becomes apparent that, as both a human resource and a source of symbolic value, Curtis' worth to industry decision-makers derived from more than her ability to convey and provoke horror. Rather, her star persona offered the American-, Canadian-, and Australian-based independents behind her early films, as well as the companies that distributed them in their principal US market, a rhetorical shield with which to protect their products from oft-leveled and potentially costly charges that the films were tarred by low production values, extreme brutality, and violent misogyny. In short, that these were reactionary, blood-soaked exploitation films.

Thus, whereas her scream queen reputation has resulted in Curtis coming to personify the purported shoddiness, sadism, and sexism of much late 1970s and early 1980s "American" horror cinema, this chapter argues that producers and distributors actually used her early star persona to undermine the credibility of claims that their films exhibited these exact characteristics.[2] The chapter therefore invites us to think more closely about how industry decision-makers utilize specific on-screen talent to increase the commercial potential of horror films—and, by extension, other genres—as well as about how the personae of

---

[2] This chapter assigns national status based on the site of circulation and consumption rather than production (see Higson, 1989). The term American is placed in inverted commas to remind us of the fact that most of Curtis' films either originated from outside of the United States or were underwritten by foreign capital, but that they were considered at the time of their release to be a part of American audiovisual culture, discussion of their overseas origins notwithstanding.

specific performers serve this strategy. Such an approach promises to enrich our understandings of the production, content, dissemination, and reception of horror cinema, through explorations of the relationships between, on one hand, the dimensions of a given star's persona, and, on the other, the situated discourses that constitute the genre in question, and those films with which a specific star is associated. In so doing, it may be possible to develop a richer appreciation of this important industrial practice by moving beyond the relevant but limiting notions that marquee casting imbues low cultural forms with the glamor of stardom or the prestige of critical applause.

Gentrification: Or, not scaring (off) the public

Although non-horrifying content dominates most horror films, and plays key roles in the ways that they are targeted to audiences (see e.g. Austin, 2002; Nowell, 2011), academic and popular accounts of their assembly and marketing typically concentrate on portrayals of threat, violence, victimization, and monstrosity. This tendency is understandable given the fact that the presence of calculatedly horrifying content—however brief—is usually seen to set horror apart from other genres of film, to a degree that, say, romantic or amusing material is not (see Deleyto, 2009). Yet, such a tendency also elides a central characteristic of horror films: that they provoke audience fear and loathing only fleetingly, if at all—often so by design.

In addition to the impracticality of producing a feature-length motion picture that comprises primarily frightening material, the fleeting and muted nature of audience horror is driven by one of the most pressing economic imperatives underwriting the production and distribution of horror films: expanding marketability and audience appeal. It needs to be stressed that, as a form of commercial filmmaking, horror is distinguished from most other non-pornographic entertainment insofar as its reputation is sufficiently fearsome to put off much of the movie-watching public, at least in the United States and Canada. A survey of the North American box office charts of the last half-century supports Robin Wood's observation that horror remains a polarizing genre which resonates with a minority of fans but usually fails to secure a general audience (1985 [1979], p. 202). These data reveal that scary movies have rarely accrued the imperious ticket sales needed to catapult a film into the upper echelons of the annual rentals charts. Thus, bona fide horror mega-hits of the magnitude of *Rosemary's Baby* (1968), *The Exorcist* (1973), *The Omen* (1976), *The Silence of the Lambs* (1991), and *The Sixth Sense* (1999) are truly exceptional. Unlike many other genres, breakaway horror hits have occurred on average once a decade.

The economic vulnerability that comes from the horror film's long-standing status as a niche audience product has led above-the-line talent consistently to reduce financial risk and to maximize profit potential by courting movie-watchers who typically eschew such fare. The more costly the project, the greater the incentive to do so. In addition to the light-hearted material that is mobilized to ensure the exhilaration of "recreational terror" rather than the displeasure of outright terrorization (Pinedo, 1997), gentrification represents a key way of reaching out to skeptical audiences.

Gentrification has underwritten the form, structure, themes, and the intertextual make-up of countless horror films and their marketing campaigns. It represents an industrial attempt to positively influence the struggles that take place across audiovisual cultures when claims-makers endeavor "correctly" to position films within the broader field of cultural production, and in cultural hierarchies (see also Gallagher, 2013); hierarchies that are contested with particular veracity when they involve divisive objects such as horror films (see Jancovich, 2002). Acts of gentrification use markers of prestige or distinction which a targeted public is likely to recognize with little effort: objects and ideas that unequivocally invoke cultural and economic capital. As with other types of film, producers and distributors may gentrify a horror movie by emphasizing opulent settings, valorized human resources, and reified works or movements (see also Snelson, 2009). Accordingly, upscale architecture and interior design, memories of the venerated director Alfred Hitchcock, and stylistic flourishes drawn from art cinema were used to elevate the independently produced and distributed horror film *Dressed to Kill* (1980) (see Kapsis, 1992, pp. 202–8). Here the accumulation of cultural capital is deemed to increase profit potential, much as it does with indie, quality, and art cinema (see e.g. Betz, 2003; Newman, 2009; King, 2011; Gallagher, 2013).

The incentive to gentrify horror films destined for the US theatrical market was perhaps never greater than when Jamie Lee Curtis moved into screen acting. The late 1970s and early 1980s was characterized, as a period in horror film history, by financial unpredictability and critical controversy. As Robert E. Kapsis has observed, claims of horror's economic robustness at this time are typically based on assessments of supply rather than demand; on high levels of production not consumption (1991). Notwithstanding moderate hits such as *The Amityville Horror* (1979), *The Shining*, and *Friday the 13th* (both 1980), this period saw most horror films fail at the North American box office. Market saturation certainly led ticket sales to be spread thinly, but a contemporaneous survey indicated that horror was among the American public's least-liked genres of film (Robbins, 1982).

The generally low cultural standing that horror has been historically accorded in American audiovisual culture was compounded in the late 1970s and early 1980s by several high-profile controversies. These tended to rest on claims that individual films, certain production trends, and sometimes the genre as a whole sexualized, trivialized, and commodified male-on-female violence, and inspired real-life instances thereof (see Lyons, 1997, ch. 2). Critical fire-storms erupted over sensationally advertised, micro-budget exploitation like *Snuff* (1976) and *Maniac* (1980) (see Johnson and Schaefer, 1993; Nowell, 2013). But it was backlashes against comparatively high-end glossy efforts such as the rape-revenge drama *Lipstick* (1976) and the aforementioned *Dressed to Kill* that made anti-horror discourse something of a critical leitmotif (see Johnson and Schaefer, 1993; Lyons, 1997; Nowell, 2013). This hostility had a toxic effect inasmuch as it made new horror films—especially low-budget projects like Curtis'—appear vulnerable to charges that they too showcased and provoked femicide. Such accusations compounded the long-standing suggestion that horror films featured shoddy production values, and that viewing them required perilous incursions into urban ghettos and dilapidated fleapits (see Church, 2011).

Understandably, many industry insiders believed that these claims threatened to alienate a sizable section of the movie-going public, especially the girls and women who were seen to determine the commercial success of salacious fare such as violent thrillers, sex comedies, and horror films (see Allison, 2007; Nowell, 2011, forthcoming). This scenario was in turn deemed sufficiently serious to undermine a film's chances of securing a lucrative distribution deal and a sizable theatrical audience—the very means by which the independent producers and the distributors of Curtis' films expected to generate most of their income (see Nowell, 2011). For some, a solution existed in the shape of Jamie Lee Curtis, who promised to imbue her films with three overlapping, mutually reinforcing concepts that structured her early star persona: Hollywood, neo-feminism, and innocuous horror.

Jamie Lee Curtis and innocuous horror

An uncertain market and a heated popular critical climate led producers and distributors to view Curtis as a bankable asset based in part on her relationships to exceptional horror films. Curtis' early star persona enabled industry professionals to distinguish their products from the generally devalued reputation of horror, by invoking films that boasted high levels of respectability. It initially permitted them to summon critically applauded horror pictures, and after that, youth market releases that were widely regarded to be among the most anodyne scary movies of the day. This process involved overwriting notions of urban malaise, politically and aesthetically questionable content, and the lower-class clientele that orbited exploitation cinema (see Church, 2011), with the decorum of the downtown art house, the grandeur of the picture palace, and the safety of the shopping mall multiplex.

Curtis received her first film roles thanks to a familial connection to arguably the most revered horror movie in the history of American cinema. The producer of her debut film, *Halloween*, explained: "I wanted Jamie Lee Curtis for the lead because her mother, Janet Leigh, was associated with [...] 'Psycho'" (Irwin Yablans quoted in Scott, 1981a; see also Leeder, forthcoming). Celebrated by the US critical establishment for its technical virtuosity, restraint, and wit, by the late 1970s, *Psycho* was routinely cited as a high watermark in American horror and as evidence of this genre's subsequent purported descent into blood-soaked schlock (see e.g. Canby, 1979; see also Kapsis, 1992, pp. 62–4). Janet Leigh's affiliation with the film, much like Curtis' connection to her mother, was never stronger than at this time. From 1977 to 1980, their respective star personae became increasingly intertwined thanks to a publicity campaign intended to reinvigorate Leigh's moribund film career and kick-start that of her daughter. Leigh began by name-checking Curtis in interviews (see e.g. *Chicago Tribune*, 1978, p. 12; Wilson, 1978). Subsequently, the American press printed countless publicity shots of Curtis and Leigh posing together or attending society events together (see e.g. Heilner, 1978, p. 1; Combined UPI AP, 1980). The campaign also saw the pair make numerous television appearances, including a 1977 episode of the talk-show *Dinah!* (1974–) on the subject of mother–daughter relations, on *A Tribute to Alfred Hitchcock* (1979), and, as mother and daughter, on *The Love Boat* (1977–87). Publicity for *Halloween* consistently emphasized Curtis' connection to her mother.

Avco Embassy, the financier-distributor of Curtis' next film, *The Fog*, also believed that she was marketable based on her connections to critically applauded horror, so much so in fact that reshoots focused on Curtis' hitherto marginal character, and a redesigned marketing campaign overemphasized her presence in the film. Avco Embassy continued to spotlight Curtis' links to *Psycho*. Lobby cards and publicity photographs highlighted mother and daughter's presence in *The Fog* (see e.g. Turan, 1980), and other photos showed the pair schmoozing with the star of *Psycho*, Anthony Perkins (Combined UPI AP, 1980). Moreover, recent developments had ensured that Curtis was now connected directly to a critically applauded horror picture; *Halloween* had been heralded in some quarters for its style, restraint, and humor. Crucially, the film had been compared favorably to *Psycho* and its director John Carpenter to Hitchcock (see e.g. Canby, 1979, p. D3).

Curtis was particularly appealing to Avco Embassy because her affiliations to prestige horror films meshed with the company's corporate and branding strategies. New head Robert "Bob" Rehme had been transforming this ailing supplier of quality cinema into a genre film specialist, thereby filling a niche that had been opened up by the demise of previous market leader American International Pictures (see Harmetz, 1981). Avco Embassy marketed these films as light-hearted date movies, as it did with *Phantasm*, or as prestige pictures, as it did with *Murder by Decree* (both 1979). The company employed the latter with *The Fog*, pitching this low-budget film as "a contemporary tale of supernatural terror," in which its director, John Carpenter, had married the visual bravura of *Halloween* to the suggestion of classical gothic chillers like *Cat People* (1942) (see e.g. Martin, 1981, p. 17).[3]

While the marketing and fairly positive critical reception of *The Fog* ensured that Curtis' connections to prestigious chillers remained germane throughout her time specializing in scary movies, her industrial appeal soon turned on an emerging association with anodyne horror films. This aspect of Curtis' star persona may be traced back to *Halloween*, which, as a bloodless date movie that was pitched to older children and young adults, was seen at this time as a comparatively harmless horror film. It was cemented by her headlining roles in *Prom Night* and *Terror Train*, two tales of maniacs stalking youngsters that had been modeled on *Halloween* in an effort to emulate the latter's solid box office performance. In contrast to their largely apathetic peers, the producers of both *Prom Night* and *Terror Train* felt that the presence of Curtis would increase these films' similarities to *Halloween*, and thus their commercial viability. As the producer of *Terror Train* put it, Curtis "brought a star caliber to the project because of *Halloween*" (Lamar Card quoted in Grove, 2010, p. 213). *Prom Night* and *Terror Train* were tailored to appease the Canadian state financier, and to appeal to Hollywood distributors and American youth. Both films therefore eschewed on-screen violence and bloodshed in favor of mystery, youth-oriented topics, and Curtis herself—elements that were also foregrounded in their marketing campaigns (Nowell, 2011, ch. 4). Consequently, these films largely avoided charges of brutality and sexism. For a time, at least, *Prom Night* and *Terror Train* were singled out as the acceptable face of "American" horror cinema (see e.g. Siskel, 1980; Thomas, 1980b).

Around the time that it released *Prom Night*, Avco Embassy leveraged the producers of *Road Games* to offer Curtis a role in the film. The company would underwrite and distribute this nominally Australian production as long as its makers increased the film's marketability in the United States. *Road Games*' producer-director Richard Franklin fired a local actress who had been

---

[3] Positioning of this sort was often supported by critics who compared *The Fog* to the 1940s horror films of directors Jacques Tourneur and Val Newton (see Turan, 1980, pp. G1, G3).

signed to appear alongside leading man Stacy Keech, admitting that "[Avco Embassy] wanted a name and they told me to try Jamie Lee Curtis" (quoted in Grove, 2010, p. 274). Having twice profited from Curtis' association with prestigious and light-hearted horror—both *The Fog* and *Prom Night* had performed well—Avco Embassy overemphasized Curtis' minor role in *Road Games* in a marketing campaign that framed the film as a Hitchcockian showcase for the Bogart- and Bacall-like verbal sparring of its headline talent (see e.g. Thomas, 1980a). As this angle suggests, the boundaries between innocuous horror and the other aspects of Curtis' early star persona often blurred—a phenomenon that is illustrated by her presentation as an embodiment of tinsel town.

Jamie Lee Curtis and Hollywood

The figure of the renegade auteur that looms large in histories of late 1970s and early 1980s "American" horror represents but one of the ways in which industry decision-makers negotiated the relationships between horror and Hollywood (see Tompkins, Chapter 12, this volume). Some film makers and marketers certainly summoned the concept of Hollywood as a means of bolstering claims of their own creative autonomy, transgression, and subcultural cache. Others, however, were less concerned with cultivating distinctions from the imagined mainstream that this institution and its conduct conjured than with positing connections thereto (see Nowell, 2011). Rather than employing Hollywood as a discursive or conceptual foil against which to position themselves and their films, these independents saw the dream factory's reputation for slick, inoffensive, accessible fare as a commercial asset. By invoking relationships to Hollywood, they sought simultaneously to distance themselves and their products from their industrial origins, and this sector's reputation for micro-budget exploitation horror that was at best technically impoverished, at worst degenerate.

Above and beyond her status as both a minor celebrity and a rising star of American entertainment, it was Curtis' unique Hollywood pedigree that made her especially appealing to both the independent producers and the distributors of horror films. Her associations to the past, present, and geography of Hollywood set Curtis apart from the other aspiring or up-and-coming young actresses that these entrepreneurs could afford to recruit. From 1977 to 1981, her credentials enabled interested parties to summon the technical polish of major studio films, and to convey something of the glamor and profligacy of this talismanic media institution, even though, strictly speaking, Curtis had yet to make a major studio picture.

Curtis was presented as Hollywood royalty on account of both her personal and purported professional associations to the classical era. Beyond the aforementioned relationship to her mother, Curtis boasted unrivaled familial connections to a period in cinema that had come to be venerated in some quarters for its decency and restraint. It was well known that Curtis was a product of one of the highest profile celebrity marriages of this period: that of Leigh and the Hollywood heart-throb Tony Curtis. Publicity surrounding the couple saw "little Jamie" thrust into the public eye from an early age in family portraits featured in film magazines like *Photoplay*, *Motion Picture*, and *Screen Album*. Although the two became estranged after the break-up of the marriage in 1958, the marketers of Jamie Lee Curtis' films consistently emphasized the fact that Tony Curtis was her father (see e.g. Avco Embassy Pictures, 1980b). Debora Hill, the producer of both *Halloween* and *The Fog*, has acknowledged the importance of Curtis' parentage, revealing: "I saw a great opportunity to promote the fact that she was the product of this Hollywood marriage" (*Halloween: A Cut above the Rest*). Summoning these bloodlines allowed Curtis to be linked to her parents' major studio pictures, including well-regarded works like Orson Welles' *A Touch of Evil*, the comedy *Some like it Hot* (both 1958), and the biblical epic *Spartacus* (1960).

Curtis was also associated with the professional practices of Hollywood's classical era. Much, for example, was made of her status as a contract player at Universal (see e.g. Avco Embassy Pictures, 1980b). In reality, this arrangement involved Curtis receiving a modest monthly wage for working bit parts in television series: "girl in dressing room" in a 1977 episode of *Quincy M.E.* (1976–83), "waitress" in a 1977 episode of *Columbo* (1968–2003), a supporting role in a 1978 episode of *Charlie's Angels* (1976–81). In practice, however, the term "contract" summoned—and was intended to summon— the classical era star system, and with it the glamor, poise, and beauty of Rita Heyworth, Katharine Hepburn, Marilyn Monroe, and others. Curtis spoke of her pride in preserving the etiquette and customs of this period. "Little things like writing thank-you notes to people," she explained in a publicity interview, "its [sic] a very simple thing, but people don't know that now, whereas that was one of the standards of the old system" (quoted in Shewey, 1981, p. 35).

As much as Curtis was presented as a part of tinsel town's heritage, she was also framed as a second-generation Hollywood insider. Thus, she was introduced at the 1980 Academy Awards as "a child of Hollywood, who has become one of its loveliest young actresses." Curtis was repeatedly aligned with the modern business practices of Hollywood. For example, on one occasion, she had halted a *New York Times* interview to pitch a movie by phone to the powerful production executive Don Borchers (see Knoedelseder, 1980, p. Q4). Curtis was also portrayed as a consummate Hollywood pro.

Prom Night's press kit emphasized that "Jamie Lee Curtis brought to the set a sense of professionalism" (Avco Embassy Pictures, 1980b). Professionalism was used to explain Curtis' pragmatic stance towards her films. "I've worked for three years trying to make my own way," she explained, "I paid my dues the only way I could: by making horror films" (quoted in Beck, 1980). This apparent candor barely concealed shrewd image management. "You can sense her determination to be seen as a professional," noted one interviewer, "[s]he uses a bold public persona—steady eye-contact, studied unpretentiousness, crowd-pleasing self-deprecation—that's intended to erase any trace of 'little Jamie'" (Shewey, 1981, p. 35).

Curtis' Hollywood credentials were further cemented by her associations to the professional, residential, and leisure haunts of the tinsel town elite. Publicity materials framed Curtis as a Los Angeles native—"born and raised in Southern California" (Avco Embassy Pictures, 1980b)—who bounced between landmarks in this conceptual epicenter of high-end American moviemaking. It was also reported that she had been educated alongside the offspring of moguls and A-listers at Beverly Hills High School and at Westlake School for Girls, before beating the path of aspiring Hollywood talent to the San Fernando Valley's Studio City (Beck, 1980). Curtis' affiliation to upmarket areas of the city was repeated by journalists who dubbed her the "Girl of the Golden West Coast," and suggested that "Jamie Lee of Beverly Hills probably wore Pampers from Rodeo Drive" (Shewey, 1981, p. 35).[4] These affluent and glamorous Los Angeles locations stood in binary opposition to the city's decrepit, crime-ridden exploitation film circuit on Hollywood Boulevard and Broadway, in much the same way as Curtis' embodiment of neo-feminism stood at odds with the sexism that was said to underwrite the production, content, and consumption of such fare.

Jamie Lee Curtis and neo-feminism

Although "American" horror film makers and marketers were subject to charges that they showcased violent misogyny, most industry decision-makers deemed this practice to be a high-risk/low-gain undertaking, based on the small audiences that gravitated to such material. Granted, some entrepreneurs—such as those behind *Don't Go in the House* (1979), *Don't Answer the*

---

[4]Curtis' relationships to the city posited a number of social types, none more striking than the Valley Girl: a privileged, varnished, socially engaged Southern California female who proliferated across 1980s youth-oriented entertainment, notably Moon Zappa's 1982 song "Valley Girl" and a 1983 film of the same name.

Phone! (1980), and *Maniac*—pursued product differentiation by foregrounding content of this sort, but they were few and far between. Irrespective of personal politics, economics determined that the overwhelming majority of individuals targeting violent films to the American theatrical market went to great lengths to pre-empt suggestions that their products were misogynistic (see Allison, 2007; Nowell, 2011, 2013). One way in which they hoped to insulate their films from this damaging accusation was by casting, and highlighting in marketing campaigns, women whose star personae projected strength, poise, and agency (see Nowell, 2013); women such as Jamie Lee Curtis.

Curtis' star persona offered a larger-than-life embodiment of what Radner has called neo-feminism (2011). Neo-feminism, argues Radner, was popularized by the writings of *Cosmopolitan* editor Helen Gurly Brown and by the 1960s "single girl" phenomenon (ibid., ch. 1). This philosophy-cum-lifestyle movement posited that individualism was the key to female empowerment (ibid.). Through a self-determined combination of career, consumption, beautification, fashion, sexual gratification, and motherhood, it was suggested that women might achieve self-fulfillment (ibid.). A pragmatic solution available to a fortunate few in an otherwise male-dominated world, neo-feminism also recuperated—as both a source of pleasure and power—the concept of girlishness, thus emphasizing the notion of woman in a perpetual state of becoming; forever on the cusp, forever turning to the market to fulfill an unattainable sense of completeness (ibid.). Curtis embodied neo-feminism in three key ways: her attention to style, her girlishness, and through claims of her personal and professional self-determination.

While she is often associated with her plain, dowdy, introverted character from *Halloween*, the young Curtis was in fact presented as a fashionable, physically attractive, sexually desirable young woman.[5] Curtis sought to distance herself from her unglamorous breakthrough role. "I wouldn't have cast myself as Laurie," she proclaimed: "I wear tight jeans, [and] have a low voice and big tits" (quoted in Martin, 1981, p. 21). Aside from Laurie, Curtis was usually cast as an alluring alpha female, playing a prom queen in *Prom Night*, the girlfriend of a fraternity president in *Terror Train*, and independent-minded hitchhikers in both *The Fog* and *Road Games*. Early promotional materials for the 1981 TV movie *Death of a Centerfold: The Dorothy Stratten Story* even topped an image of Curtis stretched across a bed with the tagline "Every man's fantasy." Significant attention was paid to Curtis' look. Her hair was said to have been treated with a "vinegar rinse" during *The Fog*

---

[5] Here we are reminded of the extent to which Carol J. Clover overstates the supposed boyishness of young horror heroines (1987).

and to contain "twelve tones [of blonde] in 'Prom Night'" (Fashion79 Staff, 1979, p. H3; Fashion80 Staff, 1980, p. 18). Similarly, where some journalists believed that her fitted pants and evening gowns afforded her "a very stylish presence" on the screen (Canby, 1980), others spotlighted her "cute habits [such] as eating Apple Jacks and wearing gold pumps" off it (Shewey, 1981, p. 35). In an interview for the horror magazine *Fangoria*, Curtis was pictured sporting designer jeans, sunglasses, and a platinum-blonde feather cut (Martin, 1981, pp. 20–1).

Curtis projected girlishness both on and off the screen. The young women that she played at the start of her career usually underwent personal growth and maturation beyond that typical of teenage protagonists or those surviving mortal danger. This sense of becoming was flagged and thematized, as Curtis' characters emerged transformed from rites of passage for American girls: babysitting in *Halloween*, graduation parties in *Prom Night* and *Terror Train*, hitchhiking in *The Fog* and *Road Games*. Marketing campaigns also suggested that Curtis was on the cusp of womanhood. Publicity materials emphasized relationships associated with a girl's teenage years: a mother–daughter bond, estranged father, and flings with edgy or older men (Beck, 1980). A recurring anecdote involved Curtis receiving a piece of cautionary advice from her mother after her first taste of professional success had gone to her head, leading her to behave precociously and ostentatiously (Shewey, 1981, p. 35). Curtis deliberately cultivated this sense of girlishness. For example, in an early interview she mused, "I'll look at a lot of things I do and I think I'm a woman, but I still do a lot of kid things, too, like eating donuts at 1 am," before concluding, "I guess I am a woman child" (*Chicago Tribune*, 1979). Journalists often rose to the bait. When confronted with "rough talking bravado and unspoiled girlishness"—with a young woman who "gulp[ed] Jack Daniels and wise-crack[ed] at full speed" but "giggle[d] and blush[ed] when talking about her boyfriends"—one writer suggested that Curtis was "[p]oised between her roles as sheltered kid and harried movie star" (Shewey, 1981, pp. 35, 107).

Alongside this knowing play of gender and age, Curtis was portrayed on- and off-screen as a self-determining young woman. In her private life, she was presented as a sexually liberated individual who enjoyed casual flings but was sufficiently self-reliant and secure not to need a man. It was even reported that she had not only declined a marriage proposal from one partner, but that she had felt the need to completely unburden herself of such a clingy mate (Martin, 1981, p. 25). The control that Curtis purportedly exerted in her heterosexual interaction was even said to have stretched to confrontations with local sexists when shooting *Road Games* in the Australian outback (Thomas, 1980a). This characterization found its double on the screen, where Curtis usually played forthright, self-confident young women, for whom men were either amusing playthings, as in *The Fog* and *Road Games*, or were weak souls incapable of contributing meaningfully to a relationship, as in *Prom Night* and *Terror Train*.

Professionally, Curtis was framed as a driven career woman whose grounded upbringing, commitment to the movie business, and street smarts enabled her to thrive in the unforgiving freelance economy of screen acting. "I was raised knowing where the money came from, not like some of my friends who were driving Porsches before they were 18," publicity materials reported her as saying (Avco Embassy Pictures, 1980b).This image was crystallized by reports that Curtis had been cast in the title role of *Death of a Centerfold: The Dorothy Stratten Story*, which was based on the high-profile case of an ambitious starlet whose acting career and romance with Hollywood director Peter Bogdanovich were cut short when she was murdered by her ex-husband. This sense of agency, poise, and control stood in marked contrast to the petrified female targets that underpinned charges of horror's misogyny, leading one writer to observe that "it seems rather hard to imagine [Curtis] being intimidated by anyone—even a knife-wielding maniac" (Martin, 1981, p. 20).

Conclusion

As Richard Dyer famously argued, some public figures promise to reconcile seemingly incompatible ideas because their star personae unite otherwise contradictory notions (1998, pp. 63–4; see also e.g. Gundle, 1995; Morrison, 2010). Entertainment industry decision-makers have consistently attempted to commodify this phenomenon by transforming the symbolic value of onscreen human resources into cultural and economic capital. They have approached the reconciliatory capacity of star images as a transferable asset insofar as it promises to imbue both the films and marketing materials in which a star appears with an equally powerful reconciliatory quality. This practice undergirded the manner in which filmmakers and distributors perceived, appropriated, and contributed to the star persona of a young woman who moved into screen acting when "American" horror films were coming under sustained critical attack in their principal market.

This chapter's examination of the structure and industrial functions of Jamie Lee Curtis' early star persona has shown how this performer enabled horror film producers and distributors to insulate their products from critical hostility so as to maximize profit potential. The fulfillment of these intertwined objectives, I argued, involved countering the potentially damaging suggestion that scary movies, harmless entertainment, and female empowerment were irreconcilable concepts; a notion which circulated American audiovisual culture in the form of a critical leitmotif that condemned contemporary horror films as debased and sexist. By collaborating with Curtis, these industry decision-makers sought to gentrify their pictures—directly through content tailoring and indirectly through marketing campaigns. The presence of Curtis promised to counter the aforementioned charges because she personified, and helped to disperse, the notion that innocuous horror films, the institution of Hollywood, and the figure of the individualistic, self-empowered female or "neo-feminist" could coexist harmoniously.

The dissemination of Curtis' early star image was recognized and reinforced by industry-watchers, many of whom tried to distill its complex interplay of elements to an appropriately evocative and reader-friendly catchphrase. Perhaps the most striking efforts came from writers who drew parallels between Curtis and one of her predecessors—an actress who was known for what amounted to neo-feminist credentials and for her glittering tinsel town heritage, and who was no stranger to cinematic bloodshed, as high-profile roles in *Murder on the Orient Express* (1974) and the 1981 women-in-danger film *The Fan* both demonstrated (see Arnold, 1978, p. B5; Paul Pompain quoted in Mann, 1981). Curtis' contribution to horror and to audiovisual culture generally, they proposed, amounted to rather more than the screams of terror with which she would come to be associated. Instead, they suggested that Jamie Lee Curtis brought to her films "a kind of Bacall quality" (Paul Pompain quoted in Mann, 1981).

Acknowledgment

I would like to thank Jindriska Blahova for her feedback on earlier drafts of this chapter.

References

Allison, D. (2007), "Courting the Critics/Assuring the Audience: The Modulation of Dirty Harry in a Changing Cultural Environment," *Film International*, 5.5: 17–29.

Arnold, G. (1978), "Halloween: A Trickle of Treats," *Washington Post*, November 26, p. B5.

Austin, B. A. (ed.) (1991), *Current Research in Film: Audiences, Economics and Law Vol. 5*, Norwood: Ablex.

Austin, T. (2002), "'*Gone with the Wind* Plus Fangs': Genre, Taste and Distinction in the Assembly, Marketing and Reception of Bram Stoker's *Dracula*," in S. Neale (ed.) *Genre and Contemporary Hollywood*, London: Routledge.
Avco Embassy Pictures (1980a), "Jamie Lee Curtis (Biography): 'Hitch' in Avco Embassy's 'Road Games'," Author's private collection, pp. 1–2.
—(1980b), "*Prom Night* Presskit," London: British Film Institute.
Beck, Marilynn (1980), "Marilynn Beck's Hollywood," *Tri City Herald*, October 14, p. 8.
Betz, M. (2003), "Art, Exploitation, Underground," in Mark Jancovich et al. (eds) *Defining Cult Movies: The Cultural Politics of Oppositional Taste*, Manchester: Manchester University Press.
Canby, V. (1979), "Chilling Truths about Scaring," *New York Times*, January 21, p. D13.
—(1980), "Film: 'Prom Night,' Chiller from Canada, Masks Gore," *New York Times*, August 16, p. 11.
Chicago Tribune (1978), "Followup," September 25, p. 12.
—(1979), "People," February 12, p. 20.
Church, D. (2011), "From Exhibition to Genre: The Case of Grind-house Films," *Cinema Journal*, 50.4: 1–25.
Clover, C. J. (1987), "Her Body, Himself: Gender in the Slasher Film," *Representations*, 20: 187–228.
Combined UPI AP (1980), Untitled Photo, *Deseret News*, February 20, p. A3.
Deleyto, C. (2009), *The Secret Life of Romantic Comedy*, Manchester: Manchester University Press.
Dyer, R. (1998), *Stars*, London: BFI.
Egan, K. (2013), "A Real Horror Star: Articulating the Extreme Authenticity of Ingrid Pitt," in K. Egan and S. Thomas (eds) *Cult Film Stardom: Offbeat Attractions and Processes of Cultification*, New York: Palgrave Macmillan.
Egan K. and Thomas, S. (eds) (2013), *Cult Film Stardom: Offbeat Attractions and Processes of Cultification*, New York: Palgrave Macmillan.
Fashion79 Staff (1979), "Listen," *Los Angeles Times*, November 16, p. H3.
Fashion80 Staff (1980), "Listen," *Los Angeles Times*, January 25, p. I8.
Gallagher, M. (2013), "Discerning Independents: Steven Soderbergh and Transhistorical Taste Cultures," in G. King, C. Molloy, and Y. Tzioumakis (eds) *American Independent Cinema: Indie, Indiewood and Beyond*, New York and London: Routledge.
Goldstein, P. (1984), "Scream No More, My Lady," *Los Angeles Times*, May 16, pp. D1–D6.
Grove, D. (2010), *Jamie Lee Curtis: Scream Queen*, Albany, NY: BearManor Media.
Gundle, S. (1995), "Sophia Loren, Italian Icon," *Historical Journal of Film, Radio and Television*, 15:3: 367–85.
Halloween: A Cut Above the Rest (2003), Anchor Bay Entertainment.
Harmetz, A. (1980), "Quick End of Low-budget Horror-film Cycle Seen," *New York Times*, October 2, p. C15.
—(1981), "Robert Rehme, King of the Low-budget Shocker," *New York Times*, November 30, p. C13.
Heilner, S. (1978), "Names ... Faces," *Boston Globe*, October 26, p. 5.

Higson, A. (1989), "The Concept of National Cinema," *Screen*, 30.1: 36–46.
Jancovich, M. (2002), "Cult Fictions: Cult Movies, Subcultural Capital and the Production of Cultural Distinctions," *Cultural Studies*, 16.2: 306–22.
Johnson, E. and, Schaefer, E. (1993), "Soft Core/Hard Gore: *Snuff* as a Crisis of Meaning," *Journal of Film and Video*, 45.2/3: 40–59.
Kapsis, R. E. (1991), "Hollywood Genres and the Production of Culture Perspective," in B. A. Austin (ed.), *Current Research in Film: Audiences, Economics and Law Vol. 5*, Norwood: Ablex.
—(1992), *Hitchcock: The Making of a Reputation*, Chicago, IL: University of Chicago Press.
King, G. (2011), "Striking a Balance between Culture and Fun: 'Quality' Meets Hitman Genre in *In Bruges*," *New Review of Film and Television*, 9.2: 132–41.
Knoedelseder, W. K. Jnr. (1980), "Jamie Lee Curtis: A Scream Queen Attracts Attention," *Los Angeles Times*, November 16, p. Q4.
Leeder, M. (forthcoming), *Halloween*, Leighton Buzzard: Auteur Press.
Lyons, C. (1997), *The New Censors: Movies and the Cultural Wars*, Philadelphia, PA: Temple University Press.
McDonald, P. (1998), "Reconceptualising Stardom," in R. Dyer, *Stars*, London: BFI.
—(2000), *The Star System: Hollywood's Production of Popular Identities*, London: Wallflower.
Mann, R. (1981), "Hollywood and Doomed Playmate," *Los Angeles Times*, July 16, p. G7.
Martin, B. (1981), "Jamie Lee Curtis," *Fangoria*, 15.3: 20–5.
Morrison, J. (2010), "Shelley Winters: Camp, Abjection, and the Aging Star," in J. Morrison (ed.) *Hollywood Reborn: Movie Stars of the 1970s*, New Brunswick, NJ: Rutgers University Press.
Neale S. (ed.) (2002), *Genre and Contemporary Hollywood*, London: Routledge.
Newman, M. Z. (2009), "Indie Culture: In Pursuit of the Authentic Autonomous Alternative," *Cinema Journal*, 48.3: 16–34.
Nowell, R. (2011), *Blood Money: A History of the First Teen Slasher Film Cycle*, New York: Continuum.
—(2013), "Targeting American Women: Movie Marketing, Genre History, and the Hollywood Women-in-danger Film," *InMedia: The French Journal of Media and Media Representations in the English Speaking World*, 3. Available online at http://inmedia.revues.org/600 (accessed August 31, 2013).
—(forthcoming), "'Private School … For Girls': Young Female Theatergoers, Early-80s Teen Sex Comedies, and the 'Make-out Movie'."
Pinedo, I. C. (1997), *Recreational Terror: Women and the Pleasures of Horror Film Viewing*, Albany: State University of New York Press.
Radner, H. (2011), *Neo-feminist Cinema: Girly Films, Chick Flicks, and Consumer Culture*, New York: Routledge.
Robbins, J. (1982), "Survey Says Public Likes Sci-Fi but Really Loves Comedy," *Variety*, September 22, p. 22.
Scott, V. (1981a), "Film Mogul Turns Menace into Millions," *Chicago Tribune*, May 31, p. D32.
—(1981b), "Jamie Lee Curtis through Being Afraid," *Sarasota Herald-Tribune*, August 10, p. 6C.

Shewey, D. (1981), "Horror of Horrors, it's Jamie Lee Curtis," *Rolling Stone*, 358, December 10, pp. 34–5, 107.

Siskel, G. (1980), "Prom Night," *Chicago Tribune*, July 21, p. A6.

Snelson, T. (2009), "'From Grade B Thrillers to Deluxe Chillers': Prestige Horror, Female Audiences, and Allegories of Spectatorship in *The Spiral Staircase* (1946)," *New Review of Film and Television Studies*, 7.2: 173–88.

Thomas, K. (1980a), "Movies: 'Roadgames': Milage from International Contacts," *Los Angeles Times*, July 6, p. O26.

—(1980b), "Stylish, Scary Fun on 'Terror Train'," *Los Angeles Times*, October 3, p. H19.

Turan, K. (1980), "'The Fog's' John Carpenter: A 'Cult' Director 'Arrives'," *Chicago Tribune*, February 4, p. A1.

Wilson, E. (1978), "It Happened Last Night," *Pittsburgh Post-Gazette*, September 11, p. 11.

Wood, R. (1985 [1979]), "An Introduction to the American Horror Film," in B. Nicholls (ed.) *Movies and Methods: Volume II*, Berkeley and Los Angeles: University of California Press.

9

"New Decade, New Rules"
Rebooting the *Scream* Franchise in the Digital Age

Valerie Wee

During the 1997 launch of *Scream 2*, the producer and head of Dimension Films, Bob Weinstein, asserted that "this is not the classic case of going, 'wow, we made a lotta money, can we make another one quick?' We always saw this as a trilogy of movies" (quoted in Hochman, 1997, p. 28). When *Scream 3* was released in 2000, Wes Craven, who had directed all three films, reiterated this claim when he suggested that "[f]rom the onset, this project was conceived as a trilogy" (quoted in Kleinschrodt, 2000, p. L21). With the release of the third installment of the *Scream* franchise, one of the most profitable teen slasher film series in the history of the American film industry was ostensibly "complete." Yet, this sense of closure proved to be relatively short-lived, as 2008 saw Bob's brother Harvey announce plans for a new installment: *Scre4m* (quoted in Fouche, 2008).

In 2011, some 15 years after *Scream* (1996) debuted, *Scre4m* opened in theaters worldwide. *Scre4m* resembled its predecessors in several ways. It was an overtly inter-textual and often self-reflexive film that centered on a group of young people trying to evade and unmask a serial killer by interrogating and deconstructing the nature, form, and content of horror films. *Scre4m* also commented on the challenges confronting the teen slasher film and the media industries around the time of its production. Just as the first three films' heightened postmodern and self-referential characteristics were tied to macro-industrial forces—the rise of a new youth demographic,

Dimension's leveraging then-parent company Disney's multiple content platforms, and trends in media marketing—*Scre4m* was also a response to key social, industrial, and technological developments that unfolded prior to its production and release. Given that "genre is always implicated in larger discourses: of industrial circumstance [...] current conditions within the culture at large [...] and shifts within audiences" (Desser, 2000, p. 88), this chapter considers the following:

1 Developments in horror that unfolded between the release of *Scream 3* and the announcement of the production of *Scre4m*.

2 Dimension's development from a part of the The Disney Company to a branch of The Weinstein Company (hereafter TWC).

3 Changes in the youth audience, particularly the desire to target a new demographic that has been labeled "the Facebook generation."

4 Technological developments in new digital media, including the rise of social networking and personal digital communication devices.

The case of *Scre4m* offers an invaluable opportunity to examine how this series of films, the teen slasher film, the media industries, the entertainment market, and the industry's engagement with society at large have continued to develop. In interrogating the forces that shaped the content and themes of *Scre4m*, this chapter argues that, where the original trilogy successfully resurrected the then-defunct teen slasher film format by reworking some of its key conventions, *Scre4m* ultimately defaults on the claim of its promotional tagline: "New Decade, New Rules." By examining the various textual strategies used in the latest installment of the franchise, the chapter highlights that this film's makers' commitment to established characters and to the fans of earlier entries ultimately limited *Scre4m*'s appeal and relevance to a new generation of youth.

Resurrecting the teen slasher film in the 2010s

Scre4m was released at a point in time when the teen slasher film had declined significantly from the high point of its commercial prowess in the late 1990s and early 2000s. Many of the conditions that had driven the production of *Scre4m* echoed those that had prompted the development of the first three films.

Before *Scream*'s release in 1996, the teen slasher film, and indeed the youth entertainment market, had become marginalized, on account of being largely dismissed by major Hollywood studios and the entertainment conglomerates to which they belonged.[1] Such were the conditions in the mid-1990s, when Bob Weinstein of the successful art house/indie outfit Miramax Films set up the genre film label Dimension Films in an effort to target youth (see Perren, 2012). Weinstein noted at this time that "[t]here were no movies being made for teenagers anymore. It had become an adult oriented business. I knew there was an audience that was not being satisfied" (quoted in Eller, 1995). Speculating that this largely ignored demographic would be receptive to products that had been fashioned specifically to serve its needs, Weinstein produced *Scream*. Further motivating this decision was the view that teen slasher films were usually considered independent productions, the box office success of which was driven by their capacity to attract a niche youth audience in spite of their low budgets, and their lack of stars and special effects. Weinstein's instincts paid off when on an estimated production budget of $14 million *Scream* generated in excess of $100 million at the North American box office, and another $70 million overseas (boxofficemojo.com; for more on how *Scream* breathed new life into the moribund teen slasher film see Wee, 2006).

Scream's financial achievements helped to resurrect the dormant teen slasher film, and, in so doing, drew the American film industry's attention to the box office potential of courting the nascent millennial youth audience. Some journalists and academics praised this film and its sequels for their originality and innovation,[2] and credited the series with making the teen slasher film attractive to female youths, who were not typically considered to be a targeted audience for this type of picture.[3] By 2000, with the release of the putative final installment of the series, the support that Generation Y—generally defined as babies born between 1977 and 1994—had given to the *Scream* films had yielded a total North American theatrical gross of $293.5 million (boxofficemojo.com). Figures of this caliber ensured that the *Scream*

---

[1] For a discussion of how the commercial success of *Clueless* (1995), *Romeo + Juliet* (1996), and *Scream* re-alerted the American film industry to the purchasing power of female youth, see Klady (1997, pp. 11–12).

[2] I do not wish to imply that the *Scream* series is unequivocally deserving of acclaim. I thank Richard Nowell for pointing out that at least some proportion of the *Scream* series' critical praise and the academic interest in its "innovation" and originality is founded on carefully, and self-consciously, cultivated discourses that have been used, often by Dimension itself, to promote the series. Certainly, existing commentary on the *Scream* series' originality and innovation ignores the existence of earlier slasher films that had already featured some of the qualities that were wrongly considered to have been pioneered by *Scream* (see n. 10).

[3] Carol J. Clover argues that the 1980s teen slasher film audience "was largely young and largely male. [...] Young males are [...] the slasher film's implied audience, the object of its address" (1992, p. 23) (for an alternative view which highlights the North American film industry's recognition of female audiences see Nowell, 2011a, 2011b).

films spearheaded a cycle of new teen slasher films that included *Urban Legend* (1998) and *Valentine* (2001), and belated sequels to earlier series such as *Halloween H20: Twenty Years Later* (1998).

Yet, with its arch, self-aware, and overtly inter-textual content, *Scream* articulated a (self-)conscious negotiation of slasher film conventions that accelerated the speed at which new teen slashers descended into meta- and inter-textual cliché (see Wee, 2005). Scholars have noted that parodies—what Thomas Schatz labeled the "Baroque" phase of a genre's textual evolution—signal that a genre has reached a point of exhaustion, wherein audiences and filmmakers are left to deride the conventions they once held sacrosanct (1981, pp. 36–7).[4] Significantly, in the year that *Scream 3* was released, the teen slasher parody *Scary Movie* (2000) was a major hit. Its release and subsequent commercial success indicated that even though audiences continued to enjoy *Scream*'s playful critique of teen slasher conventions alongside moments of straight horror, they were already appreciating films that lampooned those conventions. The proliferation of teen slasher films that had been made to capitalize on *Scream* precipitated the remarginalization of this type of film. Consequently, the conclusion of this cycle resulted from the distribution of too many retreads, and from an audience that had been overwhelmed by a glut of similar product. Many of these factors had signaled the end of the teen slasher film cycle of the late 1970s and early 1980s (see Clover, 1992, p. 23; Nowell, 2011a, pp. 187–242). With the teen slasher film returned to its marginalized, critically dismissed, and derided location, sequels to successful 1990s franchises such as the *Urban Legend* (1998–2005) and *I Know What You Did Last Summer* series (1997–2006) were released direct-to-DVD.

The remarginalization of the teen slasher film and of teen horror generally coincided with a Hollywood drive to look beyond niche demographics so as to consider the financial viability of horror films which promised to appeal to a general audience. This shift is perhaps best represented by remakes of cult Asian horror pictures such as *The Ring* (2002) and *The Grudge* (2004), which critics and reviewers often heralded for their inventiveness, for focusing on dread rather than gore, and for their growing inscrutability and moral flux (see Rose, 2002; Heffernan, Chapter 4, this volume). These elements signaled a partial return to the narrative and stylistic traditions of classical Hollywood horror, and clearly departed from the self-aware, media-obsessed attitudes of contemporary youth, thereby helping these films to appeal beyond the youth audience.

---

[4] Although Schatz's model reflects the development of the teen slasher film cycle of the late 1990s and early 2000s, the rather inflexible view of genre evolution this framework provides ensures that it is not applicable to all trends.

A decade after the release of *Scream 3*, the box office prowess of the teen slasher might have plummeted, and few horror films were being targeted primarily or solely to youth, but a new generation of youngsters was coming of age. This generation comprised the tail end of Generation Y, and the earliest representatives of a new youth wave that was dubbed "Generation Z": those born between 1995 and 2012, who had been babies or young children when Gen Y was flocking to the first three *Scream* films. Like Generation Y, this demographic was attractive to the media industries. The dearth of Gen Z-oriented horror signaled the viability of products that this cohort could call its own, products like a new *Scream* film.[5]

The Weinstein Company and Dimension Films: Going back to basics

The social, cultural, and industrial factors that I outlined in the previous section coincided with developments taking place at Dimension Films and its parent TWC, which made rebooting the *Scream* franchise not just appealing but of profound importance to these companies. Specifically, the developments that led to the October 2005 launch of TWC, in conjunction with its operations in the mid- to late 2000s, explain the appeal of rebooting the franchise, and its timing.

Prior to establishing TWC, the Weinsteins had gained significant acclaim for the success they had enjoyed in two quite distinct sectors of American film production and distribution: art house cinema, which they had developed at Miramax; and medium-budget genre films which they had developed at Dimension. Between 1993 and 2005, Dimension handled a range of horror properties, including sequels to *Hellraiser* (1987) and *The Crow* (1994), and original productions such as *From Dusk 'til Dawn* (1996) and of course *Scream*.[6] In October 2005, however, the Weinsteins left Disney to establish their new company, TWC, which also absorbed Dimension. The brothers expanded into entertainment/lifestyle interests by pursuing acquisitions, in among others, fashion, new media, and publishing (see Lowry and Cox, 2010). At the same time, Dimension remained faithful to its genre film roots,

---

[5]While Gen Z was already being targeted by the American film industry, notably with the PG-13 rated *Twilight* series (2008–12), there were no significant teen horror films targeted at Gen Z in the mid-2000s.
[6]Dimension's launch took advantage of The Disney Company's new role as Miramax's parent, in particular, access to better funding and an established international video distribution network (see Wee, 2010, pp. 120–2).

with early projects including a remake of the 1979 haunted house picture, *The Amityville Horror* (2005), the Australian horror pick-up *Wolf Creek* (2005), and a 2006 remake of the Japanese chiller *Pulse* (see Wee, forthcoming). The box office performances of these films were at best uneven. Where *The Amityville Horror* scored a respectable worldwide theatrical gross of $108 million, *Wolf Creek* accrued a relatively low gross of $27.7 million, and the $20.5 million *Pulse* generated a plodding $29.8 million (boxofficemojo.com). With none of its films breaking the $100 million threshold at the North American box office, TWC fell out of the top ten distributors as ranked by theatrical market share (see Cieply, 2009). Industry watchers questioned whether multi-media diversification and expansion, coupled with mediocre theatrical returns, had put TWC in a precarious position. Under these circumstances, the resurrection of once-lucrative franchises such as *Spy Kids* (2001–11) and *Scream* made good sense from a business standpoint.

The announcement that a new *Scream* film was to be made came as TWC's coffers were so dangerously depleted that management had brought in the corporate troubleshooter Miller Buckfire & Co.[7] It was clear that several of TWC's business and creative decisions had been ill-conceived, and that both the reputations of the Weinsteins and Dimension had plummeted from their salad days of the mid- to late 1990s and early 2000s. Reports suggested that TWC was saddled with $450 million in debt, which needed to be repaid promptly if it was to stay afloat.[8] A year before *Scre4m* was scheduled for release, a top executive acknowledged the challenges the company was facing and stressed that it would attempt to mine the Weinsteins' back catalog. He promised a return to "what the Weinsteins have always done best – marketing and making great films" while pursuing "a tighter, more efficient operation," emphasizing that it was "time to go back to the basics" (quoted in Lowry and Cox, 2010).

New technologies, new media, new youth audience

While Dimension returned to tried-and-tested territory when it came to production and content, the entertainment landscape had further fragmented. The rise of new media technologies and platforms offered younger audiences

---

[7] In 2009, Miller Buckfire restructured TWC's debts and secured extra capital to cover the company's operational costs (see Verrier, 2009; McDonald, 2010).

[8] An agreement with Goldman Sachs and Assured Guarantee announced in June 2010 allowed TWC successfully to eliminate its debts (see Lowry and Cox, 2010).

a broader range of entertainment options and experiences. These developments resulted in anticipation of increased engagement and interactivity among a youth audience that exerted greater control over when, where, and how it consumed media, and which was taking up the opportunities that new media technologies and platforms were providing for consumers to adapt media to their own ends. From the vantage point of 2011, the first three *Scream* films' reliance on traditional media and communications devices seems positively "old school."

The earlier *Scream* films had focused heavily on cinematic and generic traditions, such as when film geek Randy (Jamie Kennedy) outlines the rules to surviving slasher films, and when the heroine Sidney Prescott (Neve Campbell) considers the relationships between real and reel life by musing: "if this were a movie, I'd be played by [the *Beverly Hills 90210* actress] Tori Spelling." The earlier films had reached out to adult Gen Y by invoking the conceit that only those sufficiently familiar with contemporaneous youth culture, particularly the reputation of the teen slasher film, would survive the Ghostface killer's murderous rampage. With the young and media-fixated best equipped to cope, it was the initially teenaged (later twenty-something) Sidney and the not-much-older reporter Gale Weathers (Courtney Cox) who had, with a little help from Randy, managed to survive all three films. Sidney, Gale, and Randy served as on-screen surrogates for this trilogy's targeted audience inasmuch as their familiarity with teen slasher film conventions approximated that of the media-literate youth being courted.[9]

By the time *Scre4m* was being developed, the telephones that were a primary source of menace in the earlier films had been all but superseded by new communication systems and social networking services. Skype (launched in 2003), Facebook (in 2004), Twitter (in 2006), live blogging, and webcasting could all be conducted on cellular devices and smart phones that youth rarely even used as phones any longer. Furthermore, after *Scream* and its sequels had famously questioned and undermined the "rules" of the teen slasher film, "new, new rules" needed to be established to make a new installment relevant to youth of the 2010s. In addition, the dividing line between real and reel that was so central to the earlier *Scream* films had become increasingly blurred, with countless "reality" series having redrawn that line in such a way that these hitherto dialectical notions could co-exist and blend indistinguishably within a single media product. For example,

---

[9]While *Scream*'s high school characters were clearly used to address teenagers, sequels featured characters that had 'aged up' into their college years (*Scream 2*) and into young adulthood (*Scream 3*), much as the original consumers of the first film had done. Arguably, the financial success of the first three films came from maintaining the interest of these original viewers and attracting the new Gen Y teenagers who had aged into the slasher's targeted audience.

MTV's *The Hills* (2006–10) was marketed as a reality show only for this notion to be completely negated in its final episode, which revealed that the series was scripted, staged, and in large part fictional. Clearly, the "rules" that had been established in the trilogy of 1996 to 2000 were no longer sufficient to ensure a character's survival in a new *Scream* film. Successfully rebooting the *Scream* franchise not only required careful negotiation of the new media landscape of Gen Z, but would also involve appealing to two quite distinct audiences.

Scre4m: "New Decade, New Rules"

The makers of horror and other genre films must confront the need to employ both derivative and innovative material. Accordingly, the makers of the earlier *Scream* films had balanced their use of the generic conventions of the teen slasher—a seemingly invincible killer dispatches young people before being vanquished, often by a resilient heroine—with a playful deconstruction of these features (for a discussion of teen slasher conventions see Clover, 1992, pp. 21–64). Among the perceived innovations of the *Scream* franchise was its interrogation and undermining of teen slasher film conventions.[10] This feat was achieved by depicting media-savvy, sophisticated, self-aware teenagers who openly questioned, critiqued, and deconstructed this type of film. By making actual teen slasher films a principal focus of characters' dialog, the *Scream* films both revised and reinforced many of the conventions of the genre. For example, in the first film, Sidney lambasts teen slashers for featuring "[s]ome stupid killer stalking some big-breasted girl who can't act, who's always running up the stairs when she should be going out the front door," adding, "it's insulting," but she soon finds herself in this exact situation. Conversely, the film undermines other assumed conventions, such as when a character states that in teen slashers "sex equals death," only for Sidney to survive having recently lost her virginity. The *Scream* series also reworked the teen slasher heroine or "Final Girl" and its villain, the killer (see also Wee, 2006). It was the latter who typically connected individual installments of

---

[10] Although *Scream* was praised for its self-aware, postmodern, inter-textual "critique" of slasher conventions, it should be noted that many of these qualities had already appeared two years earlier in *Wes Craven's New Nightmare* (1994), a follow-up to the *A Nightmare on Elm Street* series (1984–91). *New Nightmare* reimagines the original *A Nightmare on Elm Street* as a film and explores the events that ensue when that film's villain Freddy Krueger (Robert Englund) surfaces in the "real" world to haunt the actress who played the original film's heroine Nancy Thompson (Heather Langenkamp).

1980s teen slasher series, with the former rarely returning in sequels.[11] By contrast, the *Scream* films offered a revolving door of killers, while making its Final Girls, Sidney and Gale, recurring elements. These veritable "star" survivors defeated new villains in each installment, making the series particularly attractive to female members of Gen Y.[12] A decade after the relative commercial and critical success of *Scream 3*, Dimension needed to ensure that *Scre4m* emulated these achievements, that it too revised the teen slasher format and refreshed the self-awareness of the *Scream* property, and that it retained the now-adult viewers who in their youth had followed the first three films while also attracting the new youth audience.[13]

The targeting of specific audience niches requires that content be tailored so that the film in question is well placed to attract its intended consumers while "urging the people who do not fit the desired lifestyle profile *not* to be part of the audience" (Turow, 1997, p. 5; emphasis in original). However, the need simultaneously to angle *Scre4m* to two distinct audience constituencies—the now-adult followers of the earlier films and the new youth cohort—would shape its balance of convention and innovation. The makers of *Scre4m* ultimately attempted to "have it both ways." On the one hand, they reached out to the now-adult followers of the first three films, by retaining the now-30-something Sidney and the now-40-something Gale. On the other hand, they targeted youth by introducing new teenage characters, by foregrounding youth-oriented material such as these characters' obsessions with new media, digital communication platforms, and twenty-first-century popular culture, and by picturing the specific challenges facing Gen Z. Thus, where Sidney and Gale (and her husband Sheriff Dewey [David Arquette]) represent a resilient "old guard" that overcame multiple threats in the earlier films, younger characters like Sidney's teenage cousin Jill (Emma Roberts) and her high school friends represent the next generation of teenagers from which new victims, a new Ghostface killer, and a new Final Girl will presumably emerge.

Scre4m needed to acknowledge the slasher film convention of setting young characters apart from adult society, physically and metaphorically. In this sense, teen slashers are angled to their prime target audience by

---

[11] Tony Williams has argued that "[a] Final Woman may fight and sometimes defeat the monster. But her ultimate victory is undercut [...] by eventual death in a sequel" (1996, p. 214).
[12] According to *USA Today*: "Typically, only about 1% of moviegoers will pay to see a film more than once. With *Scream*, an estimated 16% of women age 25 and under who saw the film in theatres went more than once, according to polling by Miramax. By comparison, only 3% of young men who saw *Scream* returned for additional screenings" (see Weeks, 1997, p. 1A).
[13] TWC president of theatrical distribution Erik Lomis has admitted that "[o]ur hope obviously is to bring this to a whole new generation of fans" (quoted in Stewart, 2011a).

foregrounding a youthful perspective and a youth-dominated milieu, and by showing young characters recognizing a threat to which others are oblivious, and that they alone are equipped to confront, defeat, and survive. *Scre4m* navigates this generic demand by dramatizing conflicts between adult and teenage characters. As younger people, Sidney and Gale had responded promptly to the teen slasher conventions they encountered, based on their familiarity with such features. However, as adults, they are now out of touch and must rely on the up-to-the-minute expertise of the students attending Sidney's alma mater, Woodsboro High. *Scre4m* attempts to integrate Sidney and Gale—who are now struggling with adult issues related to work, marriage, and family—into what they see as the unfamiliar world of Gen Z, a world characterized by new relationships to new media and new communications technologies. In so doing, the film thematizes the conflicts that structure this generation gap, long before they escalate into violence and death. These interactions highlight the distance between teenage Jill and her friends and the adults around them. At its most benign, this cross-generational interaction is marked by patronizing bemusement, petulance, and rudeness. For instance, Robbie Mercer (Erik Knudsen) and Charlie Walker (Rory Culkin)—respectively Cinema Club president and vice president—respond with polite condescension to sometimes naïve and ignorant queries about their generation's media consumption and preferences. (Stereo-)typical representations of generational discord are also conveyed by Jill's unwillingness to bond with her mother and by her stilted exchanges with Sidney. *Scre4m* also attempts to connect with and appeal to Generation Z by foregrounding new media and communication technologies that have been embraced by this demographic. Its narrative is structured around webcam activities, and its look is influenced by the aesthetics of the webcast. What is more, the film emphasizes the prevalence of blogging in twenty-first-century youth culture, and even acknowledges the rise of the independent media creator, when, for example, Robbie uses a webcam strapped to his head to broadcast interactions and interviews with his cohort to an anonymous online public.

    As a product that was conceived, produced, and controlled by a corporate media player, *Scre4m* offers an explicit mediation on technology's potential to generate new entertainment products and experiences that fall outside the purview of the traditional media industries. The film even serves up a dose of dark humor when it treats its young amateur media practitioners with increasing hostility before killing them all off. Thus, things end badly for Robbie, his webcast collaborator Charlie, and the Ghostface killer, who it is revealed has recorded the killing spree to provoke the media into granting her the fame and notoriety she so desires. This violent treatment of grassroots media producers hints at the anxieties harbored by established entertainment institutions that are struggling to address dwindling consumption, and fighting to remain relevant to a generation of young people that is adept at refashioning texts from copyrighted media content and is beginning to pursue ways of generating revenue therefrom. In fact, the killer even critiques a contemporary media and celebrity culture complex involving companies like Dimension Films that enables potentially subversive notions of "success" and achievement, arguing:

> My friends? What world are you living in? I don't need friends; I need fans. Don't you get it? This has never been about killing you. It's about becoming you [....] You had your fifteen minutes, now I want mine. I mean, what am I supposed to do? Go to college? Grad school? Work? Look around. We all live in public now; we're all on the Internet. How do you think people get famous anymore? You don't have to achieve anything! You just got to have fucked up shit happen to you [....] Those are the rules.

Even though *Scre4m* strives to be relevant to Gen Z, its narrative and style is nevertheless highly derivative of its decade-plus-old predecessors. Character dialog consistently makes the claim that the film breaks from these earlier installments by suggesting "new movie, new franchise," from genre convention by asserting "[i]f you wanna be the new, new version," and from well-trodden territory by stressing that "sick is the new sane." Yet, in spite of its inclusion of new characters and the acknowledgment that new technologies are reshaping the media and communications environment, *Scre4m* is much like earlier installments insofar as it relies heavily on media-literate characters spelling out the genre "rules" that have been established by earlier teen slasher films, in this case by the *Scream* films themselves. Thus, *Scre4m* follows its predecessors by showing central characters participating in debates about teen slasher films and being guided by an authority on the subject. In the place of the film geek Randy, a new generation of experts is represented by Charlie and Robbie, who provide Sidney and Gale with insights into the rules of movie remakes, and into new media and communication technologies. Consequently, as with the earlier installments, *Scre4m* allocates a significant amount of time to diegetic discussion of how the new Ghostface killer might negotiate and reinterpret genre conventions. *Scre4m* also updates the earlier films' mediation of violent action through various media hardware, in this case a combination of webcams and other portable recording equipment. Thus, where *Scream* pictured Gale witnessing an attack being transmitted by a video camera she has hidden at a house party, in *Scre4m* her husband views Gale herself being attacked via a video feed from a barn in which the teenagers are partying.

Scre4m's commitment to "old" rules is clearly evident in its climax. In this sequence, Sidney is attacked and left for dead by the killer, who then proceeds to offer herself up as the sole survivor or Final Girl by inflicting wounds upon her own body to give the impression that she has narrowly escaped with her life. Having been hospitalized, the killer learns of Sidney's survival, setting the stage for a final standoff between the two: the first film's Final Girl and her would-be successor. This confrontation concludes with Sidney dispatching her pretender and asserting "[d]on't fuck with the original." The film therefore pits "old" against "new" in terms of the characters and the generic conventions around which the film is built, while upholding its commitment to Sidney and, by virtue of her emblematic status, to the earlier films and to the Gen Y audience that has followed the series since the 1990s. To achieve such ends, Scre4m negates its new "rules," does away with its new Final Girl, and abandons its Gen Z audience. The latest installment of this franchise therefore reverses the revolutionary and transformative trajectory of the earlier entries in favor of a more conservative and regressive resolution.

Conclusion

In their quest to attract a new youth audience, the media industries have tended to work to the logic that each generation prefers entertainment that expresses its distinct needs, desires, perspectives, and experiences. Scre4m ultimately rejects this practice by critiquing and undermining a twenty-first-century youth perspective. In navigating a generational divide between Gen Y and Gen Z, Scre4m at best negates the latter, and at worst expresses an underlying "hostility" to it. Such a position is reflected by the fact that it renders teenage characters ignorant victims or manipulative, cold-blooded killers. Efforts to retain both the initial Gen Y followers of earlier installments, and the stars of those films, result in Scre4m ignoring the desires of the new youth cohort whose on-screen surrogates are destroyed in spite of their greater mastery of new media.

This practice may account for Scre4m's failure to attract a sizable segment of the Gen Z audience. While the film retained some of the over-25 audience of the earlier films, it largely failed to secure the attendance of under-25s (see Stewart, 2011b). Scre4m grossed a paltry $38 million at the domestic box office, less than half of the amount generated by its predecessors, and, in spite of performing slightly better overseas, its worldwide haul of $97 million was 50 percent down on the earlier films. Crucially, where the first three Scream films boasted a particularly strong appeal among female youth, Scre4m attracted "just 52% [which is] somewhat surprising when considering horror pics typically see female turnout ranging from 60%–70% of opening week" (ibid.).

The fact remains that short of its increasingly convoluted and Byzantine narrative twists and turns, *Scre4m* broke little new ground beyond acknowledging that new digital technologies impacted on and posed a threat to established media, and its disturbingly insightful commentary on America's intensifying obsession with fame and notoriety.[14] Where the original *Scream* trilogy revised and renovated the "rules" and conventions of the teen slasher film, *Scre4m* abandons innovation for imitation and ultimately reneges on the claims to newness and originality that are promised by the promotional tagline "New Decade, New Rules."

References

Cieply, M. (2009), "Weinstein Company Takes Steps to Ease Debt," *New York Times*, June 8. Available online at http://www.nytimes.com/2009/06/08/business/media/08weinstein.html (accessed March 20, 2012).

Clover, Carol J. (1992), *Men, Women and Chainsaws: Gender in the Modern Horror Film*, London: BFI.

Desser, D. (2000), "From Enka to Anime: Popular Japanese Cinema, 1945–1990," in D. Slaymaker (ed.) *A Century of Popular Culture in Japan*, Lewiston: The Edwin Mellen Press.

Eller, C. (1995), "On-screen Chemistry," *Los Angeles Times*, December 1, Section D.

Fouche, G. (2008), "In Brief: *Scream 4* Peddled by Harvey Weinstein," *Guardian*, July 15. Available online at http://www.guardian.co.uk/film/2008/jul/15/news.culture2 (accessed March 20, 2013).

Hochman, D. (1997), "*Scream* and *Scream* Again," *Entertainment Weekly*, November 28, p. 28.

Klady, L. (1997), "Studios Focus on Teen Stream," *Variety*, January 13–19, pp. 11–12.

Kleinschrodt, M. H. (2000), "Audiences Enjoy Laughing Themselves to Death," *Times-Picayune*, February 4, p. L21.

Lowry, T. and Cox, G. (2010), "What Now for the Weinsteins?," *Variety*, August 2. Available online at http://variety.com/2010/film/news/what-now-for-the-weinsteins-1118022443/ (accessed March 20, 2013).

McDonald, D. (2010), "The 'Brilliance' of Harvey Weinstein," *CNN Money*, June 25. Available at http://money.cnn.com/2010/06/25/news/companies/harvey_weinstein_deal.fortune/index.htm (accessed March 20, 2012).

---

[14] *Scre4m*'s commentary on American culture's intensifying obsession with fame and notoriety was a point that emerged in my consultations with my student, Bernard Koh, who went on more fully to explore his thoughts on this topic in an Independent Study paper.

Nowell, R. (2011a), *Blood Money: A History of the First Teen Slasher Film Cycle*, New York: Continuum.

—(2011b) "'There's More Than One Way to Lose Your Heart': The American Film Industry, Early Teen Slasher Films, and Female Youth," *Cinema Journal*, 51.1: 115–40.

Perren, A. (2012), *Indie Inc.: Miramax and the Transformation of Hollywood in the 1990s*, Austin: University of Texas Press.

Rose, S. (2002), "Nightmare Scenario," *Guardian*, September 20. Available online at http://www.guardian.co.uk/culture/2002/sep/20/artsfeatures.dvdreviews (accessed April 30, 2013).

Schatz, T. (1981), *Hollywood Genres*, New York: McGraw-Hill.

Slaymaker, D. (ed.) (2000), *A Century of Popular Culture in Japan*, Lewiston: The Edwin Mellen Press.

Stewart, A. (2011a), "'Rio' Expected to Fly Over 'Scream' at Box-Office," *Variety*, April 14. Available online at http://www.variety.com/article/VR1118035472 (accessed March 20, 2012).

—(2011b), "Worldwide Auds Flock to 'Rio'," *Variety*, April 17. Available online at http://www.variety.com/article/VR1118035538?refcatid=3762 (accessed March 20, 2012).

Turow, J. (1997), *Breaking Up America: Advertisers & the New Media World*, Chicago, IL: University of Chicago Press.

Verrier, R. (2009), "Company Town: Weinstein Co. Hires Consulting Firm to Restructure its Debt and Raise Funds," *Los Angeles Times*, June 6. Available online at http://articles.latimes.com/2009/jun/06/business/fi-ct-weinstein6 (accessed March 20, 2012).

Wee, V. (2005), "The *Scream* Trilogy: 'Hyper'-Postmodernism and the late '90s Teen Slasher Film," *Journal of Film and Video*, 57.3: 44–61.

—(2006), "Resurrecting and Updating the Teen Slasher – The Case of *Scream*," *Journal of Popular Film and Television*, 34.2: 50–61.

—(2010), *Teen Media: Hollywood and the Youth Market in the Digital Age*, Jefferson, NC: McFarland.

—(forthcoming), *Japanese Horror Films and their American Remakes: Translating Fear, Adapting Culture*, New York: Routledge.

Weeks, J. (1997), "'*Scream*' Movies Cultivate Special Audience: Girls," *USA Today*, December 12, p. 1A.

Williams, T. (1996), *Hearths of Darkness: The Family in the American Horror Film*, London: Associated University Press.

PART THREE

Movie Marketing, Branding, and Distribution

10

"Hot Profits Out of Cold Shivers!"

Horror, the First-run Market, and the Hollywood Studios, 1938 to 1942

Mark Jancovich

Douglas Gomery has argued that to start a history of Hollywood with the production of films is "to miss the point," since even "colorful movie moguls who were supposed to lord it over the California studios" were not at the heart of the system (2005, p. 2). As Gomery points out, Louis B. Mayer, MGM's studio chief and head of production, "reported—daily—to Nicholas Schenck, whose office was on Times Square, New York City, and whose constituency were the stockholders of Loew's" (ibid., p. 3). Crucially, "the core of the power of the studios" lay in their control of distribution and exhibition (ibid., p. 5). Through their ownership of the key theaters in major metropolitan areas, the Big Five—Paramount, Loew's/MGM, Twentieth Century-Fox, Warner Bros., and Radio-Keith-Orpheum (hereafter RKO)—monopolized the most lucrative audiences, taking "three quarters to seven eighths of all dollars" spent on admission (Gomery, 1996, p. 51). "It was only after they granted their own theatres first runs and soaked up as much of the box-office grosses as possible did they permit smaller independently owned theatres to scramble for the remaining bookings, sometimes months, or even years, after a film's premiere," explains Gomery (ibid.). Consequently, those production companies that did not own theaters—United Artists (hereafter UA), Universal Pictures, Columbia Pictures, and the Poverty Row outfits—were either dependent on the Big Five for access to the first-run market or were effectively locked out of these profitable venues. Such arrangements are central to an understanding of horror film production in the 1940s.

It is often claimed—even by Gomery—that horror was largely left to Universal in the 1930s and 1940s. The latter in particular is routinely dismissed as a "period of comparative infertility" (Punter, 1980, p. 347), one that "simply extends the pattern already established in the 1930s" (Tudor, 1989, p. 34), and one that was "relieved only by the undoubted but minor-key successes of the Lewton/Tourneur production team [at RKO]" (ibid.), whose productions replaced spectacular monsters with psychological studies that did not assault viewers with explicit threats but instead played on their fear of the unknown.

The problems with such accounts are numerous. First, the horror films of the 1940s did not merely represent the tail end of the 1930s cycle; they constituted a wholly new cycle that lasted from 1939 to 1946, a cycle that was shaped by quite different industrial conditions. Second, this period was hardly seen at the time as one of infertility; commentators believed they were witnessing an unprecedented boom in horror film production (see e.g. Stanley, 1944, pp. 3, 23). Third, even though many of the films were produced on low budgets by smaller companies such as Universal, Columbia, and those on Poverty Row, all of the major studios contributed to this cycle. MGM, for example, put "over $2 million" into 1945's *The Picture of Dorian Gray* ("Char.," 1945)—this at a time when the average production budget was $554,386 (Schatz, 1997, p. 172). Similarly, Val Lewton's horror films were made on medium budgets for RKO, a member of the Big Five. Thus, *Cat People* (1942) cost an estimated $134,000 (Newman, 2001, p. 13), considerably more than many of Universal's projects, where films like *Man Made Monster* and *Horror Island* (both 1941) could cost as little as $84,000 to $85,000 (Dick, 1997, p. 117), to say nothing of those made at Columbia or the Poverty Row Studios.

Accordingly, this chapter examines the industrial contexts in which RKO developed the Lewton productions. It explores how, between 1938 and 1942, various studios formulated and executed horror film production strategies; these establish the context within which RKO made *Cat People*, the commercial success of which in 1942 turned out to be something of a game-changer.[1]

---

[1] In this chapter, I pay close attention to the American trade press, particularly *Variety*, in order to gain a sense of how the target markets for various productions were understood by the industry; of how the films were seen in relation to the broader strategies of the studios, and of how the structure of the horror market as a whole was imagined.

Central to these strategies was a key distinction between films that were targeted to the lucrative first-run market and those aimed at less profitable niches, a distinction in which female moviegoers were not seen as a niche, but as central to securing the desired first-run audience. Through "a conscious effort to attract middle-class women," the industry sought to "make cinema respectable" (Grieveson, 2001, p. 65; see also Ryan, 1981). Cinematic notions of "quality" were therefore directly associated with feminine tastes, and vice versa. As the moral and cultural guardians of the middle-class family, American women offered Hollywood access to the most economically profitable audience. By contrast, the lower end of the market was associated with comparatively marginal groups such as rural populations, urban transients, the working classes, children, men, and horror fans.[2]

Consequently, and as this chapter shows, Lewton did not invent the psychological horror film. This trend in prestige horror preceded *Cat People*, as did two other key features of the Lewton films: their association with legitimate culture and their female-centeredness. A key advantage of the psychological approach to horror was its capacity to circumvent the objections of the Production Code Administration (hereafter PCA), whose opposition to, and active discouragement of, horror often rested on the films' "gruesome and brutal" content (Naylor, 2011). Psychological horror was largely immune to such charges because it eschewed visual explicitness in favor of suggestion and suspense. A second strategy of avoiding the objections of the PCA and other censorious groups was to associate horror with legitimate culture. Many prestige horror films were adaptations of literary classics, including canonized examples of women's literature, whose female-centeredness provided a point of identification for women. Lewton's first two films—*Cat People* and *I Walked with a Zombie* (1943)—were both female-centered, as was *The Seventh Victim* (1943). What is more, *I Walked with a Zombie* was associated with Charlotte Brontë's novel *Jane Eyre*.

Ultimately, this chapter shows that the studios rushed to cash in on a new fad, but that they were surprised when horror made unexpected inroads into the first-run market; a phenomenon that prompted RKO to develop the Lewton unit.

---

[2]Obviously, the middle-class family included men and children. Yet, because women were seen to represent the general middle-class family audience, it followed that, as distinct demographics, children, men, and other groups were "niche," or, to be more precise, economically marginal, audiences.

Universal and the first-run market

A lack of first-run theaters underpinned the horror strategies that Universal developed in the 1940s, a situation which forced the company to focus on other aspects of the program. As Gomery puts it, "[during the studio era,] Universal only prospered with weekly serials such as *Flash Gordon* and *Jungle Jim*, a discount newsreel service, Woody Woodpecker cartoons, feature film comedies and horror films" (1996, p. 5). Furthermore, by 1938, the studio was very different to the one that had invested in the 1930s horror cycle, having been "taken over by J. Cheever Cowdin—an investor who [...] brought ailing companies to turn them around and sell them at a profit" (Gomery, 2005, p. 158). A new administration installed at Universal in 1936 quickly shut down horror production, only to renew it in 1938 after learning of the extraordinary success that a horror triple bill comprising *Frankenstein*, *Dracula* (both 1931), and *Son of Kong* (1933) was enjoying at a small Los Angeles theater, the Regina. In response, Universal made available *Frankenstein* and *Dracula* as a nationwide double bill, promoting it to exhibitors with an advert in *Variety* that read: "THROW AWAY THE BOOKS! FOR ALL YOU EVER KNEW ABOUT SHOWMANSHIP! BECAUSE HORROR IS PAYING OFF AGAIN! Smart showmen all over the country are cashing in on it!" (1938a; capitalization in original).

The following week, *Variety* had already announced that the reissue of *Dracula* and *Frankenstein* had initiated something of a box office phenomenon. "Grosses from the key cities indicate the horror revivals are mopping up pretty nearly everywhere," noted the trade paper *Variety* (1938b). This success proved to be anything but a passing fad. Nearly a month later, the trade press was reporting a "socko response" to the horror revivals (*Variety*, 1938c), and that "Universal is side-tracking all B productions in the next four weeks to keep the stages clear for four 'A' pictures," one of which was a new horror production, *Son of Frankenstein* (1939) (*Variety*, 1938d), a film the studio promoted as a "NEW Cavalcade of Profit-Horror!" featuring the "greatest fear figures in screen history" (*Variety*, 1938e; capitalization in original).

By early 1939, *Son of Frankenstein* was promoted, alongside vehicles for the studio's top stars, as one of four key Class A productions for the "smart showman's calendar" (*Variety*, 1939a). Although *Variety* noted that the film boasted "an 'A' production layout," and that it would "attract substantial business," the trade paper stopped short of proclaiming *Son of Frankenstein* a film for general audiences ("Hobe.," 1939). Elsewhere that week, reports from key cities declared the film a "smash" (*Variety*, 1939b, p. 7), and, by August, Universal was advertising another Class A horror feature, *Tower of London*

(*Variety*, 1939d), which was also predicted to "give a good account of itself," albeit largely in "runs where pictures of this type attracts" (*Variety*, 1939f).

In 1940, however, things started to change at Universal, as the studio shifted to B horror films. The company's next horror project, *The Invisible Man Returns*, was supposed to feature "eerie situations" but "without the gruesome aspects of [its] predecessor," and to be ideally suited to the "subsequents and nabes" rather than the first-run market (*Variety*, 1940a). Although *House of the Seven Gables* (1940) was an adaptation of an "American [literary] classic" that had been "lifted far above its moderate budget classification in both production artistry and merit," the film was still only deemed fit for "the lower bracket of dualers in the keys and subsequents" (*Variety*, 1940b, p. 16a). Moreover, another film, *Black Friday* (1940), was seen to "amply satisfy addicts of this type of entertainment" rather than a general audience (*Variety*, 1940b, p. 16b). By the time *The Mummy's Hand* (1940) opened, Universal was clearly seen to be developing horror unbefitting of the first-run market; this film was dismissed as "muddled in the writing and clumsy in the production" and therefore "strictly for the lesser duals" ("Hobe.," 1940a).

The year 1941 also saw Universal release precious few Class A horror productions, and few signs of the other product with which the company has come to be associated: horror series. *Son of Frankenstein* was clearly intended as a one-off Class A production, and no plans were afoot to make new *Dracula* films. Universal did make another entry in its *Invisible Man* series, *The Invisible Woman* (1940), but this film was seen as a complete change of tack that was "played in broadest farce" ("Walt.," 1941a). With *Invisible Woman*, Universal lightened horror with comedy, thereby emulating the approach with which Paramount had achieved some success in 1939, a strategy Universal also employed with *The Black Cat*—a film dismissed for being so "poorly written" and such a "bore" that it barely even qualified as a B picture ("Char.," 1941d). *Hold that Ghost* (1941) was the only horror comedy identified as boasting first-run potential. One critic predicted that the film would "hit a merry and profitable stride in boxoffices [*sic*] of the regular runs, and rate general holdovers in the summer key bookings" ("Char.," 1941e). Yet, the financial prospects of this film rested on its status as a vehicle for one of Universal's major assets at the time, the comic duo Abbott and Costello, who had been cast "against the background of a haunted house with the usual comedic and thrill situations engendered via such a setting" (ibid.). Even Universal's "straight" horror film, *Horror Island*, was condemned as a "fourth rate low-budget mystery-and-adventure flapdoodle, poorly written, [and] sloppily produced and directed" ("Char.," 1941c).

Although Universal concentrated on cheap and shoddy horror which *Variety* believed to be destined only for fans of the genre, these films actually fared better than predicted, particularly in the first-run market. By the end of 1941, the company was encouraging exhibitors to book "that horror magic that brings you hot profits out of cold shivers!" (*Variety*, 1941d). Similarly, reports noted that exhibitors of MGM's *Dr. Jekyll and Mr. Hyde* (1941) had seen ticket sales improve when it was marketed specifically as a horror film (*Variety*, 1941a). Fox found the same with *Swamp Water* (1941) (*Variety*, 1941b).

Universal's medium-term strategy was therefore changing. This change was nowhere more apparent than in the company's signing of Lon Chaney Jnr. Although he tends to be dismissed today as a poor actor, and as evidence of a decline in standards compared to the 1930s horror stalwarts Boris Karloff and Bela Lugosi, Chaney Jnr. represented a significant investment for Universal. If the studio had hoped "to whet the curiosity as to the son's ability to follow in the footsteps of his father with this type of characterization" ("Wear.," 1941a, p. 18), Chaney had also received considerable praise for his performance as Lennie in *Of Mice and Men* (1939), which promised to imbue his horror films with a measure of cachet. It was even claimed that Chaney's "excellent work" in *Man Made Monster* suggested that "he is on his way" to "follow[ing] in the footsteps of his father" (ibid.). This film may have been accused of being "a bit incredulous for average consumption," but it was also praised for being "a well-concocted programmer" that made "no pretense of being anything but a freakish chiller" that was strictly "in the groove for the horror fans" (ibid.).

Chaney's next project, *The Wolf Man* (1941), was seen as a "dual supporter," and was praised as a "tightly knit tale of its kind, with good direction and performances by an above par assemblage of players" ("Walt.," 1941g). Even more important, however, was the claim that Chaney's character was as much a "victim" as a monster, and that the film's "dramatic" focus was on the "psychological effect of Chaney's mental and physical transitions" (ibid.), a feature that clearly suggests aspiration towards the prestigious end of the horror market, or at least a desire to produce a low-budget picture with the potential to break out of the niche market.

By 1942, Universal was developing three different types of horror film: low-budget productions that were largely dismissed as barely even adequate for the niche market; low- to medium-budget productions that were carefully constructed to convey a sense of quality and which were aimed at a general market; and big-budget prestige productions that were clearly targeted to the first-run market, although, as Gomery notes, the latter was part of a broader strategy whereby its owners "poured money into assets" such as "stars and film-makers" in order to "attract a buyer" for the studio (2005, p. 159). Furthermore, while Universal had all but abandoned the production of horror comedies, most of its horror productions were still one-off stand-alone films.

In this respect, *The Ghost of Frankenstein*, *The Mummy's Tomb*, and *Invisible Agent* (all 1942) may have been opportunistic attempts to cash in on box office trends, and to tap into the studio's reputation for such fare, but there is no evidence to suggest that they were envisaged as the first films in new series. The only calculated horror film series was a new property intended as a tie-in with a long-running radio show: Sherlock Holmes.

The Mad Doctor of Market Street (1942) was seen as an example of the first type and was accused of being "an obvious case of padding to 60 minutes" with "lines and situations [that] are often ludicrous" ("Herb.," 1943), while *Variety* wondered how "such an incredulous and wearisome tale" as *The Strange Case of Doctor RX* (1942) had even "got a front office okay" from Universal, particularly given that its "quickie schedule" was all too apparent ("Walt.," 1942c). By the time of *Night Monster* (1942), the trade press was devoting precious little time to these projects, and claimed that this particular picture "carrie[d] more horror-thrills in the title than in its footage," and that it would only "drop into supporting spots to fill out the running time where the audiences want quantity [rather than quality] on screen" ("Walt.," 1942j). Put simply, this programmer was not likely to please many people, and was unlikely even to find favor with horror fans. *The Ghost of Frankenstein* fared little better. It was described as a "drab horror tale" that "only [had] a faint resemblance" to earlier *Frankenstein* films, and one that fell short of "current film requirements" ("Walt.," 1943a).

The horror films that received some praise were therefore those with higher aspirations. *Invisible Agent* was not exactly lauded as a quality production, but it was seen as a project whose "war and spy angles" promised to generate appeal beyond the horror audience, and as one that had been realized with "sufficient levity to provide strong entertainment" ("Walt.," 1942f). It was also seen as a film to be "laughed at, and with," so much so in fact that only "hyper-critical audiences" would find fault, and it was likely to "catch plenty of bookings in the nabe and family circuits" (ibid.).

The Mystery of Marie Roget (1942) may have followed the "usual program whodunit formula" but it was also an adaptation of "an Edgar Allan Poe classic" that starred Maria Montez, whom Universal was grooming for a career in A pictures ("Walt.," 1942d). That same year, Montez had appeared in *Pardon My Sarong* (1942), a vehicle for Universal's biggest money earners of the period, Abbott and Costello, and had starred in *Arabian Nights* (1942), a spectacular Technicolor adventure from Walter Wanger, whom Universal had recently acquired to produce A features.

These pictures notwithstanding, it was the announcement of a series of Sherlock Holmes films that provoked the most positive responses (see "Walt.," 1942h). The first film in the series, *Sherlock Holmes and the Voice* of Terror (1942), was described as a "well packaged concoction [...] with suspense holding to good levels throughout" that should prove "a strong programmer of type, and due for plenty of dating in the regular runs as a supporting number" (ibid.). Nor had enthusiasm for the series declined by the release of the second entry, *Sherlock Holmes and the Secret Weapon* (1942), which was supposed to feature "action of staccato tempo" and "plenty of b.o. appeal" (*Variety*, 1942b). It was therefore the first of many Holmes films to be praised for having achieved a sense of quality in spite of their low budgets.

None of these films was deemed to be as bankable as the two other horror films that Universal developed in 1942: *Saboteur* (1942) and *Shadow of a Doubt* (1943). Both were prestige horror films, with Universal investing heavily to secure the services of director Alfred Hitchcock "on a Selznick loanout" ("Hobe.," 1942a). *Saboteur* was clearly modeled on thrillers such as *The 39 Steps* (1935) and *Foreign Correspondent* (1940), and *Variety* saw Hitchcock's direction as "expert and enormously effective," to the extent that the film would invariably "get rave reviews, play holdover engagements and clean up at the box office" (ibid.). Finally, in early 1943, Universal released *Shadow of a Doubt*, which featured a number of elements that recalled *Rebecca* (1940), and starred in the role of the central female protagonist Teresa Wright, who had appeared in the most high-profile woman's picture of the previous year, *Mrs. Miniver* (1942).

Columbia, Poverty Row, and the dilemmas of low-budget horror

If Universal had started with Class A horror productions, before reverting to B productions and then becoming more ambitious after achieving success in the first-run market, the situation was more difficult for both Columbia and the Poverty Row companies. Columbia initially fared well with low-budget programmers, but its subsequent attempts to act more ambitiously provoked a mixed response from the trade press. Alternatively, Poverty Row saw an attempt at the first-run market as representing too great a risk, and simply concentrated on low-budget programmers that the trade press treated with contempt.

Despite the economic limitations under which it operated, Columbia invested fairly heavily in putting stars into horror films. In its review of *The Man They Could Not Hang* (1939), *Variety* made specific mention of Karloff, who, it felt, had given his "usual good performance" ("Char.," 1939b). This film was judged to be a "programmer," but was also deemed to be "more than the average support" that "should do fairly well" (ibid.). The studio also tried a horror comedy, *Beware Spooks* (1939), which was seen to be "adequately satisfying as support in the family houses where broad and elemental comedy is accepted" (*Variety*, 1939e). Yet, Columbia did not expand its horror comedy output through the production of similar films. Instead, it concentrated on Karloff vehicles, such as *The Man with Nine Lives* (1940)—a film that carried "plenty of sock as a horror thriller" and that "stack[ed] up with the best screen chillers," so much so in fact that, while aimed largely at horror fans, it promised to "appease the most choosey patrons of this sort of entertainment" ("Wear.," 1940a). At this point, the studio also started to develop vehicles for Peter Lorre (see Jancovich, 2012b). *Island of Doomed Men* (1940) was clearly identified as "scare-fodder," even if it was unlikely to scare anyone except "the extremely young," Lorre's "ability to put the snake into a characterization" notwithstanding ("Art.," 1940a). Another Karloff vehicle followed, and, while it may have been aimed at niche audiences, it was still seen as a "nifty title" that was "well-geared to b.o. in the action districts, patronized by youngsters and elders who spend for this kind of thriller" ("Art.," 1940b).

By 1941, however, horror production was declining at Columbia, and the quality of its output came into question. Lorre's next project for the studio was *Face Behind the Mask* (1941), "a 'horror' picture" in which the "production, acting and story [...] are all of a fairly high order" ("Herb.," 1941). Yet, its aspirations to quality were seen as its key problem: "Cheapie grind houses with patrons predominantly male would ordinarily be the best outlet, except that audiences of this type will probably prefer a story with speedier action, and a bit less psychological study" (ibid.). Such a response was extremely positive compared to that received by Columbia's next two feature films. If it was likely that "exhibitors will have a word for '[The] Devil Commands [1941],' but it can't be used in polite society" ("Char.," 1941a), noted one reviewer, another dismissed *I Was a Prisoner On Devil's Island* (1941) as a "slipshod yarn" that would make audiences "laugh at the wrong times" ("Wear.," 1941b).

In 1942, Columbia reduced its horror output to a single film: *The Boogie Man will Get You*. This horror comedy paired Lorre and Karloff, while exploiting the latter's association with *Arsenic and Old Lace*; the film was seen to be so "reminiscent" of this Broadway hit that it "generates hearty laughs from the same premise" ("Wear.," 1942). This was not the only positive aspect of *The Boogie Man will Get You*. *Variety* claimed that, "in less skillful hands," the film would have been "merely a string of implausible events testing audience credulity," but its performers, screenwriters, and "expert direction" had produced "a crazy farce" that would prove "a strong entry to bolster dual combos" (ibid.).

While Columbia's efforts to break out of the niche market for low-budget horror met with mixed results, the Poverty Row companies harbored little desire to even attempt to adopt such an approach. These outfits did invest in on-screen talent, but their stars were usually cheaper than the likes of Karloff and Lorre. For example, where producer Sam Katzman hired Bela Lugosi for a series of low-budget films for Monogram Pictures, others cast B-listers such as Lionel Atwill, George Zucco, and John Carradine. The trade press was generally dismissive of these efforts, regarding them as so shoddy that they would even be rejected by horror fans. For example, *The Ape* (1940), a Monogram film that featured a rare Poverty Row outing for Karloff, was seen to miss "by a considerable margin," to the extent that its "weight [...] as a suspenser is nil and most of the footage is extremely boring" ("Art.," 1940c). Similarly, Monogram's Bela Lugosi film *Invisible Ghost* (1941) was described as "undoubtedly one of the feeblest pictures of the season" ("Hobe.," 1941a).

Horror comedies such as *Spooks Run Wild* (1941) tended to fare better however, in large part because they were seen to be targeted at "the juvenile trade," among which they could be expected to "find ready acceptance" ("Mort.," 1941). Yet, this response was not typically afforded Monogram's horror films. Thus, *Black Dragons* (1942), a "whodunit with horror furbelows," was accused of showing scant "respect for the average picture-goer's intelligence" ("Odec.," 1942)—a claim that was also made of 1942's *The Corpse Vanishes* ("Eddy.," 1942). Other Poverty Row companies fared little better with the trade press. *The Devil Bat* (1940) received scant attention apart from a 12-line *Variety* review, in which the picture was said to be "pretty terrible" and was predicted to "hardly [...] pass muster on even the most lowly dual situations" ("Naka.," 1941). Similarly, *The Mad Monster* (1942) was seen as "a childish almost naïve" film, whose "situations, rather than being tense, are ludicrous" ("Eddy.," 1942).

United Artists, MGM, and the prestige horror film

In contrast to Columbia, United Artists boasted a solid track record in prestige productions, to the extent that it may even be seen as a pioneer of quality horror films. In 1939, UA released *Wuthering Heights*, a "grim" and "psychological" film ("Wear.," 1939a) that was promoted on its cultural cachet, its appeal to women, and its horror content. For example, a notice placed in *Variety* announced that the film's promotional poster would be reprinted as "full page color ads in Saturday Evening Post, Collier's, Ladies Home Journal,

McCalls, Life and Cosmopolitan [...] reaching 23,000,000 homes" (*Variety*, 1939c). These magazines were aimed at middle-class readers, and several were intended specifically for women. The poster that was set to appear in these glossy publications spotlighted the literary classic on which UA's film was based ("Emily Bronte's great conflict"), horror ("The mark of Hell was in their eyes!"), and the emotional drama of protagonist Cathy's internal conflict ("I was torn by Desire [...] tortured by hate!").

This strategy was repeated the following year when UA released *Rebecca*, in many respects a prototype of the quality horror film. This 1940 picture was clearly understood as a horrific tale, as a woman's picture with literary credentials, and as a film that marked the Hollywood debut of a major overseas director in Alfred Hitchcock. While *Rebecca*'s cultural aspirations made it an "artistic success" and "one of the finest production efforts of the past year," there were worries that these aspirations made the film "too tragic and deeply psychological to hit the fancy of wide audience appeal," and there were concerns that its "b.o. lure will be limited" ("Walt.," 1940a). Nonetheless, the picture proved a "smash" (*Variety*, 1940c, p. 9), with theaters across the United States announcing that it was "one of the biggest tales in the house's history" (ibid.). It was even reported that during the 1940s there were more requests from women for *Rebecca* to be released than for any other film (ARI, 1979 [1942]).

UA also experimented with other projects. These included the prehistoric adventure *One Million B.C.* (1940)—a "corny" film that proved "a big laugh" ("Char.," 1940a)—as well as the "flesh-creepy" thriller (Crowther, 1940) *Foreign Correspondent*, which was said to feature moments of "screen terror" that have "seldom been equaled" and that "Alfred Hitchcock has so successfully learned to make pay off at the box office" ("Herb.," 1940b). However, the studio did not release any more horror films until the cycle had moved into a new gear following the commercial success of *Cat People*, partly because producer David O. Selznick hired out Hitchcock, as well as the actresses Joan Fontaine and Ingrid Bergman, for similar films, and packaged projects such as *Jane Eyre* (1943) and *The Spiral Staircase* (1945) for other studios. In addition, UA did not require a factory system that produced regularized product; ironic given its lack of first-run theaters.

Nonetheless, UA firmly established trends that other studios followed. Accordingly, MGM's first contribution to the cycle was an extravagant adaptation of "Robert Louis Stevenson's classic," *Dr. Jekyll and Mr. Hyde*. This film was not only another "psychological" horror picture, but starred Spencer Tracey, who had "developed a substantial money following" ("Flin.," 1941). It was directed by Victor Fleming, who had just helmed the hit *Gone with the Wind* (1939), and it featured a new female star from Europe in the shape of the aforementioned Bergman. These features were evidence of MGM "striving to make 'Jekyll' a 'big' film" (ibid.); and *Variety* deemed the company to have been successful when it predicted "major first runs, profitable holdovers and equally strong box office in all types of subsequent showings" (ibid.).

In spite of the success that the studio had enjoyed with the film, MGM followed *Dr. Jekyll and Mr. Hyde* with only one similar production: *Fingers at the Window* (1942), a psychological "whodunit" about a demented "ax wielder" who menaces a young woman ("Walt.," 1942b). Yet, this film was seen less as a major first-run picture than as one targeted to "mystery-inclined addicts." Like UA, MGM did not develop more horror projects until after the success of *Cat People*, when it became clear that the horror cycle was not just a passing fad, and that the genre could compete in the first-run market, at which point the studio turned to psychological, female-centered horror such as *Gaslight* (1944).

Paramount, comedy, and realism

This left Paramount, Warner Bros., and Twentieth Century-Fox to formulate strategies of their own. Paramount's first contribution to the horror cycle was *The Cat and the Canary* (1939), a highly polished horror comedy that turned Bob Hope into one of the major film stars of the decade, and inspired a host of similar fare. The film offered a careful balance of "broad comedy" and "the basic spooky atmosphere and chiller situations of John Willard's original play" ("Char.," 1939c). *The Cat and the Canary* was therefore seen as sufficiently frightening to "satisfy the mystery fans and provide spine-chilling thrills for audiences generally," as well as sufficiently amusing to "provide good entertainment for general audiences" and to avoid problems with censorious bodies such as the PCA (ibid.). What is more, this film was clearly targeted to the first-run market, where it would prove "a top programmer for upper-bracket bookings in the keys" (ibid.). Paramount followed *The Cat and the Canary* with *The Ghost Breakers* (1940). Also starring Hope, this "comedy thriller" was seen to provide "solid comedy entertainment" that would "roll up some hefty b.o. figures along the way," even though it "tend[ed] strongly to the comedy angle, with the eerie chiller sequences consuming not more than a third of the footage" ("Walt.," 1940b).

As it turned away from horror comedy, Paramount briefly flirted with a special-effects spectacular *Dr. Cyclops* (1940). The film was clearly devised as a prestige picture destined for the first-run market, but was received as a "dull effort" that was too "fantastic" to be taken seriously ("Herb.,"

1940a). Next came *The Mad Doctor* (1941), in which Basil Rathbone played a psychiatrist who exploits his profession to "marry wealthy women and then get rid of them" ("Char.," 1941b). This was clearly intended as a psychological horror film that would in part evoke *Rebecca*; however, *Variety* saw it as "poor entertainment from start to finish" (ibid.). The trade paper also complained that *The Mad Doctor*'s "90 minutes [running time] could have been cut to 60" (ibid.), an observation which implied that Paramount was unsure about the film's market; of whether it was a Class A product aimed at the first-run audience, or a B picture intended for horror fans. The year 1940 also saw the studio release a more straightforward horror project, *The Monster and the Girl*, a "weak horror picture" about brain "transplants" that was seen to have been "gleaned from similar horror screen vehicles dating back to the original 'Frankenstein'," and which was judged to be poorly suited to the "first-run Broadway theatre" at which it was being screened ("Wear.," 1941a).

Then, in 1942, Paramount developed the strategy that would come to characterize most of its horror productions for the rest of the 1940s cycle. During this period, the studio specialized in horror films that jettisoned the fantastic in favor of associations with the modern world and discourses of "realism" (Jancovich, 2012a). For example, *Double Indemnity*, *Ministry of Fear* (both 1944), and *The Lost Weekend* (1945), which now tend to be thought of as film noir, were understood at the time as horror (Jancovich, 2009b). These pictures did not play to a niche of horror fans, but were instead targeted to a general, first-run audience. This trend developed largely in response to the box office success of *This Gun for Hire* (1942)—a film remembered for making a star of Alan Ladd, but which was seen contemporaneously as a female-centered vehicle for the actress Veronica Lake. Thus, a *Variety* review opens by positioning *This Gun for Hire* in relation to Lake's previous roles, before questioning whether it stood to benefit from the first-run bookings her previous films had received (ibid.).

Where *This Gun for Hire* was seen as a first-run project, albeit one that would likely encounter "difficulties ahead," Paramount's next horror project, *Street of Chance* (1942), found favor as "a modest budget effort, yet [one] so adroitly written and deftly presented that it grips attention and concern throughout" ("Hobe.," 1942b). The film was an adaptation of a novel by Cornell Woolrich, whose stories formed the basis of a number of quality horror films that followed *Phantom Lady* (1944). *Street of Chance* features a protagonist who becomes embroiled in a "terrifying" plot involving "amnesia" and "murder," which is "told entirely through the eyes of the central character" so that "the spectator is never tipped off but finds the slow unfolding of the story as baffling and terrifying as it is for the hero" (ibid.).

Warner Bros., Twentieth Century-Fox, and the horror market

Warners initially responded to the 1940s horror cycle in a fairly predictable manner—by reworking some of its previous output. For example, *The Return of Doctor X* (1939) starred Humphrey Bogart in the role of the vicious heavy that he often played during the period, although in this film he "becomes a mass-killer" due to scientific experiments conducted by a "laboratory genius touched with madness" ("Odec.," 1939). Bogart was even said to work well in a role in which he "exudes plenty of menace and pitches a makeup that should give Boris Karloff a hot run for honors" (for a discussion of the long-standing affinities between the gangster and the horror monster see Jancovich, forthcoming). *The Return of Doctor X* also featured Warners' familiar "cub reporter who accidentally stumbled into the maze of crime and [...] proceeds [...] to unravel the whodunit" ("Odee.," 1939). However, this film was not seen as suitable for a general audience: the "average drama femme customer won't cotton to the theme," although "addicts of the gory and macabre should get a kick out" of it, noted *Variety* (ibid.).

The following year saw the release of *Devil's Island* (1939). In this grim social exposé, Karloff plays a kindly medic who is "called upon to perform a brain operation": here the horror derives from the "barbarism" of a "penal colony" ("Char.," 1940b). The production of horror films increased at Warners in 1941, as the studio became increasingly confident in its ability to tailor A pictures in a manner that promised to attract horror business. For example, *The Sea Wolf* (1941) has Edward G. Robinson playing a "dominating and cruel captain who takes fiendish delight" in the numerous "horrors" he inflicts upon others ("Walt.," 1941b). The picture was understood as both a "psychological" film and a literary adaption of a Jack London classic that promised to "sail a profitable course through the theater boxoffices [sic]" (Crowther, 1941a; "Walt.," 1941b). Also associated with horror at the time was *The Maltese Falcon* (1941), which told a story of "monstrous and logical intrigue" (Crowther, 1941b), one that was deemed to be "an A attraction" destined for "hefty grosses in all runs" and "numerous holdovers in the keys" ("Walt.," 1941f). Even *Kings Row* (1942) operated as a psychological horror film on account of sharing features with the Gothic (or paranoid) woman's film. This content is particularly apparent in the early stages of the film when attention is focused on Claude Rains' character, a "stern, awesome local physician recluse" who virtually imprisons his "doomed daughter" in their mansion—an act that leads a young man to become a "pioneering psychiatrist" ("Hobe.," 1941b). The *Kings Row* was seen to showcase the "uncanny" and a number of "gruesome phases," was understood as a literary adaptation of "Henry Bellman's widely-read novel," and was predicted to do "handsome business in first runs" (ibid.).

Warner Bros. also started to develop some of its own low-budget programmers in an effort to cash in on the market for horror that Universal had discovered. *The Smiling Ghost* (1941), for example, was "a thriller-chiller B programmer" that was expected to provide "adequate support," despite featuring the familiar "melodramatics of sliding panels and doors, cobwebbed cellar and a slinking stranger who is finally unmasked" ("Walt.," 1941d). Similarly, *The Hidden Hand* (1942) concerned "a nut who escapes from an asylum and returns to his former home, committing several murders before being apprehended by the authorities"; it was seen as a "trite horror story" for "the lower half of the duals" ("Kahn.," 1942). Finally, in *The Mysterious Doctor* (1943), "hobgoblins, headless ghosts and village idiots galore flit through a mist-blanketed English landscape" ("Wear.," 1943a). The film was nevertheless derided as "strictly a witches brew concocted to scare the pants off little Johnny [...] at a special Saturday matinee" (ibid.).

Twentieth Century-Fox initially tested the waters with horror comedy in the form of *The Gorilla* (1939), another adaptation of an "original play and two previous film versions" that combined "broad slapstick, surprise situations and eerie chills," and was seen as a "good programmer" that might "catch a few top spots" in "the keys," but mainly "as an adequate supporting attraction" ("Char.," 1939a). However, this studio's key contributions to the 1940s cycle were two Sherlock Holmes films (starring Basil Rathbone and Nigel Bruce) that were marketed and reviewed as horror films, and were associated with literary classics. As a result, both pictures were seen as high-quality programmers that had been made to capitalize on the new horror cycle and to attract general audiences. Accordingly, the first of these films, *The Hound of the Baskervilles* (1939), was seen as "a startling mystery-chiller developed along logical lines without resort to implausible situations and overtheatrics," one that was destined for "bookings on top spots of key dualers," even if this was largely at venues "that attract thriller-mystery patronage" ("Wear.," 1939a). If *Variety* referred to *The Hound of the Baskervilles* as a "mystery-chiller," as a "chiller-mystery," and as a straight "chiller," it identified *The Adventures of Sherlock Holmes* (1939) as "considerably better than" its predecessor ("Wear.," 1939b), giving no sense that the audience for these pictures would be limited to "mystery devotees," but only that the mysteries were "not made too absurd or obvious" to put off fans of the genre (ibid.).

Fox did not immediately follow the two Sherlock Holmes films with any major horror productions, although the studio did not abandon the genre entirely. *Charlie Chan at the Wax Museum* (1940) mixed some horror elements into the "once-popular series" ("Hobe.," 1940b), while another Charlie Chan mystery, *Dead Men Tell* (1941), placed the "familiar ingredients of a couple of murders and a mystery" against a "backdrop of eerie situations" and "weird settings" ("Walt.," 1941b). In addition to these programmers, 1941 saw the release of *Man Hunt*, a film which reviewers strongly associated with horror, and one that was very much in the vein of Hitchcock's *Foreign Correspondent*, although in this case it is Fritz Lang—another horror specialist—whose "direction maintains excellent suspense" ("Walt.," 1941c). If the trade press worried about the film's lack of "woman appeal," *Man Hunt* was still seen to have been the subject of "'A' production mounting throughout" (ibid.).

The studio also released *I Wake Up Screaming* in 1941. Reviewed in *Variety* as "Hot Spot," this film was regarded as "an exception to the rule" that "most murder mysteries are B's regardless of budget," and as "first rate entertainment [that] may be depended upon to [per]form better than average to very good business," thanks to its "femme cast names" ("Char.," 1941f). A murder-mystery with a female investigator (Betty Grable), *I Wake Up Screaming* was associated with horror, in part because it featured a psychologically disturbed killer; an association that Fox evidently nurtured by replacing the ambiguous title of *The Hot Spot* with the unequivocal *I Wake Up Screaming*.

Fox extended this practice to its 1941 release of *Swamp Water*. This film was also associated with horror, and, while trade reviews made nothing of this angle, the studio itself actively encouraged exhibitors to sell *Swamp Water* as a horror picture. Fox took out a double-page spread in *Variety* that boasted the tagline "Terror is Terrific", and an image of a skull (*Variety*, 1941c). The ad also featured promotional artwork that referred to a "nameless terror" and challenged audiences with the familiar come-on: "We dare you to see this picture and dare you not to shudder!" (ibid.). In February 1942, *Variety* reported that the film was doing strong business, due to being marketed "as a horror picture" (*Variety*, 1941a).

Well aware of the inroads that B horror was making into the first-run market, by late 1941, Fox had responded with two distinct strategies. First, the studio took "a leaf from Paramount's experience with Bob Hope" by placing its own "wisecracking and quip-dropping comedy film star," Milton Berle, in a similar vehicle: 1942's *Whispering Ghosts* ("Walt.," 1942j). Second, it produced two moderately budgeted programmers. The first was a reworking of *The Hound of the Baskervilles* entitled *The Undying Monster* (1942), in which Scotland Yard is "dispatched to investigate" when "a phantom mysteriously attacks [two victims] on the fog-bound moor" shrouding "an old English manse" (ibid.) The second, *Dr. Renault's Secret* (1942), concerned "an ape transformed into a man through the brain and tissue transplantation experiments of anthropologist—surgeon George Zucco" (ibid.). It was also seen as an "attempt to provide thrill-chills for horror customers" (ibid.).

From prestige to restraint at RKO

It is in relation to the strategies employed by all of these companies that we can best understand the situation at RKO. Although the horror films Val Lewton produced at this studio are often referred to as low-budget efforts, this is not strictly true. RKO was certainly struggling financially in the 1940s, but the studio was still one of the Big Five that owned first-run theaters. Accordingly, its first contribution to the horror cycle was not a cut-price programmer, but *The Hunchback of Notre Dame* (1939), "a super thriller-chiller" that boasted "vivid and gruesome horror" and a "background of elaborate medieval pageantry" (*Variety*, 1939g); traits that demonstrated a "lavish outlay in costs for elaborate sets and thousands of extras for the mob scenes" (ibid.). This film was therefore an example of one of the most revered versions of the first-run, prestige film: the big-budget, historical spectacular. What is more, the picture was based on two prestigious properties: a classic novel and a classic silent era motion picture. *Variety* even went so far as to anoint *The Hunchback of Notre Dame* "one of the greatest horror tales of literature" (ibid.). Arguing that this combination of factors would ensure "ready-made audience interest," and not just among horror fans, the trade paper observed that the film "carries strong dramatic ingredients for mass audience appeal and will roll up healthy grosses at the ticket windows" (ibid.).

RKO did not rush to follow *The Hunchback of Notre Dame* with big-budget horror films, turning to other strategies instead. For example, the studio produced a moderately priced picture with Peter Lorre, *The Stranger on the Third Floor* (1940), which was widely condemned for not having "done right by Peter Lorre," who was "so subordinated to the story that his character amounts to a bit" part ("Wear.," 1940b). It was also dismissed as "too arty for average audiences and too humdrum for others," so that, its medium budget notwithstanding, the film "doubtless cost more than necessary," due to its makers wasting resources on "fancy camera effects, lighting and trick dubbing" that did not save it from being a "desultory 'B'" (ibid.). RKO then emulated Paramount's strategy of combining comic entertainment with "eerie thrills" for "general audience requirements" by producing *You'll Find Out* (1940) ("Walt.," 1940c). This film also featured Lorre, this time alongside Karloff and Lugosi, in "a strong setup of sinister villainy" that provided "plenty of trouble and conflict for" its star, the band leader and radio personality Kay Kyser, "to combat" ("Walt.," 1940c).

RKO's next horror production was also aimed squarely at the first-run market. Intended to capitalize on the box office success of *Rebecca*, *Suspicion* (1941) was a psychological horror film that not only used the comparable storyline of "a wife's development of hysteria" on the back of the "real or imagined criminal tendencies" of her husband, but also starred *Rebecca*'s female lead Joan Fontaine, and was helmed by its director Alfred Hitchcock ("Walt.," 1941e). For these reasons, *Suspicion* was predicted to be "due for critical attention and strong women patronage in the key runs" (ibid.).

By 1942, RKO was in financial crisis. It had invested heavily in prestige productions and expensive creative talent, such as the radio sensation and "spectacular genius of the show world" Orson Welles (Lasky, 1984). However, this strategy had failed to turn around the company's ailing fortunes. Charles Koerner was appointed as new production chief, and was given the task of changing studio policy in a manner that he dubbed "[s]howmanship in place of genius" (ibid.). RKO still had its sights set on the first-run market, but now it prioritized fiscal responsibility and the marketability of its product over the demands of high-cost talent.

The effect of RKO's change in policy was seen in its horror films. Welles—who had long been associated with horror even prior to his infamous 1938 *The War of the Worlds* broadcast (see Jancovich, 2009a)—followed *Citizen Kane* (1941) and *The Magnificent Ambersons* (1942) with *Journey into Fear* (1943). If his first two films had contained elements of horror in terms of their style and subject matter, then Welles' "third release from RKO" was clearly understood at the time as a horror project and little more than "a program meller that will garner most of its plays as dual supporter" ("Walt.," 1942g). In fact, RKO's wrangles with Welles resulted in the release of *Journey into Fear* being pushed back from late 1942 to early 1943, so that it came out after the film that would transform the industry's approach to horror.

In November 1942, *Variety* reviewed a small RKO picture called *Cat People*, a film that summed up the studio's ambitions perfectly. On the one hand, *Cat People* was a female-centered "psychological" horror film: "a weird drama of thrill-chill caliber, with developments of surprises confined to psychological and mental reactions rather than transformation to grotesque and marauding characters for visual impact on audiences" ("Walt.," 1942k). On the other hand, the film was clearly devised for "exploitation-minded exhibs" who would "have a good subject here to play with to hypo b.o. returns" (ibid.). Rather than being a low-budget product, *Cat People* was "well-made on a *moderate* budget [emphasis added]" and, despite being "good supporting entertainment of its type," the film was still seen as well suited to "the regular runs" that were likely to find an audience beyond devotees of horror (ibid.).

The Lewton films were not low-budget ventures but moderately priced productions that were deliberately positioned between the cut-price productions popularized by Universal and the period's big-budget prestige pictures. In turning to psychological films, Lewton and RKO were not introducing something new to horror but were associating themselves with the lavish, respectable horror films of the day. After all, RKO had hired Lewton because he had worked with Selznick, not only as a script editor on *Rebecca* but also in developing another psychological horror film for the mega-producer: *Jane Eyre*. Lewton also filled his unit with one-time Selznick associates, such as the scriptwriter DeWitt Bodeen who had collaborated with Lewton on *Jane Eyre*, and the director Jacques Tourneur, with whom Lewton had worked on *A Tale of Two Cities* (1935).

If *Cat People* can be seen as a veritable hybrid of Universal's *The Wolf Man* and Selznick's own female-centered, psychological, artistically ambitious horror films, Lewton would effectively make his own version of *Jane Eyre* the following year with *I Walked with a Zombie*, while churning out a range of similar projects: *The Leopard Man* (1943), *The Seventh Victim*, and *The Ghost Ship* (1943). The trade press clearly recognized Lewton's production model. Where *Variety* saw *I Walked with a Zombie* as failing "to measure up to the horror title" due to being "overcrowded with trite dialogue and ponderous acting" ("Wear.," 1943b), the *Motion Picture Herald* accused the film of being pretentious, observing that its "off screen narrative by a woman, à la *Rebecca*" had provoked "titters" of laughter in the audience ("V.K.," 1943).

The Leopard Man was seen to follow a "regulation formula for generating audience suspense," but also as the latest in the "group of program mystery-thrillers" that RKO was hoping "would prove profitable for both the producer and the theatres following 'Cat People'" ("Walt.," 1943b). If this film was expected to "fall far short" of its predecessor, it was still deemed "passable fare for general audiences" rather than just "horror addicts" (ibid.). However, *Variety* concluded that *The Seventh Victim* "hasn't a chance" due to a "poor script," which even "the occasional good performance can't offset" ("Kahn.," 1943). It was therefore understood as a "minor dualer" and as "totally unbelievable hocus-pocus about a strange Greenwich coterie" (ibid.). Lewton's next project, *The Ghost Ship*, may have lacked a female-centered narrative but was nevertheless concerned with "psychological struggle," and harbored cultural aspirations that "evidently aimed for a Joseph Conrad groove," even if it was seen as a failure that "never gets started so couldn't jell" ("Donn.," 1943).

Conclusion

The early development of the 1940s horror cycle was shaped by the studios' relationships to the first-run market. After a brief period in which it produced Class A features, Universal turned to programmers that were largely targeted to niche audiences; a strategy imitated by Columbia and by the Poverty Row outfits. In contrast, for a short time, UA and MGM invested heavily in a small number of prestige horror pictures before abandoning production of such fare until after the commercial success of *Cat People*. Most of the studios seemed to expect the first-run horror market to dry up fairly quickly after 1939, but Universal's low-budget programmers performed better than expected, even in first-run markets. By 1941 and 1942, then, both Universal and Columbia had started to develop a number of culturally ambitious horror properties, whereas UA and MGM backed away from the cycle. *Dr Jekyll and Mr. Hyde* was MGM's only significant contribution to it, and UA did not produce any horror films in-house after *Rebecca*.

These developments left Paramount, Warner Bros., Fox, and RKO to develop their own strategies. Where both Warners and Fox started to produce programmers, Paramount turned to an influential series of horror films that jettisoned the fantastic and supernatural, and RKO devised a hybrid of Universal's low-budget properties and Selznick's prestige horror. Like Universal's, RKO's films exceeded expectations, demonstrating even more emphatically than Universal's films had done that a first-run audience existed for horror films. This development would profoundly change the strategy that all of the other major studios implemented from 1943 to 1946. But that, as they say, is another story.

References

ARI (1979 [1942]), "ARI Report 163, Princeton 25 July 1942," in *Gallup Looks at the Movies: Audience Research Reports 1940–1950*, Delaware: Scholarly Resources.
"Art." (1940a), "Film Reviews," *Variety*, June 5, p. 14.
—(1940b), "Film Reviews," *Variety*, October 2, p. 12.
—(1940c), "Film Reviews," *Variety*, November 6, p. 18.
"Char." (1939a), "Film Reviews," *Variety*, May 24, p. 14.
—(1939b), "Film Reviews," *Variety*, September 27, p. 14.
—(1939c), "Film Reviews," *Variety*, November 1, p. 14.
—(1940a), "Film Reviews," *Variety*, May 1, pp. 18, 20.
—(1940b), "Film Reviews," *Variety*, July 17, p. 16.
—(1941a), "Film Reviews," *Variety*, February 19, p. 16.

—(1941b), "Film Reviews," *Variety*, March 5, p. 16.
—(1941c), "Film Reviews," *Variety*, April 2, p. 16.
—(1941d), "Film Reviews," *Variety*, April 30, p. 16.
—(1941e), "Film Reviews," *Variety*, July 30, pp. 18, 20.
—(1941f), "Film Reviews," *Variety*, October 22, p. 16.
—(1945), "Film Reviews," *Variety*, March 7, p. 20.
Crowther, B. (1940), "The Screen: At the Rivoli," *New York Times*, August 28, p. 15.
—(1941a), "The Screen: Edward G. Robinson Appears as Jack London's Sadistic 'Sea Wolf' at Strand," *New York Times*, March 22, p. 20.
—(1941b), "'Maltese Falcon', A Fast Mystery-thriller with Quality and Charm at the Strand," *New York Times*, October 4, p. 18.
Dick, B. F. (1993), *The Merchant Prince of Poverty Row: Harry Cohn of Columbia Pictures*, Lexington: University Press of Kentucky.
—(1997), *City of Dreams: The Making and Remaking of Universal Pictures*, Lexington: University of Kentucky Press.
"Donn." (1943), "Film Reviews," *Variety*, December 29, p. 8.
"Eddy." (1942), "Film Reviews," *Variety*, June 3, pp. 9, 24.
"Flin." (1941), "Film Reviews," *Variety*, July 23, p. 8.
—(1942), "Film Reviews," *Variety*, March 18, pp. 8, 25.
Gomery, D. (1996), "The Economics of the Horror Film," in J. B. Weaver III and R. Tamborini (eds) *Horror Films: Current Research on Audience Preferences and Reactions*, New York: Routledge.
—(2005), *The Hollywood Studio System*, London: British Film Institute.
Grieveson, L. (2001), "A Kind of Recreative School for the Whole Family: Making Cinema Respectable," 1907–1909," *Screen*, 42.1: 64–76.
"Herb." (1940a), "Film Reviews," *Variety*, March 6, p. 16.
—(1940b), "Film Reviews," *Variety*, August 28, p. 16.
—(1941), "Film Reviews," *Variety*, February 12, p. 14.
—(1942), "Film Reviews," *Variety*, January 7, p. 44.
"Hobe." (1939), "Film Reviews," *Variety*, January 18, p. 12.
—(1940a), "Film Reviews," *Variety*, September 25, p. 15.
—(1940b), "Film Reviews," *Variety*, October 2, p. 12.
—(1941a), "Film Reviews," *Variety*, May 14, p. 18.
—(1941b), "Film Reviews," *Variety*, December 24, p. 8.
—(1942a), "Film Reviews," *Variety*, April 29, p. 8.
—(1942b), "Film Reviews," *Variety*, September 30, p. 8
Jancovich, M. (2009a), "Shadows and Bogeymen: Horror, Stylization and the Critical Reception of Orson Welles during the 1940s," *Participations*, 6.1. Available online at http://www.participations.org/Volume%206/Issue%201/jancovich.htm (accessed August 21, 2013).
—(2009b), "'Thrills and Chills': Horror, The Woman's Film and the Origins of Film Noir," *New Review of Film and Television*, 7.2: 157–71.
—(2012a), "'Terrifyingly Real': Psychology, Realism and Generic Transformation in the Demise of the 1940s Horror Cycle," *European Journal of American Culture*, 31.1: 25–39.
—(2012b), "'With Conrad Veidt and Peter Lorre on their Side': German Stars, the Psychological Film and 1940s Horror," *Studies in European Cinema*, 9.2/3: 131–42.

—(forthcoming), "'The Murderer's Mind': Edward G. Robinson, Humphrey Bogart and the 1940s Horror Film," in K. Woofter, C. EllBé and M. DeGiglio-Bellemare (eds) *Fragments of the Monster: Recovering Forties Horror*.
"Kahn." (1942), "Film Reviews," *Variety*, September 23, p. 18.
—(1943), "Film Reviews," *Variety*, August 18, p. 26.
Lasky, B. (1984), *RKO: The Biggest Little Major of the Them All*, Englewood Cliffs, NJ: Prentice-Hall.
"Mort." (1941), "Film Reviews," *Variety*, November 5, p. 8.
"Naka." (1941), "Film Reviews," *Variety*, January 22, p. 24.
Naylor, A. (2011), "'A Horror Picture at this Time is a Very Hazardous Undertaking': Did British and American Censorship End the 1930s Horror Cycle?," *Irish Journal of Gothic and Horror Studies*, 9. Available online at http://irishgothichorrorjournal.homestead.com/1930shorroban.html (accessed August 21, 2013).
Newman, K. (2001), *Cat People*, London: British Film Institute.
"Odec." (1939), "Film Reviews," *Variety*, November 29, p. 14.
—(1942), "Film Reviews," *Variety*, April 29, p. 8.
Punter, D. (1980), *The Literature of Terror: A History of Gothic Fictions from 1765 to the Present*, London: Longmans.
Ryan, M. P. (1981), *Cradle of the Middle Class: The Family in Oneida County, New York, 1790–1920*, Cambridge: Cambridge University Press.
Schatz, T. (1997), *Boom and Bust: American Cinema in the 1940s*, Berkeley: University of California Press.
Stanley, F. (1944), "Hollywood Shivers," *New York Times*, May 28, pp. 3, 23.
Tudor, A. (1989), *Monsters and Mad Scientists: A Cultural History of the Horror Movie*, Oxford: Blackwell.
"V.K." (1943), "Horror Story," *Motion Picture Herald*, March 20, p. 1214.
Variety (1938a), Untitled ad, October 12, p. 14.
—(1938b), "'Horror' Pic Revivals, Chiefly Dualed, Big B.O.; U's Fresh Crop," October 19, p. 6.
—(1938c), "Horror Great $12,500 in Balto," November 9, p. 8.
—(1938d), "Gangway for the A's," November 30, p. 5.
—(1938e), Untitled ad, December 14, p. 28.
—(1939a), Untitled ad, January 4, p. 49.
—(1939b), "Chi Has Marquee Lure and B.O.; House-'Frankenstein' Smash 22G," January 18, p. 7.
—(1939c), Untitled ad, March 22, p. 21.
—(1939d), Untitled ad, August 23, p. 17.
—(1939e), "Film Reviews," October 25, p. 11.
—(1939f), "Film Reviews," November 22, p. 14.
—(1939g), "Film Reviews," December 20, p. 14.
—(1940a), "Film Reviews," January 17, p. 14.
—(1940b), "Film Reviews," March 13, p. 16a.
—(1940c), "'Rebecca' Double-Checka $115,000 on B'Way," April 9, p. 9.
—(1941a), "United Detroit again 'Horrors' up A Metro Pic and Improves the B.O.: 'Jekyll-Hyde' Bally a la Crawford," September 10, p. 12.
—(1941b), Untitled ad, November 5, pp. 12–13.
—(1941c), Untitled ad, November 19, p. 17.

—(1941d), Untitled ad, December 10, p. 12.
—(1942a), "Chatter," February 11, p. 47.
—(1942b), "Film Reviews," *Variety*, December 30, p. 23.
"Walt." (1940a), "Film Reviews," *Variety*, March 27, p. 17.
—(1940b), "Film Reviews," *Variety*, June 12, p. 14.
—(1940c), "Film Reviews," *Variety*, November 20, p. 16.
—(1941a), "Film Reviews," *Variety*, January 1, p. 14.
—(1941b), "Film Reviews," *Variety*, March 26, pp. 16, 18.
—(1941c), "Film Reviews," *Variety*, June 11, p. 16.
—(1941d), "Film Reviews," *Variety*, August 13, p. 8.
—(1941e), "Film Reviews," *Variety*, September 24, p. 8.
—(1941f), "Film Reviews," *Variety*, October 1, p. 9.
—(1941g), "Film Reviews," *Variety*, December 17, p. 8.
—(1942a), "Film Reviews," *Variety*, March 4, p. 8.
—(1942b), "Film Reviews," *Variety*, March 18, p. 8.
—(1942c), "Film Reviews," *Variety*, April 1, p. 8.
—(1942d), "Film Reviews," *Variety*, April 8, p. 8.
—(1942e), "Film Reviews," *Variety*, April 22, p. 8.
—(1942f), "Film Reviews," *Variety*, August 5, p. 27.
—(1942g), "Film Reviews," *Variety*, August 8, p. 27.
—(1942h), "Film Reviews," *Variety*, September 9, p. 14.
—(1942i), "Film Reviews," *Variety*, October 14, p. 8.
—(1942j), "Film Reviews," *Variety*, October 21, p. 8.
—(1942k), "Film Reviews," *Variety*, November 18, p. 8.
—(1943a), "Film Reviews," *Variety*, January 13, p. 8.
—(1943b), "Film Reviews," *Variety*, May 3, p. 16.
"Wear." (1939a) "Film Reviews," *Variety*, March 29, p. 14.
—(1939b), "Film Reviews," *Variety*, September 6, p. 14.
—(1940a), "Film Reviews," *Variety*, May 1, p. 18.
—(1940b), "Film Reviews," *Variety*, September 4, p. 18.
—(1941a), "Film Reviews," *Variety*, March 26, p. 18.
—(1941b), "Film Reviews," *Variety*, July 30, p. 20.
—(1942), "Film Reviews," *Variety*, October 11, p. 8.
—(1943a), "Film Reviews," *Variety*, February 24, p. 14.
—(1943b), "Film Reviews," *Variety*, March 17, p. 23.

11

Strange Enjoyments

The Marketing and Reception of Horror in the Civil Rights Era Black Press

Mikal J. Gaines

In June 1965, the *Chicago Defender* newspaper featured a short column entitled "Inquiring Photographer," in which five black moviegoers answered a decidedly loaded question: "What is the most enjoyable movie you have ever seen?" (1965, p. 13). Most of the respondents made predictable choices, such as the biblical epic *The Robe* (1953) or the Sidney Poitier vehicle *Lilies in the Field* (1963). Apart, that is, from an accountant named Lawrence Jones who confessed: "'The Tales of Edgar Allan Poe' was the best flicker I have seen. Maybe it's because I like the horror and terror that goes along with the sinister. I am not violent or weird, out [sic] these type [sic] of movies hold a strange enjoyment for me" (ibid.). Jones' tone was understandably defensive; he seemed to sense that his desire for "these type of movies [sic]" raised suspicions about his character that an affinity to another genre would not have done. The typographical error that substitutes "out" for "but" in his answer only heightens this tension, creating a slippage upon which narrating spectatorial pleasure essentially signals his "coming out" as a horror fan. Yet, Jones was not as alone in his "strange enjoyment" as he may have thought.

The film to which Jones referred is better known as *Tales of Terror* (1962), the fourth Edgar Allen Poe adaptation that Roger Corman produced for

American International Pictures (hereafter AIP).[1] Between the mid-1950s and the late 1960s, lowbrow horror films were among the most prominently advertised in black newspapers, a pattern which suggests a consistent black audience for such fare, and one which indicates that the film industry actively courted this audience even though it marginalized blacks on and off the screen. In her survey of black representations in American horror, Robin Means Coleman also draws attention to this marketing trend (2011). She notes that newspapers like the *Chicago Defender*, the *New York Amsterdam News*, and the *Los Angeles Sentinel* featured articles on, and advertisements for, horror films so frequently that they appeared to carry a "favored status in Black communities" (ibid., p. 109). This favored status is surprising both because of horror's problematic treatment of blackness and because it coincides with the height of what Jacquelyn Dowd Hall has called the "long civil rights movement" (2005); Hall expands the dominant narrative of the movement, which is typically book-ended by Brown vs. Board of Education (1954) and the 1964 Civil Rights Act, to include earlier Leftist labor protests and ongoing transnational struggles for liberation (ibid.).

Advertisements, publicity stills, and other marketing materials which appeared in black newspapers during the period reveal that horror's appeal for black audiences ran along multiple axes. At least one of these axes concerned the increased visibility of the abject body both in the films themselves and in the popular discourse surrounding civil rights. Black horror film spectators would have found themselves in the precarious position of having to reconcile fictional images of bestial black monsters, innocent white maidens, and virtuous white heroes with very real examples of black bodily abjection such as the lynching of Emmett Till (for discussion of the concept of abjection see Kristeva, 1982; Lake Crane, 1994). This chapter begins to explore the tension surrounding the ways in which horror marketing addressed black spectators, by analyzing two images from a mid-1950s issue of the *Chicago Defender*. I then turn to the 1960s in order to examine how racial mythologies persisted in horror marketing, and to consider how black spectators may have used the genre as part of a collective exercise in self-mastery. In particular, the content and marketing of William Castle's films incorporated and anticipated evolving modes of black spectatorship by encouraging highly participatory viewing practices. These practices disrupted bourgeois patterns of silent, contemplative consumption (see Levine, 1988), thereby encouraging black spectators

---

[1] Corman's Poe adaptations included *House of Usher* (1960), *Pit and the Pendulum* (1961), *Premature Burial* (1962), *Tales of Terror* (1962), *The Haunted Palace*, *The Raven* (both 1963), *The Mask of the Red Death*, and *The Tomb of Ligeia* (both 1964) (for detailed discussion of how AIP tried to use these films to improve its reputation see McGee, 1996, pp. 198–200).

to approach horror on recreational terms. Finally, I investigate how horror marketing tried to reach out to black spectators with promises of graphic sex, violence, and other spectacles of excess associated with lowbrow "body genres" (Williams, 1991). It needs to be stressed that horror did not operate within a representational vacuum, but existed in conversation with a network of genre films that trafficked in much of the same rhetoric.

By examining specific instances of horror marketing, I hope to gain a deeper understanding of how black audiences perceived the larger world of cinema around them, and how black media facilitated a dialog about the movies while being used to sell a product that had rarely been conceived with black spectators in mind. Most studies of race and the American horror film have focused on issues of representation, and how this genre has reflected and even attempted to resolve certain socio-cultural anxieties about race (see e.g. Bruce, 2001; Donaldson, 2011; Coleman, 2011). While contributing to our understanding of horror's relationships to racial questions, this approach does not account for the industrial forces that have influenced the terms under which audiences actually encountered the films. Granted, the language and images that were used to market horror to black spectators during the civil rights era—just like much of the content of the films themselves—were sexist and racist. But these hooks also appear to have attracted those audiences that should have been most offended by them, thereby prompting us to question their potential appeal. Accordingly, this chapter examines the marketing tactics employed in black newspapers as part of an economic strategy and as rhetorical cues that audiences could interpret in a variety of ways. Ultimately, I would like to encourage deeper consideration of how the notion of black spectatorship influenced the marketing—and also the content—of horror films during this important period in the genre's development.

Monsters, maidens, and anti-miscegenation

At the bottom of a March 1956 page of the *Chicago Defender* was printed a stand-alone picture of a dark-skinned, bug-eyed monster with phallic horns protruding from its head and an unconscious white woman lying in its arms (1956b). This image, which was taken from Corman's fourth film *The Day the World Ended* (1955), echoed the racial iconography found in many science fiction and horror films of the period, from *The Day the Earth Stood Still* (1951) to *Forbidden Planet* (1956) and *Invasion of the Saucer Men* (1957). All of these films featured shots of a helpless white woman in the clutches of a non-white "monster." Coleman even goes so far as to read

The Creature from the Black Lagoon (1954) as "an obviously metaphorically raced, anti-miscegenation film" that foreshadows the 1955 lynching of Emmett Till (2011, p. 98; see also Gonder, 2003, pp. 33–4; Gonder, 2004). The still draws attention to itself because there were no other references to movies on the page, and because of its unmistakable racial connotations. The brief caption below it reads: "BEAUTEOUS Lori Nelson is shown being carried to her doom by terrifying monster in 'The Day the World Ended', horror film starting Friday at the Regal" (*Chicago Defender*, 1956b; capitalization in original). Black spectators would no doubt have been familiar with the image's racial subtext of white womanhood threatened by monstrous Others. This mythology had crystallized in the infamous "Gus" sequence in D. W. Griffith's *Birth of a Nation* (1915), and was reinforced by much American visual culture thereafter; posters for *King Kong* (1933) and even some anti-Japanese propaganda produced during World War II used similar imagery.[2]

Upon closer inspection however, the still is not quite the stand-alone image that it first appears to be. A poetic juxtaposition found in the page layout situates Nelson and her monster in a column next to a "Bronze Beauty": the Nigerian-born Londoner Felicia Oladijo (*Chicago Defender*, 1956a, p. 17). As opposed to the doomed, captive image of Nelson, Oladijo is pictured alone and returns the camera's gaze with a warm smile. She even hoped to one day become "a cabaret singer on order of America's Ella Fitzgerald," we are told (ibid.). That these two images—one of white feminine beauty in peril and the other of black feminine beauty confident and lauded—appear on the same page is not the exceptional aspect of their positioning. On the contrary, it is the fact that these two images are allowed to occupy the same representational space without canceling each other out. The "Bronze Beauty's" presence neither short-circuits the incendiary nature of the Corman image, nor does it escape its own affectedness: Oladijo's pose is far too mannered and she was experiencing her success abroad in what may well have seemed a world away for the *Chicago Defender*'s readership in Chicago and other areas where the paper circulated.[3] Both images represented exercises in myth-making; condensed versions of opposing albeit familiar narratives that

---

[2] The myth of the "black beast rapist" dates back to Reconstruction and gathered momentum during the turn of the twentieth century (see Wood, 2001). The public exchange between Rebecca Latimer Felton and Alexander Manly, which helped to incite a 1898 riot in Wilmington, NC, provides one of the most salient demonstrations of how collective violence has been mobilized around the mythology of sanctified white womanhood. As Latimer notoriously claimed: "if it takes a lynching to protect woman's dearest possession from drunken, ravening human beasts—then I say lynch a thousand a week if it becomes necessary" (Felton, 2002, p. 411; see also Dower, 1993).

[3] More than two-thirds of the *Defender*'s readership was located outside Chicago (see PBS).

were being directed to black spectators at a moment of dramatic upheaval in the dominant social order.

Other discontinuities emerge from these two images. Nelson's beauty, for example, ceases to function as a self-evident, independent phenomenon and reveals itself as mutually constituted by the monster's ugliness. Beauty, it would seem, very much needs her beast. Nelson herself also inhabits a more paradoxical rhetorical position, symbolizing sexual vulnerability but incapable of expressing self-possessed sexual desire. She exists mostly as a cipher that engenders violence by spurring white patriarchal forces into action to "save" her from the monster. The voice-over narrator from the film's theatrical trailer made the sexual nature of this threat explicit: "A monster such as the eyes of man has never before seen, killing one-by-one each of the few remaining men [and] hunting the most beautiful of the remaining women to take as his mate." Most troubling of all, the image of Nelson loses none of its power for being rooted in fiction. The image in fact gains a clarifying power by resisting a clear connection between Nelson and any "real" woman. In contrast, the "real" picture of Oladijo smiling, with its aspirational claims about a future singing career, does little to acknowledge the hazards which black women actually faced. Hers is ironically an image of black beauty unburdened, one that favors a narrative of mobility and agency over immobility and powerlessness.

It is difficult to forget that the audience for these two images comprised the same *Chicago Defender* readership that only six months earlier bore witness to pictures of Till's corpse—his mangled body served as an undeniable reminder of the dangers of racist sexual mythology (see Hudson-Weems, 2006, p. 6). When black spectators saw these images, was Corman's science fiction monster haunted by the specter of Till's abject frame? Did the image of Nelson's white, girlish innocence recall that of Carolyn Bryant, the woman at which Till had purportedly whistled, and whose honor needed to be violently defended? And did the insertion of the "Bronze Beauty" disturb this familiar triangulation of animalistic black masculinity, fragile white femininity, and white patriarchy in crisis? These questions are impossible to answer with any real certainty, but they nevertheless illuminate some of the tensions that black spectators may have experienced while being hailed by horror marketing materials. Greeted with rhetoric that coded monstrosity in racial terms, it is unlikely that they could have ignored the resonances between horror films and the often ugly realities of black social, political, and civic life. The publicity still for Corman's monster movie typifies a broader anxiety in the ways horror films addressed black audiences, a mode that continued to rely on gothic iconography such as the "maiden in flight" and the monstrous racial Other in spite of changes that were occurring in the national racial landscape.[4] The "Bronze Beauty's" presence suggests that these familiar figures could also be mediated by other images and narratives which black communities were producing about themselves.

Hurled into a 1960s mood

Discussion about horror in black newspapers continued throughout the second half of the 1950s and into the 1960s. A May 1960 publicity piece printed in the *Chicago Defender* exclaimed: "Triple Horror Films Electrify Fans at Regal" (1960, p. 16; see also Coleman, 2011, p. 109). It was a somewhat misleading title inasmuch as only two of the movies in question, the Corman-directed horror comedy *A Bucket of Blood* (1959) and the 1959 creature feature *Attack of the Giant Leeches* (AKA *Demon of the Swamp*), could really be described as horror films. The genre's popularity with black audiences was apparently strong enough to warrant mischaracterizing the contemplative wartime drama *Orders to Kill* (1958) as "a shocking tale of terror that adds to the shivering impetus of the other two films" (*Chicago Defender*, 1960, p. 16). To be fair, *A Bucket of Blood* is not exactly a straight horror film either; its dark humor makes it a clear tonal precursor to Corman's *The Little Shop of Horrors* (1960). Trailers for the latter, as well as for *Attack of the Giant Leeches*, again featured white women under attack from monsters, although each to very different effect. The trailer to the former focused on the protagonist Seymour Krelboyne (Jonathan Haze) acquiescing to the whims of his "master"—a talking plant with a taste for human flesh. Black spectators would probably have recognized the irony in seeing a white man reduced to the status of a slave, and then coerced into feeding his own kind to an alien master. Another scene in which Seymour encounters a prostitute who unknowingly offers herself as a meal for the monster pushes the irony even further by deconstructing the maiden-in-flight trope. Their exchange literally turns her into a piece of meat:

Seymour: Too bony.
Prostitute: Too bony, nobody ever told me that before.

---

[4]Leslie Fiedler says of the archetype: "Chief of the gothic symbols is, of course, the Maiden in flight—understood in the spirit of *The Monk* as representing the uprooted soul of the artist, the spirit of the man who has lost his moral home. Not the violation of death which sets such a flight in motion, but the flight itself figures forth the essential meaning of the anti-bourgeois gothic, for which the girl on the run and her pursuer become only alternate versions of the same plight" (1966, p. 1960; for a systemic accounting of different instantiations of "the Other" in gothic texts see Anolick and Douglass, 2004).

Seymour: Beef is better than veal.
Prostitute: You're such a dodo. What do you call this, chop liver?

By depicting the white maiden as a willing participant—and even something of a temptress—this trailer promised black spectators a film that would poke fun at the conventions of racist horror and perhaps even turn the theme of anti-miscegenation on its head. Moreover, black women may have taken particular pleasure in the monster's rejection of the white woman's too slender figure.[5] The *Attack of the Giant Leeches* trailer took a less nuanced approach, featuring a shot of one of the slimy black creatures sucking on a white woman's neck so that it could, as the voice-over narrator suggests, "gratify [its] distorted desires." That this woman screams with a strange mix of ecstasy and horror during the attack serves further to underscore the conflation of sex and consumption in this film's marketing.

Although Corman films such as *The Day the World Ended* and *A Bucket of Blood* were publicized heavily in black newspapers, it was director William Castle who emerged in this context as a bona fide horror auteur. As an article from a June 1958 issue of the *Chicago Defender* declared: "Horror Film 'Macabre' Wins Praise" (1958b, p. 18). *Macabre* (1958) was the first in a cycle of gimmicky horror films that would confirm Castle's reputation as a master showman.[6] The short publicity piece appealed to black spectators' desire to see a movie-going phenomenon that white audiences had already experienced: "The picture based on the horrors of death, and fright is one of the most talked of films of the season. It attracted huge throngs during its runs on Broadway and in Chicago's loop and is doing the same thing in neighborhood houses" (ibid.). Castle and his co-producer Robb White also deployed a saturation advertising campaign along with a "fright insurance" gimmick as part of their marketing strategy. It seemed to work just as well on Chicago's black audiences as it did on their white counterparts (ibid., p. 97). As another article in the *Chicago Defender* promised, "[p]atrons of the 50 neighborhood theatres where the horror film is being shown are automatically insured for $1000 against shock due to watching the film" (1958a, p. 18).

Other papers also devoted space to Castle, who seemed intent on creating his own Hitchcock-style persona. For example, A *Pittsburgh Courier* article referred to him as "the master of the macabre" and claimed that "'Homicidal'

---

[5]The musical remake of *Little Shop of Horrors* (1986), which was based on the off-Broadway play, played upon racial constructions as well, by introducing a doo-wop-style Greek chorus and by having the talking plant deliver lines in street vernacular voiced by Levi Stubbs, the lead singer of the 1960s and 1970s soul group the Four Tops.
[6]The other films included *House on Haunted Hill* (1958), *The Tingler* (1959), *13 Ghosts* (1960), and *Homicidal* (1961) (see Heffernan, 2004, p. 96).

reportedly has all the shock elements to make it a worthy successor to Castle's past suspense hits" (1961, p. 18). The same page also displayed a large ad for the film, which explained his "Coward's Corner" gimmick in detail:

> A coward's certificate will be issued to you upon your arrival at the theatre. If you are too terrified to watch the blood curdling climax, follow the yellow streak to the coward's corner at the time of the 'Fright Break' and present the certificate to have your admission sneerfully [sic] refunded.
>
> (ibid.)

Ad copy of this sort promised a thrilling ending but, perhaps even more important for black audiences, it also suggested the possibility of an intensified, collective, and secular experience that would provide them with an opportunity to engage with the rhetoric of horror without exposing themselves to the psychic trauma that accompanied other, more tangible spectacles of abjection. This experience would probably have been closer to what Isabel Cristina Pinedo has called "recreational terror," wherein "controlled loss substitutes for loss of control" (1997, p. 5). In this sense, Castle's marketing strategy stood in direct experiential opposition to the campaign for *Psycho*, which had in 1960 sought to immerse the spectator in the movie-going experience by preventing anyone from entering the theater after the start of the film (Williams, 2004, p. 183). Castle, on the other hand, purposely pulled viewers "out of" his film, and then asked for their consent to their continued manipulation. This gesture did not fully compensate for the paucity or lack of black characters in the films themselves, but it did offer a form of self-mastery through spectatorship when mastery of any kind was extremely valuable to black audiences.

The popularity of Castle's self-conscious viewing environment did not foreclose the possibility of other, more absorbing and less consensual viewing experiences. In a promotional-piece-cum-critical review for the *Los Angeles Sentinel*, an unnamed author described his total absorption in Corman's second Poe adaptation, *Pit and the Pendulum* (1961): "The screenplay, a horror film giant, written by Richard Matheson [...] presents an aura of mystery from the beginning scenes and viewers are held in breathless anticipation throughout the 85-minute run of the picture," he explained (1961, p. C3). Articles on film that appeared in black papers during the period were rarely negative and sometimes borrowed language from promotional materials, but the near-mystical power that the author lends to the film, especially with flowery phrases such as "aura of mystery" and "breathless anticipation," goes beyond typical endorsement (ibid.). An even more evocative characterization of the film's supposedly enchanting power followed:

> Filmed in Panavision and in color, [the] special effects of "Pit and the Pendulum" are eerie yet beautiful, and sounds are realistic enough to *hurl the viewer into moods* when he actually seems to experience the agonizing horrors of the pit, devised by its insane owner. [The] impact of the surprise climax keeps you thinking about the picture hours after the final reel.
>
> (Ibid.; emphasis added)

Much of this critic's confessional tone recalls Lawrence Jones' aforementioned response to *Tales of Terror*, although here this instance of "strange enjoyment" derives from the visceral and dynamic experience of being "hurled into a mood" of masochistic subjection (see Studlar, 1988). There seems little doubt that he is "the viewer" who found himself flung into sublime identification with the film's victim. His slippage in the final sentence from the third to the second person may then be read as an attempt to displace the anxious sensation of spectatorial powerlessness back onto a more universal "you." As a marketing device, one could not have asked for a better testimonial to a film's power to capture the audience, and about the pleasure of allowing oneself to be taken over by it.

No such adulation accompanied a publicity still from AIP's *The Horror of Party Beach* (1964) which appeared in the April 1964 edition of the *Chicago Defender* under the caption "You Think You've Got Troubles" (1964a, p. 17). Billed as "The First Horror-Monster Musical," this film was a bizarre genre hybrid that combined into one mishmash of a plot such elements as beach party scenes, rock 'n' roll bands, biker gangs, nuclear mutations, and zombies. The publicity still avoided all of this genre confusion, and simply depicted yet another white woman being attacked by a gruesome monster. As Coleman points out (2011, pp. 100–1), *Party Beach* contained only one black character, a maid and mammy figure named Eulabelle who believes the monsters are the result of Voodoo black magic. Her presence served as a sharp reminder of the disconnect between the kinds of political representation black Americans were demanding in civil rights discourses, and the types of demeaning representation they were still receiving in films. Ironically, an article on the same page cited the white televangelist Billy Graham claiming that racial problems were "not going to be solved by demonstrations in the street, and not even by the civil rights bill" (quoted in *Chicago Defender*, 1964b, p. 17).

Passion and horror

While lowbrow horror films like *Party Beach* were representative of those advertised most often in black newspapers, it would be a mistake to assume that the industry did not also try to sell black audiences relatively sophisticated horror pictures. The *New York Amsterdam News* called the Japanese art house horror picture *Kwaidan* (1964) a "ghost film," suggested that it was "[f]ilmed in the tradition of 'Gate of Hell' [and] 'Roshomon'," and also emphasized its Jury Prize at the Cannes Film Festival (1965, p. 21). The slow-moving style, subtitles, and the elaborately constructed mise-en-scène of *Kwaidan* placed it in contrast to a hokey film like *Party Beach*. Yet, as Kevin Heffernan has discussed, such disparate movies could both garner attention in black papers because there were independent distributors attempting to respond to a product shortage that was initiated by the Hollywood majors reducing their output in the wake of the 1948 Paramount decision (2002, p. 60). *Kwaidan* was released by Walter Reade's Continental Distributing—the company best known for putting out *Night of the Living Dead* (1968)—as part of its own newly diversified line-up, which included art house films, mass appeal pictures intended for wide release, and films given special roadshow engagements (see Heffernan, 2004, p. 208). *Kwaidan* was not the only highbrow horror film to score well with black audiences in the mid-1960s. An *Amsterdam News* article also suggested that Henri-Georges Clouzot's artsy thriller *Diabolique* or *Les diaboliques* (1955) was "a tale of horror and suspense hailed by critics and film buffs as the most diabolical and frightening ever filmed" (1966, p. 23).

Perhaps the best example of a film that struck the perfect middlebrow chord with black audiences was Roman Polanski's *Rosemary's Baby* (1968). Polanski's taut direction, coupled with high production values, elevated a decidedly lowbrow premise about a woman forced to carry and give birth to the devil's child to a polished study in paranoia and occult conspiracy. A feature in the *Chicago Defender* focused on Castle's continued influence—now as a producer—in shaping the genre, as well as Mia Farrow's rising star power (1968a, p. 12). This piece declared: "When it comes to tales of cumulative horror tinged with the supernatural, Castle's instincts are perhaps the most finely honed in the film world" (ibid.). The article went on to describe the process of adapting Ira Levin's novel, and referred to Castle as a "latter-day Alfred Hitchcock" (ibid.)—a comparison that was cemented a month later by an on-set picture in which Castle aped Hitchcock by sporting the English director's signature suit and cigar (*Chicago Defender*, 1968b, p. 10). Farrow was pictured above the headline of the aforementioned piece receiving her famous pixie haircut from stylist Vidal Sassoon, along with a caption which claimed that *Rosemary's Baby* was "her most important assignment" and that it signaled her arrival as a "full-fledged star" (ibid.).

If *Rosemary's Baby* was advertised as offering the right combination of sex and the supernatural for black audiences, it is little wonder that Umberto Lenzi's even more sexually charged *Paranoia* (1969) also received a measure of attention in the *Chicago Defender*. Originally titled *Orgasmo*, this X-rated film told the story of what its trailer described as a "jet set widow [who] reaches out for thrills at any cost." One atypically long article examined how *Paranoia* dealt with genre conventions that were seen to have been established by such films as *Psycho* (*Chicago Defender*, 1969, p. 14; see also Coleman, 2011, p. 109). Strangely, the author refers to the lead actress and "victim" Carroll Baker by her full name on three separate occasions in the piece, and although it included no accompanying photo, these multiple references, in conjunction with her clear codification as a victim, create a subtext akin to that of the aforementioned publicity still from *The Day the Earth Stood Still*. As with that image, the specter of Baker's nubile, white body—invoked entirely through the written word—is troubled by a countervailing image of black feminine beauty in the adjacent column: a picture of the majestic-looking Nina Simone who was scheduled to headline a show at the Auditorium Theatre. If Baker's character was to experience torment in this horror story, Simone appeared as a dark-skinned woman with a hard-fought wisdom and an understanding of the United States' true capacity for monstrosity. Along with a host of other black artists who confronted racism in their work and through direct activism, Simone consistently suggested that the horrors being faced by many black Americans could not be dismissed as mere paranoia.

Simone's disruptive presence notwithstanding, the article about *Paranoia* demonstrated a keen awareness of horror's development as a genre, and more specifically, a recognition that horror films were increasingly being sold as much for their graphic sexual displays as their ability to solicit screams. This meant that black audiences could be assured that even more sensationalistic films would be coming their way as the strictures of the Production Code gave way to the MPAA's more permissive rating system. Illicit themes actually elevated *Paranoia* above other horror films, at least according to the article's author, who suggested that it was "more avant-garde than usual in that it also includes sexual perversion and drug abuse" (ibid.).

Whether or not *Paranoia* truly qualified as an example of the avant-garde is less interesting than the idea that this film's value as a cultural product increased because it incorporated subject matter that would have been considered exploitative only a decade earlier. The commercial success of films like *Rosemary's Baby*, *Night of the Living Dead*, and, to a certain extent, *Paranoia* suggested that the lines between art and exploitation, between highbrow and lowbrow, and between high drama and mindless escapism were becoming less meaningful. For many of the black spectators who had been uniquely positioned to see connections between horror's distilled myths and "real" American historical and political discourses, those lines of demarcation may already have been seen as arbitrary. Various forms of black expressive culture, particularly blues and jazz, traded on performer and audience knowledge of vernacular idioms while demanding a command of classical techniques. These expressive forms had also served as vital outlets for a range of different kinds of speech, from political commentary to fierce articulations of black sexuality. Black folks therefore had had no shortage of practice in either producing or interpreting cultural texts that were at once vulgar and nuanced, frightening and revelatory. However long and winding the road between Simone's refined Technicolor blues and Romero's blunt-edged, black-and-white nightmare may have been, black audiences who were studied in decoding the former would have been quite apt at also doing so with the latter.

Black audiences would need those interpretive skills to make sense of films in which sensationalized action, brutal violence, and tawdry sex fused into a conflicted jumble of spectatorial pleasures. One need look no further than the historical drama *Slaves* (1969) to get a sense of what black audiences were up against. This film starred Dionne Warwick and Ossie Davis, and played on a double bill along with *Night of the Living Dead* in New York City during the winter of 1969. Although it was not "slavesploitation" in the vein of later films such as *Mandingo* (1975), promotional materials nevertheless positioned slave beatings and coercive sexual relationships as some of *Slaves*' principal attractions. An *Amsterdam News* article featured a picture of Stephen Boyd's slave master character MacKay delivering one such beating while a group of slaves looks on in fear (1969, p. 23). The article itself described the film as "a controversial drama in Technicolor that takes a bold look at the system of American slavery and tells of Boyd's love for his slave mistress, portrayed by Miss Warwick, and its effect on the south's rigid racial system" (ibid.). It is difficult not to notice how the author deliberately attempts to distinguish Warwick from her character, but does not do the same for Boyd, who becomes conflated with his onscreen persona. This slippage is most likely attributable, on the one hand, to an awareness of the limitations facing black actors with only a narrow range of available roles to play, and, on the other, to a recognition that there was more at stake in blacks' representation in American cinema than for most whites. For performers like Davis and Warwick to play slaves during a period when black nationalism was gaining prominence would have been a fraught endeavor and all the more so in a melodrama that black audiences would have viewed on the same bill as *Night of the Living Dead*'s defiant black protagonist Ben (Duane Jones).[7]

So much has already been said about *Slaves*' co-feature *Night of the Living Dead* that there is little need to belabor its significance here; suffice it to say that Romero's film has become one of the most discussed and influential horror films of all time, prompting a litany of popular and scholarly criticism and spawning countless imitations across media. Yet, while *Night of the Living Dead* provides some of the richest social critique of any horror film before or since, it is unlikely that any of the themes that may be read into Romero's film would have prompted black spectators to see the double feature in 1969. Both *Slaves* and *Night of the Living Dead* were first and foremost marketed as films that contained spectacles of the abject body. As an ad that appeared on the same *Amsterdam News* page as the still from *Slaves* claimed, "The screen explodes with PASSION and HORROR!" (capitalization in original). It was precisely horror's willingness to trade in a kind of cinematic currency of abject bodies, to enable communal exercises in mastery, and to incorporate the pleasures of other lowbrow genres that made it such a potent source of social critique during the following decade. This characteristic also kept the genre alive among many black viewers during the civil rights movement, since if passion and horror were the order of the day one would not need to look far to find either in the horror cinema of the 1970s.

References

Anolick, R. B. and Douglass, L. H. (2004), *The Gothic Other: Racial and Social Constructions in the Literary Imagination*, Jefferson, NC: McFarland.

Bruce, B. S. (2001), "Guess Who's Going to be Dinner: Sidney Poitier, Black Militancy, and the Ambivalence of Race in George Romero's *Night of the Living Dead*," in C. M. Moremon and C. J. Rushton (eds) *Race, Oppression, and the Zombie: Essays on Cross-cultural Appropriations of the Caribbean Tradition*, Jefferson, NC: McFarland.

Chicago Defender (1956a), "Bronze Beauty," March 14, p. 17.

—(1956b), "Untitled Display Ad," March 14, p. 17.

—(1958a), "Insurance for Watching Pix 'Macabre'," June 4, p. 18.

—(1958b), "Horror Film 'The Macabre' Wins Praise," June 9, p. 18.

—(1960), "Triple Horror Films Electrify Fans at Regal," May 4, p. 16.

---

[7] I use the term "melodrama" in line with Williams' characterization: "the fundamental mode by which American mass culture has 'talked to itself' about enduring moral dilemma of race" (2001, pp. xiii–xiv).

—(1964a), "You Think You've Got Troubles," April 14, p. 17.
—(1964b), "Protests Can't End Racial Woes: Graham," April 14, p. 17.
—(1965), "Inquiring Photographer," June 8, p. 13.
—(1968a), "Chicago Slates Suspense Film," July 22, p. 12.
—(1968b), "Untitled Photos," August 13, p. 10.
—(1969), "'Paranoia' Horror Film Debuts at the Oriental," August 16–22, p. 14.
Coleman, R. M. (2011), *Horror Noire: Blacks in American Horror Films from the 1890s to the Present*, New York: Routledge.
Donaldson, L. F. (2011), "'The Suffering Black Male Body and the Threatened White Female Body': Ambiguous Bodies in *Candyman*," *Irish Journal of Gothic and Horror Studies*, 9. Available online at http://go.galegroup.com.proxy.wm.edu/ps/i.do?id=GALE%7CN2812613439&v=2.1&u=viva_wm&it=r&p=MLA&sw=w (accessed July 17, 2013).
Dower, J. (1993), *War Without Mercy: Race and Power in the Pacific War*, New York: Pantheon.
Felton, R. L. (2002), "Letter to the Atlanta Constitution," in N. Bentley and S. Gunning (eds) *The Marrow of Tradition*, Bedford Cultural Edition, New York: Bedford/St. Martin's Press.
Fiedler, L. (1966), *Love and Death in the American Novel*, New York: Dalkey Archive Press.
Gonder, P. (2003), "Like a Monstrous Jigsaw Puzzle: Genetics and Race in Horror Films of the 1950s," *The Velvet Light Trap*, 52: 33–44.
—(2004), "Race, Gender, and Terror: The Primitive in 1950s Horror Films," *Genders*, 40. Available online at http://www.genders.org/g40/g40_gondor.html (accessed April 29, 2013).
Hall J. D. (2005), "The Long Civil Rights Movement and the Political Uses of the Past," *The Journal of American History*, 91.4: 1233–63.
Heffernan, K. (2002), "Inner City Exhibition and the Genre Film: Distributing *Night of the Living Dead* (1968)," *Cinema Journal*, 41.3: 59–77.
—(2004), *Ghouls, Gimmicks, and Gold: Horror Films and the American Movie Business, 1953–1968*, Durham, NC: Duke University Press.
Hudson-Weems, C. (2006), *Emmett Till: The Sacrificial Lamb of the Civil Rights Movement*, Revised Edition, Bloomington, IN: AuthorHouse.
Kristeva, J. (1982), *Powers of Horror: An Essay on Abjection*, New York: Columbia University Press.
Lake Crane, J. (1994), *Terror and Everyday Life: Singular Moments in the History of the Horror Film*, Thousand Oaks, CA: Sage.
Levine, L. (1988), *Highbrow Lowbrow: The Emergence of Cultural Hierarchy in America*, Cambridge, MA: Harvard University Press.
Los Angeles Sentinel (1961), "'Pit and Pendulum' a Horror Film Giant," August 24, p. C3.
McGee, M. T. (1996), *Fast and Furiouser: The Revised and Fattened Fable of American International Pictures*, Jefferson, NC: McFarland.
Moremon, C. M. and Rushton, C. J. (eds) (2001), *Race, Oppression, and the Zombie: Essays on Cross-cultural Appropriations of the Caribbean Tradition*, Jefferson, NC: McFarland.
New York Amsterdam News (1965), "Japanese Ghost Film at Fine Arts," November 27, p. 21.

—(1969), "Spine Tingling, Slave Love Tops RKO Twin Showcase," December 13, p. 23.
PBS (n.d.), available online at http://www.pbs.org/blackpress/news_bios/defender.html (accessed January 11, 2013).
Pinedo, I. C. (1997), *Recreational Terror: Women and the Pleasures of Horror Film Viewing*, Albany: State University of New York Press.
Pittsburgh Courier (1961), "Castle's 'Homicidal' Appears at Gateway," June 24, p. 18.
Studlar, G. (1988), *In the Realm of Pleasure: Von Sternberg, Dietrich, and the Masochistic Aesthetic*, New York: Columbia University Press.
Williams, L. (1991), "Film Bodies: Gender, Genre, and Excess," *Film Quarterly*, 44. 4: 2–13.
—(2001), *Playing the Race Card: Melodramas of Black White from Uncle Tom to O. J. Simpson*, Princeton, NJ: Princeton University Press.
—(2004), "Discipline and Fun: *Psycho* and Postmodern Cinema," in R. Kolker (ed.) *Alfred Hitchcock's Psycho: A Casebook*, New York: Oxford University Press.
Wood, A. L. (2001), "Lynching Photography and 'The Black Beast Rapist' in the Southern White Masculine Imagination," in P. Lehman (ed.) *Masculinity: Bodies, Movies, Culture*, New York: Routledge.

12

Bids for Distinction

The Critical-industrial Function of the Horror Auteur

Joe Tompkins

Timothy Corrigan (2003) has argued that, since the 1970s, the auteur has been increasingly commodified. In suggesting that auteurism represents a viable means of both product differentiation and brand name marketing, Corrigan reminds us that the figure of the auteur remains salient to the industry because it supports the needs of distributors and marketers (ibid., p. 98). Catherine Grant (2000) has developed these ideas by considering how such practice contributes to notions of subcultural belonging. She suggests that consumers are interpellated as experts of a given subculture and as connoisseurs of the work of specific filmmakers, and that they are encouraged to support the notion of a director-centered film culture (ibid., pp. 106–7). In light of these interventions, this chapter examines what I will call the critical-industrial function of the horror auteur, which is to say the ways in which media industries use discourses of horror auteurism to marshal the critical and popular reception of films across various media. I argue that interested parties seek to legitimate aesthetically and politically certain types of horror film by faming the horror auteur as a radical artist and as an object of cult fascination, and by suggesting that their films are subversive fare that requires audiences to adopt oppositional reading protocols.[1] The chapter begins by

---

[1] Sarah Thornton (1996, pp. 10, 13–14) defines subcultural capital as a subcategory of Pierre Bourdieu's concept of "cultural capital," or "knowledge that is accumulated through upbringing

charting the emergence of the horror auteur as a critical construct, paying particular attention to the politically inflected approaches that were spearheaded by Robin Wood in the late 1970s. From there, I consider this critical development's coincidence with the rise to prominence of the concept of the cult horror film. The chapter concludes with case studies of the horror film director George A. Romero and recent 'torture porn' filmmakers. In so doing, I hope to develop our understanding of how auteurism operates as a form of product differentiation that contributes to the cult status of horror cinema.

The critical function of the horror auteur: Golden age nostalgia

The notion that horror films merit serious critical attention is bound up with the proliferation of the concept of the horror auteur. In the late 1970s, Robin Wood argued that the genre's progressive and subversive potential rested on the ways in which certain creative personnel dramatized "the struggle for all our civilization represses or oppresses" (2003, p. 68). Wood singled out contemporaneous horror filmmakers such as Tobe Hooper, Larry Cohen, Wes Craven, and Romero as uniquely equipped to mediate these repressed cultural desires, by virtue of the manner in which they dramatized clashes between normality and monstrosity in films such as *Night of the Living Dead* (1968), *The Last House on the Left* (1972), *The Texas Chainsaw Massacre*, and *It's Alive* (both 1974). For example, Wood reads *The Texas Chainsaw Massacre* as bringing to the surface otherwise hidden and horrifying aspects of society, including the exploitation of the working class, the destructive character of patriarchal authority, and the oppression of family life (ibid., pp. 79–84). By suggesting that these individuals had radicalized the genre, Wood invested the horror auteur with a transgressive status and posited the 1970s as a golden age of American horror.

The horror auteurs were also positioned as radical because they worked outside of the institutional structures of Hollywood. Romero's *Night of the*

---

and education which confers social status" (1984). In contrast to the latter, which operates primarily in the fields of high culture, subcultural capital operates decisively in the realm of popular culture. Moreover, it is not a class-bound category like Bourdieu's formulation, but rather a form of cultural distinction that takes place through media consumption, wherein distinct taste cultures are constructed commercially through the circulation of particular forms of subcultural capital. In other words, relations between media such as "mass" or "mainstream" vs. "niche" or "cult" play key roles in organizing subcultural knowledge and affiliations (Thornton, 1996, pp. 116–62). Rather than homogenizing tastes, media actually work to nurture subcultural distinctions and audience segmentation.

Living Dead was, for example, a product of regional filmmaking, and had ties to an exploitation sector that often used outrageous marketing to differentiate its films from Hollywood fare (see Heffernan, 2004, pp. 203–19). Their efforts to carve a profitable niche from the margins of American cinema helped to crystallize the notion that such filmmakers were mounting an assault on conservative tastes and values (see Becker, 2006, pp. 42–59). As Wood argued with respect to Cohen:

> the "thinking" of [his] films can lead logically only in one direction, toward a radical and revolutionary position in relation to the dominant ideological norms and the institutions that embody them, and such a position is incompatible with any definable position within mainstream cinema (or even on its exploitation fringes); it is also incompatible with any degree of comfort or security within the dominant culture.
> (Wood, 2003, p. 91)

While Wood's heralding of progressive and subversive horror hinged on the invocation of filmmakers who supposedly challenged mainstream cinema, it is important to recognize that such claims are built on conceptually infirm foundations. As Mark Jancovich has argued, they are underpinned by what amount to critical gambits, which enable critics, fans, and directors to accumulate subcultural capital via discourses of cultural distinction (2002, pp. 219–39). Thus, claims of the subcultural authenticity of a given horror film invariably rest on the invocation of cultural hierarchies that elevate non-mainstream examples of the genre on the grounds that they are more radical or challenging than their mainstream counterparts (ibid.). At the same time, the notion of "mainstream cinema" functions as a rhetorical foil; a devalued Other against which films, genres, and filmmakers associated with a putatively independent, oppositional cinema may be contrasted (ibid.; see also Hills, 2007).

This sense of distance from an imagined mainstream permits critics like Wood to argue that the 1970s horror auteurs made films that stand in opposition to "the commercial nature of cinema and the problems of financing and distribution" (Wood, 2003, p. 85), and to the supposedly facile pleasures and conformist ideology of Hollywood fare. However, the promotion of oppositional taste involves a disavowal of the financing, distribution, branding, and market segmentation that are in fact central to this "radical" horror cinema. These phenomena play key roles in the construction of 1970s Anglophone horror as an institutionally valued province of subcultural distinction; for the notion of oppositionality that underwrites the horror auteurism that is associated with this period dovetails neatly with the subcultural politics of cult fandom and of academic Film Studies, both of which have sought to distinguish themselves from a commercial mainstream (see Jancovich, 2002, p. 310).

While the dynamics of subcultural distinction are conceptually questionable, they are central to media institutions' efforts to cultivate consumer bases. Cult movie fandom, points out Jancovich, was "not developed in opposition to either the commercial or the academic but grew out of a series of economic and intellectual developments in the post-war period that were defined by a sense of distinction from 'mainstream, commercial cinema'" (ibid., p. 317). Hence, the notion that some 1970s low-budget horror films represent a historical site of radical or revolutionary filmmaking cannot be isolated from industrial concerns, such as changing distribution patterns, the growth of independent movie houses, and the rise of the youth audience, all of which underwrote the development of film markets geared to a niche of anti-mainstream consumers (see Heffernan, 2004).

Furthermore, the industry itself contributed to the circulation of horror auteurism of the 1970s. For instance, distributors sought to capitalize on the cult appeal and the relative commercial success of *Dawn of the Dead* (1978) by repackaging some of Romero's earlier work, including *Jack's Wife* (1972) and *Martin* (1976) as "new Romero films" (see Williams, 2003, p. 47). The detailed production stories that were printed in the trade and popular press at the time of these re-releases helped cement this director's growing reputation as a horror auteur (see Hoberman and Rosenbaum, 1983, pp. 110–13; King, 2002, pp. 85–115). As Peter Hutchings has argued, "horror was the only genre of the period to acquire its own customized 'movie brats'" (2004, p. 181)—a reference to a group of mainly film school-educated directors, including Francis Ford Coppola and Martin Scorsese, who had helmed several well-received pictures that had been credited with initiating a radical, progressive nuance to Hollywood's output. Accordingly, not only were directors such as Romero presented as fully committed to horror, they were called upon to demonstrate that commitment in interviews and other publicity materials. As early as 1973, Romero proclaimed his belief that horror could be used to explore serious social issues:

> I wrote a short story which dealt with, which was in fact, an allegory, a statement about society, which dealt with a siege by the living dead. It was much less contrived, I think, than the film is, from the standpoint that it was purely allegorical.
>
> (quoted in Williams, 2011, pp. 19, 21)

The 1970s horror auteurs were distinguished by "a much more emphatic presence both within the production process, with most of them writer-directors, and in the way the films were marketed and received by critics and to a certain extent audiences as well" (Hutchings, 2004, p. 181).

It follows that the auteurist narratives and star images that enabled the construction of a radical horror cinema in the 1970s have proven enduring cornerstones of cult horror fandom. Craig Bernardini has shown, for example, that in the 1980s, American horror film magazines such as *Fangoria* primed their readers to approach horror as a director's cinema, in large part by devoting significant attention to supposedly visionary directors such as Romero, Wes Craven, and David Cronenberg (2010, p. 186, n. 2). "Today, a director who makes one or two moderately interesting horror films is quickly labeled a 'horror auteur'[...] and [is] compared to the 1970s patriarchs," notes Bernardini, before stressing that "[t]his is at once a fine instance of the marketing of auteur nostalgia, and a further indication that the contemporary horror director's auteur status remains circumscribed by genre" (ibid., p. 163). Invoking the horror auteur—particularly in its more radical, oppositional incarnations—continues to consolidate the 1970s as a high watermark in terms of the genre's quality, social significance, and progressivity; as a standard to which new filmmakers must aspire and against which they are invariably measured. However, this figure has also provided ways to imbue filmmakers and their output with those qualities that characterized this supposed golden age.

The industrial functions of the horror auteur: Transmedia cult affiliation

The horror auteur permits the drawing of subcultural distinctions by designating some horror films and directors as radical or transgressive. This phenomenon is perhaps most clearly evident in touchstone figures like Romero. Whereas critics continue to affirm this filmmaker's status as the ultimate 1970s rebel horror auteur, what typically emerges in industrial framings of the genre is his brand—the sense of a vanguard director whose supposedly distinctive countercultural approach revolutionized horror by issuing a radical challenge to society. Calling forth this image continues not only to authenticate certain trends in horror film production, such as torture-porn, but also serves to organize taste formations and subcultural distinctions across media.

A striking example of the confluence of auteurist marketing and subcultural distinction is provided by Romero's appearance at the 2009 *Spike TV*

Scream Awards.[2] Romero's receipt of a lifetime achievement award was unquestionably a result of his status as a radical horror auteur. This point was made clear by the introduction he received from Quentin Tarantino: "Heart-stopping violence, explosive bloodshed, undead flesh-eaters and dismembered ghouls. That's right. I'm talking about all the shit we love in film, and all the finer things in this goddamn life. One man is responsible for all this, and that man is George A. Romero." It is unsurprising that Romero was given his award by perhaps the quintessential celebrity auteur, since ultimately this ceremony was concerned less with paying homage to a putative master of the horror genre than with establishing a lineage from one auteur to another. After all, Tarantino had received the same award three years earlier for *Grindhouse* (2007), a big-budget pastiche of the low-budget exploitation films for which Romero was famous. This sense of passing on the mantle was even spotlighted in Tarantino's fawning but ultimately self-congratulatory tribute to Romero:

> I'm here tonight to stand up for one of the coolest, the craziest, the scariest, and America's greatest regional moviemaker of all time. I owe this man a huge debt, and so does every filmmaker who ever dared to declare their own independence, because George Romero did it first, and he did it with more guts and more gore than anybody.

Tarantino's introduction of Romero illustrates that film-related media stand to gain from associating themselves with the sense of connoisseurship that underpins both cult movie fandom and the reception practices of the academy.

Furthermore, events like the *Scream* awards reveal the enduring commercial appeal of horror auteurs. They provide an opportunity to highlight and cement elements of an auteur's star image, while also attempting to appeal to specific subcultural taste formations and piggybacking the preferences of targeted audiences. Through an association with "America's greatest regional moviemaker," Spike TV is seeking to constitute its own audience and its brand identity in terms of an identifiable taste culture based around those who affiliate themselves with "heart-stopping violence, explosive bloodshed, and dismembered ghouls." It also reinforces horror's status as a disreputable cultural form, working to consolidate the subcultural distinction of "one of the coolest, the craziest, [and] scariest" of horror filmmakers, on the grounds that Romero's reputation promises audiences an authentic cult experience. Romero is thus presented as one of the "coolest, craziest,

---

[2] Portions of this section appear in Tompkins (2010).

scariest" American filmmakers less because of his institutional independence and his radical politics, than because he permits fans, critics, and filmmakers to cement their own relationships to a disreputable genre. He functions as a critical reference point for media looking to accumulate economic and subcultural capital through showcases of their allegiances to an oppositional film culture.

The presentation of Romero at the 2009 *Scream* awards is illustrative of the degree to which the horror auteur is used as a form of niche marketing. It indicates that this figure serves as shorthand for the radical associations of horror film culture. Such figures continue to function as both a saleable attraction and an authorial position; not just as a marketing strategy that is imposed on directors, but as a modality of performance to be used on behalf of those genre practitioners who are seeking to attain or to maintain auteur status for themselves. In contemporary cinematic discourse, the horror auteur thrives as a brand name and a mode of performance.

The industrial functions of the horror auteur: Brand name performance

The tendency towards brand name auteurism is nowhere more apparent than in the marketing and commentary that surrounded a recent cycle of ultra-violent horror films that came to be known as torture-porn. Some of the directors associated with the recent torture-porn cycle have invoked the figure of the horror auteur in order to position their own films and to cement their own status. Promotion and publicity materials framed filmmakers such as Eli Roth (*Hostel* [2005] and *Hostel Part II* [2007]), Darren Lynn Bousman (*Saw II* [2005], *Saw III* [2006], and *Saw IV* [2007]), Rob Zombie (*Devil's Rejects* [2005]), Alexandre Aja (*The Hills Have Eyes* [2006]), Neil Marshall (*Dog Soldiers* [2002] and *The Descent* [2005]), and Greg McLean (*Wolf Creek* [2005]) as members of an unofficial "Splat Pack" (see e.g. Jones, 2006; Keegan, 2006; McClintock, 2006). These up-and-coming directors were presented as a closely knit collective bound by a commitment to the horror genre, and specifically to the production of quite brutal horror films. The branding of the Splat Pack involves critical framings which marshal authorship, consumption, and taste around the concept of the 1970s golden age.

In order to solidify their reputations of themselves and their films, Splat Pack directors consistently framed themselves as auteurs and emphasized the influence of 1970s horror on their own work. For example, Rob Zombie claimed:

There was a real bleakness to '70s genre cinema [...] and it infiltrated the commercial arena too. [...] When violence is done right it's troubling to watch, which is the way it should be. All the kids blown away by those '70s genre shockers are old enough to be making movies themselves, and they want to emulate the same effect for today's audiences that those movies had on them.

(quoted in Jones, 2006, p. 103)

Another Splat Pack member, Neil Marshall, supported this position. "The reason why so many titles from that golden period in the '70s have stayed in my memory so long is [that] they were starkly oppressive, visually stunning and very frightening," Marshall claimed: "[Today] there's far too much terror-lite around simply reliant on CGI blood and sound effects. That's too easy. The hard part is maintaining tension" (quoted in ibid., p. 104). Invoking 1970s horror enables these filmmakers to position their own films as exemplars of an authentic horror cinema built around the transgressive display of violence and corporeal destruction.

The effectiveness of mobilizing auteurism as a framing discourse within marketing campaigns may be gauged by the recurring presence of "renaissance" rhetoric in the critical reception of the Splat Pack, whereby ultraviolent horror films were endorsed for their makers' attempts to offer "different and creative ways to draw blood" (Tucker, 2006). An early instance of this practice appears in a 2006 article from *Total Film* magazine. The article attempted to negotiate a position of distinction for what its writer, Alan Jones, calls "the next generation of horror directors" (2006, p. 100). It did so by situating their work in relation to the 1970s horror auteurs. Thus, Jones identifies an "old blood" of cult filmmakers that included Craven, Hooper, Cronenberg, and Romero, and likens their work to that of the "new blood" of Splat Pack directors (ibid., p. 106). In so doing, Jones makes a bid for subcultural distinction on behalf of "the next generation of horror directors [who] hose down the genre with lashings of old-school carnage" (ibid., p. 100). Similarly, the trade paper *Variety* stressed that these "blood brothers" were on a mission to "bring back really violent, horrific movies" (McClintock, 2006, p. 34). Critics also credited the Splat Pack with "introducing a level of terror, torture and depravity that would make [*A Nightmare on Elm Street* villain] Freddy Kruger run for cover" (ibid., p. 1), while renouncing "the blood-and-breasts-style slasher films of the early 1980s" (Boucher, 2007, p. E1), and with taking the genre "to new heights of realistically based narrative" (ibid.). The spotlighting of these qualities enabled critics to laud the Splat Pack on the grounds that it was returning horror to, what one writer dubbed, its "transgressive roots" (McIntyre, 2009, p. E1). Thus, a *Time* magazine piece answered its own rhetorical question "[Are you] [w]ondering where all those ultraviolent movies are coming from?" with the following: "[from] an emerging and collegial band of horror auteurs who are given almost free rein and usually less than $10 million by studios or producers to make unapologetically disgusting, brutally violent movies" (Keegan, 2006, p. 67). This piece echoed a generational angle that was also present in Jones' article, picturing the Splat Pack as a "gore-happy gang" united by "big-screen bloodlust" and its professed allegiance to "Old Guard" directors like Craven and Hooper (ibid., pp. 66–8).

Members of the Splat Pack also routinely attempted to distinguish their films by distancing them from a post-*Scream* (1996) teen slasher film cycle which included *I Know What You Did Last Summer* (1997) and *Urban Legend* (1998). This process involved devaluing these scary movies as watered-down horror that offered "chaste thrills" and "teen starlets," and instead championing the 1970s horror canon for being genuinely shocking and horrifying (see Jones, 2006, p. 102). Thus, Alexandre Aja explained to the *Los Angeles Times* that in the early 2000s he and his Splat Pack contemporaries—especially Roth and Zombie—had attempted to "wrest horror back from its campier, PG-13-rated tangents," and "to reinvent the grammar of the genre" (quoted in McIntyre, 2009, p. E1). "We all came with the idea of bringing back the horror, just scaring the audience as much as we can," Aja boasted. "I think we managed to revive the intensity of the genre as it was at its most powerful in the '70s" (ibid.). The notion of putting the horror back into horror cinema positions these directors as contributors to a valued tradition. It enables claims for product differentiation to be made, by heralding the Splat Pack as the heirs apparent to the 1970s horror auteurs. The effectiveness of the Splat Pack's promotional rhetoric is further evinced by the extent to which critics reproduced its claims of recuperating horror from a PG-13 rated nadir of the late 1990s and early 2000s. For example, *Time* magazine simply stated that "there's certainly innovative filmmaking under way that rises above the mindless slasher sequels of the 80s or such predictable teen-star killfests of the 90s as *I Know What You Did Last Summer*" (Keegan, 2006, p. 68).

The emphasis placed on the horror auteur as the driving force behind the aesthetic and commercial achievements of torture-porn ultimately draws attention away from the industrial structures and market forces that made viable the production and distribution of such fare. For example, in *Time* magazine the former Lionsgate president Tom Ortenberg insisted that "[g]ood horror movies don't need stars, and they don't need special effects [...] they earn their scares through twists, through intelligent writing and great up-and-coming directors" (quoted in ibid.). Yet, torture-porn meshed well with the niche audience targeting strategies of heavily capitalized independent distributors like Lionsgate. In fact, as Alisa Perren has shown, this type of film was central to the growth of this company, which generated significant amounts of revenue from the *Saw* films (2004–10), the *Hostel* films (2005, 2007), and *The Devil's Rejects* (2005), after having already enjoyed the economic rewards of handling other films that featured more extreme violence than their Hollywood counterparts: *American Psycho* (2000), *Cabin Fever* (2002), and *House of 1000 Corpses* (2003) (Perren, 2013, pp. 109, 113; see also Tulshyan, 2010). Thus, whereas the Hollywood majors and many independent companies continued to eschew torture-porn, it was Lionsgate's commercially motivated commitment to this type of product that had opened up an opportunity for filmmakers to showcase extreme violence (see Wharton, 2013; McClintock, 2006). The production of ultra-violent horror was also supported by developments in non-theatrical distribution, in particular the rise of unrated DVD releases that were free to include sequences of brutality that would otherwise have prevented a release in most multiplex theaters. This form of delivery was nevertheless transformed rhetorically by some filmmakers who recast this platform as a loophole through which renegade auteurs could push the envelope of celluloid brutality. For example, Eil Roth, the director of *Cabin Fever* and the *Hostel* films, framed the unrated DVD as a site of subcultural distinction. He stressed to the *New York Post* that this format provides unique access to a director's uncompromised "hardcore" vision (quoted in Tucker, 2006).

Conclusion

This chapter has attempted to show that auteurism remains central to the marketing of some horror films. The invocation of horror auteurs has tended to permit critics, fans, and filmmakers to accumulate subcultural capital by expressing their appreciation of, and affiliation with, ultraviolent horror. What is more, this practice has become part of industry practice, with production and distribution personnel seeking to invest themselves and their output with the subcultural authenticity that is associated with a cohort of 1970s horror directors. Such practice has enabled them subculturally to legitimate subsequent horror films and trends, as is exemplified by the promotion and publicity that accompanied a recent cycle of torture-porn films. The continued positioning of the 1970s as a benchmark in North American horror is representative of broader trends, since, as Mark Gallagher has recently argued, the notion of a Hollywood Renaissance that is associated with this period has provided a key critical reference point for "indie" filmmakers such as Steven Soderbergh (Gallagher, 2013). They have sought to invoke this artistically venerated epoch in order to legitimate themselves as artists in spite, or perhaps because of, the slightly off-mainstream position they occupy within American cinema. It is clear that summoning this widely perceived golden age constitutes a major aspect of film promotion. Yet, the enduring myth of Renaissance remains of particular relevance to the new generation of horror auteurs. For it is they, not unlike Soderbergh and other indie filmmakers, who see themselves—and are seen by industry insiders and industry watchers—as operating at the margins of mainstream cinema while nevertheless using traditional media to promote both their films and themselves. In this respect, the Splat Pack directors have for better or worse profited from the belief that they were responsible for reorienting a major genre of American cinema or, to put it differently, for "bringing back the horror."

References

Becker, M. (2006), "A Point of Little Hope: Hippie Horror Films and the Politics of Ambivalence," *The Velvet Light Trap*, 57: 42–59.

Bernardini, C. (2010), "*Auteurdammerung*: David Cronenberg, George A. Romero, and the Twilight of the (North) American Horror Auteur," in S. Hantke (ed.) *American Horror Film: The Genre at the Turn of the Millennium*, Jackson: University Press of Mississippi.

Boucher, G. (2007), "A Queasy Does it; Grown-up Kid Eli Roth Says his Stomach-wrenching Films Tackle Social Ills too," *Los Angeles Times*, June 3, p. E1.

Bourdieu, P. (1984), *Distinction: A Social Critique of the Judgment of Taste*, London: Routledge.

Corrigan, T. (2003), "The Commerce of Auteurism," in V. W. Wexman (ed.) *Film and Authorship*, Brunswick, NJ: Rutgers University Press.

Gallagher, M. (2013), "Discerning Independents: Steven Soderbergh and Transhistorical Taste Cultures," in G. King, C. Molloy, and Y. Tzioumakis (eds) *American Independent Cinema: Indie, Indiewood and Beyond*, New York and London: Routledge.

Grant, C. (2000), "www.auteur.com?," *Screen*, 41.1: 101–8.

Hantke, S. (ed.) (2010), *American Horror Film: The Genre at the Turn of the Millennium*, Jackson: University Press of Mississippi.

Heffernan, K. (2004), *Ghouls, Gimmicks, and Gold: Horror Films and the American Movie Business, 1953–1968*, Durham, NC: Duke University Press.

Hills, M. (2007), "Para-Paracinema: The *Friday the 13th* Film Series as Other to Trash and Legitimate Film Cultures," in J. Sconce (ed.) *Sleaze Artists: Cinema at the Margins of Taste, Style, and Politics*, Durham, NC: Duke University Press.

Hoberman, J. and Rosenbaum, J. (1983), *Midnight Movies*, New York: Harper and Row.

Hutchings, P. (2004), *The Horror Film*, London: Pearson.

Jancovich, M. (2002), "Cult Fictions: Cult Movies, Subcultural Capital and the Production of Cultural Distinctions," *Cultural Studies*, 16.2: 306–22.
Jones, A. (2006), "The New Blood," *Total Film*, April, pp. 100–6.
Keegan, R. W. (2006), "The Splat Pack," *Time*, October 30, pp. 66–70.
King, G. (2002), *New Hollywood Cinema: An Introduction*, New York: Columbia University Press.
King, G., Molloy C., and Tzioumakis, Y. (eds) (2013), *American Independent Cinema: Indie, Indiewood and Beyond*, New York and London: Routledge.
McClintock, P. (2006), "Blood Brothers," *Variety*, December 25, pp. 1, 34.
McIntyre, G. (2009), "The Horror ... The Horror: Shocking Fans can be Good Business, as Hollywood is Noticing (Again)," *Los Angeles Times*, January 25, p. E1.
Nicotero, S. (2011 [1973]), "Romero: An Interview with the Director of *Night of the Living Dead*," reprinted in T. Williams (ed.) *George A. Romero: Interviews*, Jackson: University Press of Mississippi.
Perren, A. (2013), "Last Indie Standing: The Special Case of Lions Gate in the New Millennium," in G. King, C. Molloy, and Y. Tzioumakis (eds) *American Independent Cinema: Indie, Indiewood and Beyond*, New York and London: Routledge.
Sconce, J. (ed.) (2007), *Sleaze Artists: Cinema at the Margins of Taste, Style, and Politics*, Durham, NC: Duke University Press.
Thornton, S. (1996), *Club Cultures: Music, Media and Subcultural Capital*, Hanover and London: Wesleyan University Press.
Tompkins, J. (2010), "'They Have the Oscars': Oppositional Telebranding and the Cult of the Horror Auteur," *Flow*, 12.4. Available online at http://flowtv.org/2010/07/oppositional-telebranding-and-the-cult-of-the-horror-auteur/ (accessed July 17, 2013).
Tucker, R. (2006), "Horrors! Torture, Mind Games, Mayhem," *New York Post*, October 22. Available online at http://www.myspace.com/robzombie/blog/183498575 (accessed June 4, 2013).
Tulshyan, R. (2010), "*Saw*: The Most Successful Horror Franchise of All Time," *Time.com*, July 25. Available online at http://newsfeed.time.com/2010/07/25/saw-the-most-successful-horror-film-of-all-time/ (accessed July 13, 2013).
Wexman, V. W. (ed.) (2003), *Film and Authorship*, New Jersey: Rutgers University Press.
Wharton, S. (2013), "Welcome to the (Neo) Grindhouse! Sex, Violence and the Indie Film," in G. King, C. Molloy, and Y. Tzioumakis (eds) *American Independent Cinema: Indie, Indiewood and Beyond*, New York and London: Routledge.
Williams, T. (2003), *The Cinema of George A. Romero: Knight of the Living Dead*, London: Wallflower Press.
—(ed.) (2011), *George A. Romero: Interviews*, Jackson: University Press of Mississippi.
Wood, R. (2003), *Hollywood: From Vietnam to Reagan ... and Beyond*, New York: Columbia University Press.

13

Low Budgets, No Budgets, and Digital-video Nasties

Recent British Horror and Informal Distribution

Johnny Walker

On February 14, 2012, British film producer Hammer released *The Woman in Black*: the company's first period Gothic horror film in over 35 years. Starring former *Harry Potter* actor Daniel Radcliffe in the lead role, this film generated global theatrical returns of $126 million, including a respectable $54 million in North America and an impressive £21.2 million (circa US$34 million) in the United Kingdom, which led some industry watchers to anoint it "the UK's highest grossing British horror film since records began" (Kemp, 2012).[1] A few weeks later, on March 22, 2012, a British horror film that bore few similarities to Hammer's picture surfaced on DVD in the UK. *Kill Keith* (2011)—a parochial horror comedy starring the English daytime TV stalwart, Keith Chegwin—prompted Stuart Heritage of London's *Guardian* newspaper to suggest that the film's "cheap" and "trashy" character made it "far more representative of the British horror scene" than *The Woman in Black* could ever be (2012). Heritage certainly had a point. As the film's promotional tagline "Not in most cinemas from 11th Nov." made clear, films like *Kill Keith* rarely receive a theatrical opening of any description, and especially not a

---

[1] All box office data obtained from Internet Movie Database Professional (www.imdb.com/pro).

wide one. Rather, they tend to be released with comparatively little fanfare to home-viewing platforms such as DVD and Video on Demand (VoD).

This chapter examines direct-to-video (hereafter DTV) British horror as an example of what Ramon Labato (2012) has recognized as "informal" distribution practices. As Labato argues, such releases are often characterized by handshake deals, flat-fee sales, and piracy, and are therefore quite distinct from the revenue-sharing business models, systems of statistical enumeration, and staggered "windowing" patterns of post-theatrical releases associated with formal distribution (ibid.). As such, this chapter assesses the centrality of home video and associated platforms to the production of British horror cinema in the twenty-first century, from the high street and the web store to YouTube and beyond. Thus, where the British filmmaker Richard Stanley was not alone in suggesting that, in the 1990s, DTV horror had brought an end to what he deemed to be the "great British horror film" (2002, p. 193), this chapter shows that "fan boy fluff," as Stanley called it, actually sustained British horror across the following decade.

The horrors of direct-to-video

A DTV release is often derided or dismissed as the Other of feature film distribution. As Barbara Klinger has argued, in some critical circles, "[the] big-screen performance is marked as authentic, as representing bona fide cinema," while a video release by comparison remains a "regrettable triumph of convenience" (2006, p. 2; also Labato, 2012, pp. 32–6). Yet, as Linda Ruth Williams has pointed out, low-budget horror is well suited to home video because of the genre's well-established low cultural status, because its targeted audiences are prepared to actively seek out such fare, and because the small screen is more forgiving than the big screen of these films' low production values (2005, p. 290).

About 70 percent of the 500 or so feature-length horror films produced by British companies in the twenty-first century bypassed theatrical distribution. These films are typically shot on a shoestring budget of £500,000 (circa US$800,000) or less, and can sometimes cost as little as £5,000 (circa US$8,000), or even, in some cases, a few hundred pounds, to make. Their UK home video distribution is handled by companies such as Revolver Films, which released *Broken* (2006), and Safecracker Pictures, which released *Nazi Zombie Death Tales* (AKA *Battlefield Death Tales*) (2012).[2] Others have

---

[2]Some of these films were picked up in the United States by distributors specializing in low-budget, low-prestige niche audience fare, such as The Weinstein Company's subsidiary Dimension Extreme, which released *Broken* (2006), *Mum & Dad*, and *Gnaw* (both 2008).

either circulated on recordable DVD-Rs obtained through self-managed websites, as was the case with *Ouija Board* (2009), or are available through YouTube, as was the case with *Zombie Village* (2005), or VoD websites such as LOVEFiLM Instant, as with *Red Canopy* (2006). Most, however, circulate beyond mainstream circles, reminding us of a paradox that characterizes low-end cinema, wherein "[e]very year, thousands of movies are released into nontheatrical markets, and most disappear off the radar without having made any kind of mark. [...] There is an incommensurability of *scale* here: the nontheatrical market is enormous, yet obscure" (Labato, 2012, p. 21; emphasis in original).

In the early 2000s, the appeal of releasing a film DTV in the UK was undermined by the establishment of the UK Film Council as a means of helping the British film industry to perform well internationally (Leggott, 2008, p. 17). At this time, British horror film producers were seeking to emulate the box office success that some of their American contemporaries had enjoyed by modeling films on the hit teen slasher movie *Scream* (1996) (Walker, 2012, pp. 438–40). Even for those filmmakers who shot on video, the idea of releasing the likes of *My Little Eye* and *28 Days Later* (both 2002) DTV was undesirable because it may have upheld an oft-leveled criticism that, as Julian Petley has put it, most "Brit flicks" of the time were considered to be "shit flicks" (2002, pp. 44–50). The stigma attached to such a release was expressed by the director of *My Little Eye*, Marc Evans, who suggested that a UK DTV release of the film would have ruined his career (*My Little Eye*, DVD).

With the consumption of films on home-viewing formats surpassing theatrical attendance in 2003 (UK Film Council, 2004), it became clear that most British horror films were not destined for success at UK theaters. Unlike their Hollywood counterparts, these films were produced for significantly less than the £1 million (circa US$1.6 million) that had financed such comparatively high-end British horror films as *The Hole* (2001) and *Long Time Dead* (2002). What is more, their makers did not have access to the generous marketing budgets that had contributed to the financial achievements of the low-budget, major studio-backed hits *28 Days Later*, *Shaun of the Dead* (2004), and *The Descent* (2005) (see e.g. Mitchell, 2002; Minns, 2004). Without the exposure afforded by a lengthy theatrical engagement, most British horror films were forced to generate revenue exclusively from their long "shelf life" in high street and online stores. For example, *F* (2010) was left to make money on home video after its two-week theatrical release accrued a mere £13,000 gross (circa US$23,400) (see Walker, 2011).

Not unlike other forms of low-budget cinema, such as the Poverty Row horrors of the 1940s or the Italian exploitation movies of the 1970s, films released on DTV have often been made to capitalize on those that boasted a strong track record in the theatrical market (see Labato, 2012, p. 25). In this respect, British horror's wholesale shift from the silver screen to the small screen was accelerated by the strong box office performance of Neil Marshall's 2005 film *The Descent*, which fared well in the UK and surpassed all expectations in North American theaters. At a time when most British producers saw horror films either as pin-brained gorefests aimed at men or as "mature" psychological and emotional dramas angled to women (Macnab, 2004, p. 6), the makers of *The Descent* shrewdly pitched their tale of women encountering bloodthirsty troglodytes in the Appalachians to a mixed-sex audience. On the one hand, they used a heavy dose of gore to evoke the recent horror hit *The Texas Chainsaw Massacre* (2003) and cannibalistic creatures to recall the zombies of *Dawn of the Dead* (2004). On the other, themes of child loss, motherhood, and female malady opened up *The Descent* to audiences seeking more subtle, cerebral, and thus "sophisticated" forms of horror in the vein of the female-centered horror hits *The Ring* (2002) and *The Grudge* (2004). This dual mode of address and audience targeting perhaps indicates why *The Descent* became the first horror movie to attract about as many women to British theaters as it did men (UK Film Council, 2006, p. 54). Yet, in spite of its noted similarities to other contemporary horror films, *The Descent* was an anomaly as far as British film production was concerned. If the generally poor track record of the nation's horror cinema was anything to go by, *The Descent*'s achievements at the international box office were unlikely to be emulated by other British horror films, not least because US distributors were already flooding these markets with similar fare, such as the *Saw* series (2004–2010).

To capitalize on *The Descent*'s local and international profile, producers therefore turned to the home video market, where distribution rights are cheaper, where distributors can easily acquire lower budgeted films, and where some profits are almost always guaranteed for distributors. Under these circumstances, the market was flooded with an array of similar films that either went DTV or that, in an effort to generate exposure, received very limited theatrical releases. These included gory rural horrors like *Broken*, *Wilderness* (2006), and *Eden Lake* (2008); chillers about child loss and female mental instability such as *Venus Drowning* (2006), *Shrooms* (2007), and *The Daisy Chain* (2008); creature features à la *Salvage* (2009), *Splintered*, and *Outcast* (both 2010); and family-centered horror, including *Mum & Dad* and *Gnaw*.[3] These films were often compared unfavorably to *The Descent*, in both critical and commercial terms.[4] Moreover, those films that opened theatrically

---

[3] This list is offered as a guide. There are inevitable sub-generic cross-overs.
[4] Most did not receive mainstream coverage at all, but relied on websites such as DreadCentral.

usually only did so for a few days before appearing on DVD and VoD. Examples include *Salvage*, *Surviving Evil*, and *Tony* (both 2009). The exception was *Mum & Dad*, which on December 26, 2008 was made available simultaneously across multiple platforms: theaters, the pay-per-view service Sky Box Office, VoD, and DVD. In bypassing the standard 16-week gap that separates a film's theatrical release from its home video release (see Henderson, 2009, pp. 475–6), this strategy represented a tacit acknowledgment that the audience for British horror was too small to offset the substantial costs of theatrical distribution.

A spate of hybrid genre pictures was also made with a view to securing a DVD release. These films were typically funded by first-time private investors who were trying their luck in the movie business. Most of the films were either furnished with slapstick comedy, as was the case with *Evil Aliens* (2005), or with the gangsters and hooligans of contemporary British crime movies such as *The Football Factory* (2004) and *The Business* (2005). As the CEO of Black and Blue Films, Jonathan Sothcott, explained to me, the presence of British crime film star Danny Dyer on a DVD cover could almost guarantee the sale of between 60,000 to 100,000 units, more than double that of the company's other releases (2011). This form of British exploitation cinema was again often closely modeled on commercially successful cultural products. For example, Black and Blue's *Devil's Playground* (2010) imbeds into the crime film format a tale of zombies spawned by a virus caused by corporate malpractice, which its makers drew from the *Resident Evil* series (2002–) and *28 Weeks Later* (2007). Similarly, the filmmakers behind the vampire/gangster picture *Dead Cert* (2010) borrowed elements of content from HBO's hit television drama series *The Sopranos* (1999–2007) and *True Blood* (2008–). While genre-mixing permitted the makers and distributor of these films to maximize their profits by invoking a range of previously lucrative fare, it was their availability on DVD that truly facilitated the measure of success they enjoyed. Had the films incurred substantial losses from a wide theatrical run, the profits they made on DVD would have plummeted or been erased entirely. The same was also true of the first film to be released by the newly relaunched Hammer, *Beyond the Rave* (2008), which was designed specifically for the social networking site Myspace.com, where it also premiered (see Hills, Chapter 14, this volume). The fact that Britain's most internationally recognizable producer of horror films chose to use a web-based platform to launch a hotly anticipated comeback provides perhaps the clearest indication that British horror would continue to be sustained not by theatrical exhibition but by home viewing.

---

com, BloodyDisgusting.com, and Twitchfilm.com for exposure. Despite being screened at various festivals, *Venus Drowning* has yet to receive an official release.

Doing it yourself, for yourself

The proliferation of British horror on home-viewing formats incentivized semi-professionals or amateurs to produce similar movies in their home towns on practically non-existent budgets, using friends and family as casts and crews. For instance, in 1999, Jonathon Ash established the production company Digital Nasties with a view to making backyard fare such as *Zombie Ferox* (2002) and *The Graveyard of Death* (2005). Similarly, Jason Impey set up J. I. Productions and its horror arm Exploitation Pictures in the southern English town of Milton Keynes in order to specialize in micro-budget efforts like *Sick Bastard* (2007) and 2009's *Tortured* (AKA *Sex Slave*). Meanwhile in 2005, Andrew Senior filmed his £1,000 (circa US$1,600) horror comedy, *The Evolved: Part One* (2006), on digital video in and around London, and Bryn Hammond—who would become somewhat infamous for his widely despised horror magazine *Gorezone* (see Carruthers, 2010)—shot a Northamptonshire-set slasher movie called *The Summer of the Massacre* (2006) for £50 (circa US$80). At the risk of stating the obvious, the chances of such films securing traditional forms of distribution are very remote. Unsurprisingly then, with the exception of the £45 (circa US$72) zombie movie *Colin* (2008), which was granted a theatrical run in 2009 after it became the subject of international media coverage (see Manzoor, 2009), these films are invariably made available online through small distributors' catalogs or on the DVD-R format, or on VoD streaming platforms.

As one might expect, the companies comprising this cottage industry—Exploitation Pictures, Digital Nasties, Revolt Films, Midnight Films, Opiate of the People Films, Arrogant Films, and others—have not produced a large number of films. Their projects are in effect a hobby, one that requires a fairly large amount of time (if not always money), but one that can be fitted around full-time jobs and other responsibilities. The filmmakers involved also tend not to be focused on capital gain or the esthetic proficiency of their films. Thus, in a particularly memorable moment from Exploitation Pictures' *The Turning* (2011), little effort is made to mask the fact that a collapsing woodland hut is in fact a garden toolshed surrounded by fencing.

These rough-and-ready films boast many of the traits that Jeffrey Sconce (1995) famously identified as characteristic of "paracinema." They are cheap, technically inept (characterized by poor sound quality, poor image resolution, and clumsy editing), and they appeal to an extremely small audience niche. Yet, as Ernest Mathijs and Jamie Sexton have argued, this "badness" is central to the pleasures that some audiences derive from such films; fare that "is frequently approached ironically" (2011, p. 18). The valorization of the trashy that is central to such consumption is in turn commodified by the distributors of these films, who often use this feature as a selling point.

Online cult branding

As Mark Jancovich has argued, some fan communities draw distinctions between what they term "authentic" and "inauthentic" horror (2000). Where the former is said to comprise transgressive films, and those that are subject to alternative forms of production and delivery, the latter is derided as "sanitized tripe" consumed by the "moronic victims of mass culture" (ibid., p. 25). The invocation of this binary opposition is central to the circulation of many informally distributed British horror films, nowhere more so than in the instances of cult branding that take place online.

This phenomenon is exemplified by the circulation of *The Evolved: Part One*, a light-hearted tale of cops tracing a series of dog disappearances to a London fast-food company called Burger Priest, and by *The Summer of the Massacre*, a straight-faced slasher about teenagers stalked by the masked maniac Hammerhead. *The Evolved: Part One* is only available as a stand-alone film from retailers based in the United States, where it is handled by the DTV exploitation specialist Troma Releasing. *The Summer of the Massacre* is available in the UK as one of 26 horror films in *The Dead of Night Collection* of DVDs, and in the US through Brain Damage Films, a company that, in conjunction with its subsidiary labels Maxim Media, Nocturnal Features, and Midnight Releasing, releases micro-budget horror films.[5] Both of the films are positioned in such a way that they reflect the brand identity of their respective distributors; identities that derive from each company's film library, and which reject "mainstream" conceptions of cinematic quality rooted in technical proficiency while embracing the rough-and-ready traits of exploitation cinema (for an analysis of North American DTV horror's negotiation of this terrain see Badley, 2010). Through their alignment with established forms of cult cinema, *The Evolved: Part One* and *The Summer of the Massacre* are invested with a measure of subcultural authenticity which belies the fact that neither film can lay claim to the cult following or the controversy that would support such a reputation.

---

[5]The film also appears in the box set *Bloody Nightmares*, which showcases 100 amateur horror films over 24 discs. There are two other prominent distributors of this kind of material in the United States, both of which distribute British films: World Wide Multi Media and Chemical Burn Entertainment.

Troma positions *The Evolved: Part One* in such a way as to suggest that it embodies the brand identity that the company developed in the 1980s and 1990s through relatively high-profile releases such as the *Toxic Avenger* series (1984–2003) and *Class of Nuke 'em High* (1986). Consequently, the film's DVD cover projects a similar sense of wackiness by situating a Nazi puppet carrying a corpse alongside incongruously colorful neon surroundings. In line with other Troma DVDs, the film's title is capitalized and rendered in a bold green font surrounded by a yellowish hue. This color scheme approximates Troma's house style inasmuch as it is also used for the company's corporate logo, as well as its most well-known product: the *Toxic Avenger* movies. *The Evolved: Part One* is therefore associated with examples of canonized paracinema, and imbued with an aura that this British obscurity would be unlikely to develop autonomously. Put differently, Troma's seal of approval elevates this film to the status of a cult work that demands the attention of trash aficionados.

Before considering the positioning of *The Summer of the Massacre*, a few words on its US distributor, Brain Damage Films, are needed. As a newer player in film distribution, Brain Damage has sought to generate awareness of, and interest in, its portfolio of films among targeted consumers. It has therefore advertised on internet forums such as the Underground Horror Network in an effort to complement the passing trade that no doubt drives sales of its products at online retailers such as amazon.com. Moreover, the company's own website proclaims it to be the "Number 1 in Indie Horror and Shock," while the website of its sister label, Maxim Media (through which Brain Damage's titles are also available), claims it to be "[t]he largest worldwide distributor of independent horror and shock films [whose] library of indie horror, thriller, paranormal, and reality/shock films is unparalleled in size—and always growing!" Such hyperbole is played very much tongue-in-cheek: Brain Damage's official forum indicates that it has only one member (me!), and the company's 500 followers on Twitter pale in comparison to Troma's 4,500. This is not to suggest that the company is in a state of denial over its own marginality. Quite the contrary: this marginality is transformed into a selling point for the niche of consumers who see themselves as indulging in the forbidden fruit in which the company trades. A keen awareness of the product and its market is in operation here, one that places exclusive emphasis on the consumer of "shot-on-video, low-budget horror"—the "Gorehound"—and one which openly acknowledges that the standard of the films on offer will be found wanting when judged by established indices of quality and value relating to production values, narrative coherence, and acting competency (Brain Damage Films). Accordingly, Brain Damage's claim that *The Summer of the Massacre* will "sicken even the hardest of horror fans" is not to be taken too seriously, especially if one is aware that this company also handles the similarly schlocky and absurdly titled *Motor Home Massacre* (2005), *RetarDead*, and *Bachelor Party in the Bungalow of the Damned* (both 2008). The foregrounding of badness as a selling point thus aligns *The Summer of the Massacre* to the other paracinematic oddities in Brain Damage's portfolio in a manner that angles discourse of cult to those "Gorehounds" who are very much in on the joke.

The UK release of *The Summer of the Massacre* also mobilized discourses of cult. In its domestic market the film was, as I noted above, issued as part of *The Dead of Night* collection of DVDs; a collection that mixes obscurities like 1973's *Dr Tarr's Torture Dungeon* (AKA *The Mansion of Madness*), *Birds of Prey* (1987), and *Oliver Twisted* (2000) with a number of famous older titles—from American cheapies such as *Don't Look in the Basement* (1973), *Massacre at Central High* (1976), and *Chopping Mall* (1986), to the revered Italian exploitation pictures *Kill, Baby … Kill* (AKA *Curse of the Dead*) (1966), *Zombie Flesh Eaters* (1979), and *Zombie Holocaust* (1980). In this respect, the DVD series echoes Troma's output, since it places under a single banner both celebrated cult films and largely unknown fare. *The Summer of the Massacre* DVD was, like the other films in the collection, adorned with a black cover that featured "The Dead of Night Collection" at the top, and the film's title across the middle. This uniformity of style serves to unite otherwise disparate films; unlike those in Arrow Video's cult horror series or in Shameless DVD's sex and exploitation catalog, these do not in all cases share a director, a single genre, reputations, or contexts of production. This form of branding validates each film in the collection as what we might term a "cult film by association."

Where it has been argued that DTV films are disposable artifacts, that they offer "the audience what they like (and nothing more)," and that they are "something to be bought, sold and forgotten" (Labato, 2012, pp. 25, 34), it could also be argued that Troma, Brain Damage, and *The Dead of Night* collection operate in a quite different way. At a point in time when the major Hollywood companies and their sister labels have peppered the theatrical and home-viewing markets with comparatively glossy remakes of cult horror films such as *The Hills Have Eyes* (1977, 2006) and *The Last House on the Left* (1972, 2009), these small companies have traded in a form of subcultural authenticity that the heavyweights of motion picture distribution could not marshal based on their corporate power. This (desired) subcultural authenticity derives from a sense of sleaze and the forbidden which itself derives from a new generation of exploitation cinema that eschews the respectability and overt commerciality of the Hollywood re-envisaging or even that of the newly re-mastered widescreen collectors' editions of the films of cult Italian exploitation filmmakers such as Mario Bava and Lucio Fulci. As one user of the online forum Cult Labs stated of *The Dead of Night* collection: "ok the transfers [are] not up to Shameless standard, nor [are] the covers (the actual cover feels like its been printed from a home printer), but I kinda feel that this adds to the whole feel of the sleeziness [sic] of these films, if you know what I mean" ("iluvdvds@Cult_Labs", 2008). In other words, while a film like *The Summer of the Massacre* may well have been lost amid the thousands of films in international circulation, it is preserved amid the otherwise disparate films in *The Dead of Night* collection. Sleaziness is seen as a positive, and cheap packaging as appropriate to the films in question; they complement an aura of the low in a way that a widescreen HD restoration or a glossy Hollywood remake could never do.

While many British horror filmmakers feel that the benefits of working with a distributor outweigh their concerns that their films may be mis-marketed, for others the prospect that their work could be misrepresented is too much to bear, leading them to assert a greater measure of control over their output through various forms of self-distribution.

Self-distribution

The internet has opened up multiple opportunities for filmmakers to distribute their films themselves, and British horror filmmakers have adopted three main approaches. First, the cottage industry DVD approach involves a collective (usually the director and his friends) paying for its film to be glass-mastered and reproduced at a professional pressing plant, after it has been submitted for certification to the British Board of Film Classification (hereafter BBFC). An example of this fairly atypical means of distribution is provided by *Hacked Off* (2005), 1,000 copies of which were available from high street stores and online retailers (see Brown, 2005). Second is the VHS/VCD/DVD-R approach, whereby home-made copies of a film are disseminated on one of these formats either via events such as fairs or from online retailers like amazon.com, which, through its CreateSpace subsidiary, handles the duplication and sale of DVD-Rs. Films that have been made available in this manner include *Written in Blood* (1998), *Cycle* (2005), *The Lost* (2006), and *Ouija Board*. Third, films are released online through video-sharing services such as YouTube or Vimeo, through a film's official website, as with the 2009 "online theatrical premiere" of *Stag Night of the Dead* (2010) at stagnightofthedead.com, or through an affiliate such as dreadcentral.com, which premiered *Pig* in 2010.

Self-distribution is both a product of, and a solution to, the economic constraints under which most British horror filmmakers must work. The

CreateSpace option, for example, enables producers to "retain copyright through a non-exclusive license," while also incorporating a "fixed revenue-sharing split" that is initiated at the point of first sale (Cunningham and Silver, 2012, p. 56). Of particular relevance to horror filmmakers is the fact that such an arrangement, like most of the others described above, provides a way of circumventing the costly submission of films to censorship boards. In particular, the fact that amazon.com is based in the United States, a country in which filmmakers are not legally bound to submit their work for certification, allows Britons to sidestep the costly submission of their films to the BBFC—a prerequisite of releasing a film commercially in the United Kingdom. Alternatively, to acquire a DVD certificate in the UK, the makers of a film like *The Lost*, which was shot for £3,000 (circa US$4,800) in 48 hours, would have been charged an impedimentary £600 (circa US$960) as a result of a "handling fee of £75 [circa US$120] per submission plus £6.00 [c. US$10] per minute for full length of work" (BBFC, 2013). To this expenditure would be added the cost of prints, of cover art, and of the DVD interface, all of which must themselves also pass through the BBFC at a cost to the distributor (or in this case to the filmmakers themselves).

These forms of independence have also afforded British horror filmmakers several advantages over conventional means of delivery. They have enabled them to distribute their work across the globe quickly, conveniently, and affordably, thus allowing them to determine the exchange value of their products rather than have third parties do so on their behalf. It has also enabled filmmakers to retain the rights to their intellectual property, thereby ensuring that it is they who decide upon the cut of the film that reaches audiences as opposed to third parties who may re-cut it to make it fit better into their own corporate branding exercises, as happened with *The Evolved: Part One* and *The Summer of the Massacre*. The sense of comfort, achievement, and self-determination that filmmakers feel comes with such practices is expressed by the director of *Ouija Board*, Matt "M. J." Stone, who revealed: "I've loved every aspect of making the film, designing the DVD cover, the DVD menus, the website, editing and shooting myself, coming up with the idea and building it up to a full script with only myself to please" (2011).

Conclusion

This chapter has examined the centrality of home video to the distribution of twenty-first-century British horror films. By addressing the economic imperatives that underwrote the production of such films, I argue that the relative financial success of *The Descent* incentivized the production of low-budget fare intended for non-theatrical distribution. The filmmakers behind this type of British horror cinema have either negotiated or embraced the subcultural credentials of DTV releases by cutting deals with specialist DVD distributors or by releasing the films themselves. The chapter has also shown that DVD labels pitched the films to a niche of web users as cult cinema, and that self-distribution enabled the films' makers to stay true to their creative visions, by ensuring that it was they and not third parties who determined the final cut of the film.

Unlike in the 1970s, when the British film industry all but collapsed following the withdrawal of American capital, in the twenty-first century, the internet, along with affordable filmmaking and editing equipment, has enabled horror film production to continue albeit outside of what we might think of as traditional spheres of production and conventional channels of distribution. Of course, DTV horror is not only a British phenomenon, with informal distribution underwriting the circulation of films such as Italy's *The Shunned House* (2003), Pakistan's *Hell's Ground* (2007), and Spain's *Juan of the Dead* (2011). New research will shed light on the precise manner in which nationally specific, genre-specific, and transnational industrial conditions shape the production, content, distribution, and promotion of these films. Such undertakings promise to reveal the extent to which the case of the United Kingdom is fairly distinct, or whether it is emblematic of practices taking place across the globe.

Horror movies released on DTV may well be "impressively bad," as Stuart Heritage has suggested of the British contributions, but they are "still impressive" when we consider the constraints under which they are made (Heritage, 2012). Therefore, while subsequent UK offerings may not ultimately be as visible or as broadly appealing as, say, Hammer's *The Woman in Black* or the next Hollywood horror blockbuster, the Gorehounds who seek out this material are likely to find it, and, in so doing, ensure that the reels keep turning for DTV British horror.

References

Badley, L. (2010), "Bringing it All Back Home: Horror Cinema and Video Culture," in I. Conrich (ed.) *Horror Zone: The Cultural Experience of Contemporary Horror Cinema*, London: I. B. Tauris.

Brain Damage Films (2013), available online at http://braindamagefilms.com/about/ (accessed July 18, 2013).

British Board of Film Classification (BBFC) (2013), available online at http://www.bbfc.co.uk/industry-services/additional-information/fee-tariff (accessed July 18, 2013).

Brown, P. (2005), "Andrew Weild," *Horror Asylum*. Available online at http://www.horror-asylum.com/interview/andrewweild/interview.asp (accessed January 11, 2011).

Carruthers, J. (2010), "An Open Letter to *Gorezone* Magazine," *Let's Get Dangerous!*, January 13. Available online at http://letsgetdangerous.wordpress.com/2010/01/13/an-open-letter-to-gorezone-magazine (accessed April 7, 2011).

Cunningham, S. and Silver, J. (2012), "On-line Film Distribution: Its History and Global Complexion," in D. Iordanova and S. Cunningham (eds) *Digital Disruption: Cinema Movies On-line*, St. Andrews: St. Andrews Film Studies.

Henderson, S. (2009), "From Screen to Shelf: Perspectives on Independent Distribution," *Journal of British Cinema and Television*, 6.3: 468–80.

Heritage, S. (2012), "*Kill Keith*: Cheggers' Horror is a Film to Die for," *Guardian*, March 22. Available online at http://www.guardian.co.uk/film/filmblog/2012/mar/22/kill-keith-british-horror (accessed July 2, 2012).

"iluvdvds@Cult_Labs" (2008), Untitled Blog Post. Available online at http://www.cult-labs.com/forums/horror-today/652-dead-night.html (accessed August 13, 2013).

Jancovich, M. (2000), "'A Real Shocker': Authenticity, Genre and the Struggle for Cultural Distinctions," *Cultural Studies*, 14.1: 22–35.

Kemp, S. (2012), "*The Woman in Black* is the Most Successful British Horror Film in 20 Years," *Hollywood Reporter*, Febuary 28. Available online at http://www.hollywoodreporter.com/news/daniel-radcliffe-woman-in-black-box-office-295641 (accessed November 28, 2012).

Klinger, B. (2006), *Beyond the Multiplex: Cinema, New Technologies, and the Home*, Berkeley: University of California Press.

Labato, R. (2012), *Shadow Economies of Cinema: Mapping Informal Film Distribution*, London: BFI.

Leggott, J. (2008), *From Heritage to Horror: Contemporary British Cinema*, London: Wallflower.

Macnab, G. (2004), "The Wages of Fear," *Screen International*, 1438, p. 6.

Manzoor, S. (2009), "My £45 Hit Film: Marc Price on his Zombie Movie *Colin*," *Guardian*, July 30. Available online at http://www.guardian.co.uk/film/2009/jul/30/marc-price-zombie-film-colin (accessed November 11, 2012).

Mathijs, E. and Sexton, J. (2011), *Cult Cinema: An Introduction*, Oxford: Wiley-Blackwell.

Minns, A. (2004), "Distributing Support," *Screen International*, 1451, p. 8.

Mitchell, R. (2002), "Marketing Drives *28 Days Later*," *Screen International*, 1380, November 8–14, p. 6.

Nesselon, L. (2006), "Review: *The Evolved: Part One*," *Variety*, June 18. Available online at http://variety.com/2006/film/reviews/the-evolved-part-one-1200515405 (accessed May 1, 2012).

Petley, J. (2002), "From Brit-flicks to Shit-flicks: The Cost of Public Subsidy," *Journal of Popular British Cinema*, 5: 37–52.

Reinhold, C. (2009), "*The Summer of the Massacre*," *Horror Unrated*. Available online at http://www.horrorunrated.com/reviews/s/THE%20SUMMER%20OF%20THE%20MASSACRE.htm (accessed May 1, 2013).

Sconce, J. (1995), "'Trashing' the Academy: Taste, Excess and an Emerging Politics of Cinematic Style," *Screen*, 36.4: 371–93.

Sothcott, J. (2011) Email Interview with Author, November 11.
Stanley, R. (2002), "Dying Light: An Obituary for the Great British Horror Film," in S. Chibnall and J. Petley (eds) *British Horror Cinema*, London: Routledge.
Stone, M. (2011), Email Interview with Author, November 11.
Tilley, D. (2011), "Blood Nightmares #34: *The Summer of the Massacre*," *Movie Feast*, May 23. Available online at http://moviefeast.blogspot.co.uk/2011/05/bloody-nightmares-34-summer-of-massacre.html (accessed May 1, 2013).
UK Film Council (2004), *UK Film Council Statistical Year Book: Annual Review 2003–2004*. Available online at http://www.ukfilmcouncil.org.uk/media/pdf/l/r/Final_Yearbook_0304.pdf (accessed January 7, 2011).
—(2006), *UK Film Council Statistical Year Book 2005–2006*. Available online at http://www.ukfilmcouncil.org.uk/media/pdf/l/r/Statistical_Yearbook_05-06.pdf (accessed January 7, 2011).
Walker, J. (2011), "*F* for 'Frightening'?: Johannes Roberts Takes on Hoodie Horrors," *Diabolique*, 3: 24–32.
—(2012), "A Wilderness of Horrors? – British Horror Cinema in the New Millennium," *Journal of British Cinema and Television*, 9.3: 436–46.
Williams, L. R. (2005), *The Erotic Thriller in Contemporary Cinema*, Edinburgh: Edinburgh University Press.

14

Hammer 2.0

Legacy, Modernization, and Hammer Horror as a Heritage Brand

Matt Hills

The British company Hammer was once a prolific producer of horror films; yet, as David Pirie notes, "[the year] 1979 was the last moment of the old Hammer" (2008, p. 191). Michael Carreras resigned as director that April, and within days the firm had fallen into receivership (Hearn and Barnes, 2007, p. 171). Although several buyouts and re-launches followed (Hutchings, 1993; Meikle, 2009; Rose, 2009), a 1979 remake of *The Lady Vanishes* would be Hammer's last new theatrically released film until *Let Me In* (2010) 31 years later. As Marcus Hearn has stated, the late 1970s "was the end of an historic bloodline, but the brand would outlive its creators" (2011, p. 167).

My interest in this chapter lies with the twenty-first-century resurrection of Hammer under CEO Simon Oakes, or what has been dubbed "Hammer 2.0" (Scargill, 2011).[1] The "new Hammer" is the custodian of an extensive back catalog of audiovisual content that can be licensed, merchandised, and

---

[1] While the development of Hammer 2.0 is linked to "the emergence of branding *as a discourse*" (Moor, 2007, p. 5; emphasis in original), it needs to be remembered that branding "is hardly new to the film industry. Historically, it can be traced to the use of company trademarks in the early 1900s and to the formalization of product branding around stars and serials in the 1910s" (Grainge, 2008, p. 8). That said, branding "has become linked to key transformations and developments within contemporary cultural industries" taking place from the 1980s onwards (ibid., p. 9).

monetized. It is now involved in the production of new films, web content, books, theater plays, and audio projects. Oakes' entry in the program for Hammer's stage version of *The Turn of the Screw* (2013) describes his company's activity thus:

> After the acquisition of Hammer Films in 2007, Simon and his partners rebooted this beloved British heritage brand with a new slate of films. This is Hammer's first foray into theatre having previously extended the brand into publishing with Random House and the digital media space with Hammer YouTube channel.
> (Almeida Theatre Programme, 2013, p. 19)

But what does it mean for Hammer to be positioned industrially and discursively as a "heritage brand" that operates across media in the age of convergence? In the first section of this chapter, I focus on the tensions that have arisen out of Hammer's attempts to trade on its past and to position itself as contemporary. I argue that such practice has resulted in a contradictory identity for the present-day Hammer, one marked both by modernization and nostalgia.[2]

Part of Hammer's value as a brand derives not only from its history and its cultural status, but also from its dedicated fan following. I consider this phenomenon in the second section of the chapter, in which I address "brand community" (Kornberger, 2010, p. 131), conflicts between fans and company management, and the ways in which Hammer horror fandom exceeds and transgresses brand discourses. As Heather Hendershot has observed, "the rise of media convergence has created both problems and solutions for horror" (2011, p. 161). At the corporate level, problems occur when companies look to develop cross-platform franchises over stand-alone films. The industrial environment in which the former has developed nevertheless offers solutions to such challenges, because niche platforms like premium cable television can show horror that does not need to worry about Broadcast Standards and Practices, unlike US network TV. As Hendershot points out, the issue becomes one of "developing [...] brands [...] that function equally

---

[2] It should be noted that "[i]dentifying branding remains difficult [...] because branding proceeds in different ways in different institutional contexts, and because new accounts of, and prescriptions for, branding are being produced all the time by various marketing gurus and branding consultancies. Branding is assembled or 'put together' differently in these different contexts" (Moor, 2007, p. 7). Referring to "the brand" therefore risks the spurious reduction of diverse activities to a "single thing" (Lury, 2004, p. 16). Nonetheless, such practice may be analyzed in specific institutional contexts and it is this more focused approach that I adopt here, rather than offering a master theory of branding in relation to horror's merchants of menace.

well as films, TV, and games" (ibid.). Yet, strictly speaking, Hammer has not engaged in transmedia storytelling. It has instead concentrated on developing distinct projects intended for individual media rather than multiple platforms. As a heritage brand, Hammer boasts a portfolio of legacy and newer properties. This focus on brand extension has created difficulties related to coherence and integrity (see Jenkins, 2006, p. 19; Arvidsson, 2006, p. 77). As this chapter shows, branding discourses have led to a curiously doubled effect whereby Hammer 2.0 has oscillated uneasily between a reaction to the present and a loyalty to the past.

Modernized ... or classic British horror? The perils and possibilities of doubled branding

Initially, the twenty-first-century rebirth of Hammer was surprisingly low-key. One of its first new titles, *Beyond the Rave* (2008), was not earmarked for theatrical release, but was a web-based serial produced by Puregrass, a company that had previously worked on the horror web serial *When Evil Calls* (2008). This practice permitted the employment of a low-budget, promised strong appeal to the youth demographic, and enabled collaborations with social media such as the MySpace website. *Beyond the Rave* also made extensive use of dance music that had been selected by the celebrity DJ Pete Tong, and boasted profiles of its vampire characters on myspace.com. Conversely, it gestured to Hammer's past. The horror icon Ingrid Pitt featured in one installment, and the crew commentary that accompanied the DVD release of *Beyond the Rave* spotlighted "Hammer references," including shooting at the traditional Hammer location of Black Park in the English county of Buckinghamshire, and the 1957 release of *Quatermass 2* (Crew Commentary). We are told that these "specific [...] moments [...] directly relate to the Hammer legacy" (ibid.), illustrating that the producers of *Beyond the Rave* were aware of the need to also include material that might appeal to long-term fans.

Predictably, Hammer was anxious to reassert its pop cultural kudos after such a long period of inactivity. *Beyond the Rave*, with its MySpace/DJ tie-ins, represented a rather heavy-handed attempt to mark the title as "now" and youthful, its more traditionally Hammer elements notwithstanding. *Dracula A.D. 1972* (1972) is also discussed in the aforementioned commentary, albeit without any sense that this film was part of an earlier struggle to update Hammer. *Dracula A.D. 1972* went into production as "Dracula Today"(Rigby, 2000, p. 194), and used pop music "as a signifier of 'modernity', explicitly levelled at a young audience" (Donnelly, 2005, p. 101). With this film and several other projects, "pop songs were only a momentary attraction, an attempt to furnish the films with a pop culture credibility" (ibid.). Attempting paratextually to frame *Beyond the Rave* as carrying brand coherence by invoking *Dracula A.D. 1972* is therefore rather ironic: it fails to consider the extent to which Hammer's output had by the 1970s already become incoherent and reactive. As Martin Kornberger (2010, p. 112) notes of problematic branding:

> [I]f one puts too much emphasis on the external environment, this leads to hyper-adaptation: an organisation involved in hyper-adaptation follows every fashion trend head over heels. An example is LEGO in the 1990s, which opened up theme parks, went into LEGO TV, lifestyle, retail, dolls, robotics, software, and so on. In the end, this was a disastrous strategy because LEGO mimicked trends that did not resonate with its legacy.

This discourse of legacy was thoroughly internalized by those working on *Beyond the Rave*. It also underwrote the production of DVD/Blu-ray extras, the copyright of which was attributed to "Hammer Films Legacy Limited." Yet, *Beyond the Rave* only really resembles *Dracula A.D. 1972* insofar as it appears hyper-adaptive. Its makers emphasize the "external environment," to use Kornberger's terms, rather than fashioning an innovative film. Film historians such as Peter Hutchings have made a strong case for reading breakthrough Hammer releases like *The Curse of Frankenstein* (1957) as innovative horror (Hutchings, 2001, pp. 85–6). But if Hammer partly made its name in unearthing new shock effects—allied with "upscale […] period setting[s]" (Heffernan, 2004, p. 58)—the novelty of *Beyond the Rave* derived from its status as a web series. As a result of relying on MySpace profiles to develop its characters, *Beyond the Rave*'s protagonists come across as underdeveloped ciphers in the film itself. The outcome was a Hammer title that while derivative still looks and sounds like a product of its techno-cultural moment. By veering towards dance music as an unstable marker of modernization—Tong's involvement was evidently intended to mark the soundtrack as credible—*Beyond the Rave* detaches itself from Hammer's past, and the company's celebrated recruitment of composers such as James Bernard (see Mathijs and Sexton, 2011, p. 180). As such, the makers of *Beyond the Rave* self-consciously abandon a musical legacy and a cult of Hammer soundtracks that was built on ostinato motifs and rises in pitch (Donnelly, 2005, pp. 99–100), in favor of a radically different DJ-led "sonic branding" (Powers, 2010, p. 293). Rather than contributing to Hammer's "brand awareness, appeal and cohesion" (ibid.), this deployment of dance music "relies on

[...] longstanding assumptions about the power of musical sound [...] [as] a vector of pure affect" (ibid., p. 288), but in a way that has no connection to its past. The choice of music therefore collides with the brand, glancing off it as a connotative irrelevance that fails to reinforce any of the qualities traditionally associated with Hammer. For Devon Powers, sonic branding is very much about targeting consumers with a "totalizing" brand experience (ibid., p. 300). Far from achieving such a state however, the extension of Hammer into low-budget web serialization fractures and fragments this experience. Black Park, Ingrid Pitt, and vampiric figures are overwritten with instances of formal "now-ness" such as short bursts of online narrative, and by sonic or musical credibility. Hammer's desire not to belong to the past results in a failure to consider how its ostensive golden years were linked to generic innovation at the textual level rather than with technical innovation, while generating a marked tension between subordinated legacy and hyper-adaptive modernization.

Its music may have sought pop credibility, but Hammer was ill-served by *Beyond the Rave*'s uneasy mix of vampires and club culture. The project has been marginalized in Hammer's subsequent brand discourses. The afore-mentioned résumé of CEO Simon Oakes makes no mention of the MySpace serial. Moreover, Marcus Hearn's official publication *The Hammer Vault* devotes only a single sentence to *Beyond the Rave*, before concluding that Hammer's new production, *Wake Wood* (2010), had "helped to re-establish Hammer as a credible brand for the new century" (2011, p. 171). The impli-cation is that *Beyond the Rave* did no such thing.

In contrast to the British-centered *Beyond the Rave*, Hammer's first theatri-cally released film since its re-emergence was distanced from the company's national origins: 2010's *Let Me In* relocated *Let the Right One In* (2008) from Sweden to the United States of the early 1980s. Directed by Matt Reeves, *Let Me In* was promoted as "from the director of *Cloverfield* [2008]." *Let Me In* appears to have been calibrated to resemble J. J. Abrams' style of US multiplex-friendly productions due to its use of lens flare, its small-town American setting, and references to Abrams' Bad Robot production company (such as the incor-poration of the fictional brand "Slusho" (Reeves, 2011)). If Hammer's legacy of British horror was submerged by pop signifiers of modernity in *Beyond the Rave*, on this occasion, Hollywood conventions overwhelmed the possibility that *Let Me In* might contribute to the construction of Hammer as a coherent brand. *Let Me In* explicitly Americanizes Hammer. So seamless is this assimi-lation of Hollywood convention that, as Ken Gelder (2012, p. 38) recognizes:

> very few film reviewers had a good word to say about Reeves's *Let Me In* [...] For Ryan Gilbey in the *New Statesman*, *Let Me In* is "reconstituted

cinema, a computer's idea of what made the original tick and click". For Terrence Rafferty in the *New York Times*, "All remakes feed guiltily on the blood of their originals". [...] Here, it is as if Reeves's relation to *Let the Right One in* is exactly like Oskar's relation to Eli: neighbourly and vampiric.

Whether machinic or vampiric, *Let Me In* was certainly not linked discursively with notions of art or transgression. As Hutchings (1993, p. 87) has lamented of the cultural memories and celebratory narratives that have surrounded Hammer:

> we must constantly be aware of British horror's disreputability, for this quality comprises an integral part of the genre's working. It is a fundamental condition of British horror's existence that no one 'really' takes it seriously; therein lies dispensation for its transgressions. [...] Rendering these films worthy and respectable would be doing them a disservice. More, it would be like forcing them into the light and then watching helplessly as they crumble into dust.

The final sentence references one of Hammer's most (in)famous moments: the defeat of Dracula (Christopher Lee) by Peter Cushing's Van Helsing at the conclusion of the 1958 version of *Dracula*. Hutchings reminds us that Hammer's 1950s putative golden age was accompanied by a keen sense of cultural transgression and generic innovation. *Dracula*, like 1957's *The Curse of Frankenstein*, was hardly an on-trend or respectable title even if it has been elevated over the years to the status of a horror classic. *Let Me In* remakes a vampire film that was taken seriously by critics for its blend of social realism and chilling ambivalence: it is therefore a pre-sold property rooted in respectable horror and reworked in a "US mainstream/multiplex" visual style. These characteristics are the antithesis of Hammer's historical dimensions, apart from the fact that the film focuses on vampires and therefore summons the figure of Dracula. Hyper-adaptive brand modernization again triumphs over brand "legacy": "Hammer is returned in name only" (Meikle, 2009, p. 226). This type of modernization is concerned with fitting into contemporary Hollywood horror trends rather than risking generic transgression or marked textual development.

Filmed partly in New Mexico, set in New York, and starring Hilary Swank along with Christopher Lee in a supporting role, *The Resident* (2011) represented another component in Hammer's aggressive pursuit of the American market. Strong paratextual attempts were made to align this film with Hammer traditions. Hammer archivist Marcus Hearn narrates it as "a modern take on Hammer's stylish legacy of suspense thrillers," drawing parallels between Lee's appearance in the film and his role in *Taste of Fear* (1961): "still cast as the red herring some 50 years later" (Hearn, 2011, p. 173). Similarly, other official brand discourses positioned *The Resident* as part of Hammer's lineage:

> *The Resident* may seem to be an unusual fit for the Hammer production slate. [...] But at various stages in the history of Hammer, thrillers have provided an alternative backbone and staple diet. [...][S]criptwriter Jimmy Sangster [...] initiated the group of films often labelled as "mini-Hitchcocks". Beginning with *Taste of Fear*, Hammer would produce a series of films [...] which [...] clearly drew their influence [...] from Hitchcock's thrillers. [...] So as Hammer returned to production some 25 years later, it was perhaps little surprise that they [*sic*] honed-in on another 'Woman in Terror' story.
>
> (Simpson, 2011)

This attempt to reconcile brand legacy and modernization remains somewhat unconvincing if one contrasts official paratexts to the film itself. Despite attempts to align *The Resident* with *Taste of Fear*, its use of Christopher Lee is comparatively restrained. In the role of August, Lee never constitutes a convincing threat to Swank's Juliet. The notion that she finds him unnerving seems to derive more from the self-referential concept of Lee as a Hammer favorite than his character in this movie. Moreover, about 30 minutes into *The Resident* it is revealed that August's grandson Max (Jeffrey Dean Morgan) has in fact been stalking Juliet. This twist sidelines any focus on Lee as the potential villain of the piece. By contrast, Francis Cottam's novelization focuses more intently on Lee's character:

> August looked probingly into Juliet's face. [...] [H]e was probably about eighty years old, tall and gaunt and with the frailness of old age, but with a strong mental energy, an emotional alertness that came off him like heat. [...] He stretched out his hand to her and she shook it, surprised at the strength of his grip.
>
> (Cottam, 2011, p. 61)

The film does not clearly convey August's "emotional alertness"; nor does it provide a reaction shot to indicate that Juliet has been surprised by his fierce grip. The potency invested in August by Cottam's rendering seems to draw on Lee's "intertextual (sub)cultural capital" as an icon of horror cinema (Hills, 2005, p. 187), thereby granting him a more forceful and threatening presence: his casting gestures to Hammer's past, raising the possibility of tying together old and new incarnations of the company. Yet, *The Resident* plays like an unremarkable psycho-thriller; its use of a renovating nail gun à la the home invasion thriller *Pacific Heights* (1990), like its shift in perspective via a rewind effect, feel like well-worn devices. The New York setting remains a world away from the British NSS Newsagent chain depicted in *Straight on till Morning* (1972) or the boys' school of *Fear in the Night* (1972). Whether in its gothic horror or women-in-peril guises, Hammer has rarely relied so heavily on such obvious Hollywood shorthand. Instead, it typically showcased Britishness via details of ingrained actorly habitus, the Buckinghamshire countryside, and country houses like Oakley Court.

The Resident and *Let Me In* both display tensions between legacy and modernization through their courting of American and international audiences for whom New York City serves as a default urban space and Abrams-esque lens flare a default visual style. Set against these titles, 2010's *Wake Wood* and *The Woman in Black* retreated towards Hammer's past by restoring a sense of Britishness. But even this practice could not recuperate a coherent brand identity, since it merely created an additional level of brand doubling: Hammer seemed torn between contemporary-feeling US pieces and backward-looking UK representations of pastoral landscapes. For instance, in contrast to the prevailing now-ness of *Beyond the Rave* and *The Resident*, CEO Simon Oakes describes *Wake Wood* as "a throwback [...] to the sort of [...] more Pagan, Occult films that Hammer was famous for in the sixties and seventies" (Cast and Crew Interviews, 2011). This film features a couple who, after the death of their daughter, discover that rituals performed in the sleepy town of Wake Wood may be able to bring back their offspring, but at the cost of never being able to leave the place. *Wake Wood* is preoccupied with an inability to move on; its lead characters Patrick (Aiden Gillen) and Louise (Eva Birthistle) seek to restore the past through mystical means. This theme is made explicit in the chilling words with which K. A. John closes her novelization: "Patrick would [...] be [...] more tied to the town than ever" (2011, p. 295). Oakes' emphasis on a "throwback" seemingly blurs diegetic and extra-diegetic meanings: characters are trapped in the titular town of Wake Wood because it allows them to hold onto deceased loved ones, while Hammer must also avoid becoming trapped in its own past. The Hammer 2.0 film that is most explicitly linked to the company's legacy is thus itself a fable, one that warns of the need both to honor the past and let go of it. Hearn suggests that *Wake Wood* was "on the appropriate subject of rebirth" (2011, p. 171) forming part of Hammer's reinvention. Even more appropriately however, this film is about the need to fuse past and present rather than about subordinating the latter to the former.

The Woman in Black, a gothic chiller adapted from a Susan Hill (1983) novel of the same name, is Hammer 2.0's biggest commercial success. A major factor in the box office achievements of *The Woman in Black* was its status as a star vehicle for the *Harry Potter* (2001–11) actor Daniel Radcliffe. In this case, Hammer's notable hit was less a result of generic innovation or textual transgression than piggybacking on Harry Potter's brand equity. The *Harry Potter* films, operating as what Paul Grainge terms a "'calculated' [...] franchise" (2008, p. 142), had "sought to establish a base of consumer loyalty, preparing the way for the frequent, near annual, re-promotion of the Harry Potter brand. [...] Central to this strategy was the idea that (child) consumers would grow with the franchise and its characters as sequels were produced, a principle of maturation" (Grainge 2008, p. 140). With *The Woman in Black*, Hammer aimed to exploit this strategy by ostensibly completing the arc of the *Harry Potter* brand, implying that Radcliffe had matured into full adulthood by moving genres from juvenile fantasy to a harder-edged ghost story. Hammer thus appropriated (*Harry Potter*) brand discourses that had become attached to Radcliffe's growth from boy to man. This shrewd parabranding amounts to one brand amorphously deriving value from another, without the industrial agents involved licensing the intellectual property and without a co-branding agreement. *The Woman in Black* was thus a highly opportunistic project, one that was once again hyper-adaptive to external environments. Casting of this sort ensures that even though *The Woman in Black* complements Hammer's legacy, it too responds to the perceived need for modernization. The film's denouement plays to norms of contemporary mainstream cinema: screenwriter Jane Goldman's adaptation replaces the downbeat conclusion of Hill's book with a feel-good ending in which the family unit is magically restored, albeit beyond the grave. Hollywood ideology aimed at the restoration of connotative normality is thus recuperated, despite the death of Radcliffe's character.

The tension between legacy and modernization that has plagued Hammer 2.0 has led to a crucial difference between Hammer's putative golden age and its new discursive framing. Such was Hammer's intense production schedule in the 1950s and 1960s that it was almost singlehandedly responsible for the generation of certain cycles of film. Consequently, Hammer could occupy the different stages of a film cycle, creating both a "Trailblazer Hit"—commercially successful films that exhibit a high degree of textual innovation to which new cycles can be traced—and "Prospector Cash-ins" i.e. similar films made quickly to capitalize on such hits—before its own sequels finally saturated the market (see Nowell, 2011, pp. 46, 52). This situation differs markedly from subsequent horror film cycles such as the slasher films of the 1980s and 1990s, wherein films were made by different producers. No longer emulating its predecessor's factory-like production, Hammer 2.0 occupies a far weaker position economically. Not only is the company unable singlehandedly to generate cycles, it has also failed to create any significant Trailblazer Hits. Instead, and as a result of its desire to be seen as a current brand, rather than trading exclusively on past glories, Hammer 2.0 has focused on inexpensive Cash-ins as it seeks to emulate patterns in horror production such as producing a low-budget web serial with a more experienced partner; a remake of a critically acclaimed "serious" vampire movie; an urban thriller/star vehicle; character-driven rural horror, or a ghost story/star vehicle that once again emphasizes the sanctity of the conventional family unit. The problem with brand discourses here is that they encourage an emulative position; Hammer seeks to jump on trends and copy "mainstream" successes. As such, the company has fused contemporary horror film conventions with (usually marginalized) nods to its past without ever looking to lead the market or innovate, as it did with its 1950s gothic horrors and reworking of *Frankenstein* (see Heffernan, 2004, p. 49). Caught between emulating its own past and the contemporaneous genre concerns of others, Hammer's post-2007 audiovisual output has recurrently cultivated brand legacy and modernization.

Retro ... or neo-chillers? The pleasures and pains of commodified nostalgia

Not only is Hammer's output characterized by fissures and fractures; the company's engagement with "fan nostalgia" (Garde-Hansen, 2011, p. 132) is marked by tension as well. A reduction in risk-taking innovation has been a problem for Hammer as a contemporary brand, but long-term fans have also vocally opposed some of Hammer 2.0's output, suggesting that so-called "brand communities" may also pose a threat to the company's reinvention (Arvidsson, 2006, p. 80; Kornberger, 2010, p. 131).

As a heritage brand, Hammer complements its new projects by exploiting its back catalog. Brigid Cherry has pointed out that Hammer uses information about the company in a manner intended to feed fans' yearnings to increase their supply of subcultural capital: "the Hammer [web]site offers a history of the studio and archival material on every Hammer film [...] [T]hese features allow fans to build on their knowledge and competencies" (2010, pp. 78–9). Such a combination of promotional and fan discourse is also apparent in reference publications such as *The Hammer Vault* (Hearn, 2011) and *The Hammer Story: The Authorised History of Hammer Films* (Hearn and Barnes, 2007), as well as in DVD/Blu-ray extras and at events such as the 2013 "BFI Monster Weekend," which premiered a newly restored print of *The Mummy* (1959) at the British Museum. It is nonetheless imperative that we avoid concluding that Hammer's mobilization of its own past means that the company is merely catering to nostalgic fans, and that they embrace its actions en masse. Theories of branding have stressed that if a media text is very long-running it can facilitate effective branding (Johnson, 2012, p. 159), and furthermore that branding represents an attempt to elicit "modes of consumer engagement, turning [...] potentially distracted feelings into emotional and fully exploitable commercial commitments" (Grainge, 2008, p. 26). Given its vast back catalog of material, and a history that is tied to fans' memories of watching TV double bills or sneaking into theatrical screenings in their youth (see e.g. Gatiss, 2011, pp. 6–7; Gallagher, 2013a), Hammer's brand management is not just intended to "guide the investment of affect on the part of consumers [...] creating an affective intensity" (Arvidsson, 2006, p. 93), but also to use fans' memories and nostalgia as a way of maintaining their affection for the brand. As Sarah Banet-Weiser observes:

> building a brand is about building an affective, authentic *relationship* with a consumer, one based [...] on the accumulation of memories, emotions, personal narratives, and expectations. Brands create what Raymond Williams called a structure of feeling, an ethos of intangible qualities. [...] These affective relationships with brands are slippery, mobile, and often ambivalent, which makes them as powerful and profitable as they are difficult to predict.
> (Banet-Weiser, 2012, pp. 8–9; emphasis in original)

Hammer's "atmosphere" as much as narrative content (Morris, 2006, pp. 64–5; Kermode, 2001) leads to fan nostalgia for its films. But the more fans embrace a brand through cherished memories, the more likely it is that their sense of that brand will be contradicted or challenge the new directions it takes. Kornberger notes that for "purists [...] certain products are actually not 'real' [...] products" that belong to a particular brand (2010, p. 153), and for some devotees certain aspects of Hammer 2.0 may not convey what they feel the "real" Hammer represents.

Consequently, Hammer's efforts to cater to its established fan base have not been without difficulties. The high-definition remastering of *The Curse of Frankenstein* proved particularly controversial, with, for example, one amazon. co.uk reviewer dismissing it as a "tarnished jewel":

> I have been really pleased with the successful revival of the Hammer brand, especially the fact that the "new" Hammer has shown a welcome commitment to their legacy by investing in this restoration programme.

> [...] However [...] I don't think this Blu-Ray transfer [...] is going to satisfy either the old Hammer fan or the new devotee. [...] [C]omparing the image quality of the older Warner Bros DVD version with both the Academy and widescreen versions on the BR here [...] the image quality [...] is undoubtedly better on the older DVD.
>
> (Floyd, 2012)

The official Hammer blog responded to such criticism by arguing that the choice of 1.37:1 aspect ratio offered the "perfectly framed" version (Hammer, 2012a), and that "the HD encode, due to its higher resolution, shows more of the artefacts present in the source material, including softness, grain and high contrast. The SD encode may [...] look smoother as these artefacts are less visible" (Hammer, 2012b). Nevertheless, fans continued to grumble that "the quality of the transfer is horrible. Colors are bland when compared to the US Warner DVD. [...] The transfer needs some serious TLC" ("Scott", 2012).

The remastering of Hammer's back catalogue therefore does not meet with the automatic approval of fans. This is especially true when they feel that, rather than delivering a sharper image, High Definition has drawn attention to problems with the original print, and when there is no definitive record of a film's original aspect ratio. Fans do not simply celebrate Hammer's past, while lambasting its new ventures as inauthentic; they also scrutinize the restoration of this material. Although reissuing such films represents an attempt to commodify fans' nostalgia, as well as an attempt to present Hammer in the best possible light to a new generation of fan consumers, it cannot, as certain brand theorists would have it, unproblematically "capture the productivity of the social and subsume it as a form of value-generating immaterial labour" (Arvidsson, 2006, p. 94). Bloggers, commenters, and reviewers are no doubt caught up in "the production of meaning [and] [...] in adding to the value of those films [...] [b]y perpetuating the life of a text" (Tryon, 2009, p. 136), but this is not always a smooth process: fan reviewers may powerfully criticize or even savage a film, for example.

Although branding experts accept that brand communities sometimes come into conflict with the companies they follow, because they see themselves as engaged in a non-commercial practice and because they harbor different investments in the brand than the company does (Kornberger, 2010, pp. 157–8), it is not uncommon for theorists to claim that "internal" production/marketing cultures may be aligned with "external" brand communities, suggesting harmonious relations between companies like Hammer and their fans (ibid., p. 131). Even though they differ from each other, "organizational cultures and brand communities [...] are compatible. Structurally, they are mirror images of each other, both emanating from the brand" (ibid., p. 142).

Yet, Hammer's fandom does not simply "emanate" from the brand. Hammer may constitute a hub from which fan associations and memories flow outwards both intertextually and experientially, but this process exceeds Hammer as a brand. Thus, while the writer Mark Gatiss celebrates Hammer, his memories of childhood fandom derive in large part from the pleasure he took from repeated consumption of two reference books rather than from the Hammer brand itself:

> Like many boys of our age, it turned out Jonathan Rigby and I had both owned Denis Gifford's ghoulishly green-tinged *A Pictorial History of Horror Movies* and Alan J Frank's impossibly lush but clumsily titled *Movie Treasury of Horror Movies*, the latter virtually my bible as a child. [...] Years later and Jonathan and I are in Black Park [...] filming the Hammer-heavy second episode of my BBC documentary *A History of Horror*. [...] The response to the documentary was genuinely heart-warming. Almost all fans of a certain age, it seems, owned both the Gifford and Frank books.
>
> (Gatiss, 2011, pp. 6–7)

Along with these treasured artifacts, the shooting location Black Park is also commemorated nostalgically. Overseen by Buckinghamshire County Council, the Park represents a space that is powerfully meaningful to Hammer devotees, without being commercialized by Hammer itself. Yet, Black Park barely exists outside Hammer's economic and branding circuits; it costs money to visit this site as a result of travel expenses and so on, but none of this is tied back to profit-generation for Hammer. Similarly, Hammer's other filming locations, such as Oakley Court, have also become objects of fans' "affective intensity" (Arvidsson, 2006, p. 93) without being encapsulated by the Hammer brand. Staying at Oakley Court is very much a commercial activity as it has been turned into a hotel and conference venue. Once again, however, this commerce exceeds Hammer's brand management:

> The country house, Oakley Court, features in both [*The*] *Plague of the Zombies* [1966] (as Squire Hamilton's house) and *The Reptile* [1966] (home of Dr Franklyn and the title creature). [...] The fascia of the building is the same now as it was then, but these days it's a rather expensive hotel. When I reached a "certain age", my wife treated us to a weekend there—and you can see our bedroom at the top left of the screen as Sir James Forbes approaches Squire Hamilton's house at night for his confrontation with the zombie-master.
>
> (Laws, 2006, p. 63)

Both Black Park and Oakley Court enable fans imaginatively to enter into Hammer's structure of feeling, yet they are cathected with the brand without being branded. Thus, although brand communities may emanate from an intellectual property, their interest in that property is not merely different from that of corporate owners; it affectively outruns the brand. Devotees both contest Hammer's restorations and nostalgically commemorate the brand to such an extent that they become intrigued by "external" experiences, places, and commodities over which Hammer has little or no control, and in which it has no stake. To focus only on the "co-creation" of value fails to take into account the degree to which fans' collective and personal memories (Garde-Hansen, 2011, p. 123) can also independently create brand-connected, but non-branded, value. Since it cannot monetize parabranding, this may be of no interest to Hammer: it is the owners of Oakley Court that benefit directly from the custom of people such as the British horror writer and Hammer fan Stephen Laws.[3]

Hammer's brand community can also escape the company's branding strategies by reading unofficial books. Both Christopher Fowler and Stephen Volk have published works of fiction that involve Hammer, either explicitly or connotatively. For example, Fowler's 2012 novel *Hell Train* concerns an "unmade Hammer film" and features "cameos" from Christopher Lee and Peter Cushing (2012, p. 210). It also portrays the former Hammer executive Michael Carreras as mysterious, and Hammer as manipulative and devious:

> "I suppose I should be thankful that Michael didn't turn out to be the Devil."
> "Maybe he did. If you'd gone to Amicus first, they would probably have hired you for an anthology film. Instead you came to us, and now you've promised not to go to them."
> [...] "Were you a part of the deal?"
> She smiled sadly. "We had to make sure you produced a script, so that we could stop it."
>
> (Fowler, 2012, p. 269)

Pirie refers to Hammer as a "semi-magical" brand, one that is surrounded by urban legends which circulate paratextually as a cluster of unofficial, scurrilous, and rumored meanings (2008, p. 225). Fowler and Volk align Hammer with unofficial and darker meanings. Where Fowler represents the

---

[3] Just as Hammer may itself derive value from other brands, including the aforementioned *Harry Potter* franchise through the casting of Daniel Radcliffe. Given this fact, the gray area of parabranding requires greater exploration in relation to corporate and fan activities.

company's internal processes as sinister machinations, Volk (2013) merges fantastical and real-world monstrosities in a tale of former Hammer star Cushing investigating child abuse in his adopted home town of Whitstable. Both *Hell Train* and *Whitstable* (2013) may have been hard sells for the Hammer/Arrow Books imprint since they are not straightforwardly on-brand. Under such circumstances, branding discourses mitigate risk by restricting the circulation of unappealing discourses related to Hammer.

Having said this, Hammer's extension into publishing has shifted since its initial new releases in March 2011: a new edition of Peter Curtis' 1960 novel *The Witches* (AKA *The Devil's Own*), and Francis Cottam's novelization of *The Resident*. Beginning with a programmatic combination of new and old and of legacy and modernization, Hammer Books has gradually diversified its output. It has, for example, commissioned "literary" ghost stories from big-name authors whom one might not associate with Hammer, such as Helen Dunmore's *The Greatcoat*, Jeanette Winterson's *Daylight Gate* (both 2012), Julie Myerson's *The Quickening*, and Sophie Hannah's *The Orphan Choir* (both 2013).These titles also represent an effort to reposition the Hammer brand in order to imbue it with a measure of literary-aesthetic respectability. Thus, Dunmore's work includes an afterword in which she only refers to Hammer as sending "an email […] asking if I would consider writing a ghost or horror story" (2012, p. 241). Otherwise, the author's meditations focus on avoiding cliché (ibid., pp. 247, 249), and referencing ghosts in works of classical literature, such as those in Dickens and Shakespeare (ibid., 251–4). This rather over-the-top bid for literary value is extended to Shakespeare's inclusion as a character in *The Daylight Gate* (Winterson, 2012, pp. viii, 101). Yet, by the time Julie Myerson's *The Quickening* was published the following year, Hammer had evidently retreated from this parade of gothic literary greatness. Myerson's author biography instead suggests an archetypal Hammer fan of her generation, one who enjoyed "watching Friday night Hammer horror movies as a teenager in the 70s" and who was "haunted by the cult 1972 TV play *The Stone Tape*" (2013, p. 277). Pairing literary value with a more traditionally fan-friendly outlook that acknowledges Hammer's legacy, *The Quickening* endeavors paratextually to bridge "retro" Hammer and "neo" Hammer, although its attempt to align legacy and modernization would be destabilized by Sophie Hannah's *The Orphan Choir*. Rather than pursuing a hermetic literary agenda, or seeking to align the retro and neo aspects of the Hammer brand, this book was tailored to exemplify the modern incarnation of the company. *The Orphan Choir* boasts a sticker on its cover which reads "If you liked *The Woman in Black* You'll Love this." It also contains a brief essay that emphasizes ghost films over literature, and that singles out Hammer's recent *The Woman in Black* for praise (Hannah, 2013, p. 290).Where Hammer's first big-name novellas were purely "literary" and medium-specific, as if they were hermetically sealed from film and television, Hannah's book wears its cross-media credentials quite literally on its sleeve. Hammer's expansion into different media typically proceeded along single paths, thereby eschewing the transmedia storytelling and cross-media promotion that are the hallmarks of synergy; the established practice of novelization is the closest the company previously came to such practice. But with *The Orphan Choir*, Hammer's use of an original novel to cross-promote a neo-Hammer film pushed this property firmly in the direction of modernization.

Hammer's publishing imprint contributes additional dimensions to its brand activity. While it may be assumed that novelizations of films such as *Vampire Circus* and *X The Unknown* (both 2012) would be designed to tap into fan nostalgia, they are in fact hybridized updates set in the present day:

> Arrow Books [...] were [sic] considering doing some [...] updated novelisations of some of the old films. [...] [T]he reason that they wanted the books updated was just because they wanted to appeal to a modern audience, and that was the directive we got down from the guys at Hammer. [...] They didn't want books that were kind of set in the seventeenth, eighteenth, nineteenth centuries. They wanted books that had characters that [...] a modern horror audience would identify with.
>
> (Morris, 2013)

These awkward neo-retro books capture perfectly Hammer's own brand doubling: while seeking to leverage its archive, the company cannot afford to side with a niche fan readership over a broader mainstream market. Such a tension is further evinced by Hammer's acquisition of Young Adult (YA) novels that are indebted to the bestselling *Twilight* series. Post-*Twilight* Hammer horror novels include Melvin Burgess' *Hunger* (2013), which bills this author as "the godfather of YA fiction," as well as the first two parts of a Swedish school-based fantasy trilogy: *The Circle* (2012) and *Fire* (2013), both of which were written by Sara Bergmark Elfgren and Mats Strandberg. These books again demonstrate Hammer's hyper-adaptive responsiveness to external trends. Although some older male horror fans may position themselves in opposition to *Twilight* by positing Hammer's 1950s output as 'true' vampire fiction (Bode, 2010), the company's jumping on board the YA fantasy bandwagon destabilizes the Hammer versus YA fantasy binary. Fan nostalgia leads to older horror texts being constructed as authentic:

> Because cinematic horror [...] is primarily directed toward a youth market, we may spend time gaining (sub-)cultural capital surrounding the genre,

only to eventually find ourselves distanced in age and (sub-)cultural competence from the audience currently being catered to—hence the tendency to distrust current trends and seek refuge in nostalgia.
(Church, 2010, p. 236; see also Egan, 2007, p. 167)

Hammer's brand doubling and relative incoherence reflects this process, as it consistently seeks to accumulate fractured forms of (sub)cultural capital linked to different generations of horror fans and to imagined mainstream/fan audiences. Hammer's oscillation between neo and retro branding is threaded through its "Hammer Chiller" audios, just as much as through its updated novelizations, with British horror writer Mark Morris confirming that the "Chiller" series followed a similar brief to his *Vampire Circus* novelization: "the only directive again I was given was that they wanted something kind of modern, something [...] that wasn't [...] entrenched in the past" (Morris, 2013). Unlike films, the lower budgets on which novels/audios are produced permit the targeting of fan niches. It is therefore unsurprising that, rather than courting older Hammer fans, Hammer addresses multiple imagined audiences. For example, *The Box*, the opening "Hammer Chiller" (Gallagher, 2013b), adapts Stephen Gallagher's earlier (2010) short story by shifting it from the post-World War II years to the present day, thereby fulfilling Hammer's brief for "something kind of modern." This is modernization run amok, as if Hammer's brand management is afraid of reminding listeners of the company's history. Like the literary exonimation of Hammer in its first original novels, this "presentist" exonimation of the legacy brand amounts to a strangely self-negating practice whereby Hammer seeks simultaneously to capitalize on, and to deny, its own cultural histories.

Conclusion

In this chapter I have considered how Hammer returned to production and brand extension in 2007. Strongly marked by branding discourses, Hammer 2.0's range extends across web serialization, films, remastered Blu-rays, events, theater, new and adapted books, audio stories, and merchandise. Despite a theoretical emphasis on coherence, as a brand, twenty-first-century Hammer has been insistently self-divided and doubled. The company has hesitated over modernization and commodification of its legacy, and it has sought to hybridize or to align the two, rarely, if ever, successfully. Brand discourses have not generated coherence, due largely to Hammer's hyper-adaptive and externally responsive strategies. One moment the company targets "literary" readers, the next YA fans; first it competes on the mainstream US movie market before releasing a "throwback" to British folk horror; initially it tries to appear techno-culturally 'now', then novelizing old films. Yet, despite these tensions, Hammer continues to enjoy a dedicated fan following or brand community. I have argued that this method of understanding Hammer horror fandom is rather limited however, and not only because fans come into conflict with Hammer over issues such as remastering. The concept of the brand community also fails to consider parabranding and how fan practices can exceed brand management without being non- or anti-commercial.

Perhaps the strongest thread of coherence stemming from Hammer's brand discourses has been its apparent unwillingness to take risks. In one way or another, all of its projects have played it safe. Even the technologically innovative *Beyond the Rave* was textually unadventurous. Unlike its predecessor, Hammer 2.0 has yet to generate any "Trailblazer Hits"—commercially successful films that are marked by generic innovation or transgression—although its brand equity and fan nostalgia surely rely in large part on the place in film history that was won for Hammer by its prolific, transgressive output of the 1950s and 1960s. The curse of Hammer is precisely what grants it (undead) life: the shadow of a previous golden age looms large over its output. Not purely a merchant of menace, Hammer 2.0 is also an ambivalent merchant of nostalgia.

References

Almeida Theatre Programme (2013), *The Turn of the Screw by Henry James, adapted by Rebecca Lenkiewicz*, Islington: Almeida.

Arvidsson, A. (2006), *Brands: Meaning and Value in Media Culture*, London and New York: Routledge.

Banet-Weiser, S. (2012), *Authentic: The Politics of Ambivalence in a Brand Culture*, New York and London: New York University Press.

Barker, M. and Petley, J. (eds) (2001), *Ill Effects: The Media/Violence Debate—Second Edition*, London and New York: Routledge.

Bode, L. (2010), "Transitional Tastes: Teen Girls and Genre in the Critical Reception of *Twilight*," *Continuum*, 24.5: 707–19.

Burgess, M. (2013), *Hunger*, London: Hammer/Arrow.

Cast and Crew Interviews (2011), *Wake Wood*, Hammer/Momentum Pictures/Vertigo Films.

Cherry, B. (2010), "Stalking the Web: Celebration, Chat and Horror Film Marketing on the Internet," in I. Conrich (ed.) *Horror Zone: The Cultural Experience of Contemporary Horror Cinema*, London and New York: I. B. Tauris.

Church, D. (2010), "Afterword: Memory, Genre, and Self-Narrativisation; Or, Why I Should be a More Content Horror Fan," in Steffen Hantke (ed.) *American*

Horror Film: The Genre at the Turn of the Millennium, Jackson: University Press of Mississippi.
Cottam, F. (2011), *The Resident*, London: Hammer/Arrow.
Crew Commentary (2010), *Beyond the Rave* DVD, Hammer/MySpace/Channel Four/Puregrass Films.
Curtis, P. (2011), *The Witches*, London: Hammer/Arrow.
Donnelly, K. J. (2005), *The Spectre of Sound: Music in Film and Television*, London: BFI.
Dunmore, H. (2012), *The Greatcoat*, London: Hammer/Arrow.
Egan, K. (2007), *Trash or Treasure? Censorship and the Changing Meanings of the Video Nasties*, Manchester: Manchester University Press.
Elfgren, S. B. and Strandberg, M. (2012), *The Circle*, London: Hammer/Arrow.
—(2013), *Fire*, London: Hammer/Arrow.
Floyd, T. (2012), "Amazon Customer Review: Tarnished Jewel," October 23. Available online at http://www.amazon.co.uk/The-Curse-Frankenstein-BlurayDVD/dp/B008LU8MME/ref=sr_1_1?ie=UTF8&qid=1373543026&sr=81&keywords=the+curse+of+frankenstein (accessed July 29, 2013).
Fowler, C. (2012), *Hell Train*, Oxford: Solaris.
Gallagher, S. (2010), *The Box*, Kindle: Brooligan Press.
—(2013a), "Hammer Chillers—The Box," June 5. Available online at http://brooligan.blogspot.co.uk/2013/06/hammer-chillers-box.html (accessed July 29, 2013).
—(2013b), *Hammer Chillers: The Box*, June 7. Available online at http://www.hammerchillers.com/releases.asp?id=1 (accessed July 29, 2013).
Garde-Hansen, J. (2011), *Media and Memory*, Edinburgh: Edinburgh University Press.
Gatiss, M. (2011), "Foreword," in J. Rigby, *Studies in Terror: Landmarks of Horror Cinema*, Cambridge: Signum Books.
Gelder, K. (2012), *New Vampire Cinema*, London: BFI/Palgrave-Macmillan.
Grainge, P. (2008), *Brand Hollywood: Selling Entertainment in a Global Media Age*, London and New York: Routledge.
Grass, B. (2008), "Power to the Pixel 2008: Ben Grass," October 29. Available online at http://www.youtube.com/watch?v=OAZgUwzUKO4 (accessed July 4, 2013).
Hammer (2012a), "The Curse of Aspect Ratios!," October 15. Available online at http://blog.hammerfilms.com/?p=166 (accessed July 29, 2013).
—(2012b), "A Note on the Restoration, Mastering and Authoring of *The Curse of Frankenstein*," October 17. Available online at http://blog.hammerfilms.com/?p=321 (accessed July 29, 2013).
Hannah, S. (2013), *The Orphan Choir*, London: Hammer/Arrow.
Hearn, M. (2011), *The Hammer Vault*, London: Titan.
Hearn, M. and Barnes, A. (2007), *The Hammer Story: The Authorised History of Hammer Films*, London: Titan.
Heffernan, K. (2004), *Ghouls, Gimmicks, and Gold: Horror Films and the American Movie Business, 1953–1968*, Durham, NC, and London: Duke University Press.
Hendershot, H. (2011), "*Masters of Horror*: TV Auteurism and the Progressive Potential of a Disreputable Genre," in M. Kackman, M. Binfield, M. Thomas

Payne, A. Perlman, and B. Sebok (eds) *Flow TV: Television in the Age of Media Convergence*, New York and London: Routledge.
Hill, S. (1983), *The Woman in Black*, London: Hamish Hamilton.
Hills, M. (2005), *The Pleasures of Horror*, London and New York: Continuum.
Hutchings, P. (1993), *Hammer and Beyond: The British Horror Film*, Manchester and New York: Manchester University Press.
—(2001), *Terence Fisher*, Manchester: Manchester University Press.
Hutson, S. (2012), *X The Unknown*, London: Hammer/Arrow.
Jenkins, H. (2006), *Convergence Culture: Where Old and New Media Collide*, New York and London: New York University Press.
John, K. A. (2011), *Wake Wood*, London: Hammer/Arrow.
Johnson, C. (2012), *Branding Television*. London and New York: Routledge.
Kackman, M., Binfield, M., Thomas Payne, M., Perlman, A., and Sebok, B. (eds) (2011), *Flow TV: Television in the Age of Media Convergence*, New York and London: Routledge.
Kermode, M. (2001), "I Was a Teenage Horror Fan: Or, 'How I Learned to Stop Worrying and Love Linda Blair'," in M. Barker and J. Petley (eds) *Ill Effects: The Media/Violence Debate—Second Edition*, London and New York: Routledge.
Kornberger, M. (2010), *Brand Society: How Brands Transform Management and Lifestyle*, Cambridge: Cambridge University Press.
Laws, S. (2006), "*Plague of the Zombies* (1966)," in M. Morris (ed.) *Cinema Macabre*, Hornsea: PS Publishing.
Lury, C. (2004), *Brands: The Logos of the Global Economy*, London and New York: Routledge.
Mathijs, E. and Sexton, J. (2011), *Cult Cinema: An Introduction*, Malden, MA, and Oxford: Wiley-Blackwell.
Meikle, D. (2009), *A History of Horrors: The Rise and Fall of the House of Hammer*, Lanham, MD: Scarecrow.
Moor, L. (2007), *The Rise of Brands*, Oxford and New York: Berg.
Morris, M. (2006 [1966]), "*The Reptile*," in *Cinema Macabre*, Hornsea: PS Publishing.
—(ed.) (2006), *Cinema Macabre*, Hornsea: PS Publishing.
—(2012), *Vampire Circus*, London: Hammer/Arrow.
—(2013), "Hammer Chillers 2: Mark Morris." Available online at https://soundcloud.com/bafflegabble (accessed July 4, 2013).
Myerson, J. (2013), *The Quickening*, London: Hammer/Arrow.
Nowell, R. (2011), *Blood Money: A History of the First Teen Slasher Film Cycle*, New York and London: Continuum.
Pirie, D. (2008), *A New Heritage of Horror: The English Gothic Cinema*, London and New York: I. B. Tauris.
Powers, D. (2010), "Strange Powers: The Branded Sensorium and the Intrigue of Musical Sound," in M. Aronczyk and D. Powers (eds) *Blowing up the Brand*, New York: Peter Lang.
Reeves, M. (2011), "Writer/Director Commentary," *Let Me In*, Region, Hammer/Icon Home Entertainment.
Rigby, J. (2000), *English Gothic: A Century of Horror Cinema*, London: Reynolds and Hearn.

—(2011), *Studies in Terror: Landmarks of Horror Cinema*, London: Signum.
Rose, J. (2009), *Beyond Hammer: British Horror Cinema since 1970*, Leighton Buzzard: Auteur Press.
Scargill, N. (2011), "Hammer 2.0—CEO Simon Oakes Reveals Studio's Future Plans," *MovieScope Magazine*, August 26. Available online at http://www.moviescopemag.com/features/hammer-2-0-ceo-simon-oakes-reveals-studios-future-plans (accessed July 29, 2013).
"Scott" (2012), "Hello Hammer!," November 14. Available online at http://blog.hammerfilms.com/?p=166 (accessed July 29, 2013).
Simpson, R. (2011), "Hammer's Women in Peril," March 11. Available online at http://www.hammerfilms.com/news/article/newsid/278/hammers-women-in-peril (accessed July 29, 2013).
Tryon, C. (2009), *Reinventing Cinema: Movies in the Age of Media Convergence*, New Brunswick, NJ: Rutgers University Press.
"Uncle Creepy" (2012), "Hammer Thinking Franchise with *The Woman in Black*; Daniel Radcliffe Back for Part 2?," *Dread* Central, June 18. Available online at http://www.dreadcentral.com/news/56509/hammer-thinking-franchise-woman-black-daniel-radcliffe-back-part-2 (accessed July 29, 2013).
Volk, S. (2013), *Whitstable*, London: Spectral Press.
Winterson, J. (2012), *The Daylight Gate*, London: Hammer/Arrow.

Index

13 Ghosts (1960) 65, 193
28 Days Later (2002) 217
28 Weeks Later (2007) 219

Abbott and Costello 167, 169
Abraham Lincoln: Vampire Hunter (2012) 82, 83
Abrams, J. J. 233, 236
adaptation
    literature to film 16–17, 18–19, 20, 33–4, 45–59, 165, 167, 173, 176, 177, 179, 243–5
    of South East Asian horror films 67–72, 150, 218
Adventures of Sherlock Holmes, The (1939) 177
AIP *see* American International Pictures
Aja, Alexandre 66, 209, 211
Alien (1979) 64
Allen, Irwin 53
All Quiet on the Western Front (1930) 16
American International Pictures (AIP) 136, 188, 195
American Psycho (2000) 212
Amityville Horror, The (1977 [novel]) 53, 57
Amityville Horror, The (1979) 53, 67, 72, 133
Amityville Horror, The (2005) 66, 67, 72, 152
Amusement Securities Corporation 35n. 3
Andromeda Strain, The (1971) 54
Anson, Jay 53
Ape, The (1940) 172
Arabian Nights (1942) 169

Arrogant Films 220
Ash, Jonathon 220
Asher, E. M. 22n. 6, 23
Attack of the Giant Leeches (AKA *Demon of the Swamp*) (1959) 192–3
Attenborough, Richard 53, 56
Atwill, Lionel 172
audiences
    black 187–99
    family 165, 169, 171,
    female 4, 34, 57–8, 70–1, 134, 165, 172–3, 180, 218
    female youth 70, 134, 155, 149, 155, 158–9
    horror fans 63, 65, 70, 82, 83, 132, 155, 165, 167, 168, 169, 171, 172, 173, 174, 175, 177, 179, 187, 205–9, 212, 221–2, 230–1, 238–46
    male 70, 134, 149n. 3, 244
    online 76, 79, 81, 217, 224, 231–3
    rural 15, 17, 32, 39, 85, 165
    working-class 165
Audrey Rose (1975 [novel]) 52, 54, 55, 56–8
Audrey Rose (1977) 52, 55, 56–9
Australian Film Industry 75–88, 136–7, 141, 152
Australian Film, Television and Radio School 78
Avco Embassy Pictures 129, 135–7

Bacall, Lauren 137, 143
Bachelor Party in the Bungalow of the Damned (2008) 223
Bad Robot 233
Badham, John 53

Bait (2012) 76, 84, 87–8
Baker, Carroll 197
Banet-Weiser, Sarah 239
Bava, Mario 223
Bay, Michael 61, 66
Beaumont, Charles 48n. 2
Beck, Steve 66
Before I Hang (1940) 37
Behind the Door (1940) see *Man with Nine Lives, The*
Beneath the Planet of the Apes (1970) 54
Benighted (1927) 48
Bergstrom, Janet 93
Berle, Milton 178
Bernardini, Craig 207
Beware Spooks (1939) 171
Bewitched (1945) 98
Beyond the Rave (2008) 219, 231–3, 236, 246
BFI Monster Weekend 238–9
Bill & Ted's Excellent Adventure (1989) 66
Bing, Jonathan 61
Birds of Prey (AKA *Beaks: The Movie*) (1987) 223
Birth of a Nation (1915) 190
Black Alibi (1942) 48
Black and Blue Films 219
Black Cat, The (1934) 14, 20, 22–4, 167
Black Dragons (1942) 172
Black Friday (1940) 167
Black Water (2007) 76, 80–1, 84, 85
Blatty, William Peter 50, 52, 55
Bloch, Robert 48, 50
Block-Booking 36, 38, 41
Bloodmoon (1990) 78
Bodeen, DeWitt 181
Body Melt (1993) 78
Body Snatcher, The (1945) 63
Bogart, Humphrey 137, 176
Bogdanovich, Peter 142
Böhme, Gernot 111n. 2, 116
Boogie Man will Get You, The (1942) 171
Borchers, Don 138
Bourdieu, Pierre 217–18n. 1
Bousman, Darren Lynn 209

Box, The (2013) 245
Brain Damage Films 221, 222–3
Brandner, Gary 53
'*Breaker' Morant* (1980) 78
Breen, Joseph 98
Bride of Frankenstein, The (1935) 22, 24n. 8, 26, 109
Bridge too Far, A (1977) 56
British Board of Film Classification (BBFC) 224–5
British film industry 48n. 2, 54, 56, 75, 80, 122, 215–26, 229–46
Broadway (1929) 16
Broken (2006) 216, 218
Brontë, Charlotte 165
Bronte, Emily 173
Brown, Helen Gurly 140
Brown vs. Board of Education (1954) 188
Browning, Tod 17
Bruce, Nigel 177
Bucket of Blood, A (1959) 192, 193
Bug (AKA *The Hephaestus Plague*) (1975) 52, 55
Bureau of Motion Pictures, The 97n. 3, Burgess, Melvyn 244
Burnt Offerings (1973 [novel]) 51, 52, 57
Burnt Offerings (1976) 51, 52
Business, The (2005) 219
Butterfield 8 (1960) 55

Cabin Fever (2002) 212
Cabin in the Woods (2012) 82, 83
Calling Dr. Death (1943) 93
Cammell, Donald 52
Campbell, John W. 53
Captive Wild Woman (1943) 96, 97
Carpenter, John 53, 55, 135, 136
Carradine, John 40, 96, 172
Carreras, Michael 229, 242
Carrie (1974 [novel]) 52
Carrie (1976) 52, 55
Carroll, Noel 2
Case of Charles Dexter Ward, The (1927 [novel]) 48n. 3
Case of the Missing Brides, The see *Corpse Vanishes, The*

Castle in Flanders (1936) 110
Castle, William 49, 51, 65, 66, 188, 193–4, 196
Cat and the Canary, The (1939) 37, 112, 174
Cat People (1942) 63, 93, 96n. 2, 114, 136, 164, 165, 173–4, 180–1, 182
Cavalcanti, Alberto 114
Chan, Jackie 81
Chaney, Lon 15, 17, 47n. 1
Chaney, Lon Junior 168
Charlie Chan at the Wax Museum (1940) 177–8
Charlie's Angels (1976–81) 138
Chemical Burn Entertainment 221n. 5
Cherry, Brigid 238
Chopping Mall (1986) 223
Circle, The (2012) 244
Citizen Kane (1941) 180
City of the Dead, The (AKA *Horror Hotel*) (1960) 117–26
Civil Rights Act (1964) 188
Class of Nuke 'em High (1986) 222
Clover, Carol. J. 58, 140n. 5, 149n. 3
Cloverfield (2008) 233
Clueless (1995) 149n. 1
Cochrane, Robert H. 25
Cohen, Larry 67, 204, 205
Columbia Pictures 32n. 2, 35n. 3, 164, 170–2, 182
Columbo (1968–2003) 138
Coma (1977 [novel]) 52
Coma (1978) 52, 53
Conjure Wife (1943) 48
Cook, David A. 45, 46, 51
Cook, Robin 53
Coppola, Francis Ford 206
Corman, Roger 48n. 3, 187, 188n. 1, 189, 190, 191, 192–4
Corpse Vanishes, The (AKA *The Case of the Missing Brides*) (1942) 172
Corrigan, Timothy 203
Cowdin, Cheever 166
Craven, Wes 66, 147, 154n. 10, 204, 207, 210, 211

Creature from the Black Lagoon, The (1954) 26, 190
Creature with the Atom Brain, The (1955) 41
Crichton, Michael 52
Crocodile Dundee (1986) 86
Cronenberg, David 207, 210
Crow, The (1994) 151
Crowther, Bosley 94, 97, 99–100, 104–5
cultural capital (and subcultural capital) 133, 203n. 1, 205, 209, 212, 235, 238, 244–5
Curse of Frankenstein, The (1957) 232, 234, 239
Curtis, Dan 52, 55
Curtis, Jamie Lee 129–43
Curtis, Peter 243
Curtis, Tony 138
Cushing, Peter 234, 242, 243,
Cycle (2005) 224

Daisy Chain, The (2008) 218
Dakota Kid, The (1951) 40–1
Dante, Joe 53, 55
Dark Castle Entertainment 65–6
Dark Mirror, The (1946) 93–4, 102–3
Dark Water (2005) 66
Davis, Ossie 198
Dawn of the Dead (1978) 61, 206
Dawn of the Dead (2004) 66, 218
Day the Earth Stood Still, The (1951) 189, 197
Day the World Ended, The (1955) 189–90, 193
Daybreakers (2009) 76, 80, 84
Daylight Gate (2012) 243
Death of a Centerfold: The Dorothy Stratten Story (1981) 130, 140, 142
De Bont, Jan 63–4
De Palma, Brian 52, 55
De Havilland, Olivia 102
Dead Cert (2010) 219
Dead Men Tell (1941) 178
Dead of Night Collection, The 221, 223–4
Demon Seed (1975 [novel]) 52

Demon Seed (1977) 52
Descent, The (2005) 209, 217, 218, 225
Devil Bat, The (1940) 37, 172
Devil Commands, The (1941) 171
Devil Inside, The (2012) 82, 83
Devil's Island (1939) 37, 176
Devil's Own, The (1960) see *Witches, The*
Devil's Playground (2010) 219
Devil's Rejects (2005) 209, 212
Diaboliques, Les (1955) 196
Die Hard (1988) 63
Digital Nasties 220
digital technologies 64, 79, 81, 148, 155–7
Dimension Films 66, 147–59
Direct-to-Video release see DTV
Disney Company, The 148, 151
Doctor Doolittle (1967) 51
Doctor X (1932) 22n. 5, 37
Dog Soldiers (2002) 209
Don't Answer the Phone! (1979) 139–40
Don't Go in the House (1979) 139
Don't Look in the Basement (1973) 223
Double Indemnity (1944) 175
Dr. Cyclops (1940) 174
Dr. Jekyll and Mr. Hyde (1931) 22n. 5, 34, 47
Dr. Jekyll and Mr. Hyde (1941) 47, 168, 173, 174, 182
Dr. Renault's Secret (1942) 178–9
Dr. Tarr's Torture Dungeon (AKA *The Mansion of Madness*) (1973) 223
Dracula (1897 [novel]) 16, 47, 53
Dracula (1931) 16–26, 34, 47, 54, 166–7
Dracula (1958) 234
Dracula (1979) 53, 54
Dracula A.D. 1972 (1972) 231–2
Dracula-Frankenstein double bill see *Frankenstein-Dracula* double bill
Dressed to Kill (1980) 4, 133, 134,
Dreyer, Carl Theodor 114
DTV (Direct-to-Video release) 81, 216–26

Dunmore, Helen 243
Durbin, Deanna 25
Dyer, Danny 219
Dyer, Richard 130, 142

Egan, Kate 130n. 1
Ehrlich, Max 52
Elfgren, Sara Bergmark 244
Emmerich, Toby 67
Entity, The (1978 [novel]) 53, 55
Entity, The (1982) 53
Evans, Marc 217
Evil Aliens (2005) 219
Evil Dead, The (1981) 70
Evolved: Part One, The (2006) 220, 221–2, 225
Exorcist, The (1971 [novel]) 50, 52, 54, 57
Exorcist, The (1973) 46, 52, 54, 55, 57–8, 70, 132,
exploitation cinema 4, 45, 59, 131, 134–5, 137, 139, 198, 205, 208, 217, 219
Exploitation Pictures (company) 220
Eye, The (2002) 68
Eye, The (2006) 67, 69

F (2010) 217
Face Behind the Mask, The (1941) 171
Face of Marble, The (1946) 31n. 1, 38, 40
family-based horror 4, 62, 63–5, 70, 218, 237–8
Family Demons (2009) 81
Fan, The (1981) 143
Fangoria 141, 207
Farris, John 52
Farrow, Mia 196
Faust (1926) 34
Fear in the Night (1972) 236
Federal Bureau of Investigation (FBI) 103
Feed (2005) 87
Felitta, Frank de 52, 53, 55, 56, 57
Field, Ted 66
Final Girl see Clover, Carol J.
Fingers at the Window (1942) 174

Finney, Jack 48, 52
Fire (2013) 244
first run market, The 15–16, 18, 20, 23, 35, 163–82
Fly, The (1986) 63
Fog, The (1980) 129, 130, 135–6, 137, 138, 140, 141, 142
Fontaine, Joan 173, 180
Football Factory, The (2004) 219
Forbes, Brian 52, 56,
Forbidden Planet (1956) 189
Foreign Correspondent (1940) 170, 173, 178
Form, Andrew 66
Foucault, Michel 94, 97
Fowler, Christopher 242–3
Fox-Searchlight 66
Frankenstein (1818 [novel]) 18–19, 47,
Frankenstein (1931) 19–26, 34, 37, 114, 166
    Frankenstein-Dracula double bill 37, 47, 166
    Frankenstein-Dracula-Son of Kong triple bill 166
Frankenstein Meets the Wolf Man (1943) 40
Freaks (1932) 22n. 5
Freud, Sigmund 95–7, 103, 104
Friday the 13th (1980) 58, 147
Friday the 13th (2009) 72
Friedkin, William 52
Friend, Tad 68–9
From Dusk 'til Dawn (1996) 151
Fulci, Lucio 223
Full Circle (1975 [novel]) 52
Full Circle (1977) 52, 55
Fuller, Brad 66
Furie, Sidney J. 53
Fury, The (1976 [novel]) 52, 55
Fury, The (1978) 52, 55

Gallagher, Mark 212
Gaslight (1944) 174
Gates of Hell, The (2008) 87
Gelder, Ken 243–4
Generation Y (Gen-Y) 149, 151–8
Generation Z (Gen-Z) 151, 155–8
genre theory 1–5, 32–41, 150

Gessner, Nicolas 52
Ghost Breakers, The (1940) 31n. 1, 35, 36n. 4, 37, 39, 174
Ghost of Frankenstein, The (1942) 25, 169
Ghost Ship, The (1943) 181
Ghost Story (1979 [novel]) 53, 55
Ghost Story (1981) 53, 55
Ghoul, The (1933) 22n. 5
Girdler, William 53, 55
Gitlin, Todd 37
Gnaw (2008) 216n. 2, 218
Goddard, Paulette 37
Godfather, The (1969 [novel]) 51
Goldman, Jane 237
Goldman, William 53, 55
Golem, The (1920) 112
Gomery, Douglas 163, 164, 166, 168
Gone with the Wind, The (1939) 173
Gorilla, The (1939) 177
Graebner, William 95
Graham, Billy 195
Grainge, Paul 237
Grandview, U.S.A. (1984) 130
Grant, Catherine 203
Graveyard of Death, The (2005) 220
Greatcoat, The (2012) 243
Grindhouse (2007) 208
Grudge, The (2004) 67, 69, 71, 150, 218
Guillermin, John 56

Hacked Off (2005) 224
Hall, Charles D. 17, 21
Hall, Jacquelyn Dowd 188
Halloween (1978) 1, 58, 64, 72, 110, 130, 135, 136, 138, 140, 141
Halloween II (1980) 130
Halloween (2007) 72
Halloween H20: Twenty Years Later (1998) 150
Halperin, Victor see Halperins, The
Halperin, Edward see Halperins, The
Halperins, The 22n. 5, 34–5
Hammer Films 54n. 4, 80, 130n. 1, 215, 219, 226, 229–46
Hands of Orlac, The (1920 [novel]) 48
Hanich, Julian 111

INDEX

Hannah, Sophie 243–4
Harlequin (1980) 87
Harris, Julie 63
Harry Potter series of films (2001–11) 215, 237, 242n. 3
Harvest Home (1973 [novel]) 50
Haute Tension (2003) 66
Haunted Palace, The (1963) 48n. 3, 188n. 1
Haunting, The (1963) 48, 56, 63–5
Haunting, The (1999) 61, 63–5
Haunting of Hill House, The (1959 [novel]) 48, 63
Heffernan, Kevin 4, 196, 232
Hell House (1971) 52, 54
Hell Train (2012) 242–3
Hello Dolly! (1969) 51
Hellraiser (1987) 151
Hell's Ground (2007) 226
Hendershot, Heather 230–1
Hepburn, Katharine 138
Herzog, Arthur 53
Heyworth, Rita 138
Hidden Hand, The (1942) 177
Hill, Debora 138
Hiller, Arthur 53, 55–6
Hills, The (2006–10) 154
Hills Have Eyes, The (1977) 2, 66, 223
Hills Have Eyes, The (2006) 66, 209, 223
Hitchcock, Alfred 4, 48, 49, 50, 104n. 6, 121, 133, 135,137, 170, 173, 178, 180, 193, 196, 235
Hitcher, The (1986) 67
Hitcher, The (2007) 67
Hold that Ghost, The (1941) 167
Hole, The (2001) 217
Hollywood Quarterly 100
Homicidal (1961) 65, 193–4
Hood, Robert 87
Hooper, Tobe 67, 204, 210, 211
Hope, Bob 37, 174, 178
Horror comedy 150, 167, 171, 174, 177, 193, 215, 220
Horror Island (1941) 164, 167
Horror of Party Beach, The (1964) 41, 195–6

Hostel (2005) 3, 62, 72, 209, 212
Hostel Part II (2007) 209, 212
Hough, John 52, 53, 56
Hound of the Baskervilles, The (1939) 47, 177, 178
House of 1000 Corpses (2003) 212
House of Dracula (1945) 25–6,
House of Frankenstein (1944) 25–6
House of Horrors (AKA *Joan Medford is Missing*) (1946) 25
House of the Seven Gables, The (1940) 167
House of Usher (1960) 188n. 1
House of Wax (2005) 66
House on Haunted Hill (1958) 65, 193n. 1
House on Haunted Hill (1999) 65, 66
Howling, The (1977 [novel]) 53
Howling, The (1981) 53
Howling III: Marsupials, The (1987) 78, 85
Hunchback of Notre Dame, The (1831 [novel]) 47
Hunchback of Notre Dame, The (1923) 15
Hunchback of Notre Dame, The (1939) 47, 179
Hunger (2013) 244
Hunt for Red October, The (1990) 63
Hussein, Waris 52
Huston, John 100
Hutchings, Peter 34, 206, 207, 232, 234

I Am Legend (1954 [novel]) 52, 54
I Know how many Runs You Scored Last Summer (2008) 81
I Know What You Did Last Summer (1997) 211
I Know What You Did Last Summer series of films (1997–2006) 150
I Shot Andy Warhol (1995) 64
I Wake Up Screaming (1941) 178
I Walked with a Zombie (1943) 31n. 1, 32, 35, 36n. 4, 37, 38n. 5, 39, 115, 165, 181
I Was a Prisoner on Devil's Island (1941) 171

Ichise, Taka 69
Impey, Jason 220
Incredibly Strange Creatures who Stopped Living and Became Mixed-Up Zombies, The (1964) 41
Incubus (1976 [novel]) 53
Incubus (1982) 53
Inn of the Damned (1975) 78
Invasion of the Body Snatchers (1956) 48
Invasion of the Body Snatchers (1978) 52, 53, 63
Invasion of the Saucer Men (1957) 189
Invisible Agent (1942) 169
Invisible Ghost (1941) 172
Invisible Invaders (1959) 41
Invisible Man, The (1933) 22, 26
Invisible Man Returns, The (1940) 167
Invisible Woman, The (1940) 167
Irvin, John 53, 56
Island of Doomed Men (1940) 171
Island of Dr. Moreau, The (1896 [novel]) 47, 52
Island of Dr. Moreau, The (1977) 52, 53
Island of Lost Souls (1932) 22n. 5, 47
It's Alive (1974) 67, 204

J. I. Productions 220
Jack's Wife (1972) 206
Jackson, Shirley 48, 63
Jancovich, Mark 48, 50, 94n. 1, 205–6, 221
Jane Eyre (1943) 165, 173, 181
Japanese horror *see* J-horror
Jaws (1975 [novel]) 52, 55
Jaws (1975) 52, 53, 55
J-horror 62, 66, 68–72, 150
Journey into Fear (1943) 180
Journey's End (1930) 19
Juan of the Dead (2011) 226
Junior Laemmle *see* Laemmle, Carl 'Junior'
Ju-On (2002) 70n. 1

Kapsis, Robert E. 4, 133
Karloff, Boris 19, 22, 23, 24, 36n. 4, 37, 168, 170, 171, 172, 176, 179

Kattan, Chris 66
Katzman, Sam 172
Kaufman, Philip 52
Keech, Stacy 136–7
Kenny (2006) 86
Kerruish, Jesse Douglas 48
Kill, Baby … Kill (AKA *Curse of the Dead*) (1966) 223
Kill Keith (2011) 215
Killbillies, The (2012) 81
Killer Elite (2011) 77
King Kong (1933) 190
King of the Underworld (1939) 37
King of the Zombies (1941) 31n. 1, 32, 38, 39
Kings Row (1942) 176
King, Stephen 52, 53, 55
Kitano, Takeshi 67
Klinger, Barbara 216
Knowing (2009) 77
Koenig, Laird 52
Koerner, Charles 180
Kongo (1932) 22n. 5
Konvitz, Jeffrey 52
Koontz, Dean 52
Kornberger, Martin 232, 239
Kracauer, Siegfried 98n. 4
Kruger, Ehren 69
Kubrick, Stanley 53
Kwaidan (1964) 196
Kyser, Kay 179

Labato, Roman 216–18, 223
Ladd, Alan 175
Lady in the Dark (1944) 104n. 6
Lady Vanishes, The (1979) 229
Laemmle, Carl 14–15, 16–17, 18, 19, 20, 25
Laemmle, Carl 'Junior' (Junior Laemmle) 15–16, 17, 18, 20, 21n. 4, 22, 25, 26
Lang, Fritz 178
Last House on the Left, The (1972) 204, 223
Last House on the Left, The (2009) 223
Last Man on Earth, The (1964) 41, 54n. 4

Lee, Christopher 234, 235, 242
Lee, Roy 68–9
Legend of Hell House, The (1973) 52, 54
Lenzi, Umberto 197
Leopard Man, The (1943) 48–9, 63, 115, 181
Let Me In (2010) 110, 229, 233–4, 236
Let the Right One In (2008) 233–4
Let there be Light (1946) 100
Levin, Ira 49–50, 52, 196
Lewton, Val 37–8n. 5, 48, 56, 63, 114–17, 126, 164, 165, 179, 181
Li, Jet 67
Lilies in the Field (1963) 187
Lionsgate (also previously Lions Gate) 80, 211–12
Little Girl who Lives down the Lane, The (1974 [novel]) 52
Little Girl who Lives down the Lane, The (1976) 52
Little Shop of Horrors (1986) 193n. 5
Little Shop of Horrors, The (1960) 192
Lipstick (1976) 134
Logan's Run (1976) 56
Lomis, Erik 155n. 13
Loncraine, Richard 52
London, Jack 176
Long Time Dead (2002) 217
Lorre, Peter 171, 172, 179
Los Angeles, City of 139
Lost, The (2006) 224, 225
Lost Weekend, The (1945) 175
Love Boat, The (1978–87) 135
Love Story (1970) 56
Love Wanga (AKA *Ouanga*) (1934) 31n. 1, 35
Lovecraft, H. P. 48n. 3, 110, 117, 118, 121,
Loved Ones, The (2009) 76
Lugosi, Bela 17, 21, 22–4, 34–5, 40, 168, 172, 179
Lundberg, Ferdinand and Marynia Farnham 95, 102

McLean, Greg 80, 85, 209
Macabre (1958) 65, 193
Macbeth (1948) 41

Mad Doctor, The (1941) 175
Mad Doctor of Market Street, The (1942) 169
Mad Love (1935) 48
Mad Monster, The (1942) 172
Magic (1976 [novel]) 53, 55
Magic (1978) 53, 55, 56, 57
Magic Island, The (1929) 33–4
Magnificent Ambersons, The (1942) 180
Maltese Falcon, The (1941) 176
Man Hunt (1941) 178
Man who Dared, The (1939) 37
Man with Nine Lives, The (AKA *Behind the Door*) (1940) 37, 171
Man Made Monster (1941) 164, 168
Man They Could Not Hang, The (1939) 37, 170
Mandingo (1975) 198
Maniac (1980) 134, 140
Manitou, The (1975 [novel]) 53
Manitou, The (1978) 53, 57
Mann, Daniel 52, 55
Marasco, Robert 51, 52
Married to the Mafia (2002) 68
Marshall, Neil 209, 210, 218
Martin (1976) 206
Mask of Fu Manchu, The (1932) 22n. 5
Mask of the Red Death, The (1964) 188n. 1
Mask of Zorro, The (1998) 64
Massacre at Central High (1976) 223
Masterton, Graham 53
Matheson, Richard 48n. 2, 52, 54, 194
Matrix, The (1999) 67
Maxim Media 221, 222
Mayer, Geoff 77
Mayer, Louis B. 15, 163
Mephisto Waltz, The (1969 [novel]) 50, 52
Mephisto Waltz, The (1971) 50, 52, 57
Mexican, The (2001) 69
MGM 15, 17, 22n. 5, 32, 98, 163, 164, 168, 172–4, 182,
Midnight Films 220
Midnight Releasing 221
Miller Buckfire & Co. 152
Ministry of Fear (1944) 175

Miramax Films 66, 68, 149, 151, 155n. 12
Modern Women: The Lost Sex (1947) 95
Monogram Pictures 39, 40, 172
Monroe, Marilyn 138
Monster and the Girl, The (1941) 175
Monsters Inc. (2001) 67
Montez, Maria 169
Moonrise (1948) 41
Motion Picture Association of America (MPAA) 51, 70, 97, 98, 197
Motor Home Massacre (2005) 223
MPAA *see* Motion Picture Association of America
Mrs. Miniver (1942) 170
Mulligan, Robert 52, 55
Mum & Dad (2008) 216n. 2, 218–19
Mummy, The (1932) 22, 24, 26
Mummy, The (1959) 238–9
Mummy's Hand, The (1940) 167
Mummy's Tomb, The (1942) 169
Murder by Decree (1979) 136
Murders in the Rue Morgue (1932) 14, 20–2, 47, 113
Museum of Modern Art, The 100
My Brilliant Career (1979) 78
My Little Eye (2002) 217
My Sassy Girl (2001) 68
My Wife is a Gangster (2001) 68
Myerson, Julie 243
Mysterious Doctor, The (1943) 177
Mystery of Marie Roget, The (1942) 169
Mystery of the Wax Museum (1933) 22n. 5

Nakata, Hideo 66, 69
Nazi Zombie Death Tales (AKA *Battlefield Death Tales*) (2012) 216
NBCUniversal 26
Needle (2010) 80, 87
Neeson, Liam 64
Nelson, Lori 190–1
neo-feminism 139–43
New Line Cinema 61–2, 66, 67
Night Monster (1942) 169

Night of Fear (1972) 78
Night of the Eagle (1962) 48n. 2
Night of the Living Dead (1968) 49, 54, 61, 196, 198, 199, 204
Nightmare on Elm Street, A series of films (1984–91) 154n. 10, 210
Nightwing (1977 [novel]) 53
Nightwing (1979) 53, 56
Nocturnal Features 221
Nowell, Richard 4, 32–3, 39, 58, 149n. 2

Oakes, Simon 229–30, 233, 236
Old Dark House, The (1932) 22, 48, 110
Oliver Twisted (2000) 223
Omega Man, The (1971) 52, 53, 54,
One Million B.C. (1940) 173
Opiate of the People Films 220
Orders to Kill (1958) 192
Orgasmo (1969) *see Paranoia*
Orphan Choir, The (2013) 243–4
Ortenberg, Tom 211
Other, The (1971 [novel]) 50, 52, 54, 55
Other, The (1972) 50, 52, 54, 55, 57
Others, The (2001) 70
Ouija Board (2009) 217, 224, 225
Our Man Flint (1966) 55
Outcast (2010) 218
"Ozploitation" 75, 78, 84, 86

Pacific Heights (1990) 236
Page, Thomas 52
Paracinema 220–3
Paramount Decrees (United States vs. Paramount Pictures Inc.) 41
Paranoia (1969) 197–8
Paranormal Activity 4 (2012) 82, 83
Pardon My Sarong (1942) 169
Patrick (1978) 78
PCA *see* Production Code Administration
Perfect (1985) 130
Perkins, Anthony 135
Perren, Alissa 211–12
Petley, Julian 217
Phantasm (1979) 136

Phantom Lady (1942) 175
Phantom of the Opera (1910 [novel]) 47
Phantom of the Opera (1925) 47n. 1
Phantom of the Opera (1943) 47, 48
Phillips, Arthur 83–4
Picnic at Hanging Rock (1975) 85
Picture of Dorian Gray, The (1890 [novel]) 47
Picture of Dorian Gray, The (1945) 47–8
Pinedo, Isabel Cristina 133, 194
Pirie, David 229, 242
Pit and the Pendulum (1961) 188n.1, 194–5,
Pitt, Ingrid 130n. 1
Plague of the Zombies, The (1966) 241
Planet of the Apes (1968) 54
Platinum Dunes 66–7
Poe, Edgar Allan 20, 22, 23, 47, 48n. 3, 169, 187, 188n. 1, 194
Polan, Dana 96
Polanski, Roman 49, 50, 52, 196
Possessed (1947) 93, 103, 104,
Possession, The (2012) 82, 83
Possession of Joe Delaney, The (1970 [novel]) 52, 57
Possession of Joe Delaney, The (1972) 52, 57
Poverty Row 32n. 2, 38–40, 164, 170–2, 182, 217
Powers, Devon 232–3
Premature Burial (1962) 188n. 1
Price, Vincent 65, 98
Priestley J. B. 48
Primal (2010) 80, 85
Producer Offset (Australia) 77, 80, 81
Production Code Administration 35, 97, 165, 174, 197
Production-of-culture perspective 31n. 2
Prom Night (1980) 2n. 2, 129, 130, 136, 137, 139, 140, 141, 142
Prometheus (2012) 82, 83
Psychiatry 93–105
Psycho (1959 [novel]) 48, 50
Psycho (1960) 48, 49, 50, 110, 114, 121, 135, 194, 197

Pulse (2006) 152
Puzo, Mario 51

Quatermass 2 (1957) 231
Quickening, The (2013) 243
Quincy M.E. (1976–83) 138

Radar Pictures 66
Radcliffe, Daniel 215, 237, 242n. 3
Radio-Keith-Orpheum *see* RKO
Radner, Hilary 131, 140
Raimi, Sam 61, 70
Random House Publishing 230
Rathbone, Basil 175, 177
Ratman's Notebooks (1969) 52
Raven, The (1935) 14, 20, 23–4
Raven, The (1963) 188n. 1
Razorback (1984) 78, 85, 86
Rebecca (1940) 170, 173, 175, 180, 181, 182
Reception Studies 2, 3, 4, 203–7
Red Canopy (2006) 217
Reef, The (2010) 76, 80, 84
Rehme, Robert 'Bob' 135–6
Reign in Darkness (2002) 81, 82, 87
Reincarnation of Peter Proud, The (1973 [novel]) 52, 55, 57
Reincarnation of Peter Proud, The (1975) 52, 55, 57
remakes 55, 61–72, 114–15, 150, 152, 193n. 5, 223, 224, 229, 234, 238
Reptile, The (1966) 241
Republic Pictures 40
Resident, The (2011) 234–6, 243
Resident Evil series of films (2002–) 219
Resident Evil: Apocalypsa (2004) 61
RetarDead (2008) 223
Return of Doctor X, The (1939) 31n. 1, 35, 36n. 4, 37, 176
Revenge of the Nerds (1984) 66
Revenge of the Zombies (AKA *The Corpse Vanished*) (1943) 31n. 1, 32, 38, 39
Revolt Films 220
Revolt of the Zombies (1936) 31n. 1, 32, 35

Revolution Pictures 70
Revolver Films 216
Rialto Theater, New York City 100, 101n. 5, 105
Ring, The (2002) 61, 62, 67, 68, 69, 71, 150, 218
Ring Two, The (2005) 62, 69, 70, 71
Ringu (1998) 68, 69
RKO 25, 31–2n. 2, 37n. 5, 63, 95, 114, 163, 164, 165, 179–81, 182
Road Games (1981) 130, 136–7, 140, 141, 142
Road Warrior, The (1981) 86
Robe, The (1953) 187
Rogers, Charles 25
Rogue (2007) 76, 80, 84, 85,
romance 34, 36n. 4, 37, 132,
Romeo + Juliet (1996) 149n. 1
Romero, George A. 54, 61, 198–9, 204, 206–10
Rosemary's Baby (1967 [novel]) 47–52, 57
Rosemary's Baby (1968) 47–52, 132, 196–7, 198
Rosenberg, Stuart 179
Roth, Eli 209, 211, 212
run-zone-clearance 36, 41
Ruric, Peter 22–3n. 6
Rush, Geoffrey 65–6
Russell, Jamie 35
Russell, Ray 53
Ryan, Michael and Douglas Kellner 46
Rydstrom, Gary 64

Saboteur (1942) 170
Safecracker Pictures 216
Sagal, Boris 52
Salles, Walter 66
Salvage (2009) 218, 219
Saw (series of films) (2004–10) 212, 218
Saw (2004) 62, 72, 76, 77
Saw II (2005) 209
Saw III (2006) 209
Saw IV (2007) 209
Scared Stiff (1953) 41
Scary Movie (2000) 150
Schatz, Thomas 15, 16, 17n. 2, 150

Schenck, Aubrey 99
Schenck, Nicholas 163
Schrader, Paul 114–15
Sconce, Jeffrey 220–1
Scorsese, Martin 206
Scream (series of films) (1996–2011) 62, 66, 72, 147, 149n. 2, 151, 152, 153, 154, 155, 157, 158
Scream (1996) 4, 129, 143, 148–50, 151, 153, 154, 155, 157, 159, 211, 217
Scream 2 (1997) 147, 153n. 9
Scream 3 (2000) 69, 147, 148, 150, 151, 153n. 9, 155
Scre4m (2011) 148, 154–9
Sea Wolf, The (1941) 176
Seabrook, William 33
self-distribution 224–5
Selznick, David O. 170, 173, 181, 182
Senior, Andrew 220
Sentinel, The (1974 [novel]) 52
Sentinel, The (1977) 52
Seventh Victim, The (1943) 93, 116, 165, 181
Shadow of a Doubt (1943) 170
Shaun of the Dead (2004) 217
Shameless DVD 223, 224
Shelley, Mary 18, 47, 109
Sherlock Holmes and the Secret Weapon (1942) 170
Sherlock Holmes and the Voice of Terror (1942) 169–70
Sherlock Holmes series of films 169–70, 177–8
Shimizu, Takashi 66, 70n. 1
Shining, The (1977 [novel]) 53
Shining, The (1980) 53, 133
Shock (1946) 94, 98–105
Shot in the Dark, A (1964) 55
Show Boat (1936) 25
Shrooms (2007) 218
Shunned House, The (2003) 226
Shutter (2008) 67
Sick Bastard (2007) 200
Silence of the Lambs, The (1991) 59, 132
Silver, Joel 65–6
Simone, Nina 197–8

Sisters (1973) 46
Sixth Sense, The (1999) 62, 70, 132
Skal, David J. 32
Slaves (1969) 198–9
Smiling Ghost, The (1941) 177
Smith, Greg M. 113n. 3
Smith, Martin Cruz 53, 55
Snake Pit, The (1948) 93, 94, 104–5
Snuff (1976) 134
social media 148, 153, 156, 219, 231–3, 240
Soderbergh, Steven 212–13
Some Like it Hot (1958) 138
Some Must Watch (1933/1941) 48
Son of Dracula (1943) 25
Son of Frankenstein (1939) 25, 166–7
Son of Kong (1933) 166
Sopranos, The (1999–2007) 219
Sothcott, Jonathan 219
Sound of Music, The (1965) 56
Spartacus (1960) 138
special effects 19, 22–3n. 6, 62–5, 104, 114, 116, 149, 179, 195, 210, 211, 232
Speed (1994) 64
Spellbound (1945) 104n. 6
Spider Woman Strikes Back, The (1946) 97
Spider-Man (2002) 67
Spierig Brothers, the 80
Spike TV Scream Awards 207–9
Spiral Staircase, The (1945) 48, 49, 173
Splat Pack, the 209–11, 213
Splintered (2010) 218
Spooks Run Wild (1941) 37, 172
Spy Kids (series of films) (2001–11) 152
Stag Night of the Dead (2010) 224
Stallybrass, Peter 96
Stepford Wives, The (1972 [novel]) 52
Stepford Wives, The (1975) 52
Stepford Wives, The (2004) 61, 63
Stewart, Fred Mustard 50, 52
Stewart, Ramona 52
Stoker, Bram 16, 47, 53
Stone Tape, The (1972) 243
Storm Warning (2007) 76
Straight on till Morning (1972) 236
Strandberg, Mats 244

Strange Case of Doctor RX, The (1942) 169
Stranger on the Third Floor, The (1940) 179
Strangler of the Swamp, The (1946) 126
Straub, Peter 52, 53, 55
streaming 220
Street of Chance (1942) 175
Streiber, Whitley 53
subcultural capital *see* cultural capital
Subterano (2003) 87
Summer of the Massacre, The (2006) 220, 221, 222–5
Sunday too far Away (1975) 78
Surviving Evil (2009) 219
Suspicion (1941) 180
Svengali (1931) 34, 37
Swamp Water (1941) 168, 178
Swank, Hilary 234–5
Swarm, The (1974 [novel]) 53
Swarm, The (1977) 53
symptomatic analysis 3, 5

Tales of Terror (1962) 187, 188n. 1, 195
Tappert, Rob 70n. 1
Tarantino, Quentin 75, 208
Taste of Fear (1961) 235
Taylor, Don 52
Taylor, Elizabeth 55
Taylor, Lili 64–5
Teenage Zombies (1959) 41
teen slasher films 4, 58, 62, 69, 70, 72, 110, 129, 147–59, 210, 211, 217, 220–1
television 50, 54, 55, 61, 65, 66, 69, 81, 135, 138, 219, 230, 244
Terminator, The (1984) 64
Terror Train (1980) 129, 130, 136, 140, 141, 142
Terwilliger, George 35
Texas Chainsaw Massacre, The (1974) 2, 46, 66, 204
Texas Chainsaw Massacre, The (2003) 61, 66, 218
Thalberg, Irving 15–16
Thing, The (1982) 53, 55
Thirst (1979) 78

INDEX

Thir13en Ghosts (2001) 65, 66
This Gun for Hire (1942) 175
Thompson, J. Lee 52, 56
Thornton, Sarah 203–4n. 1
Three Men and a Baby (1987) 66
Three Smart Girls (1936) 25
Till, Emmett 188, 190–1
Tingler, The (1959) 65, 193n. 6
Tippet, Phil 64
Titanic (1997) 67
To Kill a Mockingbird (1962) 55
Tomb of Ligeia, The (1964) 188n. 1
Tong, Pete 231, 232
Tong, Stanley 67
Tony (2009) 219
Tora! Tora! Tora! (1970) 51
Tortured (AKA *Sex Slave*) (2009) 220
Total Film 210
Touch of Evil, A (1958) 138
Tower of London (1939) 166–7
Towering Inferno, The (1974) 56
Toxic Avenger series of films (1984–2003) 222
Trading Places (1983) 130
Traffic in Souls (1913) 15
Triangle, (2009) 76, 80, 84, 87
Tribute to Alfred Hitchcock, A (1979) 135
Troma Releasing 221–3
True Blood (2008–) 219
Tryon, Thomas 50, 52
Tunnel, The (2011) 76
Turn of the Screw (2013 [stageplay]) 230
Turning, The (2011) 220
Twentieth Century-Fox (later Twentieth Century Fox) 32, 67, 94, 98–100, 104–5, 167, 168, 174, 176–9, 182
Twilight series of films (2008–12) 59, 151n. 5, 244
Twisted Pictures 80
Twister (1996) 64
Tzioumakis, Yannis 38

Ulmer, Edgar 22–3n. 6
Undead (2003) 80
Underground Horror Network 222
Undying Monster, The (AKA *The Hammond Mystery*) (1942) 48, 178
Uninvited, The (2009) 67
United Artists (UA) 31–2 n. 2, 35, 57, 163–4, 172–4, 182
Universal-International 102–3
Universal Pictures 13–26, 32n. 2, 35n. 3, 38n. 6, 40, 61 95–6, 97, 138, 164, 166–70, 177, 181, 182
Universal Studios Hollywood 26
Urban Legend series of films (1998–2005) 150
Urban Legend (1998) 150, 211

Valley Girl (1982 [song]) 139n. 4
Valley Girl (1983) 139n. 4
Valley of the Zombies (1946) 31n. 1, 38, 40
Vampire Bat, The (1933) 22n. 5
Vampire Circus, The (2012) 244–5
Vampire films see also *Dracula* 18, 22, 40, 54, 76, 78, 80, 82, 83, 85, 114, 219, 231, 233, 234, 238, 244, 245
Vampyr (1932) 114
Van Helsing (2004) 26
Variety 18, 22, 24n. 8, 25n. 9, 35, 36n. 4, 40, 61, 63, 65, 67, 95, 164n. 1, 166, 167, 169, 170, 171, 172, 174, 175, 176, 177, 178, 179, 180, 181, 210
Venus Drowning (2006) 218, 218–19n. 4
Verbinski, Gore 69
Vertigo Entertainment 68–9
VoD (Video on Demand) 216–20
online release 224
Volk, Stephen 242–3
Voodoo Man (1944) 31n. 1, 38, 40

Wadleigh, Michael 53
Wake Wood (2010) 233, 236
Walking Dead, The (1936) 31n. 1, 35, 36n. 4, 37
Wan, James 78
Wanger, Walter 169
War of the Worlds, The (1938) (radio broadcast) 180

Warner Bros. 22n. 5, 32n. 2, 57, 65, 68, 163, 174, 176–7, 182, 240
Warwick, Dionne 198
Waterloo Bridge (1931) 19
Watts, Naomi 69
Weinstein, Bob 147, 149
Weinstein Company, The (TWC) 80, 148, 151–2, 216n. 2
Weinstein, Harvey 147
Weird Woman (1944) 48
Wells, H. G. 47, 52
Welles, Orson 63, 138, 180
Wendkos, Paul 52
Wes Craven's New Nightmare (1994) 154n. 10
West Side Story (1961) 56
Whale, James 19, 20
Whannell, Leigh 76
When Evil Calls (2008) 231
Whispering Ghosts (1942) 178
White, Allon 96
White, Ethel Lina 48
White, Robb 193
White Zombie (1932) 22n. 5, 31n. 1, 32–5, 39
Whitstable (2013) 243
Who Goes There? (1938) 53
Wigley, Mark 111
Wilderness (2006) 218
Willard (1971) 52, 55
Willard, John 174
Williams, Linda 189, 199n. 7,
Williams, Linda Ruth 216
Williams, Tony 155n. 11
Winner, Michael 52, 56
Winterson, Janette 243
Wise, Robert 48, 52, 56, 63
Witches, The (1960) (AKA *Devil's Own, The*) 243
Wolf Creek (2005) 75, 77, 80, 84–6, 152, 209

Wolfen (1978 [novel]) 53
Wolfen (1981) 53
Wolf Man, The (1941) 26, 40, 168, 181
Woman in Black, The (1983 [novel]) 236
Woman in Black, The (2012) 215, 226, 236–7, 243
Woo, John 67
Woo-Ping, Yuen 68
Wood, Robin 2, 46, 132, 204–5
Woolrich, Cornell 48, 175
World Wide Multi Media 221n. 5
Written in Blood (1998) 224
Wuthering Heights (1939) 172

X The Unknown (2012) 244

Yeoh, Michelle 67
You'll Find Out (1940) 179
Yun-Fat, Chow 67

Zanetti, Eugenio 64
Zanuck, Darryl F. 99
Zemeckis, Robert 61, 65, 66
Zeta-Jones, Catherine 64
Zombie Ferox (2002) 220
Zombie films 22, 31–41, 61, 80, 115, 165, 181, 195, 216, 217, 218, 219, 220, 223, 241
Zombie Flesh Eaters (1979) 223
Zombie Holocaust (1980) 223
Zombie, Rob 209, 211
Zombie Village (2005) 217
Zombies of the Stratosphere (1952) 41
Zombies on Broadway (1945) 31n. 1, 35, 36n. 4, 37
Zucco, George 40, 172, 179

Lightning Source UK Ltd.
Milton Keynes UK
UKHW020348100720
366312UK00008B/147